SRA
Reading Mastery
Signature Edition

Presentation Book C
Grade K

Siegfried Engelmann
Elaine C. Bruner

 McGraw Hill **SRA**

Columbus, OH

The McGraw-Hill Companies

18 LKV 21

ISBN: 978-0-07-612196-0
MHID: 0-07-612196-8

Columbus, OH 43219
4400 Easton Commons
SRA/McGraw-Hill
Send all inquiries to this address:

Printed in the United States of America.

SRAonline.com

READING MASTERY® is a registered trademark of The McGraw-Hill Companies, Inc.

Table of Contents

*Individual Checkout Lessons

Curriculum Map *at the back of the book*

p

d

g

t

SOUNDS

EXERCISE 1

Teaching **p** as in **pat**

a. (Point to **p.**) Here's a new sound. It's a quick sound.

b. My turn. (Pause. Touch **p** for an instant, saying:) **p.** (Do not say **puuh.**)

c. Again. (Touch **p** and say:) **p.**

d. (Point to **p.**) Your turn. When I touch it, you say it. (Pause.) Get ready. (Touch **p.**) *p.*

e. Again. (Touch **p.**) *p.*

f. (Repeat *e* until firm.)

EXERCISE 2

Individual test

(Call on individual children to identify **p.**)

EXERCISE 3

Sounds firm-up

a. Get ready to say the sounds when I touch them.

b. (Alternate touching **p** and **d.** Point to the sound. Pause one second. Say:) Get ready. (Touch the sound.) *The children respond.*

c. (When **p** and **d** are firm, alternate touching **p, g, d,** and **t** until all four sounds are firm.)

EXERCISE 4

Individual test

(Call on individual children to identify **p, g, d,** or **t.**)

EXERCISE 5

Sounds firm-up

a. (Point to **p.**) When I touch the sound, you say it.

b. (Pause.) Get ready. (Touch **p.**) *p.*

c. Again. (Repeat *b* until firm.)

d. Get ready to say all the sounds when I touch them.

e. (Alternate touching **k, v, u, ō, p, sh, h,** and **n** three or four times. Point to the sound. Pause one second. Say:) Get ready. (Touch the sound.) *The children respond.*

p

k

v

u

ō

sh

h

n

EXERCISE 6

Individual test

(Call on individual children to identify one or more sounds in exercise 5.)

READING VOCABULARY

EXERCISE 7

Children rhyme with **mop**

a. (Touch the ball for **mop.**) You're going to read this word the fast way. (Pause three seconds.) Get ready. (Move your finger quickly along the arrow.) *Mop.*

b. (Touch the ball for **cop.**) This word rhymes with (pause) **mop.** (Move to **c,** then quickly along the arrow.) *Cop.*

• Yes, what word? (Signal.) *Cop.*

c. (Touch the ball for **top.**) This word rhymes with (pause) **mop.** (Move to **t,** then quickly along the arrow.) *Top.*

• Yes, what word? (Signal.) *Top.*

EXERCISE 8

Children identify, then sound out an irregular word (**was**)

a. (Touch the ball for **was.**) Everybody, you're going to read this word the fast way. (Pause three seconds.) Get ready. (Move your finger quickly along the arrow.) *Was.* Yes, **was.**

b. Now you're going to sound out the word. Get ready. (Quickly touch **w, a, s** as the children say *wwwaaasss.*)

c. Again. (Repeat *b.*)

d. How do we say the word? (Signal.) *Was.* Yes, **was.**

e. (Repeat *b* and *d* until firm.)

EXERCISE 9

Individual test

(Call on individual children to do *b* and *d* in exercise 8.)

EXERCISE 10

Children read the fast way

(Touch the ball for **ōld.**) Get ready to read this word the fast way. (Pause three seconds.) Get ready. (Signal.) *Old.*

EXERCISE 11

Children read the words the fast way

(Have the children read the words on this page the fast way.)

EXERCISE 12

Individual test

(Call on individual children to read one word the fast way.)

mop

cop

top

was

ōld

EXERCISE 13

Children identify, then sound out an irregular word (**of**)

a. (Touch the ball for **of.**) Everybody, you're going to read this word the fast way. (Pause three seconds.) Get ready. (Move your finger quickly along the arrow.) *Of.* Yes, **of.**

b. Now you're going to sound out the word. Get ready. (Quickly touch **o, f** as the children say *ooofff.*)

c. Again. (Repeat *b.*)

d. How do we say the word? (Signal.) *Of.* Yes, **of.**

e. (Repeat *b* and *d* until firm.)

f. (Call on individual children to do *b* and *d.*)

EXERCISE 14

Children identify, then sound out an irregular word (**to**)

(Repeat the procedures in exercise 13 for **to.**)

EXERCISE 15

Children read the fast way

(Touch the ball for **that.**) Get ready to read this word the fast way. (Pause three seconds.) Get ready. (Signal.) *That.*

EXERCISE 16

Children sound out the word and tell what word

a. (Touch the ball for **cōat.**) Sound it out.

b. Get ready. (Touch **c, ō, t** as the children say *cōōōt.*)

• (If sounding out is not firm, repeat *b.*)

c. What word? (Signal.) *Coat.* Yes, **coat.**

EXERCISE 17

Children sound out the word and tell what word

a. (Touch the ball for **gōat.**) Sound it out.

b. Get ready. (Touch **g, ō, t** as the children say *gōōōt.*)

• (If sounding out is not firm, repeat *b.*)

c. What word? (Signal.) *Goat.* Yes, **goat.**

EXERCISE 18

Children read the words the fast way

(Have the children read the words on this page the fast way.)

EXERCISE 19

Individual test

(Call on individual children to read one word the fast way.)

STORY 108

EXERCISE 20

First reading—children read the story the fast way

(Have the children reread any sentences containing words that give them trouble. Keep a list of these words.)

a. (Pass out Storybook.)

b. Open your book to page 37 and get ready to read. ✔

c. We're going to read this story the fast way.

d. Touch the first word. ✔

e. Reading the fast way. First word. (Pause three seconds.) Get ready. (Tap.) *Thē.*

f. Next word. ✔

• (Pause three seconds.) Get ready. (Tap.) *Old.*

g. (Repeat *f* for the remaining words in the first sentence. Pause at least three seconds between taps. The children are to identify each word without sounding it out.)

h. (Repeat *d* through *g* for the next two sentences. Have the children reread the first three sentences until firm.)

i. (The children are to read the remainder of the story the fast way, stopping at the end of each sentence.)

j. (After the first reading of the story, print on the board the words that the children missed more than one time. Have the children sound out each word one time and tell what word.)

k. (After the group's responses are firm, call on individual children to read the words.)

EXERCISE 21

Individual test

a. I'm going to call on individual children to read a whole sentence the fast way.

b. (Call on individual children to read a sentence. Do not tap for each word.)

EXERCISE 22

Second reading—children read the story the fast way and answer questions

a. You're going to read the story again the fast way and I'll ask questions.

b. First word. ✔

• Get ready. (Tap.) *Thē.*

c. (Tap for each remaining word. Pause at least three seconds between taps. Pause longer before words that gave the children trouble during the first reading.)

d. (Ask the comprehension questions below as the children read.)

After the children read:	You ask:
The old goat had an old coat.	What did she have? (Signal.) *An old coat.*
The old goat said, "I will eat this old coat."	What did she say? (Signal.) *I will eat this old coat.*
So she did.	What did she do? (Signal.) *She ate the old coat.*
"That was fun," she said.	What did she say? (Signal.) *That was fun.*
"I ate the old coat."	What did the goat say? (Signal.) *I ate the old coat.*
"And now I am cold."	What did she say? (Signal.) *And now I am cold.*
Now the old goat is sad.	How does she feel? (Signal.) *Sad.*
	• Why? (Signal.) *The children respond.*

EXERCISE 23

Picture comprehension

a. What do you think you'll see in the picture? *The children respond.*

b. Turn the page and look at the picture.

c. (Ask these questions:)

   1. How does that goat feel? *The children respond.*

   • Cold and sad.

   2. Why is she out in the cold without a coat? *The children respond.*

   • Because she ate her coat.

   3. Did you ever go outside without a coat when it was cold? *The children respond.*

WORKSHEET 108

SUMMARY OF INDEPENDENT ACTIVITY
EXERCISE 24

Introduction to independent activity

a. (Pass out Worksheet 108 to each child.)

b. Everybody, you're going to do this worksheet on your own. (Tell the children when they will work the items.)

• Let's go over the things you're going to do.

Sentence copying

a. (Hold up side 1 of your worksheet and point to the first line in the sentence-copying exercise.)

b. Everybody, here's the sentence you're going to write on the lines below.

c. Get ready to read the words in this sentence the fast way. First word. ✔

• Get ready. (Tap.) *Thē.*

d. Next word. ✔

• Get ready. (Tap.) *Goat.*

e. (Repeat *d* for the remaining words.)

f. After you finish your worksheet, you get to draw a picture about the sentence, **thē gōat āte thē cōat.**

Sound writing

a. (Point to the sound-writing exercise.) Here are the sounds you're going to write today. I'll touch the sounds. You say them.

b. (Touch each sound.) *The children respond.*

c. (Repeat the series until firm.)

Matching

a. (Point to the column of words in the Matching Game.)

b. Everybody, you're going to follow the lines and write these words.

c. Reading the fast way.

d. (Point to the first word. Pause.) Get ready. (Signal.) *The children respond.*

e. (Repeat *d* for the remaining words.)

f. (Repeat *d* and *e* until firm.)

Cross-out game

(Point to the boxed word in the Cross-out Game.) Everybody, here's the word you're going to cross out today. What word? (Signal.) *Not.* Yes, **not.**

Pair relations

a. (Point to the pair-relations exercise on side 2.) You're going to circle the picture in each box that shows what the words say.

b. (Point to the space at the top of the page.) After you finish, remember to draw a picture that shows **thē gōat āte thē cōat.**

★INDIVIDUAL CHECKOUT: STORYBOOK
EXERCISE 25

2½–minute individual fluency checkout: rate/accuracy—whole story

(Make a permanent chart for recording results of individual checkouts. See Teacher's Guide for sample chart.)

a. As you are doing your worksheet, I'll call on children one at a time to read the **whole story.** If you can read the whole story the fast way in less than two and a half minutes and if you make no more than three errors, I'll put two stars after your name on the chart for lesson 108.

b. If you make too many errors or don't read the story in less than two and a half minutes, you'll have to practice it and do it again. When you do read it in under two and a half minutes with no more than three errors, you'll get one star. Remember, two stars if you can do it the first time, one star if you do it the second or third time you try.

c. (Call on a child. Tell the child:) Read the whole story very carefully the fast way. Go. (Time the child. If the child makes a mistake, quickly tell the child the correct word and permit the child to continue reading. As soon as the child makes more than three errors or exceeds the time limit, tell the child to stop.) You'll have to read the story to yourself and try again later. (Plan to monitor the child's practice.)

d. (Record two stars for each child who reads appropriately. Congratulate those children.)

e. (Give children who do not earn two stars a chance to read the story again before the next lesson is presented. Award one star to each of those children who meet the rate and accuracy criterion.)

41 words/**2.5 min** = 16 wpm [**3 errors**]

END OF LESSON 108

SOUNDS

EXERCISE 1

Teaching **p** as in **pat**

a. (Point to **p.**) My turn. When I touch it, I'll say it. (Pause. Touch **p** for an instant, saying:) p. (Do not say **puuh.**)

b. (Point to **p.**) Your turn. When I touch it, you say it. (Pause.) Get ready. (Touch **p.**) p.

c. Again. (Touch **p.**) p.

d. (Repeat c until firm.)

p

g

d

k

EXERCISE 2

Sounds firm-up

a. Get ready to say the sounds when I touch them.

b. (Alternate touching **g** and **p.** Point to the sound. Pause one second. Say:) Get ready. (Touch the sound.) *The children respond.*

c. (When **g** and **p** are firm, alternate touching **d, g, k,** and **p** until all four sounds are firm.)

EXERCISE 3

Individual test

(Call on individual children to identify **d, g, k,** or **p.**)

EXERCISE 4

Teacher introduces cross-out game

a. (Use transparency and crayon.)

b. I'll cross out the sounds on this part of the page when you can tell me every sound.

c. Remember—when I touch it, you say it.

d. (Go over the sounds until the children can identify all the sounds in order.)

EXERCISE 5

Individual test

(Call on individual children to identify two or more sounds in exercise 4.)

EXERCISE 6

Teacher crosses out sounds

a. You told me every sound. Get ready to do it again. This time I'll cross out each sound when you tell me what it is.

b. (Point to each sound. Pause. Say:) Get ready. (Touch the sound.) *The children respond.*

• (As you cross out the sound, say:) Goodbye, _____.

I

v

w

ā

ō

READING VOCABULARY
EXERCISE 7

Children read the fast way

a. Get ready to read these words the fast way.

b. (Touch the ball for **got.** Pause three seconds.) Get ready. (Signal.) *Got.*

c. (Repeat *b* for the remaining words on the page.)

EXERCISE 8

Children read the fast way again

a. Get ready to do these words again. Watch where I point.

b. (Point to a word. Pause one second. Say:) Get ready. (Signal.) *The children respond.*

• (Point to the words in this order: **have, not, got, ship.**)

c. (Repeat *b* until firm.)

EXERCISE 9

Individual test

(Call on individual children to read one word the fast way.)

WORKSHEET 160

SUMMARY OF INDEPENDENT ACTIVITY
EXERCISE 19

Introduction to independent activity

a. (Pass out sides 1 and 2 of Worksheet 160 to each child.)

b. Everybody, do a good job on your worksheet today and I'll give you a bonus worksheet.

c. (Hold up side 1 of your worksheet.) You're going to do this worksheet on your own. (Tell the children when they will work the items.)

• Let's go over the things you're going to do.

Story items

a. (Point to the story-items exercise.)

b. Everybody, here are items about the story we read today.

c. Think about what happened in the story and circle the right answer for each item.

Picture comprehension

a. (Point to the pictures in the picture-comprehension exercise.) Everybody, you're going to look at the picture. Then you're going to read each item and write the missing word.

b. Remember—the first sound of each missing word is already written in the blank.

Reading comprehension

a. (Point to the reading-comprehension exercise on side 2.)

b. Everybody, get ready to read the sentences in the box the fast way.

c. First word. ✔

• Get ready. (Tap for each word as the children read the sentences *He fell in the mud. His nose had mud on it.*)

d. (Point to items 1 and 2.) These items tell about the story in the box. You're going to read each item and circle the right answer.

Sound writing

a. (Point to the sound-writing exercise.) Here are the sounds you're going to write today. I'll touch the sounds. You say them.

b. (Touch each sound.) *The children respond.*

c. (Repeat the series until firm.)

Sentence copying

a. (Point to the dotted sentence in the sentence-copying exercise.)

b. You're going to trace the words in this sentence. Then you're going to write the sentence on the other lines.

c. Reading the fast way. First word. ✔

• Get ready. (Tap for each word.)

d. After you finish your worksheet, you get to draw a picture about the sentence, **"I ēat fast," hē said.** You'll draw your picture on a piece of plain paper. (When the children finish their worksheets, give them sheets of plain paper.)

INDIVIDUAL CHECKOUT: STORYBOOK
EXERCISE 20

2½-minute individual fluency checkout: rate/accuracy

a. As you are doing your worksheet, I'll call on children one at a time to read the **whole story.** Remember, you get two stars if you read the story in less than two and a half minutes and make no more than three errors.

b. (Call on a child. Tell the child:) Start with the title and read the story carefully the fast way. Go. (Time the child. Tell the child any words the child misses. Stop the child as soon as the child makes the fourth error or exceeds the time limit.)

c. (If the child meets the rate-accuracy criterion, record two stars on your chart for lesson 160. Congratulate the child. Give children who do not earn two stars a chance to read the story again before the next lesson is presented.)
95 words/**2.5 min** = 38 wpm [**3 errors**]

EXERCISE 21

Bonus worksheet: sides 3 and 4

(After the children have completed their worksheet exercises, give them sides 3 and 4 of Worksheet 160. Tell them they may keep the stories and read them.)

END OF LESSON 160

END OF PRESENTATION BOOK C

EXERCISE 10

Children identify, then sound out an irregular word (**said**)

a. (Touch the ball for **said**.) Everybody, you're going to read this word the fast way. (Pause three seconds.) Get ready. (Move your finger quickly along the arrow.) *Said.* Yes, **said**.

b. Now you're going to sound out the word. Get ready. (Quickly touch **s, a, i, d** as the children say *sssaaaiiid*.)

c. Again. (Repeat *b.*)

d. How do we say the word? (Signal.) *Said.* Yes, **said**.

e. (Repeat *b* and *d* until firm.)

f. (Call on individual children to do *b* and *d*.)

EXERCISE 11

Children sound out the word and tell what word

a. (Touch the ball for **cop**.) Sound it out.

b. Get ready. (Touch **c, o, p** as the children say *cooop*.)

• (If sounding out is not firm, repeat *b*.)

c. What word? (Signal.) *Cop.* Yes, **cop**.

EXERCISE 12

Children sound out the word and tell what word

(Repeat the procedures in exercise 11 for **dip**.)

EXERCISE 13

Children sound out the word and tell what word

(Repeat the procedures in exercise 11 for **down**.)

EXERCISE 14

Children identify, then sound out an irregular word (**of**)

a. (Touch the ball for **of**.) Everybody, you're going to read this word the fast way. (Pause three seconds.) Get ready. (Move your finger quickly along the arrow.) *Of.* Yes, **of**.

b. Now you're going to sound out the word. Get ready. (Quickly touch **o, f** as the children say *ooofff*.)

c. Again. (Repeat *b.*)

d. How do we say the word? (Signal.) *Of.* Yes, **of**.

e. (Repeat *b* and *d* until firm.)

f. (Call on individual children to do *b* and *d*.)

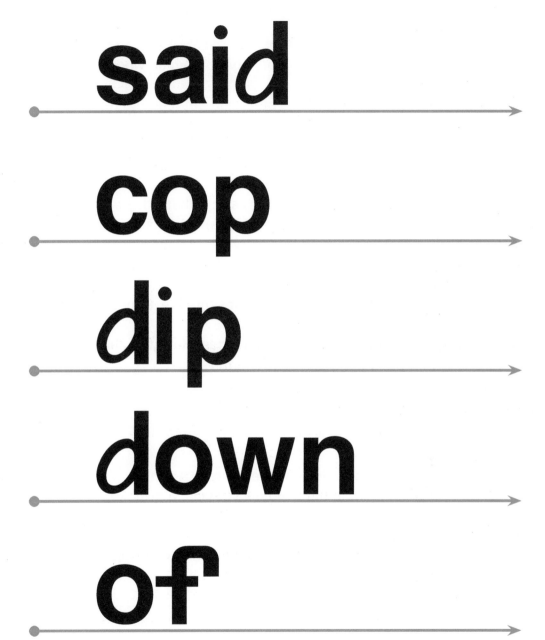

EXERCISE 15

Children read the words the fast way

(Have the children read the words on this page the fast way.)

STORY 160
EXERCISE 15

First reading—children read the title and first three sentences

a. Now you're going to finish the story about the man who went so fast.

b. Everybody, touch the title of the story and get ready to read the words in the title the fast way.

c. First word. ✔

• (Pause two seconds.) Get ready. (Tap.) *A.*

d. (Tap for each remaining word in the title.)

e. (After the children have read the title, ask:) What's this story about? (Signal.) *A man liked to go fast.* Yes, **a man liked to go fast.**

f. Everybody, get ready to read this story the fast way.

g. First word. ✔

• (Pause two seconds.) Get ready. (Tap.) *A.*

h. (Tap for the remaining words in the first sentence. Pause at least two seconds between taps.)

i. (Repeat *g* and *h* for the next two sentences. Have the children reread the first three sentences until firm.)

EXERCISE 16

Individual children or the group read sentences to complete the first reading

a. I'm going to call on individual children to read a sentence. Everybody, follow along and point to the words. If you hear a mistake, raise your hand.

b. (Call on a child.) Read the next sentence. (Do not tap for the words. Let children read at their own pace, but be sure they read the sentence correctly.)

To Correct
(Have the child sound out the word. Then return to the beginning of the sentence.)

c. (Repeat *b* for most of the remaining sentences in the story. Occasionally have the group read a sentence. When the group is to read, say:) Everybody, read the next sentence. (Pause two seconds.) Get ready. (Tap for each word in the sentence. Pause at least two seconds between taps.)

EXERCISE 17

Second reading—individual children or the group read each sentence; the group answer questions

a. You're going to read the story again. This time I'm going to ask questions.

b. Starting with the first word of the title. ✔

• Get ready. (Tap as the children read the title. Pause at least two seconds between taps.)

c. (Call on a child.) Read the first sentence. *The child responds.*

d. (Repeat *b* and *c* in exercise 16. Present the following comprehension questions to the entire group.)

After the children read:	You say:
"I will not do things fast."	What did the man say? *The children respond.* He said, "I will slow down. I will not do things fast."
And he did not eat so fast that he got fish cake on his nose.	Name the things that the man did not do fast any more. *The children respond.* He didn't go fast in his car. He did not walk fast. He did not talk fast. And he did not eat fast.

EXERCISE 18

Picture comprehension

a. What do you think you'll see in the picture? *The children respond.*

b. Turn the page and look at the picture.

c. (Ask these questions:)

1. Does the man look like he's going fast in that picture? *No.*

2. Is his wife happy? *Yes.*

• Why do you think she doesn't like him to go fast when he eats? *The children respond.*

3. Did you ever eat so fast that you got food on your nose? *The children respond.*

STORY 109
EXERCISE 16

First reading—children read the story the fast way

(Have the children reread any sentences containing words that give them trouble. Keep a list of these words.)

a. (Pass out Storybook.)

b. Open your book to page 39 and get ready to read. ✔

c. We're going to read this story the fast way.

d. Touch the first word. ✔

e. Reading the fast way. First word. (Pause three seconds.) Get ready. (Tap.) *Thē.*

f. Next word. ✔

• (Pause three seconds.) Get ready. (Tap.) *Fat.*

g. (Repeat *f* for the remaining words in the first sentence. Pause at least three seconds between taps. The children are to identify each word without sounding it out.)

h. (Repeat *d* through *g* for the next two sentences. Have the children reread the first three sentences until firm.)

i. (The children are to read the remainder of the story the fast way, stopping at the end of each sentence.)

j. (After the first reading of the story, print on the board the words that the children missed more than one time. Have the children sound out each word one time and tell what word.)

k. (After the group's responses are firm, call on individual children to read the words.)

EXERCISE 17

Individual test

a. Turn back to page 39. I'm going to call on individual children to read a whole sentence the fast way.

b. (Call on individual children to read a sentence. Do not tap for each word.)

EXERCISE 18

Second reading—children read the story the fast way and answer questions

a. You're going to read the story again the fast way and I'll ask questions.

b. First word. ✔

• Get ready. (Tap.) *Thē.*

c. (Tap for each remaining word. Pause at least three seconds between taps. Pause longer before words that gave the children trouble during the first reading.)

d. (Ask the comprehension questions below as the children read.)

After the children read:	You say:
The fat man and his fat cow got on a little rock.	Who got on the rock? (Signal.) *The fat man and his fat cow.*
A cat said, "Fat man, that rock will not hold a fat man and his cow."	What did the cat say? (Signal.) *Fat man, that rock will not hold a fat man and his cow.*
"That rock will go down the hill."	What did the cat say? (Signal.) *That rock will go down the hill.*
Did the rock go down the hill with the fat man and his fat cow?	What do you think? *The children respond.*

EXERCISE 19

Picture comprehension

a. Everybody, look at the picture.

b. (Ask these questions:)

  1. Did the rock go down the hill with the fat man and his fat cow? *Yes.*
  2. How do you think that fat man feels? *The children respond.*
  3. What would you do if you were that fat man? *The children respond.*

STORYBOOK

READ THE ITEMS 160
EXERCISE 12

Children read items 1 and 2

a. (Pass out Storybook.)

b. Open your book to page 190. ✔

c. Get ready to read the items and play the game.

d. Finger under the first word of the title. ✔

e. When I tap, read the title. (Pause.) Get ready. (Tap.) *Read the items.*

f. Touch item 1 and get ready to read. ✔

• First word. (Tap for each word as the children read
When the teacher says "Touch your head," hold up your hands.)

• (Repeat until firm.)

g. Everybody, get ready to say item 1. (Pause and signal.)
The children say the sentence.

• (Repeat four times or until firm.)

h. Touch item 2 and get ready to read. ✔

• First word. (Tap for each word as the children read
If the teacher picks up a book, say "Now.")

• (Repeat until firm.)

i. Everybody, get ready to say item 2. (Pause and signal.)
The children say the sentence.

• (Repeat four times or until firm.)

EXERCISE 13

Children reread items 1 and 2 and answer questions

a. Everybody, touch item 1. ✔

b. Read item 1 to yourself. Raise your hand when you know what you're going to do and when you're going to do it.

c. (After the children raise their hands, say:) Everybody, what are you going to do when I say **"Touch your head"**? (Signal.) *Hold up my hands.*

> **To Correct**
> 1. Everybody, read item 1 out loud. (Tap as the children read each word.)
> 2. What are you going to do when I say **"Touch your head"**? (Signal.) *Hold up my hands.*

d. Everybody, when are you going to **hold up your hands?** (Signal.)
When the teacher says "Touch your head."

> **To Correct**
> 1. Everybody, read item 1 out loud. (Tap as the children read each word.)
> 2. When are you going to **hold up your hands?** (Signal.) *When the teacher says "Touch your head."*

e. (Repeat *c* and *d* until firm.)

f. Everybody, touch item 2. ✔

g. Read item 2 to yourself. Raise your hand when you know what you're going to do and when you're going to do it.

h. (After the children raise their hands, say:) Everybody, what are you going to do if I **pick up a book?** (Signal.) *Say "Now."*

> **To Correct**
> 1. Everybody, read item 2 out loud. (Tap as the children read each word.)
> 2. What are you going to do if I **pick up a book?** (Signal.) *Say "Now."*

i. Everybody, when are you going to **say "Now"?**
(Signal.) *If the teacher picks up a book.*

> **To Correct**
> 1. Everybody, read item 2 out loud. (Tap as the children read each word.)
> 2. When are you going to **say "Now"?** (Signal.) *If the teacher picks up a book.*

j. (Repeat *h* and *i* until firm.)

EXERCISE 14

Children play the game

a. Everybody, touch item 1. ✔

b. Read the item to yourself. Raise your hand when you know what you're going to do and when you're going to do it.

c. (After the children raise their hands, say:) Let's play the game. Think about what you're going to do (pause) and when you're going to do it.

d. (Hold out your hand. Pause.) Get ready. **Touch your head.** (Pause. Drop your hand.) *The children hold up their hands immediately.*

> **To Correct**
> 1. What did I say? (Signal.) *Touch your head.*
> 2. What are you supposed to do when I say **"Touch your head"**? (Signal.) *Hold up my hands.*
> 3. (If the children's responses are not firm, have them read item 1 aloud.)
> 4. (Repeat exercise 14.)

WORKSHEET 109

SUMMARY OF INDEPENDENT ACTIVITY
EXERCISE 20

Introduction to independent activity

a. (Pass out Worksheet 109 to each child.)

b. Everybody, you're going to do this worksheet on your own. (Tell the children when they will work the items.)

• Let's go over the things you're going to do.

Sentence copying

a. (Hold up side 1 of your worksheet and point to the first line in the sentence-copying exercise.)

b. Everybody, here's the sentence you're going to write on the lines below.

c. Get ready to read the words in this sentence the fast way. First word. ✔

• Get ready. (Tap.) *A.*

d. Next word. ✔

• Get ready. (Tap.) *Cow.*

e. (Repeat *d* for the remaining words.)

f. After you finish your worksheet, you get to draw a picture about the sentence, **a cow got on a rock.**

Sound writing

a. (Point to the sound-writing exercise.) Here are the sounds you're going to write today. I'll touch the sounds. You say them.

b. (Touch each sound.) *The children respond.*

c. (Repeat the series until firm.)

Matching

a. (Point to the column of words in the Matching Game.)

b. Everybody, you're going to follow the lines and write these words.

c. Reading the fast way.

d. (Point to the first word. Pause.) Get ready. (Signal.) *The children respond.*

e. (Repeat *d* for the remaining words.)

f. (Repeat *d* and *e* until firm.)

Cross-out game

(Point to the boxed word in the Cross-out Game.) Everybody, here's the word you're going to cross out today. What word? (Signal.) *Man.* Yes, **man.**

Pair relations

a. (Point to the pair-relations exercise on side 2.) You're going to circle the picture in each box that shows what the words say.

b. (Point to the space at the top of the page.) After you finish, remember to draw a picture that shows **a cow got on a rock.**

INDIVIDUAL CHECKOUT: STORYBOOK
EXERCISE 21

2-minute individual fluency checkout: rate/accuracy—first page

a. As you are doing your worksheet, I'll call on children one at a time to read the **first page** of the story. If you can read the first page of the story the fast way in less than two minutes and if you make no more than three errors, I'll put two stars after your name on the chart for lesson 109.

b. If you make too many errors or don't read the page in less than two minutes, you'll have to practice it and do it again. When you do read it in under two minutes with no more than three errors, you'll get one star. Remember, two stars if you can do it the first time, one star if you do it the second or third time you try.

c. (Call on a child. Tell the child:) Read the first page of the story very carefully the fast way. Go. (Time the child. If the child makes a mistake, quickly tell the child the correct word and permit the child to continue reading. As soon as the child makes more than three errors or exceeds the time limit, tell the child to stop.) You'll have to read the page to yourself and try again later. (Plan to monitor the child's practice.)

d. (Record two stars for each child who reads appropriately. Congratulate those children.)

e. (Give children who do not earn two stars a chance to read the page again before the next lesson is presented. Award one star to each of those children who meet the rate and accuracy criterion.)

35 words/**2 min** = 18 wpm [**3 errors**]

END OF LESSON 109

EXERCISE 7

Children sound out an irregular word (**took**)

a. (Touch the ball for **took.**) Sound it out.

b. Get ready. (Quickly touch each sound as the children say *toook.*)

c. Again. (Repeat *b* until firm.)

d. That's how we <u>sound out</u> the word. Here's how we <u>say</u> the word. **Took.** How do we <u>say</u> the word? (Signal.) *Took.*

e. Now you're going to <u>sound out</u> the word. Get ready. (Touch each sound as the children say *tooook.*)

f. Now you're going to say the word. Get ready. (Signal.) *Took.*

g. (Repeat *e* and *f* until firm.)

h. Yes, this word is **took.** I **took** your pencil.

EXERCISE 8

Individual test

(Call on individual children to do *e* and *f* in exercise 7.)

EXERCISE 9

Children sound out the word and tell what word

a. (Touch the ball for **moon.**) Sound it out.

b. Get ready. (Touch **m, oo, n** as the children say *mmmoooonnn.*)

• (If sounding out is not firm, repeat *b.*)

c. What word? (Signal.) *Moon.* Yes, **moon.**

EXERCISE 10

Children read the words the fast way

a. Now you get to read the words on this page the fast way.

b. (Touch the ball for **moon.** Pause three seconds.) Get ready. (Move your finger quickly along the arrow.) *Moon.*

c. (Repeat *b* for **took.**)

EXERCISE 11

Individual test

(Call on individual children to read one word the fast way.)

SOUNDS

EXERCISE 1

Sounds firm-up

a. Get ready to say the sounds when I touch them.

b. (Alternate touching **p** and **t.** Point to the sound. Pause one second. Say:) Get ready. (Touch the sound.) *The children respond.*

c. (When **p** and **t** are firm, alternate touching **g, v, p,** and **t** until all four sounds are firm.)

p

t

g

v

EXERCISE 2

Individual test

(Call on individual children to identify **g, v, p,** or **t.**)

p

k

n

sh

o

c

ō

u

EXERCISE 3

Sounds firm-up

a. (Point to **p.**) When I touch the sound, you say it.

b. (Pause.) Get ready. (Touch **p.**) *p.*

c. Again. (Repeat *b* until firm.)

d. Get ready to say all the sounds when I touch them.

e. (Alternate touching **k, n, sh, o, c, p, ō,** and **u** three or four times. Point to the sound. Pause one second. Say:) Get ready. (Touch the sound.) *The children respond.*

EXERCISE 4

Individual test

(Call on individual children to identify one or more sounds in exercise 3.)

EXERCISE 4

Children read the fast way

a. Get ready to read these words the fast way.

b. (Touch the ball for **bent**. Pause three seconds.) Get ready. (Signal.) *Bent.*

c. (Repeat *b* for the remaining words on the page.)

EXERCISE 5

Children read the fast way again

a. Get ready to do these words again. Watch where I point.

b. (Point to a word. Pause one second. Say:) Get ready. (Signal.) *The children respond.*

• (Point to the words in this order: **crȳ, whȳ, room, bent.**)

c. (Repeat *b* until firm.)

EXERCISE 6

Individual test

(Call on individual children to read one word the fast way.)

bent

crȳ

room

whȳ

READING VOCABULARY

EXERCISE 5

Children read the fast way

a. Get ready to read these words the fast way.

b. (Touch the ball for **fog.** Pause three seconds.) Get ready. (Signal.) *Fog.*

c. (Repeat *b* for the remaining words on the page.)

EXERCISE 6

Children read the fast way again

a. Get ready to do these words again. Watch where I point.

b. (Point to a word. Pause one second. Say:) Get ready. (Signal.) *The children respond.* (Point to the words in this order: **fog, log, lots, sand, ēars.**)

c. (Repeat *b* until firm.)

EXERCISE 7

Individual test

(Call on individual children to read one word the fast way.)

fog

sand

ēars

lots

log

Groups that are firm on Mastery Tests 29 and 30 should skip this lesson.

READING VOCABULARY

EXERCISE 1

Children read the fast way

a. Get ready to read these words the fast way.

b. (Touch the ball for **think.** Pause three seconds.) Get ready. (Signal.) *Think.*

c. (Repeat *b* for the remaining words on the page.)

EXERCISE 2

Children read the fast way again

a. Get ready to do these words again. Watch where I point.

b. (Point to a word. Pause one second. Say:) Get ready. (Signal.) *The children respond.*

• (Point to the words in this order: **faster, thing, down, slōwer, think.**)

c. (Repeat *b* until firm.)

EXERCISE 3

Individual test

(Call on individual children to read one word the fast way.)

think

thing

faster

slōwer

down

EXERCISE 8

Children identify, then sound out an irregular word (**to**)

a. (Touch the ball for **to.**) Everybody, you're going to read this word the fast way. (Pause three seconds.) Get ready. (Move your finger quickly along the arrow.) *To.* Yes, **to.**

b. Now you're going to sound out the word. Get ready. (Quickly touch **t, o** as the children say *tooo.*)

c. Again. (Repeat *b.*)

d. How do we say the word? (Signal.) *To.* Yes, **to.**

e. (Repeat *b* and *d* until firm.)

EXERCISE 9

Individual test

(Call on individual children to do *b* and *d* in exercise 8.)

EXERCISE 10

Children sound out the word and tell what word

a. (Touch the ball for **dog.**) Sound it out.

b. Get ready. (Touch **d, o, g** as the children say *dooog.*)

• (If sounding out is not firm, repeat *b.*)

c. What word? (Signal.) *Dog.* Yes, **dog.**

EXERCISE 11

Children sound out the word and tell what word

a. (Touch the ball for **tāil.**) Sound it out.

b. Get ready. (Touch **t, ā, l** as the children say *tāāālll.*)

• (If sounding out is not firm, repeat *b.*)

c. What word? (Signal.) *Tail.* Yes, **tail.**

EXERCISE 12

Children read the words the fast way

a. Now you get to read the words on this page the fast way.

b. (Touch the ball for **to.** Pause three seconds.) Get ready. (Move your finger quickly along the arrow.) *To.*

c. (Repeat *b* for each word on the page.)

to

dog

tāil

EXERCISE 13

Individual test

(Call on individual children to read one word the fast way.)

EXERCISE 22

Picture comprehension

a. Everybody, look at the picture.

b. (Ask these questions:)
   1. Does he look like he's going fast? *Yes.*
   - Where's the meat pie? *The children respond.*
     Yes, it's flying toward his wife.
   2. What's that stuff on his feet? *The children respond.*
   - Egg.
   3. Does he even have food all over his nose? *Yes.*
   - Fish cake.

c. I think he'd better slow down. We'll see what happens when we read the rest of the story.

WORKSHEET 159

SUMMARY OF INDEPENDENT ACTIVITY
EXERCISE 23

Introduction to independent activity

a. (Pass out Worksheet 159 to each child.)

b. Everybody, you're going to do this worksheet on your own. (Tell the children when they will work the items.)
   - Let's go over the things you're going to do.

Story items

a. (Hold up side 1 of your worksheet and point to the story-items exercise.)

b. Everybody, here are items about the story we read today.

c. Think about what happened in the story and circle the right answer for each item.

Picture comprehension

a. (Point to the pictures in the picture-comprehension exercise.) Everybody, you're going to look at the picture. Then you're going to read each item and write the missing word.

b. Remember—the first sound of each missing word is already written in the blank.

Reading comprehension

a. (Point to the reading-comprehension exercise on side 2.)

b. Everybody, get ready to read the sentences in the box the fast way.

c. First word. ✔

   - Get ready. (Tap for each word as the children read the sentences *A girl walked down the road. She met a big fox.*)

d. (Point to items 1 and 2.) These items tell about the story in the box. You're going to read each item and circle the right answer.

Sound writing

a. (Point to the sound-writing exercise.) Here are the sounds you're going to write today. I'll touch the sounds. You say them.

b. (Touch each sound.) *The children respond.*

c. (Repeat the series until firm.)

Sentence copying

a. (Point to the dotted sentence in the sentence-copying exercise.)

b. You're going to trace the words in this sentence. Then you're going to write the sentence on the other lines.

c. Reading the fast way. First word. ✔

   - Get ready. (Tap for each word.)

d. After you finish your worksheet, you get to draw a picture about the sentence, **hē āte a mēat pīe.** You'll draw your picture on a piece of plain paper. (When the children finish their worksheets, give them sheets of plain paper.)

END OF LESSON 159

STORYBOOK

STORY 110
EXERCISE 14

First reading—children read the story the fast way

(Have the children reread any sentences containing words that give them trouble. Keep a list of these words.)

a. (Pass out Storybook.)

b. Open your book to page 42 and get ready to read. ✔

c. We're going to read this story the fast way.

d. Touch the first word. ✔

e. Reading the fast way. First word. (Pause three seconds.) Get ready. (Tap.) *Thē.*

f. Next word. ✔
- (Pause three seconds.) Get ready. (Tap.) *Rat.*

g. (Repeat *f* for the remaining words in the first sentence. Pause at least three seconds between taps. The children are to identify each word without sounding it out.)

h. (Repeat *d* through *g* for the next two sentences. Have the children reread the first three sentences until firm.)

i. (The children are to read the remainder of the story the fast way, stopping at the end of each sentence.)

j. (After the first reading of the story, print on the board the words that the children missed more than one time. Have the children sound out each word one time and tell what word.)

k. (After the group's responses are firm, call on individual children to read the words.)

EXERCISE 15

Individual test

a. Look at page 42. I'm going to call on individual children to read a whole sentence the fast way.

b. (Call on individual children to read a sentence. Do not tap for each word.)

EXERCISE 16

Second reading—children read the story the fast way and answer questions

a. You're going to read the story again the fast way and I'll ask questions.

b. First word. ✔
- Get ready. (Tap.) *Thē.*

c. (Tap for each remaining word. Pause at least three seconds between taps. Pause longer before words that gave the children trouble during the first reading.)

d. (Ask the comprehension questions below as the children read.)

After the children read:	You say:
Thē rat had fun.	Who is this story about? (Signal.) *A rat.*
He ran in thē sand.	What did he do? (Signal.) *He ran in the sand.*
He had sand on his feet.	Where did he have sand? (Signal.) *On his feet.*
He had sand on his ears.	Tell me all the places he had sand. (Signal.) *On his feet and ears.*
He had sand on his nose.	Tell me all the places he had sand. (Signal.) *On his feet, ears, and nose.*
He had sand on his tail.	Tell me all the places he had sand. (Signal.) *On his feet, ears, nose, and tail.*
He said, "I have a lot of sand on me."	What did he say? (Signal.) *I have a lot of sand on me.*

EXERCISE 17

Picture comprehension

a. What do you think you'll see in the picture? *The children respond.*

b. Turn the page and look at the picture.

c. Show me the little specks of sand.

d. (Ask these questions:)

   1. What is that rat doing? *The children respond.* Running in the sand.

   2. How do you think it feels to run through the sand? *The children respond.*

STORY 159
EXERCISE 19

First reading—children read the title and first three sentences

a. Look at page 187. ✔
You're going to read the first part of this story today.

b. Everybody, touch the title of the story and get ready to read the words in the title the fast way.

c. First word. ✔

• (Pause two seconds.) Get ready. (Tap.) *A.*

d. (Tap for each remaining word in the title.)

e. (After the children have read the title, ask:) What's this story about? (Signal.) *A man liked to go fast.* Yes, **a man liked to go fast.**

f. Everybody, get ready to read this story the fast way.

g. First word. ✔

• (Pause two seconds.) Get ready. (Tap.) *A.*

h. (Tap for the remaining words in the first sentence. Pause at least two seconds between taps.)

i. (Repeat *g* and *h* for the next two sentences. Have the children reread the first three sentences until firm.)

EXERCISE 20

Individual children or the group read sentences to complete the first reading

a. I'm going to call on individual children to read a sentence. Everybody, follow along and point to the words. If you hear a mistake, raise your hand.

b. (Call on a child.) Read the next sentence. (Do not tap for the words. Let children read at their own pace, but be sure they read the sentence correctly.)

To Correct
(Have the child sound out the word. Then return to the beginning of the sentence.)

c. (Repeat *b* for most of the remaining sentences in the story. Occasionally have the group read a sentence. When the group is to read, say:) Everybody, read the next sentence. (Pause two seconds.) Get ready. (Tap for each word in the sentence. Pause at least two seconds between taps.)

EXERCISE 21

Second reading—individual children or the group read each sentence; the group answer questions

a. You're going to read the story again. This time I'm going to ask questions.

b. Starting with the first word of the title. ✔

• Get ready. (Tap as the children read the title. Pause at least two seconds between taps.)

c. (Call on a child.) Read the first sentence. *The child responds.*

d. (Repeat *b* and *c* in exercise 20. Present the following comprehension questions to the entire group.)

After the children read:	You say:
A man liked to go fast.	What's this story about? (Signal.) *A man liked to go fast.*
He even talked fast.	Name some things that the man did fast. *The children respond.* He went fast in his car. He walked fast and ran fast. He even talked fast.
He sat down to eat an egg and a fish cake and a meat pie.	What did he eat? (Signal.) *An egg, a fish cake, and a meat pie.*
But he ate so fast that the egg slipped and fell on his feet.	What happened? (Signal.) *He ate so fast that the egg slipped and fell on his feet.*
The meat pie hit his wife.	Tell me all the things that happened when he went to eat the fish cake and the meat pie. *The children respond.* His nose went into the fish cake. He hit the meat pie. And the meat pie hit his wife.

WORKSHEET 110

SUMMARY OF INDEPENDENT ACTIVITY
EXERCISE 18

Introduction to independent activity

a. (Pass out sides 1 and 2 of Worksheet 110 to each child.)

b. Everybody, do a good job on your worksheet today and I'll give you a bonus worksheet.

c. (Hold up side 1 of your worksheet.) You're going to do this worksheet on your own. (Tell the children when they will work the items.)

• Let's go over the things you're going to do.

Sentence copying

a. (Point to the first line in the sentence-copying exercise.)

b. Everybody, here's the sentence you're going to write on the lines below.

c. Get ready to read the words in this sentence the fast way. First word. ✔

• Get ready. (Tap.) *He.*

d. Next word. ✔

• Get ready. (Tap.) *Had.*

e. (Repeat *d* for the remaining words.)

f. After you finish your worksheet, you get to draw a picture about the sentence, **hē had sand on him.**

Sound writing

a. (Point to the sound-writing exercise.) Here are the sounds you're going to write today. I'll touch the sounds. You say them.

b. (Touch each sound.) *The children respond.*

c. (Repeat the series until firm.)

Matching

a. (Point to the column of words in the Matching Game.)

b. Everybody, you're going to follow the lines and write these words.

c. Reading the fast way.

d. (Point to the first word. Pause.) Get ready. (Signal.) *The children respond.*

e. (Repeat *d* for the remaining words.)

f. (Repeat *d* and *e* until firm.)

Cross-out game

(Point to the boxed word in the Cross-out Game.) Everybody, here's the word you're going to cross out today. What word? (Signal.) *Sand.* Yes, **sand.**

Pair relations

a. (Point to the pair-relations exercise on side 2.) You're going to circle the picture in each box that shows what the words say.

b. (Point to the space at the top of the page.) After you finish, remember to draw a picture that shows **hē had sand on him.**

INDIVIDUAL CHECKOUT: STORYBOOK
EXERCISE 19

2-minute individual fluency checkout: rate/accuracy—whole story

a. As you are doing your worksheet, I'll call on children one at a time to read the **whole story.** Remember, you get two stars if you read the story in less than two minutes and make no more than three errors.

b. (Call on a child. Tell the child:) Read the whole story very carefully the fast way. Go. (Time the child. Tell the child any words the child misses. Stop the child as soon as the child makes the fourth error or exceeds the time limit.)

c. (If the child meets the rate-accuracy criterion, record two stars on your chart for lesson 110. Congratulate the child. Give children who do not earn two stars a chance to read the story again before the next lesson is presented.)

43 words/**2 min** = 22 wpm [**3 errors**]

EXERCISE 20

Bonus worksheet: sides 3 and 4

(After the children have completed their worksheet exercises, give them sides 3 and 4 of Worksheet 110. Tell them they may keep the stories and read them.)

END OF LESSON 110

Before presenting lesson 111, give Mastery Test 21 to each child. Do not present lesson 111 to any groups that are not firm on this test.

STORYBOOK

READ THE ITEMS 159
EXERCISE 16

Children read items 1 and 2

a. (Pass out Storybook.)

b. Open your book to page 186. ✔

c. Get ready to read the items and play the game.

d. Finger under the first word of the title. ✔

e. When I tap, read the title. (Pause.) Get ready. (Tap.) *Read the items.*

f. Touch item 1 and get ready to read. ✔

• First word. (Tap for each word as the children read *If the teacher says "Touch your nose," touch your feet.*)

• (Repeat until firm.)

g. Everybody, get ready to say item 1. (Pause and signal.) *The children say the sentence.*

• (Repeat four times or until firm.)

h. Touch item 2 and get ready to read. ✔

• First word. (Tap for each word as the children read *When the teacher says, "Give me your book," give the teacher your book.*)

• (Repeat until firm.)

i. Everybody, get ready to say item 2. (Pause and signal.) *The children say the sentence.*

• (Repeat four times or until firm.)

EXERCISE 17

Children reread items 1 and 2 and answer questions

a. Everybody, touch item 1. ✔

b. Read item 1 to yourself. Raise your hand when you know what you're going to do and when you're going to do it.

c. (After the children raise their hands, say:) Everybody, what are you going to do if I say **"Touch your nose"**? (Signal.) *Touch my feet.*

> **To Correct**
> 1. Everybody, read item 1 out loud. (Tap as the children read each word.)
> 2. What are you going to do when I say **"Touch your nose"**? (Signal.) *Touch my feet.*

d. Everybody, when are you going to **touch your feet**? (Signal.) *If the teacher says "Touch your nose."*

> **To Correct**
> 1. Everybody, read item 1 out loud. (Tap as the children read each word.)
> 2. When are you going to **touch your feet**? (Signal.) *If the teacher says "Touch your nose."*

e. (Repeat c and d until firm.)

f. Everybody, touch item 2. ✔

g. Read item 2 to yourself. Raise your hand when you know what you're going to do and when you're going to do it.

h. (After the children raise their hands, say:) Everybody, what are you going to do when I say **"Give me your book?** (Signal.) *Give you my book.*

> **To Correct**
> 1. Everybody, read item 2 out loud. (Tap as the children read each word.)
> 2. What are you going to do when I say **"Give me your book"**? (Signal.) *Give you my book.*

i. Everybody, when are you going to **give me your book?** (Signal.) *When the teacher says "Give me your book."*

> **To Correct**
> 1. Everybody, read item 2 out loud. (Tap as the children read each word.)
> 2. When are you going to **give me your book?** (Signal.) *When the teacher says "Give me your book."*

j. (Repeat h and i until firm.)

EXERCISE 18

Children play the game

a. Everybody, touch item 1. ✔

b. Read the item to yourself. Raise your hand when you know what you're going to do and when you're going to do it.

c. (After the children raise their hands, say:) Let's play the game. Think about what you're going to do (pause) and when you're going to do it.

d. (Hold out your hand. Pause.) Get ready. **Touch your nose.** (Drop your hand.) *The children touch their feet immediately.*

> **To Correct**
> 1. What did I say? (Signal.) *Touch your nose.*
> 2. What are you supposed to do when I say **"Touch your nose"**? (Signal.) *Touch my feet.*
> 3. (If the children's responses are not firm, have them read item 1 aloud.)
> 4. (Repeat exercise 18.)

MASTERY TEST 21 — after lesson 110, before lesson 111

a. Get ready to read these words the fast way.

b. (test item) (Touch the ball for **have**. Pause three seconds.)
Get ready. (Signal.) *Have.*

c. (test item) (Touch the ball for **gōats**. Pause three seconds.)
Get ready. (Signal.) *Goats.*

d. (test item) (Touch the ball for **shāve**. Pause three seconds.)
Get ready. (Signal.) *Shave.*

e. (test item) (Touch the ball for **cow**. Pause three seconds.)
Get ready. (Signal.) *Cow.*

f. (test item) (Touch the ball for **was**. Pause three seconds.)
Get ready. (Signal.) *Was.*

Total number of test items: **5**
A group is weak if more than one-third of the children missed any of the items on the test.

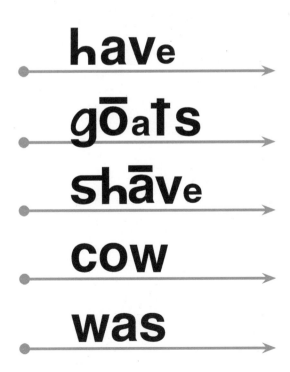

If the group is firm on Mastery Test 21 and was firm on Mastery Test 20:

Skip lesson 111 and present lesson 112 to the group during the next reading period. If more than one child missed any of the items on the test, present the firming procedures specified below to those children.

If the group is firm on Mastery Test 21 but was weak on Mastery Test 20:

Present lesson 111 to the group during the next reading period. If more than one child missed any of the items on the test, present the firming procedures specified below to those children.

If the group is weak on Mastery Test 21:

A. Present these firming procedures to the group during the next reading period.
   1. Lesson 105, Reading Vocabulary, page 312 (Book B), exercises 16, 17.
   2. Lesson 107, Reading Vocabulary, pages 324–325 (Book B), exercises 6 through 16.
   3. Lesson 109, Reading Vocabulary, page 7, exercises 7 through 9.
B. After presenting the above exercises, again give Mastery Test 21 individually to members of the group who failed the test.
C. If the group is firm (less than one-third of the total group missed any items on the retest), present lesson 111 to the group during the next reading period.
D. If the group is still weak (more than one-third of the total group missed any items on the retest), repeat *A* and *B* during the next reading period.

EXERCISE 12

Children rhyme with **fell** and **tell**

a. (Touch the ball for **fell.**) You're going to read this word the fast way. (Pause three seconds.) Get ready. (Move your finger quickly along the arrow.) *Fell.*

b. (Touch the ball for **tell.**) This word rhymes with (pause) **fell.** (Move to **t,** then quickly along the arrow.) *Tell.* Yes, what word? (Signal.) *Tell.*

EXERCISE 13

Children sound out the word and tell what word

a. (Touch the ball for **fast.**) Sound it out.

b. Get ready. (Touch **f, a, s, t** as the children say *fffaaassst.*)

• (If sounding out is not firm, repeat *b.*)

c. What word? (Signal.) *Fast.* Yes, **fast.**

EXERCISE 14

Children read the words the fast way

a. Now you get to read the words on this page the fast way.

b. (Touch the ball for **fell.** Pause three seconds.) Get ready. (Move your finger quickly along the arrow.) *Fell.*

c. (Repeat *b* for each word on the page.)

EXERCISE 15

Individual test

(Call on individual children to read one word the fast way.)

fell

tell

fast

(Groups that are firm on Mastery Tests 20 and 21 should skip this lesson and do lesson 112 today.)

SOUNDS

EXERCISE 1

Teacher and children play the sounds game

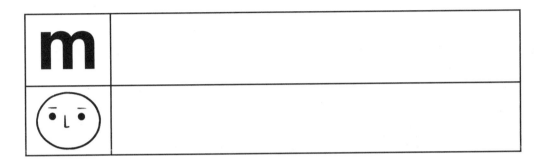

a. (Use transparency and crayon. Write the sounds in the symbol box. Keep score in the score box.)

b. I'm smart. I think I can beat you in a game.

c. Here's the rule. When I touch a sound, you say it.

d. (Play the game. Make one symbol at a time in the symbol box. Use the symbols **l, w,** I, and **h.**)
(Make each symbol quickly. Pause. Touch the symbol. Play the game for about two minutes.)
(Then ask:) Who won? (Draw a mouth on the face in the score box.)

EXERCISE 2

Teacher introduces cross-out game

a. (Use transparency and crayon.)

b. I'll cross out the sounds on this page when you can tell me every sound.

c. Remember—when I touch it, you say it.

d. (Go over the sounds until the children can identify all the sounds in order.)

EXERCISE 3

Individual test

(Call on individual children to identify two or more sounds in exercise 2.)

EXERCISE 4

Teacher crosses out sounds

a. You told me every sound. Get ready to do it again. This time I'll cross out each sound when you tell me what it is.

b. (Point to each sound. Pause. Say:) Get ready. (Touch the sound.) *The children respond.*

• (As you cross out the sound, say:) Goodbye, _____.

EXERCISE 9

Children read the fast way

a. Get ready to read these words the fast way.

b. (Touch the ball for **went.** Pause three seconds.) Get ready. (Signal.) *Went.*

c. (Repeat *b* for the remaining words on the page.)

EXERCISE 10

Children read the fast way again

a. Get ready to do these words again. Watch where I point.

b. (Point to a word. Pause one second. Say:) Get ready. (Signal.) *The children respond.*

• (Point to the words in this order: **went, wīpe, slipped, slōw.**)

c. (Repeat *b* until firm.)

EXERCISE 11

Individual test

(Call on individual children to read one word the fast way.)

went

slōw

slipped

wīpe

READING VOCABULARY

EXERCISE 5

Children read the fast way

a. Get ready to read these words the fast way.

b. (Touch the ball for **lots.** Pause three seconds.) Get ready. (Signal.) *Lots.*

c. (Repeat *b* for the remaining words on the page.)

EXERCISE 6

Children read the fast way again

a. Get ready to do these words again. Watch where I point.

b. (Point to a word. Pause one second. Say:) Get ready. (Signal.)
The children respond.

• (Point to the words in this order: **with, us, fog, have, lots.**)

c. (Repeat *b* until firm.)

EXERCISE 7

Individual test

(Call on individual children to read one word the fast way.)

lots

fog

us

have

with

READING VOCABULARY
EXERCISE 6

Children read the fast way

a. Get ready to read these words the fast way.
b. (Touch the ball for **pīe.** Pause three seconds.) Get ready. (Signal.) *Pie.*
c. (Repeat *b* for the remaining words on the page.)

EXERCISE 7

Children read the fast way again

a. Get ready to do these words again. Watch where I point.
b. (Point to a word. Pause one second. Say:) Get ready. (Signal.) *The children respond.*
• (Point to the words in this order: **wīfe, pīe, ēven, bent, thing.**)
c. (Repeat *b* until firm.)

EXERCISE 8

Individual test

(Call on individual children to read one word the fast way.)

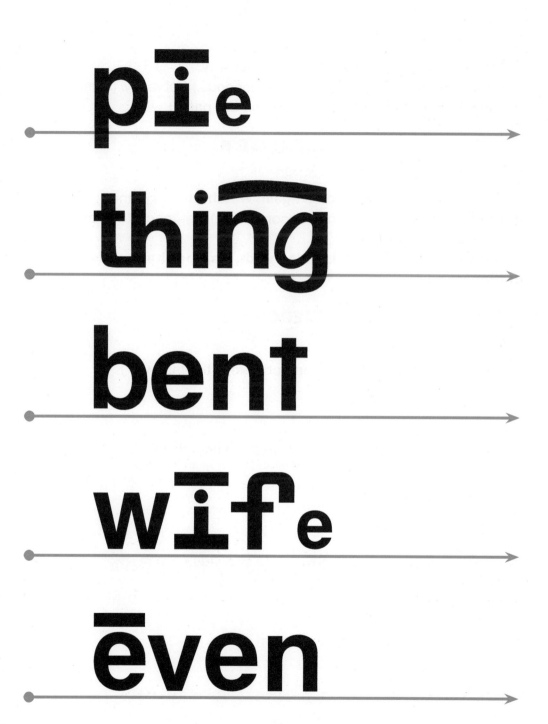

EXERCISE 8

Children rhyme with **log**

a. (Touch the ball for **log.**) You're going to read this word the fast way. (Pause three seconds.) Get ready. (Move your finger quickly along the arrow.) *Log.*

b. (Touch the ball for **dog.**) This word rhymes with (pause) **log.** (Move to **d,** then quickly along the arrow.) *Dog.* Yes, what word? (Signal.) *Dog.*

EXERCISE 9

Children identify, then sound out an irregular word (**of**)

a. (Touch the ball for **of.**) Everybody, you're going to read this word the fast way. (Pause three seconds.) Get ready. (Move your finger quickly along the arrow.) *Of.* Yes, **of.**

b. Now you're going to sound out the word. Get ready. (Quickly touch **o, f** as the children say *ooofff.*)

c. Again. (Repeat *b.*)

d. How do we say the word? (Signal.) *Of.* Yes, **of.**

e. (Repeat *b* and *d* until firm.)

EXERCISE 10

Individual test

(Call on individual children to do *b* and *d* in exercise 9.)

EXERCISE 11

Children read the words the fast way

a. Now you get to read the words on this page the fast way.

b. (Touch the ball for **log.** Pause three seconds.) Get ready. (Move your finger quickly along the arrow.) *Log.*

c. (Repeat *b* for each word on the page.)

EXERCISE 12

Individual test

(Call on individual children to read one word the fast way.)

of

Groups that are firm on Mastery Tests 29 and 30 should skip this lesson.

SOUNDS

EXERCISE 1

Teaching **ū** as in **ūse**

a. (Point to **ū**.) My turn. (Pause. Touch **ū** and say:) ū̄ū̄ū̄.
b. (Point to **ū**.) Your turn. When I touch it, you say it. (Pause.) Get ready. (Touch **u**.) ū̄ū̄ū̄.
•   (Lift your finger.)
c. Again. (Touch **ū**.) ū̄ū̄ū̄ū̄.
•   (Lift your finger.)
d. (Repeat *c* until firm.)

EXERCISE 2

Sounds firm-up

a. Get ready to say the sounds when I touch them.
b. (Alternate touching **ū** and **oo**. Point to the sound. Pause one second. Say:) Get ready. (Touch the sound.) *The children respond.*
c. (When **ū** and **oo** are firm, alternate touching **ū, oo, u,** and **z** until all four sounds are firm.)

EXERCISE 3

Individual test

(Call on individual children to identify **ū, oo, u,** or **z**.)

EXERCISE 4

Sounds firm-up

a. (Point to **ū**.) When I touch the sound, you say it.
b. (Pause.) Get ready. (Touch **ū**.) ū̄ū̄ū̄.
c. Again. (Repeat *b* until firm.)
d. Get ready to say all the sounds when I touch them.
e. (Alternate touching **ū, qu, ȳ, wh, j, y, er,** and **ī** three or four times. Point to the sound. Pause one second. Say:) Get ready. (Touch the sound.) *The children respond.*

EXERCISE 5

Individual test

(Call on individual children to identify one or more sounds in exercise 4.)

STORYBOOK

STORY 111

EXERCISE 13

First reading—children read the story the fast way

(Have the children reread any sentences containing words that give them trouble. Keep a list of these words.)

a. (Pass out Storybook.)

b. Open your book to page 45 and get ready to read. ✔

c. We're going to read this story the fast way.

d. Touch the first word. ✔

e. Reading the fast way. First word. (Pause three seconds.) Get ready. (Tap.) *She.*

f. Next word. ✔

• (Pause three seconds.) Get ready. (Tap.) *Said.*

g. (Repeat *f* for the remaining words in the first sentence. Pause at least three seconds between taps. The children are to identify each word without sounding it out.)

h. (Repeat *d* through *g* for the next two sentences. Have the children reread the first three sentences until firm.)

i. (The children are to read the remainder of the story the fast way, stopping at the end of each sentence.)

j. (After the first reading of the story, print on the board the words that the children missed more than one time. Have the children sound out each word one time and tell what word.)

k. (After the group's responses are firm, call on individual children to read the words.)

EXERCISE 14

Individual test

a. Turn back to page 45. I'm going to call on individual children to read a whole sentence the fast way.

b. (Call on individual children to read a sentence. Do not tap for each word.)

EXERCISE 15

Second reading—children read the story the fast way and answer questions

a. You're going to read the story again the fast way and I'll ask questions.

b. First word. ✔

• Get ready. (Tap.) *She.*

c. (Tap for each remaining word. Pause at least three seconds between taps. Pause longer before words that gave the children trouble during the first reading.)

d. (Ask the comprehension questions below as the children read.)

After the children read:	You say:
She said, "I have a fan."	Who said that? (Signal.) *She did.*
He said, "I have sand."	Who had the sand? (Signal.) *He did.*
She said, "We can run the sand in the fan."	What did she say? (Signal.) *We can run the sand in the fan.*
So he ran the fan near the sand.	What did he do? (Signal.) *He ran the fan near the sand.*
He had sand in his ears.	Where did he have sand? (Signal.) *In his ears.*
He said, "I can not hear."	What did he say? (Signal.) *I can not hear.* Why couldn't he hear? (Signal.) *He had sand in his ears.*
He had sand on his seat.	Where did he have sand? (Signal.) *On his seat.*
She said, "We have sand on us."	Who said that? (Signal.) *She did.*

EXERCISE 16

Picture comprehension

a. Everybody, look at the picture.

b. (Ask these questions:)

1. Why do they have their hands over their faces? *The children respond.*

• So they won't get sand in their faces.

2. Does that look like fun to you? *The children respond.*

EXERCISE 30

Picture comprehension

a. Everybody, look at the picture.

b. (Ask these questions:)

1. What's the fat eagle doing? *The children respond.*
   - He's jumping on top of the tiger.
   - I'll bet that hurts.
2. What's the tiger going to do? *The children respond.*
   - Run far away.
   - Look at how happy the other eagles are. I sure am glad the tiger didn't get that little eagle.

WORKSHEET 158
SUMMARY OF INDEPENDENT ACTIVITY
EXERCISE 31

Introduction to independent activity

a. (Pass out Worksheet 158 to each child.)

b. Everybody, you're going to do this worksheet on your own. **(Tell the children when they will work the items.)**
   - Let's go over the things you're going to do.

Story items

a. (Hold up side 1 of your worksheet and point to the story-items exercise.)

b. Everybody, here are items about the story we read today.

c. Think about what happened in the story and circle the right answer for each item.

Picture comprehension

a. (Point to the pictures in the picture-comprehension exercise.) Everybody, you're going to look at the picture. Then you're going to read each item and write the missing word.

b. Remember—the first sound of each missing word is already written in the blank.

Reading comprehension

a. (Point to the reading-comprehension exercise on side 2.)

b. Everybody, get ready to read the sentences in the box the fast way.

c. First word. ✔
   - Get ready. (Tap for each word as the children read the sentences *A tiger sat under a tree. He was looking for rabbits.*)

d. (Point to items 1 and 2.) These items tell about the story in the box. You're going to read each item and circle the right answer.

Sound writing

a. (Point to the sound-writing exercise.) Here are the sounds you're going to write today. I'll touch the sounds. You say them.

b. (Touch each sound.) *The children respond.*

c. (Repeat the series until firm.)

Sentence copying

a. (Point to the dotted sentence in the sentence-copying exercise.)

b. You're going to trace the words in this sentence. Then you're going to write the sentence on the other lines.

c. Reading the fast way. First word. ✔
   - Get ready. (Tap for each word.)

d. After you finish your worksheet, you get to draw a picture about the sentence, **they give him cāke.** You'll draw your picture on a piece of plain paper. **(When the children finish their worksheets, give them sheets of plain paper.)**

END OF LESSON 158

Worksheet 111

SUMMARY OF INDEPENDENT ACTIVITY
EXERCISE 17

Introduction to independent activity

a. (Pass out Worksheet 111 to each child.)

b. Everybody, you're going to do this worksheet on your own. (Tell the children when they will work the items.)

• Let's go over the things you're going to do.

Sentence copying

a. (Hold up side 1 of your worksheet and point to the first line in the sentence-copying exercise.)

b. Everybody, here's the sentence you're going to write on the lines below.

c. Reading the fast way. First word. ✔

• Get ready. (Tap.) *He.*

d. Next word. ✔

• Get ready. (Tap.) *Ran.*

e. (Repeat *d* for the remaining words.)

f. After you finish your worksheet, you get to draw a picture about the sentence, **hē ran thē fan.**

Sound writing

a. (Point to the sound-writing exercise.) Here are the sounds you're going to write today. I'll touch the sounds. You say them.

b. (Touch each sound.) *The children respond.*

c. (Repeat the series until firm.)

Matching

a. (Point to the column of words in the Matching Game.)

b. Everybody, you're going to follow the lines and write these words.

c. Reading the fast way.

d. (Point to the first word. Pause.) Get ready. (Signal.) *The children respond.*

e. (Repeat *d* for the remaining words.)

f. (Repeat *d* and *e* until firm.)

Cross-out game

(Point to the boxed word in the Cross-out Game.) Everybody, here's the word you're going to cross out today. What word? (Signal.) *Run.* Yes, **run.**

Pair relations

a. (Point to the pair-relations exercise on side 2.) You're going to circle the picture in each box that shows what the words say.

b. (Point to the space at the top of the page.) After you finish, remember to draw a picture that shows **hē ran thē fan.**

END OF LESSON 111

STORY 158
EXERCISE 27

First reading—children read the title and first three sentences

a. Now you're going to finish the story about the fat eagle.

b. Everybody, touch the title of the story and get ready to read the words in the title the fast way.

c. First word. ✔

• (Pause two seconds.) Get ready. (Tap.) *The.*

d. (Tap for each remaining word in the title.)

e. (After the children have read the title, ask:) What's this story about? (Signal.) *The fat eagle.* Yes, **the fat eagle.**

f. Everybody, get ready to read this story the fast way.

g. First word. ✔

• (Pause two seconds.) Get ready. (Tap.) *A.*

h. (Tap for the remaining words in the first sentence. Pause at least two seconds between taps.)

i. (Repeat *g* and *h* for the next two sentences. Have the children reread the first three sentences until firm.)

EXERCISE 28

Individual children or the group read sentences to complete the first reading

a. I'm going to call on individual children to read a sentence. Everybody, follow along and point to the words. If you hear a mistake, raise your hand.

b. (Call on a child.) Read the next sentence. (Do not tap for the words. Let children read at their own pace, but be sure they read the sentence correctly.)

> **To Correct**
> (Have the child sound out the word. Then return to the beginning of the sentence.)

c. (Repeat *b* for most of the remaining sentences in the story. Occasionally have the group read a sentence. When the group is to read, say:) Everybody, read the next sentence. (Pause two seconds.) Get ready. (Tap for each word in the sentence. Pause at least two seconds between taps.)

EXERCISE 29

Second reading—individual children or the group read each sentence; the group answer questions

a. You're going to read the story again. This time I'm going to ask questions.

b. Starting with the first word of the title. ✔

• Get ready. (Tap as the children read the title. Pause at least two seconds between taps.)

c. (Call on a child.) Read the first sentence. *The child responds.*

d. (Repeat *b* and *c* in exercise 28. Present the following comprehension questions to the entire group.)

After the children read:	You say:
"I must save the little eagle."	What did the fat eagle say? (Signal.) *I must save the little eagle.* I wonder what he can do to save the little eagle.
He came down like a fat rock on the tiger.	What did the fat eagle do? (Signal.) *He came down like a fat rock on the tiger.* Do you suppose the tiger liked that? *The children respond.*
And the tiger ran far away.	What did the tiger do? (Signal.) *He ran far away.*
They give him cake and ham and corn.	What do the other eagles do? (Signal.) *They give him cake and ham and corn.* Why don't they make fun of him any more? *The children respond.* Because he saved the little eagle.

SOUNDS
EXERCISE 1

Teacher and children play the sounds game

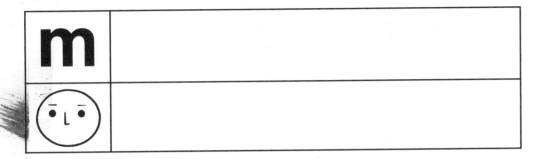

a. (Use transparency and crayon. Write the sounds in the symbol box. Keep score in the score box.)

b. I'm smart. I think I can beat you in a game.

c. Here's the rule. When I touch a sound, you say it.

d. (Play the game. Make one symbol at a time in the symbol box. Use the symbols **ē, i, n,** and **ā.**) (Make each symbol quickly. Pause. Touch the symbol. Play the game for about two minutes.) (Then ask:) Who won? (Draw a mouth on the face in the score box.)

EXERCISE 2

Child plays teacher

a. (Use transparency and crayon.)

b. [Child's name] is going to be the teacher.

c. [Child] is going to touch the sounds. When [child] touches a sound, you say it.

d. (The child points to and touches the sounds.) *The children respond.* (You circle any sound that is not firm.)

e. (After the child has completed the page, present all the circled sounds to the children.)

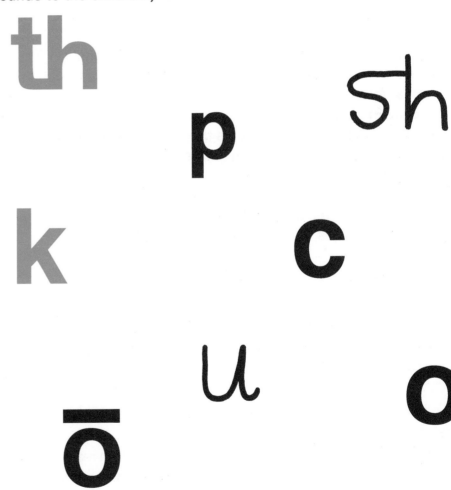

EXERCISE 3

Individual test

(Call on individual children.) If you can say the sound when I call your name, you may cross it out.

STORYBOOK

READ THE ITEMS 158
EXERCISE 24

Children read items 1 and 2

a. (Pass out Storybook.)
b. Open your book to page 183. ✔
c. Get ready to read the items and play the game.
d. Finger under the first word of the title. ✔
e. When I tap, read the title. (Pause.) Get ready. (Tap.) *Read the items.*
f. Touch item 1 and get ready to read. ✔
• First word. (Tap for each word as the children read *When the teacher says "Touch your feet," stand up.*)
• (Repeat until firm.)
g. Everybody, get ready to say item 1. (Pause and signal.) *The children say the sentence.*
• (Repeat four times or until firm.)
h. Touch item 2 and get ready to read. ✔
• First word. (Tap for each word as the children read *If the teacher says "Go," touch your ears.*)
• (Repeat until firm.)
i. Everybody, get ready to say item 2. (Pause and signal.) *The children say the sentence.*
• (Repeat four times or until firm.)

EXERCISE 25

Children reread items 1 and 2 and answer questions

a. Everybody, touch item 1. ✔
b. Read item 1 to yourself. Raise your hand when you know what you're going to do and when you're going to do it.
c. (After the children raise their hands, say:) Everybody, what are you going to do when I say **"Touch your feet"**? (Signal.) *Stand up.*

To Correct
1. Everybody, read item 1 out loud. (Tap as the children read each word.)
2. What are you going to do when I say **"Touch your feet"**? (Signal.) *Stand up.*

d. Everybody, when are you going to **stand up?** (Signal.) *When the teacher says "Touch your feet."*

To Correct
1. Everybody, read item 1 out loud. (Tap as the children read each word.)
2. When are you going to **stand up?** (Signal.) *When the teacher says "Touch your feet."*

e. (Repeat *c* and *d* until firm.)
f. Everybody, touch item 2. ✔
g. Read item 2 to yourself. Raise your hand when you know what you're going to do and when you're going to do it.
h. (After the children raise their hands, say:) Everybody, what are you going to do if I say **"Go"**? (Signal.) *Touch my ears.*

To Correct
1. Everybody, read item 2 out loud. (Tap as the children read each word.)
2. What are you going to do when I say **"Go"**? (Signal.) *Touch my ears.*

i. Everybody, when are you going to **touch your ears?** (Signal.) *If the teacher says "Go."*

To Correct
1. Everybody, read item 2 out loud. (Tap as the children read each word.)
2. When are you going to **touch your ears?** (Signal.) *If the teacher says "Go."*

j. (Repeat *h* and *i* until firm.)

EXERCISE 26

Children play the game

a. Everybody, touch item 1. ✔
b. Read the item to yourself. Raise your hand when you know what you're going to do and when you're going to do it.
c. (After the children raise their hands, say:) Let's play the game. Think about what you're going to do (pause) and when you're going to do it.
d. (Hold out your hand. Pause.) Get ready. **Touch your feet.** (Pause. Drop your hand.) *The children stand up immediately.*

To Correct
1. What did I say? (Signal.) *Touch your feet.*
2. What are you supposed to do when I say **"Touch your feet"**? (Signal.) *Stand up.*
3. (If the children's responses are not firm, have them read item 1 aloud.)
4. (Repeat exercise 26.)

READING VOCABULARY
EXERCISE 4

Children sound out an irregular word (**are**)

a. (Touch the ball for **are.**) Sound it out.

b. Get ready. (Quickly touch each sound as the children say *aaarrr.*)

c. Again. (Repeat *b* until firm.)

d. That's how we <u>sound out</u> the word. Here's how we <u>say</u> the word. **Are.** How do we <u>say</u> the word? (Signal.) *Are.*

e. Now you're going to <u>sound out</u> the word. Get ready. (Touch each sound as the children say *aaarrr.*)

f. Now you're going to <u>say</u> the word. Get ready. (Signal.) *Are.*

g. (Repeat *e* and *f* until firm.)

EXERCISE 5

Children rhyme with an irregular word (**are**)

a. (Touch the ball for **are.**) Everybody, you're going to read this word the fast way. Get ready. (Signal.) *Are.*

b. (Touch the ball for **car.**) This word rhymes with (pause) **are.** Get ready. (Move to **c,** then quickly along the arrow.) *Car.*

c. (Touch the ball for **tar.**) This word rhymes with (pause) **are.** Get ready. (Move to **t,** then quickly along the arrow.) *Tar.*

d. (Repeat *a* through *c* until firm.)

EXERCISE 6

Children sound out **car** and **tar**

a. (Have the children sound out **car.**) *Caaarrr.*

- How do we say the word? (Signal.) *Car.*
- Yes, **car.** Ride in my **car.**

b. (Have the children sound out **tar.**) *Taaarrr.*

- How do we say the word? (Signal.) *Tar.*
- Yes, **tar. Tar** is black.

ar_e

car

tar

EXERCISE 18

Children sound out an irregular word (**took**)

a. (Touch the ball for **took.**) Sound it out.

b. Get ready. (Quickly touch each sound as the children say *toook.*)

c. Again. (Repeat *b* until firm.)

d. That's how we <u>sound out</u> the word. Here's how we <u>say</u> the word. **Took.** How do we <u>say</u> the word? (Signal.) *Took.*

e. Now you're going to <u>sound out</u> the word. Get ready. (Touch each sound as the children say *tooook.*)

f. Now you're going to say the word. Get ready. (Signal.) *Took.*

g. (Repeat *e* and *f* until firm.)

h. Yes, this word is **took.** She **took** my book.

EXERCISE 19

Individual test

(Call on individual children to do *e* and *f* in exercise 18.)

EXERCISE 20

Children sound out the word and tell what word

a. (Touch the ball for **head.**) Sound it out.

b. Get ready. (Touch **h, e, d** as the children say *heeed.*)

• (If sounding out is not firm, repeat *b.*)

c. What word? (Signal.) *Head.* Yes, **head.**

EXERCISE 21

Children read the fast way

(Touch the ball for **thing.**) Get ready to read this word the fast way. (Pause three seconds.) Get ready. (Signal.) *Thing.*

EXERCISE 22

Children read the words the fast way

(Have the children read the words on this page the fast way.)

EXERCISE 23

Individual test

(Call on individual children to read one word the fast way.)

EXERCISE 7

Children identify, then sound out an irregular word (**of**)

a. (Touch the ball for **of**.) Everybody, you're going to read this word the fast way. (Pause three seconds.) Get ready. (Move your finger quickly along the arrow.) *Of.* Yes, **of.**

b. Now you're going to sound out the word. Get ready. (Quickly touch **o, f** as the children say *ooofff.*)

c. Again. (Repeat *b.*)

d. How do we say the word? (Signal.) *Of.* Yes, **of.**

e. (Repeat *b* and *d* until firm.)

EXERCISE 8

Individual test

(Call on individual children to do *b* and *d* in exercise 7.)

EXERCISE 9

Children sound out the word and tell what word

a. (Touch the ball for **dog**.) Sound it out.

b. Get ready. (Touch **d, o, g** as the children say *dooog.*)

• (If sounding out is not firm, repeat *b.*)

c. What word? (Signal.) *Dog.* Yes, **dog.**

EXERCISE 10

Children sound out the word and tell what word

a. (Touch the ball for **pot**.) Sound it out.

b. Get ready. (Touch **p, o, t** as the children say *pooot.*)

• (If sounding out is not firm, repeat *b.*)

c. What word? (Signal.) *Pot.* Yes, **pot.**

EXERCISE 11

Children read the words the fast way

a. Now you get to read the words on this page the fast way.

b. (Touch the ball for **of**. Pause three seconds.) Get ready. (Move your finger quickly along the arrow.) *Of.*

c. (Repeat *b* for each word on the page.)

of

dog

pot

EXERCISE 12

Individual test

(Call on individual children to read one word the fast way.)

EXERCISE 15

Children read the fast way

a. Get ready to read these words the fast way.

b. (Touch the ball for **under.** Pause three seconds.) Get ready. (Signal.) *Under.*

c. (Repeat *b* for the remaining words on the page.)

EXERCISE 16

Children read the fast way again

a. Get ready to do these words again. Watch where I point.

b. (Point to a word. Pause one second. Say:) Get ready. (Signal.) *The children respond.*

• (Point to the words in this order: **shōw, ōver, under, fast, after.**)

c. (Repeat *b* until firm.)

EXERCISE 17

Individual test

(Call on individual children to read one word the fast way.)

under

ōver

after

shōw

fast

EXERCISE 13

Children read the fast way

a. Get ready to read these words the fast way.

b. (Touch the ball for **us.** Pause three seconds.) Get ready. (Signal.) *Us.*

c. (Touch the ball for **log.** Pause three seconds.) Get ready. (Signal.) *Log.*

EXERCISE 14

Children identify, then sound out an irregular word (**to**)

a. (Touch the ball for **to.**) Everybody, you're going to read this word the fast way. (Pause three seconds.) Get ready. (Move your finger quickly along the arrow.) *To.* Yes, **to.**

b. Now you're going to sound out the word. Get ready. (Quickly touch **t, o** as the children say *tooo.*)

c. Again. (Repeat *b.*)

d. How do we say the word? (Signal.) *To.* Yes, **to.**

e. (Repeat *b* and *d* until firm.)

EXERCISE 15

Individual test

(Call on individual children to do *b* and *d* in exercise 14.)

EXERCISE 16

Children read the words the fast way

a. Now you get to read the words on this page the fast way.

b. (Touch the ball for **us.** Pause three seconds.) Get ready. (Move your finger quickly along the arrow.) *Us.*

c. (Repeat *b* for each word on the page.)

EXERCISE 17

Individual test

(Call on individual children to read one word the fast way.)

EXERCISE 9

Children identify, then sound out an irregular word (**look**)

a. (Touch the ball for **look.**) Everybody, you're going to read this word the fast way. (Pause three seconds.) Get ready. (Move your finger quickly along the arrow.) *Look.* Yes, **look.**

b. Now you're going to sound out the word. Get ready. (Quickly touch **l, oo, k** as the children say *lllooook.*)

c. Again. (Repeat *b.*)

d. How do we say the word? (Signal.) *Look.* Yes, **look.**

e. (Repeat *b* and *d* until firm.)

look

EXERCISE 10

Individual test

(Call on individual children to do *b* and *d* in exercise 9.)

EXERCISE 11

Children rhyme with **wīfe** and **līfe**

a. (Touch the ball for **wīfe.**) You're going to read this word the fast way. (Pause three seconds.) Get ready. (Move your finger quickly along the arrow.) *Wife.*

b. (Touch the ball for **līfe.**) This word rhymes with (pause) **wife.** (Move to **l,** then quickly along the arrow.) *Life.*

• Yes, what word? (Signal.) *Life.*

wīfe

EXERCISE 12

Children sound out the word and tell what word

a. (Touch the ball for **picks.**) Sound it out.

b. Get ready. (Touch **p, i, c, s** as the children say *piiicsss.*)

• (If sounding out is not firm, repeat *b.*)

c. What word? (Signal.) *Picks.* Yes, **picks.**

līfe

picks

EXERCISE 13

Children read the words the fast way

(Have the children read the words on this page the fast way.)

EXERCISE 14

Individual test

(Call on individual children to read one word the fast way.)

STORY 112
EXERCISE 18

First reading—children read the story the fast way

(Have the children reread any sentences containing words that give them trouble. Keep a list of these words.)

a. (Pass out Storybook.)

b. Open your book to page 48 and get ready to read. ✔

c. We're going to read this story the fast way.

d. Touch the first word. ✔

e. Reading the fast way. First word. (Pause three seconds.) Get ready. (Tap.) *A.*

f. Next word. ✔

• (Pause three seconds.) Get ready. (Tap.) *Dog.*

g. (Repeat *f* for the remaining words in the first sentence. Pause at least three seconds between taps. The children are to identify each word without sounding it out.)

h. (Repeat *d* through *g* for the next two sentences. Have the children reread the first three sentences until firm.)

i. (The children are to read the remainder of the story the fast way, stopping at the end of each sentence.)

j. (After the first reading of the story, print on the board the words that the children missed more than one time. Have the children sound out each word one time and tell what word.)

k. (After the group's responses are firm, call on individual children to read the words.)

EXERCISE 19

Individual test

a. I'm going to call on individual children to read a whole sentence the fast way.

b. (Call on individual children to read a sentence. Do not tap for each word.)

EXERCISE 20

Second reading—children read the story the fast way and answer questions

a. You're going to read the story again the fast way and I'll ask questions.

b. First word. ✔

• Get ready. (Tap.) *A.*

c. (Tap for each remaining word. Pause at least three seconds between taps. Pause longer before words that gave the children trouble during the first reading.)

d. (Ask the comprehension questions below as the children read.)

After the children read:	You say:
A dog sat in a little car.	What did the dog do? (Signal.) *Sat in a little car.*
The dog said, "I need to eat."	What did he say? (Signal.) *I need to eat.*
Will the dog eat a fish?	What do you think? *The children respond.* Let's read and find out.
No.	Will he eat a fish? (Signal.) *No.*
Will the dog eat a log?	What do you think? *The children respond.* Let's read and find out.
No.	Will he eat a log? (Signal.) *No.*
Will the dog eat a pot of tar?	What's a pot of tar? *The children respond.* Let's see if he'll eat that.
No.	Will he eat a pot of tar? (Signal.) *No.*
The dog will eat the car.	What will he do? (Signal.) *He will eat the car.* That's silly.

READING VOCABULARY
EXERCISE 5

Children read a word beginning with two consonants (**slōw**)

a. (Cover **s.** Point to **lōw.**) You're going to read this part of the word the fast way. (Pause three seconds.) Get ready. (Signal.) *Lōw.* Yes, **lōw.**

b. (Uncover **s.** Point to **s.**) You're going to say this first. (Move your finger quickly under **lōw.**) Then you're going to say (pause) **low.**

c. (Point to **s.**) What are you going to say first? (Signal.) *sss.*

• What are you going to say next? (Signal.) *Lōw.*

d. (Repeat *c* until firm.)

e. (Touch the ball for **slōw.**) Get ready. (Move to **s,** then quickly along the arrow.) *Ssslow.*

f. Say it fast. (Signal.) *Slow.*

• Yes, what word? (Signal.) *Slow.* Yes, **slow.**

• Good reading.

g. Again. (Repeat *e* and *f* until firm.)

h. Now you're going to sound out (pause) **slow.** Get ready. (Touch **s, l, ō, w** as the children say *ssslllōōōwww.*)

• What word? (Signal.) *Slow.* Yes, **slow.**

EXERCISE 6

Children read the fast way

a. Get ready to read these words the fast way.

b. (Touch the ball for **when.** Pause three seconds.) Get ready. (Signal.) *When.*

c. (Repeat *b* for the remaining words on the page.)

EXERCISE 7

Children read the fast way again

a. Get ready to do these words again. Watch where I point.

b. (Point to a word. Pause one second. Say:) Get ready. (Signal.) *The children respond.*

• (Point to the words in this order: **when, from, then.**)

c. (Repeat *b* until firm.)

EXERCISE 8

Individual test

(Call on individual children to read one word on the page the fast way.)

slōw

when

then

from

EXERCISE 21

Picture comprehension

a. Everybody, look at the picture.

b. (Ask these questions:)
1. Is he eating part of the car? *Yes.*
- What part? *The children respond.*
- The steering wheel.
2. Do you think that silly dog will eat the whole car? *The children respond.*
- I don't think a car would taste very good.

WORKSHEET 112

SUMMARY OF INDEPENDENT ACTIVITY
EXERCISE 22

Introduction to independent activity

a. (Pass out Worksheet 112 to each child.)

b. Everybody, you're going to do this worksheet on your own. (Tell the children when they will work the items.)
- Let's go over the things you're going to do.

Sentence copying

a. (Hold up side 1 of your worksheet and point to the first line in the sentence-copying exercise.)

b. Everybody, here's the sentence you're going to write on the lines below.

c. Reading the fast way. First word. ✔
- Get ready. (Tap.) *Thē.*

d. Next word. ✔
- Get ready. (Tap.) *Dog.*

e. (Repeat *d* for the remaining words.)

f. After you finish your worksheet, you get to draw a picture about the sentence, **thē dog āte thē car.**

Sound writing

a. (Point to the sound-writing exercise.) Here are the sounds you're going to write today. I'll touch the sounds. You say them.

b. (Touch each sound.) *The children respond.*

c. (Repeat the series until firm.)

Matching

a. (Point to the column of words in the Matching Game.)

b. Everybody, you're going to follow the lines and write these words.

c. Reading the fast way.

d. (Point to the first word. Pause.) Get ready. (Signal.) *The children respond.*

e. (Repeat *d* for the remaining words.)

f. (Repeat *d* and *e* until firm.)

Cross-out game

(Point to the boxed word in the Cross-out Game.) Everybody, here's the word you're going to cross out today. What word? (Signal.) *Hand.* Yes, **hand.**

Pair relations

a. (Point to the pair-relations exercise on side 2.) You're going to circle the picture in each box that shows what the words say.

b. (Point to the space at the top of the page.) After you finish, remember to draw a picture that shows **thē dog āte thē car.**

END OF LESSON 112

SOUNDS

EXERCISE 1

Teacher firms up **u**

a. (Point to **u**.) Everybody, get ready to tell me this sound. Get ready. (Touch **u**.) *uuu.*

b. (Point to **ū**.) Everybody, look at the line over this sound. This is not **uuu**. Is it **uuu**? (Signal.) *No.*

c. (Point to each sound and ask:) Is this **uuu**? *The children respond.*

d. (Repeat *c* until firm.)

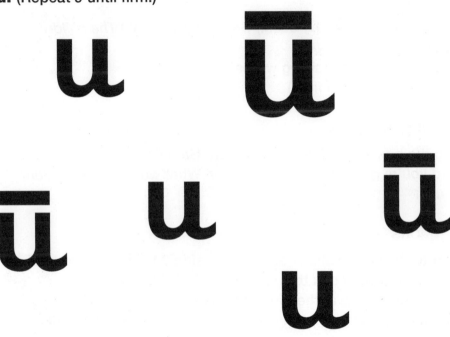

EXERCISE 2

Teaching **ū** as in **ūse**; children discriminate **u—ū**

a. (Point to the first **ū**.) Everybody, this is **ūūū**.

b. When I touch it, you say it. (Pause.) Get ready. (Touch **ū**.) *ūūū.*

c. Again. (Touch **ū**.) *ūūū.*

d. (Repeat *c* until firm.)

e. Get ready to do all these sounds. When I touch the sound, you say it. (Alternate touching the sounds. Before touching each **ū**, trace the line and say:) Remember—this is not **uuu**.

f. (Repeat *e* until all the sounds are firm.)

EXERCISE 3

Sounds firm-up

a. (Point to **ū**.) When I touch the sound, you say it.

b. (Pause.) Get ready. (Touch **ū**.) *ūūū.*

c. Again. (Repeat *b* until firm.)

d. Get ready to say all the sounds when I touch them.

e. (Alternate touching **ū, ō, ȳ, z, qu,** and **j** three or four times. Point to the sound. Pause one second. Say:) Get ready. (Touch the sound.) *The children respond.*

EXERCISE 4

Individual test

(Call on individual children to identify one or more sounds in exercise 3.)

ch

sh

c

th

SOUNDS

EXERCISE 1

Teaching **ch** as in **chat**

a. (Point to **ch**.) Here's a new sound. It's a quick sound.

b. My turn. (Pause. Touch **ch** for an instant, saying:) **ch.** (Do not say **chuh.**)

c. Again. (Touch **ch** and say:) ch.

d. (Point to **ch**.) Your turn. When I touch it, you say it. (Pause.) Get ready. (Touch **ch**.) *ch.*

e. Again. (Touch **ch**.) *ch.*

f. (Repeat *e* until firm.)

EXERCISE 2

Individual test

(Call on individual children to identify **ch**.)

EXERCISE 3

Sounds firm-up

a. Get ready to say the sounds when I touch them.

b. (Alternate touching **ch** and **sh**. Point to the sound. Pause one second. Say:) Get ready. (Touch the sound.) *The children respond.*

c. (When **ch** and **sh** are firm, alternate touching **ch, c, sh,** and **th** until all four sounds are firm.)

EXERCISE 4

Individual test

(Call on individual children to identify **ch, c, sh,** or **th**.)

EXERCISE 5

Sounds firm-up

a. (Point to **ch**.) When I touch the sound, you say it.

b. (Pause.) Get ready. (Touch **ch**.) *ch.*

c. Again. (Repeat *b* until firm.)

d. Get ready to say all the sounds when I touch them.

e. (Alternate touching **p, v, ō, l, w, k, r,** and **ch** three or four times. Point to the sound. Pause one second. Say:) Get ready. (Touch the sound.) *The children respond.*

EXERCISE 6

Individual test

(Call on individual children to identify one or more sounds in exercise 5.)

EXERCISE 28

Picture comprehension

a. What do you think you'll see in the picture? *The children respond.*

b. Turn the page and look at the picture.

c. (Ask these questions:)

    1. Where's the little eagle? *The children respond.* Under the tree.

    2. Where's the fat eagle? *The children respond.* In the tree.

    3. Where is the tiger? *The children respond.* Behind the tree.

    4. What's he doing? *The children respond.* He's getting ready to grab the little eagle.

    • It looks bad for that little eagle.

WORKSHEET 157

SUMMARY OF INDEPENDENT ACTIVITY

EXERCISE 29

Introduction to independent activity

a. (Pass out Worksheet 157 to each child.)

b. Everybody, you're going to do this worksheet on your own. **(Tell the children when they will work the items.)**

    • Let's go over the things you're going to do.

Story items

a. (Hold up side 1 of your worksheet and point to the story-items exercise.)

b. Everybody, here are items about the story we read today.

c. Think about what happened in the story and circle the right answer for each item.

Picture comprehension

a. (Point to the pictures in the picture-comprehension exercise.) Everybody, you're going to look at the picture. Then you're going to read each item and write the missing word.

b. Remember—the first sound of each missing word is already written in the blank.

Reading comprehension

a. (Point to the reading-comprehension exercise on side 2.)

b. Everybody, get ready to read the sentences in the box the fast way.

c. First word. ✔

    • Get ready. (Tap for each word as the children read the sentences *A girl liked to talk. She talked to the mail man.*)

d. (Point to items 1 and 2.) These items tell about the story in the box. You're going to read each item and circle the right answer.

Sound writing

a. (Point to the sound-writing exercise.) Here are the sounds you're going to write today. I'll touch the sounds. You say them.

b. (Touch each sound.) *The children respond.*

c. (Repeat the series until firm.)

Sentence copying

a. (Point to the dotted sentence in the sentence-copying exercise.)

b. You're going to trace the words in this sentence. Then you're going to write the sentence on the other lines.

c. Reading the fast way. First word. ✔

    • Get ready. (Tap for each word.)

d. After you finish your worksheet, you get to draw a picture about the sentence, **a fat ēagle sat.** You'll draw your picture on a piece of plain paper. (When the children finish their worksheets, give them sheets of plain paper.)

END OF LESSON 157

READING VOCABULARY

EXERCISE 7

Children sound out an irregular word (**car**)

a. (Touch the ball for **car.**) Sound it out.

b. Get ready. (Quickly touch each sound as the children say *caaarrr.*)

c. Again. (Repeat *b* until firm.)

d. That's how we <u>sound out</u> the word. Here's how we <u>say</u> the word. **Car.** How do we <u>say</u> the word? (Signal.) *Car.*

e. Now you're going to <u>sound out</u> the word. Get ready. (Touch each sound as the children say *caaarrr.*)

f. Now you're going to say the word. Get ready. (Signal.) *Car.*

g. (Repeat *e* and *f* until firm.)

h. Yes, this word is **car.** A dog sat in the **car.**

EXERCISE 8

Individual test

(Call on individual children to do *e* and *f* in exercise 7.)

EXERCISE 9

Children sound out the word and tell what word

a. (Touch the ball for **cāme.**) Sound it out.

b. Get ready. (Touch **c, ā, m** as the children say *cāāāmmm.*)

• (If sounding out is not firm, repeat *b.*)

c. What word? (Signal.) *Came.* Yes, **came.**

EXERCISE 10

Children sound out the word and tell what word

(Repeat the procedures in exercise 9 for **chops.**)

EXERCISE 11

Children read the words the fast way

a. Now you get to read the words on this page the fast way.

b. (Touch the ball for **car.** Pause three seconds.) Get ready. (Move your finger quickly along the arrow.) *Car.*

c. (Repeat *b* for each word on the page.)

EXERCISE 12

Individual test

(Call on individual children to read one word the fast way.)

car

cāme

chops

STORY 157
EXERCISE 25

First reading—children read the title and first three sentences

a. You're going to read the first part of this story today.

b. Everybody, touch the title of the story and get ready to read the words in the title the fast way.

c. First word. ✔

• (Pause two seconds.) Get ready. (Tap.) *The.*

d. (Tap for each remaining word in the title.)

e. (After the children have read the title, ask:) What's this story about? (Signal.) *The fat eagle.* Yes, **the fat eagle.**

f. Everybody, get ready to read this story the fast way.

g. First word. ✔

• (Pause two seconds.) Get ready. (Tap.) *An.*

h. (Tap for the remaining words in the first sentence. Pause at least two seconds between taps.)

i. (Repeat *g* and *h* for the next two sentences. Have the children reread the first three sentences until firm.)

EXERCISE 26

Individual children or the group read sentences to complete the first reading

a. I'm going to call on individual children to read a sentence. Everybody, follow along and point to the words. If you hear a mistake, raise your hand.

b. (Call on a child.) Read the next sentence. (Do not tap for the words. Let children read at their own pace, but be sure they read the sentence correctly.)

> **To Correct**
> (Have the child sound out the word. Then return to the beginning of the sentence.)

c. (Repeat *b* for most of the remaining sentences in the story. Occasionally have the group read a sentence. When the group is to read, say:) Everybody, read the next sentence. (Pause two seconds.) Get ready. (Tap for each word in the sentence. Pause at least two seconds between taps.)

EXERCISE 27

Second reading—individual children or the group read each sentence; the group answer questions

a. You're going to read the story again. This time I'm going to ask questions.

b. Starting with the first word of the title. ✔

• Get ready. (Tap as the children read the title. Pause at least two seconds between taps.)

c. (Call on a child.) Read the first sentence. *The child responds.*

d. (Repeat *b* and *c* in exercise 26. Present the following comprehension questions to the entire group.)

After the children read:	You say:
The fat eagle.	What's this story about? (Signal.) *The fat eagle.*
He ate cake and ham and corn.	What did he eat? (Signal.) *Cake and ham and corn.*
He ate and ate, and he got fatter and fatter.	What happened? (Signal.) *He ate and ate, and he got fatter and fatter.* Why did he get fatter? (Signal.) *Because he ate and ate.*
"Ho ho."	What did the other eagles say? *The children respond.*
A little eagle sat under a tree.	Where was the little eagle? (Signal.) *Under a tree.* Where was the fat eagle? (Signal.) *In a tree.* And what was the tiger doing? (Signal.) *Hunting for eagles.* Better watch out, little eagle.
The other eagles yelled and yelled, but the little eagle did not hear them.	Who was yelling? (Signal.) *The other eagles.* Why? *The children respond.* Did the little eagle hear them? (Signal.) *No.* Poor little eagle. We'll see what happens when we finish the story.

EXERCISE 13

Children sound out an irregular word (**are**)

a. (Touch the ball for **are.**) Sound it out.

b. Get ready. (Quickly touch each sound as the children say *aaarrr.*)

c. Again. (Repeat *b* until firm.)

d. That's how we <u>sound out</u> the word. Here's how we <u>say</u> the word. **Are.** How do we <u>say</u> the word? (Signal.) *Are.*

e. Now you're going to <u>sound out</u> the word. Get ready. (Touch each sound as the children say *aaarrr.*)

f. Now you're going to <u>say</u> the word. Get ready. (Signal.) *Are.*

g. (Repeat *e* and *f* until firm.)

h. Yes, this word is **are.** **Are** you working hard?

EXERCISE 14

Individual test

(Call on individual children to do *e* and *f* in exercise 13.)

EXERCISE 15

Children read the fast way

a. Get ready to read these words the fast way.

b. (Touch the ball for **shops.** Pause three seconds.) Get ready. (Signal.) *Shops.*

c. (Repeat *b* for the remaining words on the page.)

EXERCISE 16

Children read the fast way again

a. Get ready to do these words again. Watch where I point.

b. (Point to a word. Pause one second. Say:) Get ready. (Signal.) *The children respond.*

• (Point to the words in this order: **cops, shops, dog.**)

c. (Repeat *b* until firm.)

EXERCISE 17

Individual test

(Call on individual children to read one word on the page the fast way.)

are

shops

dog

cops

STORYBOOK

READ THE ITEMS 157
EXERCISE 22

Children read items 1 and 2

a. (Pass out Storybook.)
b. Open your book to page 180. ✔
c. Get ready to read the items and play the game.
d. Finger under the first word of the title. ✔
e. When I tap, read the title. (Pause.) Get ready. (Tap.) *Read the items.*
f. Touch item 1 and get ready to read. ✔
- First word. (Tap for each word as the children read *If the teacher stands up, touch your hand.*)
- (Repeat until firm.)
g. Everybody, get ready to say item 1. (Pause and signal.) *The children say the sentence.*
- (Repeat four times or until firm.)
h. Touch item 2 and get ready to read. ✔
- First word. (Tap for each word as the children read *If the teacher says "Stand up," touch your nose.*)
- (Repeat until firm.)
i. Everybody, get ready to say item 2. (Pause and signal.) *The children say the sentence.*
- (Repeat four times or until firm.)

EXERCISE 23

Children reread items 1 and 2 and answer questions

a. Everybody, touch item 1. ✔
b. Read item 1 to yourself. Raise your hand when you know what you're going to do and when you're going to do it.
c. (After the children raise their hands, say:) Everybody, what are you going to do if I **stand up?** (Signal.) *Touch my hand.*

To Correct
1. Everybody, read item 1 out loud. (Tap as the children read each word.)
2. What are you going to do if I **stand up?** (Signal.) *Touch my hand.*

d. Everybody, when are you going to **touch your hand?** (Signal.) *If the teacher stands up.*

To Correct
1. Everybody, read item 1 out loud. (Tap as the children read each word.)
2. When are you going to **touch your hand?** (Signal.) *If the teacher stands up.*

e. (Repeat *c* and *d* until firm.)
f. Everybody, touch item 2. ✔
g. Read item 2 to yourself. Raise your hand when you know what you're going to do and when you're going to do it.
h. (After the children raise their hands, say:) Everybody, what are you going to do if I say **"Stand up"?** (Signal.) *Touch my nose.*

To Correct
1. Everybody, read item 2 out loud. (Tap as the children read each word.)
2. What are you going to do if I say **"Stand up"?** (Signal.) *Touch my nose.*

i. Everybody, when are you going to **touch your nose?** (Signal.) *If the teacher says "Stand up."*

To Correct
1. Everybody, read item 2 out loud. (Tap as the children read each word.)
2. When are you going to **touch your nose?** (Signal.) *If the teacher says "Stand up."*

j. (Repeat *h* and *i* until firm.)

EXERCISE 24

Children play the game

a. Everybody, touch item 1. ✔
b. Read the item to yourself. Raise your hand when you know what you're going to do and when you're going to do it.
c. (After the children raise their hands, say:) Let's play the game. Think about what you're going to do (pause) and when you're going to do it.
d. (Hold out your hand. Pause.) Get ready. (Stand up. Pause. Drop your hand.) *The children touch their hands immediately.*

To Correct
1. What did I do? (Signal.) *Stand up.*
2. What are you supposed to do if I **stand up?** (Signal.) *Touch my hand.*
3. (If the children's responses are not firm, have them read item 1 aloud.)
4. (Repeat exercise 24.)

EXERCISE 18

Children sound out an irregular word (**art**)

a. (Touch the ball for **art.**) Sound it out.

b. Get ready. (Quickly touch each sound as the children say *aaarrrt.*)

c. Again. (Repeat *b* until firm.)

d. That's how we <u>sound out</u> the word. Here's how we <u>say</u> the word. **Art.** How do we <u>say</u> the word? (Signal.) *Art.*

e. Now you're going to <u>sound out</u> the word. Get ready. (Touch each sound as the children say *aaarrrt.*)

f. Now you're going to <u>say</u> the word. Get ready. (Signal.) *Art.*

g. (Repeat *e* and *f* until firm.)

EXERCISE 19

Children rhyme with an irregular word (**art**)

a. (Touch the ball for **art.**) Everybody, you're going to read this word the fast way. Get ready. (Signal.) *Art.*

b. (Touch the ball for **part.**) This word rhymes with (pause) **art.** Get ready. (Move to **p,** then quickly along the arrow.) *Part.*

c. (Repeat *a* and *b* until firm.)

EXERCISE 20

Children sound out **part**

(Have the children sound out **part.**) *Paaarrrt.*

- How do we say the word? (Signal.) *Part.* Yes, **part.**
- This **part** of the pencil is the point.

EXERCISE 21

Children read a word beginning with two consonants (**slōw**)

a. (Cover **s.** Point to **lōw.**) You're going to read this part of the word the fast way. (Pause three seconds.) Get ready. (Signal.) *Lōw.* Yes, **lōw.**

b. (Uncover **s.** Point to **s.**) You're going to say this first. (Move your finger quickly under **lōw.**) Then you're going to say (pause) **lōw.**

c. (Point to **s.**) What are you going to say first? (Signal.) *sss.*

• What are you going to say next? (Signal.) *Lōw.*

d. (Repeat *c* until firm.)

e. (Touch the ball for **slōw.**) Get ready. (Move to **s,** then quickly along the arrow.) *Ssslow.*

f. Say it fast. (Signal.) *Slow.*

• Yes, what word? (Signal.) *Slow.* Yes, **slow.**

• Good reading.

g. Again. (Repeat *e* and *f* until firm.)

h. Now you're going to sound out (pause) **slow.** Get ready. (Touch **s, l, ō, w** as the children say *ssslllōōōwww.*)

• What word? (Signal.) *Slow.* Yes, **slow.**

STORY 113
EXERCISE 21

First reading—children read the story the fast way

(Have the children reread any sentences containing words that give them trouble. Keep a list of these words.)

a. (Pass out Storybook.)

b. Open your book to page 50 and get ready to read. ✔

c. We're going to read this story the fast way.

d. Touch the first word. ✔

e. Reading the fast way. First word. (Pause three seconds.) Get ready. (Tap.) *A.*

f. Next word. ✔

• (Pause three seconds.) Get ready. (Tap.) *Dog.*

g. (Repeat *f* for the remaining words in the first sentence. Pause at least three seconds between taps. The children are to identify each word without sounding it out.)

h. (Repeat *d* through *g* for the next two sentences. Have the children reread the first three sentences until firm.)

i. (The children are to read the remainder of the story the fast way, stopping at the end of each sentence.)

j. (After the first reading of the story, print on the board the words that the children missed more than one time. Have the children sound out each word one time and tell what word.)

k. (After the group's responses are firm, call on individual children to read the words.)

EXERCISE 22

Individual test

a. Look at page 50. I'm going to call on individual children to read a whole sentence the fast way.

b. (Call on individual children to read a sentence. Do not tap for each word.)

EXERCISE 23

Second reading—children read the story the fast way and answer questions

a. You're going to read the story again the fast way and I'll ask questions.

b. First word. ✔

• Get ready. (Tap.) *A.*

c. (Tap for each remaining word. Pause at least three seconds between taps. Pause longer before words that gave the children trouble during the first reading.)

d. (Ask the comprehension questions below as the children read.)

After the children read:	You say:
A dog was in the fog.	What's a fog? *The children respond.*
A goat was in the fog.	Name everybody who was in the fog. (Signal.) *A dog, a cat, and a goat.*
The cat and the dog sat on the log.	Who sat on the log? (Signal.) *The cat and the dog.* Who didn't sit on the log? (Signal.) *The goat.*
"Ha-ha."	What did the goat say? *The children respond.* How could he be in the log? *The children respond.*

EXERCISE 24

Picture comprehension

a. What do you think you'll see in the picture? *The children respond.*

b. Turn the page and look at the picture.

c. (Ask these questions:)

  1. Is the goat in the log? *The children respond.* Yes, that log is hollow.
  2. Did you ever see a hollow log? *The children respond.*
  3. Did you ever see an animal go into a hollow log? *The children respond.*

EXERCISE 17

Children read a word beginning with two consonants (**trēē**)

a. (Cover **t.** Run your finger under **rēē.**) You're going to sound out this part. Get ready. (Touch **r,** between the **ē**'s as the children say *rrrēēē.*)

b. Say it fast. (Signal.) *Rēē.* Yes, this part is **rēē.**

c. (Uncover **t.** Point to **t.**) You're going to say this first. (Move your finger quickly under **rēē.**) Then you're going to say (pause) **rēē.**

d. (Point to **t.**) What are you going to say first? (Signal.) *t.*

• What are you going to say next? (Signal.) *Rēē.*

e. (Repeat *d* until firm.)

f. (Touch the ball for **trēē.**) Get ready. (Move to **t,** then quickly along the arrow.) *Tree.*

g. Say it fast. (Signal.) *Tree.*

• Yes, what word? (Signal.) *Tree.* Yes, **tree.**

• Good reading.

h. Again. (Repeat *f* and *g* until firm.)

i. Now you're going to sound out (pause) **tree.** Get ready. (Touch **t, r,** between the **ē**'s as the children say *trrrēēē.*)

• What word? (Signal.) *Tree.* Yes, **tree.**

EXERCISE 18

Children sound out the word and tell what word

a. (Touch the ball for **things.**) Sound it out.

b. Get ready. (Touch **th, ing, s** as the children say *thththiiingsss.*)

• (If sounding out is not firm, repeat *b.*)

c. What word? (Signal.) *Things.* Yes, **things.**

EXERCISE 19

Children sound out the word and tell what word

(Repeat the procedures in exercise 18 for **ēven.**)

EXERCISE 20

Children read the words the fast way

a. Now you get to read the words on this page the fast way.

b. (Touch the ball for **things.** Pause three seconds.) Get ready. (Move your finger quickly along the arrow.) *Things.*

c. (Repeat *b* for **trēē.**)

Individual test

(Call on individual children to read one word the fast way.)

WORKSHEET 113

SUMMARY OF INDEPENDENT ACTIVITY
EXERCISE 25

Introduction to independent activity

a. (Pass out Worksheet 113 to each child.)

b. Everybody, you're going to do this worksheet on your own. (Tell the children when they will work the items.)

• Let's go over the things you're going to do.

Sentence copying

a. (Hold up side 1 of your worksheet and point to the first line in the sentence-copying exercise.)

b. Everybody, here's the sentence you're going to write on the lines below.

c. Reading the fast way. First word. ✔

• Get ready. (Tap.) *The.*

d. Next word. ✔

• Get ready. (Tap.) *Goat.*

e. (Repeat *d* for the remaining words.)

f. After you finish your worksheet, you get to draw a picture about the sentence, **thē gōat sat on a log.**

Sound writing

a. (Point to the sound-writing exercise.) Here are the sounds you're going to write today. I'll touch the sounds. You say them.

b. (Touch each sound.) *The children respond.*

c. (Repeat the series until firm.)

Matching

a. (Point to the column of words in the Matching Game.)

b. Everybody, you're going to follow the lines and write these words.

c. Reading the fast way.

d. (Point to the first word. Pause.) Get ready. (Signal.) *The children respond.*

e. (Repeat *d* for the remaining words.)

f. (Repeat *d* and *e* until firm.)

Cross-out game

(Point to the boxed word in the Cross-out Game.) Everybody, here's the word you're going to cross out today. What word? (Signal.) *Dog.* Yes, **dog.**

Pair relations

a. (Point to the pair-relations exercise on side 2.) You're going to circle the picture in each box that shows what the words say.

b. (Point to the space at the top of the page.) After you finish, remember to draw a picture that shows **thē gōat sat on a log.**

END OF LESSON 113

EXERCISE 14

Children read the fast way

a. Get ready to read these words the fast way.

b. (Touch the ball for **under.** Pause three seconds.) Get ready. (Signal.) *Under.*

c. (Repeat *b* for the remaining words on the page.)

EXERCISE 15

Children read the fast way again

a. Get ready to do these words again. Watch where I point.

b. (Point to a word. Pause one second. Say:) Get ready. (Signal.) *The children respond.*

• (Point to the words in this order: **fast, tēēth, tiger, whȳ, under.**)

c. (Repeat *b* until firm.)

EXERCISE 16

Individual test

(Call on individual children to read one word the fast way.)

under

tīger

tēēth

whȳ

fast

SOUNDS

EXERCISE 1

Teaching **ch** as in **chat**

a. (Point to **ch.**) My turn. When I touch it, I'll say it. (Pause. Touch **ch** for an instant, saying:) ch.

b. (Point to **ch.**) Your turn. When I touch it, you say it. (Pause.) Get ready. (Touch **ch.**) *ch.*

c. Again. (Touch **ch.**) *ch.*

d. (Repeat *c* until firm.)

EXERCISE 2

Sounds firm-up

a. Get ready to say the sounds when I touch them.

b. (Alternate touching **g** and **ch.** Point to the sound. Pause one second. Say:) Get ready. (Touch the sound.) *The children respond.*

c. (When **g** and **ch** are firm, alternate touching **g, th, ch,** and **sh** until all four sounds are firm.)

EXERCISE 3

Individual test

(Call on individual children to identify **g, th, ch,** or **sh.**)

ch

v

ā

ō

n

p

d

k

ch

g

th

sh

EXERCISE 4

Sounds firm-up

a. (Point to **ch.**) When I touch the sound, you say it.

b. (Pause.) Get ready. (Touch **ch.**) *ch.*

c. Again. (Repeat *b* until firm.)

d. Get ready to say all the sounds when I touch them.

e. (Alternate touching **v, ā, ō, n, p, d, k,** and **ch** three or four times. Point to the sound. Pause one second. Say:) Get ready. (Touch the sound.) *The children respond.*

EXERCISE 5

Individual test

(Call on individual children to identify one or more sounds in exercise 4.)

EXERCISE 10

Children read a word beginning with two consonants (**stands**)

a. (Cover **s.** Run your finger under **tands.**) You're going to sound out this part. Get ready. (Touch **t, a, n, d, s** as the children say *taaannndsss.*)

b. Say it fast. (Signal.) *Tands.* Yes, this part is **tands.**

c. (Uncover **s.** Point to **s.**) You're going to say this first. (Move your finger quickly under **tands.**) Then you're going to say (pause) **tands.**

d. (Point to **s.**) What are you going to say first? (Signal.) *sss.*

• What are you going to say next? (Signal.) *Tands.*

e. (Repeat *d* until firm.)

f. (Touch the ball for **stands.**) Get ready. (Move to **s,** then quickly along the arrow.) *Ssstands.*

g. Say it fast. (Signal.) *Stands.*

• Yes, what word? (Signal.) *Stands.* Yes, **stands.**

• Good reading.

h. Again. (Repeat *f* and *g* until firm.)

i. Now you're going to sound out (pause) **stands.** Get ready. (Touch **s, t, a, n, d, s** as the children say *ssstaaannndsss.*)

• What word? (Signal.) *Stands.* Yes, **stands.**

EXERCISE 11

Children read the fast way

a. Get ready to read these words the fast way.

b. (Touch the ball for **after.** Pause three seconds.) Get ready. (Signal.) *After.*

c. (Repeat *b* for the remaining words on the page.)

EXERCISE 12

Children read the fast way again

a. Get ready to do these words again. Watch where I point.

b. (Point to a word. Pause one second. Say:) Get ready. (Signal.) *The children respond.*

• (Point to the words in this order: **smīle, after, ēagle.**)

c. (Repeat *b* until firm.)

EXERCISE 13

Individual test

(Call on individual children to read one word on the page the fast way.)

stands

after

smīle

ēagle

READING VOCABULARY

EXERCISE 6

Children sound out an irregular word (**car**)

a. (Touch the ball for **car.**) Sound it out.

b. Get ready. (Quickly touch each sound as the children say *caaarrr.*)

c. Again. (Repeat *b* until firm.)

d. That's how we <u>sound out</u> the word. Here's how we <u>say</u> the word. **Car.** How do we <u>say</u> the word? (Signal.) *Car.*

e. Now you're going to <u>sound out</u> the word. Get ready. (Touch each sound as the children say *caaarrr.*)

f. Now you're going to say the word. Get ready. (Signal.) *Car.*

g. (Repeat *e* and *f* until firm.)

h. Yes, this word is **car.** A **car** has wheels.

EXERCISE 7

Individual test

(Have children do *e* and *f* in exercise 6.)

EXERCISE 8

Children sound out the word and tell what word

a. (Touch the ball for **chips.**) Sound it out.

b. Get ready. (Touch **ch, i, p, s** as the children say *chiiipsss.*)

• (If sounding out is not firm, repeat *b*.)

c. What word? (Signal.) *Chips.* Yes, **chips.**

EXERCISE 9

Children sound out an irregular word (**far**)

a. (Touch the ball for **far.**) Sound it out.

b. Get ready. (Quickly touch each sound as the children say *fffaaarrr.*)

c. Again. (Repeat *b* until firm.)

d. That's how we <u>sound out</u> the word. Here's how we <u>say</u> the word. **Far.** How do we <u>say</u> the word? (Signal.) *Far.*

e. Now you're going to <u>sound out</u> the word. Get ready. (Touch each sound as the children say *fffaaarrr.*)

f. Now you're going to say the word. Get ready. (Signal.) *Far.*

g. (Repeat *e* and *f* until firm.)

h. Yes, this word is **far.** I live **far** from here.

EXERCISE 10

Individual test

(Have children do *e* and *f* in exercise 9.)

EXERCISE 11

Children read the words the fast way

(Have the children read the words on this page the fast way.)

EXERCISE 12

Individual test

(Have children read one word the fast way.)

READING VOCABULARY

EXERCISE 6

Children read a word beginning with two consonants (**steps**)

a. (Cover **s.** Run your finger under **teps.**) You're going to sound out this part. Get ready. (Touch **t, e, p, s** as the children say *teeepsss.*)

b. Say it fast. (Signal.) *Teps.* Yes, this part is **teps.**

c. (Uncover **s.** Point to **s.**) You're going to say this first. (Move your finger quickly under **teps.**) Then you're going to say (pause) **teps.**

d. (Point to **s.**) What are you going to say first? (Signal.) *sss.*

• What are you going to say next? (Signal.) *Teps.*

e. (Repeat *d* until firm.)

f. (Touch the ball for **steps.**) Get ready. (Move to **s,** then quickly along the arrow.) *Sssteps.*

g. Say it fast. (Signal.) *Steps.*

• Yes, what word? (Signal.) *Steps.* Yes, **steps.**

• Good reading.

h. Again. (Repeat *f* and *g* until firm.)

i. Now you're going to sound out (pause) **steps.** Get ready. (Touch **s, t, e, p, s** as the children say *sssteeepsss.*)

• What word? (Signal.) *Steps.* Yes, **steps.**

EXERCISE 7

Children read the fast way

a. Get ready to read these words the fast way.

b. (Touch the ball for **when.** Pause three seconds.) Get ready. (Signal.) *When.*

c. (Repeat *b* for the remaining words on the page.)

EXERCISE 8

Children read the fast way again

a. Get ready to do these words again. Watch where I point.

b. (Point to a word. Pause one second. Say:) Get ready. (Signal.) *The children respond.*

• (Point to the words in this order: **where, there, when.**)

c. (Repeat *b* until firm.)

steps

when

where

there

EXERCISE 9

Individual test

(Call on individual children to read one word on the page the fast way.)

EXERCISE 13

Children read the fast way

a. Get ready to read these words the fast way.

b. (Touch the ball for **ships.** Pause three seconds.) Get ready. (Signal.) *Ships.*

c. (Repeat *b* for the remaining words on the page.)

EXERCISE 14

Children read the fast way again

a. Get ready to do these words again. Watch where I point.

b. (Point to a word. Pause one second. Say:) Get ready. (Signal.) *The children respond.* (Point to the words in this order: **rōad, ships, sō, gō.**)

c. (Repeat *b* until firm.)

EXERCISE 15

Individual test

(Call on individual children to read one word the fast way.)

Groups that are firm on Mastery Tests 29 and 30 should skip this lesson and do lesson 158 today.

SOUNDS

EXERCISE 1

Teaching **z** as in **zoo**

a. (Point to **z**.) My turn. (Pause. Touch **z** and say:) zzz.
b. (Point to **z**.) Your turn. When I touch it, you say it. (Pause.) Get ready. (Touch **z**.) *zzz*.
• (Lift your finger.)
c. Again. (Touch **z**.) *zzz*.
• (Lift your finger.)
d. (Repeat *c* until firm.)

EXERCISE 2

Sounds firm-up

a. Get ready to say the sounds when I touch them.
b. (Alternate touching **z** and **v**. Point to the sound. Pause one second. Say:) Get ready. (Touch the sound.) *The children respond.*
c. (When **z** and **v** are firm, alternate touching **z, v, s,** and **qu** until all four sounds are firm.)

z

v

s

EXERCISE 3

Individual test

(Call on individual children to identify **z, v, s,** or **qu.**)

z   ā

u   *qu*

J   g

EXERCISE 4

Sounds firm-up

a. (Point to **z**.) When I touch the sound, you say it.
b. (Pause.) Get ready. (Touch **z**.) *zzz*.
c. Again. (Repeat *b* until firm.)
d. Get ready to say all the sounds when I touch them.
e. (Alternate touching **z, ā, u, qu, j, g, wh,** and **ȳ** three or four times. Point to the sound. Pause one second. Say:) Get ready. (Touch the sound.) *The children respond.*

wh

EXERCISE 5

Individual test

(Call on individual children to identify one or more sounds in exercise 4.)

EXERCISE 16

Children sound out an irregular word (**farm**)

a. (Touch the ball for **farm.**) Sound it out.
b. Get ready. (Quickly touch each sound as the children say *fffaaarrrmmm.*)
c. Again. (Repeat *b* until firm.)
d. That's how we <u>sound out</u> the word. Here's how we <u>say</u> the word. **Farm.** How do we <u>say</u> the word? (Signal.) *Farm.*
e. Now you're going to <u>sound out</u> the word. Get ready. (Touch each sound as the children say *fffaaarrrmmm.*)
f. Now you're going to say the word. Get ready. (Signal.) *Farm.*
g. (Repeat *e* and *f* until firm.)
h. Yes, this word is **farm.** We see cows on a **farm.**

EXERCISE 17

Individual test

(Call on individual children to do *e* and *f* in exercise 16.)

EXERCISE 18

Children sound out an irregular word (**are**)

a. (Touch the ball for **are.**) Sound it out.
b. Get ready. (Quickly touch each sound as the children say *aaarrr.*)
c. Again. (Repeat *b* until firm.)
d. That's how we <u>sound out</u> the word. Here's how we <u>say</u> the word. **Are.** How do we <u>say</u> the word? (Signal.) *Are.*
e. Now you're going to <u>sound out</u> the word. Get ready. (Touch each sound as the children say *aaarrr.*)
f. Now you're going to say the word. Get ready. (Signal.) *Are.*
g. (Repeat *e* and *f* until firm.)
h. Yes, this word is **are.** You **are** in school.

EXERCISE 19

Individual test

(Call on individual children to do *e* and *f* in exercise 18.)

EXERCISE 20

Children read the words the fast way

a. Now you get to read the words on this page the fast way.
b. (Touch the ball for **farm.** Pause three seconds.) Get ready. (Move your finger quickly along the arrow.) *Farm.*
c. (Repeat *b* for **are.**)

EXERCISE 21

Individual test

(Call on individual children to read one word the fast way.)

WORKSHEET 156

SUMMARY OF INDEPENDENT ACTIVITY
EXERCISE 30

Introduction to independent activity

a. (Pass out Worksheet 156 to each child.)

b. Everybody, you're going to do this worksheet on your own. (Tell the children when they will work the items.)

• Let's go over the things you're going to do.

Story items

a. (Hold up side 1 of your worksheet and point to the story-items exercise.)

b. Everybody, here are items about the story we read today.

c. Think about what happened in the story and circle the right answer for each item.

Picture comprehension

a. (Point to the pictures in the picture-comprehension exercise.) Everybody, you're going to look at the picture. Then you're going to read each item and write the missing word.

b. Remember—the first sound of each missing word is already written in the blank.

Reading comprehension

a. (Point to the reading-comprehension exercise on side 2.)

b. Everybody, get ready to read the sentences in the box the fast way.

c. First word. ✔

• Get ready. (Tap for each word as the children read the sentences *Bill went to the park. He went in the big pool.*)

d. (Point to items 1 and 2.) These items tell about the story in the box. You're going to read each item and circle the right answer.

Sound writing

a. (Point to the sound-writing exercise.) Here are the sounds you're going to write today. I'll touch the sounds. You say them.

b. (Touch each sound.) *The children respond.*

c. (Repeat the series until firm.)

Sentence copying

a. (Point to the dotted sentence in the sentence-copying exercise.)

b. You're going to trace the words in this sentence. Then you're going to write the sentence on the other lines.

c. Reading the fast way. First word. ✔

• Get ready. (Tap for each word.)

d. After you finish your worksheet, you get to draw a picture about the sentence, **the girl smīled.** You'll draw your picture on a piece of plain paper. (When the children finish their worksheets, give them sheets of plain paper.)

END OF LESSON 156

STORY 114

EXERCISE 22

First reading—children read the story the fast way

(Have the children reread any sentences containing words that give them trouble. Keep a list of these words.)

a. (Pass out Storybook.)

b. Open your book to page 53 and get ready to read. ✔

c. We're going to read this story the fast way.

d. Touch the first word. ✔

e. Reading the fast way. First word. (Pause three seconds.) Get ready. (Tap.) *Thē.*

f. Next word. ✔

• (Pause three seconds.) Get ready. (Tap.) *Fat.*

g. (Repeat *f* for the remaining words in the first sentence. Pause at least three seconds between taps. The children are to identify each word without sounding it out.)

h. (Repeat *d* through *g* for the next two sentences. Have the children reread the first three sentences until firm.)

i. (The children are to read the remainder of the story the fast way, stopping at the end of each sentence.)

j. (After the first reading of the story, print on the board the words that the children missed more than one time. Have the children sound out each word one time and tell what word.)

k. (After the group's responses are firm, call on individual children to read the words.)

EXERCISE 23

Individual test

a. Turn back to page 53. I'm going to call on individual children to read a whole sentence the fast way.

b. (Call on individual children to read a sentence. Do not tap for each word.)

EXERCISE 24

Second reading—children read the story the fast way and answer questions

a. You're going to read the story again the fast way and I'll ask questions.

b. First word. ✔

• Get ready. (Tap.) *Thē.*

c. (Tap for each remaining word. Pause at least three seconds between taps. Pause longer before words that gave the children trouble during the second reading.)

d. (Ask the comprehension questions below as the children read.)

After the children read:	You say:
The fat man and his dog had a car.	What did the fat man and his dog have? (Signal.) *A car.*
The car did not run.	What was wrong with the car? (Signal.) *It didn't run.*
The fat man and his dog sat on the goat.	Who sat on the goat? (Signal.) *The fat man and his dog.*
The fat man said, "The goat will not go."	What did the fat man say? (Signal.) *The goat will not go.*
So the fat man and his dog sat on the road.	What happened? (Signal.) *The fat man and his dog sat on the road.*

EXERCISE 25

Picture comprehension

a. Everybody, look at the picture.

b. (Ask these questions:)

1. Who's sitting on the road? *The children respond.* A fat man and his dog.

2. What's the goat doing? *The children respond.*

3. What would you do if you were that dog? *The children respond.*

STORY 156
EXERCISE 26

First reading—children read the title and first three sentences

a. Now you're going to finish the story about the girl and her red tooth brush.

b. Everybody, touch the title of the story and get ready to read the words in the title the fast way.

c. First word. ✔

• (Pause two seconds.) Get ready. (Tap.) *The.*

d. (Tap for each remaining word in the title.)

e. (After the children have read the title, ask:) What's this story about? (Signal.) *The red tooth brush.* Yes, **the red tooth brush.**

f. Everybody, get ready to read this story the fast way.

g. First word. ✔

• (Pause two seconds.) Get ready. (Tap.) *A.*

h. (Tap for the remaining words in the first sentence. Pause at least two seconds between taps.)

i. (Repeat *g* and *h* for the next two sentences. Have the children reread the first three sentences until firm.)

EXERCISE 27

Individual children or the group read sentences to complete the first reading

a. I'm going to call on individual children to read a sentence. Everybody, follow along and point to the words. If you hear a mistake, raise your hand.

b. (Call on a child.) Read the next sentence. (Do not tap for the words. Let children read at their own pace, but be sure they read the sentence correctly.)

To Correct

(Have the child sound out the word. Then return to the beginning of the sentence.)

c. (Repeat *b* for most of the remaining sentences in the story. Occasionally have the group read a sentence. When the group is to read, say:) Everybody, read the next sentence. (Pause two seconds.) Get ready. (Tap for each word in the sentence. Pause at least two seconds between taps.)

EXERCISE 28

Second reading—individual children or the group read each sentence; the group answer questions

a. You're going to read the story again. This time I'm going to ask questions.

b. Starting with the first word of the title. ✔

• Get ready. (Tap as the children read the title. Pause at least two seconds between taps.)

c. (Call on a child.) Read the first sentence. *The child responds.*

d. (Repeat *b* and *c* in exercise 27. Present the following comprehension questions to the entire group.)

After the children read:	You say:
The girl went back to her room.	What did she do? (Signal.) *She went back to her room.*
She slipped on her dog.	What did she slip on? (Signal.) *Her dog.*
Her dog was brushing his teeth with her red tooth brush.	What was that dog doing? (Signal.) *He was brushing his teeth with her red tooth brush.*
They said, "Now we both have teeth that shine like the moon."	What did they say? (Signal.) *Now we both have teeth that shine like the moon.*

EXERCISE 29

Picture comprehension

a. Everybody, look at the picture.

b. (Ask these questions:)

1. Look at those teeth. They really shine. What did the girl and the dog say about their teeth? *The children respond.* Yes, **we both have teeth that shine like the moon.**

2. What would you do if you had a dog that used your tooth brush? *The children respond.*

WORKSHEET 114

PAIR RELATIONS

The children will need pencils.

EXERCISE 26

Children draw a line through the incorrect words

a. (Pass out Worksheet 114 to each child.)

b. (Point to the picture of the ear in the pair-relations exercise on side 2.) Everybody, what does this picture show? (Signal.) *An ear.*

c. (Point to the words next to the picture.) Let's find the word that tells about this picture. Reading the fast way.

d. (Point to the word **nōse**. Pause.) Everybody, what word? (Signal.) *Nose.*

• Does that word tell about this picture? (Signal.) *No.*

• It's wrong. So I'll draw a line through it. (Do it.)

e. (Point to the word **tēēth**. Pause.) Everybody, what word? (Signal.) *Teeth.*

• Does that word tell about this picture? (Signal.) *No.*

• It's wrong. So I'll draw a line through it. (Do it.)

f. (Point to the word **ēar**. Pause.) Everybody, what word? (Signal.) *Ear.*

• Does that word tell about this picture? (Signal.) *Yes.*

• It's right. So I won't draw a line through it.

g. (Point to the word **car**. Pause.) Everybody, what word? (Signal.) *Car.*

• Does that word tell about this picture? (Signal.) *No.*

• So what do I do? (Signal.) *Draw a line through it.* Yes, I'll draw a line through it.

• (Do it.)

h. (Point to the picture of the ear.) Everybody, draw a line through the words that do not tell about this picture. ✔

i. (Hold up your worksheet. Point to the picture of the cow.) Everybody, what does this picture show? (Signal.) *A cow.* Yes, a cow.

• Draw a line through the words that do not tell about this picture. ✔

j. You'll do the rest of the boxes later.

SUMMARY OF INDEPENDENT ACTIVITY
EXERCISE 27

Introduction to independent activity

a. (Hold up Worksheet 114.)

b. Everybody, you're going to finish this worksheet on your own. (Tell the children when they will work the remaining items.)

• Let's go over the things you're going to do.

Sentence copying

a. (Point to the first line in the sentence-copying exercise on side 1.)

b. Everybody, here's the sentence you're going to write on the lines below.

c. Reading the fast way. First word. ✔

• Get ready. (Tap.) *A.*

d. Next word. ✔

• Get ready. (Tap.) *Man.*

e. (Repeat *d* for the remaining words.)

f. After you finish your worksheet, you get to draw a picture about the sentence, **a man sat on a gōat.**

Sound writing

a. (Point to the sound-writing exercise.) Here are the sounds you're going to write today. I'll touch the sounds. You say them.

b. (Touch each sound.) *The children respond.*

c. (Repeat the series until firm.)

Matching

a. (Point to the column of words in the Matching Game.)

b. Everybody, you're going to follow the lines and write these words.

c. Reading the fast way.

d. (Point to the first word. Pause.) Get ready. (Signal.) *The children respond.*

e. (Repeat *d* for the remaining words.)

f. (Repeat *d* and *e* until firm.)

Cross-out game

(Point to the boxed word in the Cross-out Game.) Everybody, here's the word you're going to cross out today. What word? (Signal.) *Pot.* Yes, **pot.**

Pair relations

a. (Point to the pair-relations exercise on side 2.) Remember—you're going to draw a line through the words in each box that do not tell about the picture.

b. (Point to the space at the top of the page.) After you finish, remember to draw a picture that shows **a man sat on a gōat.**

END OF LESSON 114

STORYBOOK

READ THE ITEMS 156
EXERCISE 23

Children read items 1 and 2

a. (Pass out Storybook.)

b. Open your book to page 177. ✔

c. Get ready to read the items and play the game.

d. Finger under the first word of the title. ✔

e. When I tap, read the title. (Pause.) Get ready. (Tap.) *Read the items.*

f. Touch item 1 and get ready to read. ✔

• First word. (Tap for each word as the children read *When the teacher says "Stand up," pick up your book.*)

• (Repeat until firm.)

g. Everybody, get ready to say item 1. (Pause and signal.) *The children say the sentence.*

• (Repeat four times or until firm.)

h. Touch item 2 and get ready to read. ✔

• First word. (Tap for each word as the children read *If the teacher says "Now," hold up your hands.*)

• (Repeat until firm.)

i. Everybody, get ready to say item 2. (Pause and signal.) *The children say the sentence.*

• (Repeat four times or until firm.)

EXERCISE 24

Children reread items 1 and 2 and answer questions

a. Everybody, touch item 1. ✔

b. Read item 1 to yourself. Raise your hand when you know what you're going to do and when you're going to do it.

c. (After the children raise their hands, say:) Everybody, what are you going to do when I say **"Stand up"**? (Signal.) *Pick up my book.*

┌─ **To Correct** ──────────────────────┐
1. Everybody, read item 1 out loud. (Tap as the children read each word.)
2. What are you going to do when I say **"Stand up"**? (Signal.) *Pick up my book.*
└────────────────────────────────────┘

d. Everybody, when are you going to **pick up your book?** (Signal.) *When the teacher says "Stand up."*

┌─ **To Correct** ──────────────────────┐
1. Everybody, read item 1 out loud. (Tap as the children read each word.)
2. When are you going to **pick up your book?** (Signal.) *When the teacher says "Stand up."*
└────────────────────────────────────┘

e. (Repeat *c* and *d* until firm.)

f. Everybody, touch item 2. ✔

g. Read item 2 to yourself. Raise your hand when you know what you're going to do and when you're going to do it.

h. (After the children raise their hands, say:) Everybody, what are you going to do if I say **"Now"**? (Signal.) *Hold up my hands.*

┌─ **To Correct** ──────────────────────┐
1. Everybody, read item 2 out loud. (Tap as the children read each word.)
2. What are you going to do if I say **"Now"**? (Signal.) *Hold up my hands.*
└────────────────────────────────────┘

i. Everybody, when are you going to **hold up your hands?** (Signal.) *If the teacher says "Now."*

┌─ **To Correct** ──────────────────────┐
1. Everybody, read item 2 out loud. (Tap as the children read each word.)
2. When are you going to **hold up your hands?** (Signal.) *If the teacher says "Now."*
└────────────────────────────────────┘

j. (Repeat *h* and *i* until firm.)

EXERCISE 25

Children play the game

a. Everybody, touch item 1. ✔

b. Read the item to yourself. Raise your hand when you know what you're going to do and when you're going to do it.

c. (After the children raise their hands, say:) Let's play the game. Think about what you're going to do (pause) and when you're going to do it.

d. (Hold out your hand. Pause.) Get ready. **Stand up.** (Pause. Drop your hand.) *The children pick up their books immediately.*

┌─ **To Correct** ──────────────────────┐
1. What did I say? (Signal.) *Stand up.*
2. What are you supposed to do when I say **"Stand up"**? (Signal.) *Pick up my book.*
3. (If the children's responses are not firm, have them read item 1 aloud.)
4. (Repeat exercise 25.)
└────────────────────────────────────┘

SOUNDS

EXERCISE 1

Sounds firm-up

a. Get ready to say the sounds when I touch them.
b. (Alternate touching **ch** and **c.** Point to the sound. Pause one second. Say:) Get ready. (Touch the sound.) *The children respond.*
c. (When **ch** and **c** are firm, alternate touching **h, c, v,** and **ch** until all four sounds are firm.)

 c

v

EXERCISE 2

Individual test

(Call on individual children to identify **h, c, v,** or **ch.**)

EXERCISE 3

Teacher introduces cross-out game

a. (Use transparency and crayon.)
b. I'll cross out the sounds on this part of the page when you can tell me every sound.
c. Remember—when I touch it, you say it.
d. (Go over the sounds until the children can identify all the sounds in order.)

EXERCISE 4

Individual test

(Call on individual children to identify two or more sounds in exercise 3.)

EXERCISE 5

Teacher crosses out sounds

a. You told me every sound. Get ready to do it again. This time I'll cross out each sound when you tell me what it is.
b. (Point to each sound. Pause. Say:) Get ready. (Touch the sound.) *The children respond.*
• (As you cross out the sound, say:) Goodbye, _____.

w

k

ō

r

i

u

EXERCISE 19

Children sound out an irregular word (**looked**)

a. (Touch the ball for **looked.**) Sound it out.

b. Get ready. (Quickly touch each sound as the children say *lllooookd.*)

c. Again. (Repeat *b* until firm.)

d. That's how we <u>sound out</u> the word. Here's how we <u>say</u> the word. **Looked.** How do we <u>say</u> the word? (Signal.) *Looked.*

e. Now you're going to <u>sound out</u> the word. Get ready. (Touch each sound as the children say *lllooookd.*)

f. Now you're going to say the word. Get ready. (Signal.) *Looked.*

g. (Repeat *e* and *f* until firm.)

h. Yes, this word is **looked.** I **looked** under the chair.

i. (Call on individual children to do *e* and *f.*)

EXERCISE 20

Children read **fat** and **fatter**

a. (Touch the ball for **fat.**) You're going to read this word the fast way. (Pause three seconds.) Get ready. (Move your finger quickly along the arrow.) *Fat.*

b. (Return to the ball for **fat.**) Yes, this word is **fat.**

c. (Touch the ball for **fatter.**) So this must be **fat . . .** (Touch **er.**) *Er.*

• What word? (Signal.) *Fatter.* Yes, **fatter.**

d. Again. (Repeat *b* and *c* until firm.)

e. (Touch the ball for **fat.**) This word is **fat.**

f. (Touch the ball for **fatter.**) So this must be . . . (Quickly run your finger under **fat** and tap **er.**) *Fatter.* Yes, **fatter.**

g. Again. (Repeat *e* and *f* until firm.)

h. Now you're going to sound out (pause) **fatter.** Get ready. (Touch **f, a,** between the **t**'s, **er** as the children say *fffaaaterrr.*)

• Yes, what word? (Signal.) *Fatter.* Yes, **fatter.**

EXERCISE 21

Children read the fast way

(Touch the ball for **broom.**) Get ready to read this word the fast way. (Pause three seconds.) Get ready. (Signal.) *Broom.*

EXERCISE 22

Children read the words the fast way

(Have the children read the words on this page the fast way.)

Individual test

(Call on individual children to read one word the fast way.)

looked

fat

fatter

broom

READING VOCABULARY
EXERCISE 6

Children identify, then sound out an irregular word (**are**)

a. (Touch the ball for **are.**) Everybody, you're going to read this word the fast way. (Pause three seconds.) Get ready. (Move your finger quickly along the arrow.) *Are.* Yes, **are.**

b. Now you're going to sound out the word. Get ready. (Quickly touch **a, r** as the children say *aaarrr.*)

c. Again. (Repeat *b.*)

d. How do we say the word? (Signal.) *Are.* Yes, **are.**

e. (Repeat *b* and *d* until firm.)

EXERCISE 7

Individual test

(Call on individual children to do *b* and *d* in exercise 6.)

EXERCISE 8

Children read the fast way

a. Get ready to read these words the fast way.

b. (Touch the ball for **ēach.** Pause three seconds.) Get ready. (Signal.) *Each.*

c. (Repeat *b* for the remaining words on the page.)

EXERCISE 9

Children read the fast way again

a. Get ready to do these words again. Watch where I point.

b. (Point to a word. Pause one second. Say:) Get ready. (Signal.) *The children respond.*

• (Point to the words in this order: **cop, ēach, lots.**)

c. (Repeat *b* until firm.)

EXERCISE 10

Individual test

(Call on individual children to read one word on the page the fast way.)

cop

lots

EXERCISE 15

Children sound out the word and tell what word

a. (Touch the ball for **yelled.**) Sound it out.

b. Get ready. (Touch **y, e,** between the **l**'s, **d** as the children say *yyyeeellld.*)

• (If sounding out is not firm, repeat *b.*)

c. What word? (Signal.) *Yelled.* Yes, **yelled.**

EXERCISE 16

Children sound out the word and tell what word

(Repeat the procedures in exercise 15 for **after.**)

EXERCISE 17

Children read the fast way

a. Get ready to read these words the fast way.

b. (Touch the ball for **slipped.** Pause three seconds.) Get ready. (Signal.) *Slipped.*

c. (Repeat *b* for the remaining words on the page.)

EXERCISE 18

Children read the words the fast way

a. Now you get to read the words on this page the fast way.

b. (Touch the ball for **yelled.** Pause one second.) Get ready. (Move your finger quickly along the arrow.) *Yelled.*

c. (Repeat *b* for each word on the page.)

Individual test

(Call on individual children to read one word the fast way.)

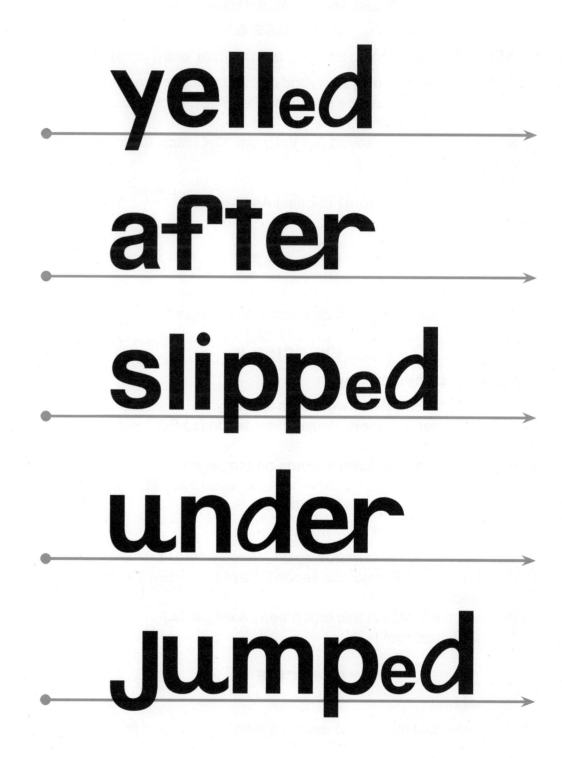

EXERCISE 11

Children sound out an irregular word (**arm**)

a. (Touch the ball for **arm.**) Sound it out.

b. Get ready. (Quickly touch each sound as the children say *aaarrrmmm.*)

c. Again. (Repeat *b* until firm.)

d. That's how we <u>sound out</u> the word. Here's how we <u>say</u> the word. **Arm.** How do we <u>say</u> the word? (Signal.) *Arm.*

e. Now you're going to <u>sound out</u> the word. Get ready. (Touch each sound as the children say *aaarrrmmm.*)

f. Now you're going to <u>say</u> the word. Get ready. (Signal.) *Arm.*

g. (Repeat *e* and *f* until firm.)

EXERCISE 12

Children rhyme with an irregular word (**arm**)

a. (Touch the ball for **arm.**) Everybody, you're going to read this word the fast way. Get ready. (Signal.) *Arm.*

b. (Touch the ball for **farm.**) This word rhymes with (pause) **arm.** Get ready. (Move to **f,** then quickly along the arrow.) *Farm.*

c. (Repeat *a* and *b* until firm.)

EXERCISE 13

Children sound out **farm**

(Have the children sound out **farm.**) *Fffaaarrrmmm.* How do we say the word? (Signal.) *Farm.* Yes, **farm.** Do you live on a **farm?**

EXERCISE 14

Children sound out the word and tell what word

a. (Touch the ball for **tēach.**) Sound it out.

b. Get ready. (Touch **t, ē, ch** as the children say *tēēēch.*)

• (If sounding out is not firm, repeat *b.*)

c. What word? (Signal.) *Teach.* Yes, **teach.**

EXERCISE 15

Children read the words the fast way

a. Now you get to read the words on this page the fast way.

b. (Touch the ball for **arm.** Pause three seconds.) Get ready. (Move your finger quickly along the arrow.) *Arm.*

c. (Repeat *b* for each word on the page.)

arm

farm

tēach

EXERCISE 16

Individual test

(Call on individual children to read one word the fast way.)

EXERCISE 10

Children read a word beginning with two consonants (**tree**)

a. (Cover **t.** Run your finger under **rēē.**) You're going to sound out this part. Get ready. (Touch **r,** between the **ē**'s as the children say *rrrēēē.*)

b. Say it fast. (Signal.) *Rēē.* Yes, this part is **rēē.**

c. (Uncover **t.** Point to **t.**) You're going to say this first. (Move your finger quickly under **rēē.**) Then you're going to say (pause) **rēē.**

d. (Point to **t.**) What are you going to say first? (Signal.) *t.*

• What are you going to say next? (Signal.) *Rēē.*

e. (Repeat *d* until firm.)

f. (Touch the ball for **trēē.**) Get ready. (Move to **t,** then quickly along the arrow.) *Trēē.*

g. Say it fast. (Signal.) *Tree.*

• Yes, what word? (Signal.) *Tree.* Yes, **tree.**

• Good reading.

h. Again. (Repeat *f* and *g* until firm.)

i. Now you're going to sound out (pause) **tree.** Get ready. (Touch **t, r,** between the **ē**'s as the children say *trrrēēē.*)

• What word? (Signal.) *Tree.* Yes, **tree.**

EXERCISE 11

Children sound out the word and tell what word

a. (Touch the ball for **from.**) Sound it out.

b. Get ready. (Touch **f, r, o, m** as the children say *fffrrrooommm.*)

• (If sounding out is not firm, repeat *b.*)

c. What word? (Signal.) *From.* Yes, **from.**

EXERCISE 12

Children sound out the word and tell what word

(Repeat the procedures in exercise 11 for **tīger.**)

EXERCISE 13

Children read the words the fast way

(Have the children read the words on this page the fast way.)

EXERCISE 14

Individual test

(Call on individual children to read one word the fast way.)

EXERCISE 17

Children identify, then sound out an irregular word (**of**)

a. (Touch the ball for **of**.) Everybody, you're going to read this word the fast way. (Pause three seconds.) Get ready. (Move your finger quickly along the arrow.) *Of.* Yes, **of.**

b. Now you're going to sound out the word. Get ready. (Quickly touch **o, f** as the children say *ooofff.*)

c. Again. (Repeat *b*.)

d. How do we say the word? (Signal.) *Of.* Yes, **of.**

e. (Repeat *b* and *d* until firm.)

EXERCISE 18

Individual test

(Call on individual children to do *b* and *d* in exercise 17.)

EXERCISE 19

Children sound out an irregular word (**cars**)

a. (Touch the ball for **cars**.) Sound it out.

b. Get ready. (Quickly touch each sound as the children say *caaarrrsss.*)

> **To Correct**
> If the children do not say the sounds you touch
> 1. (Say:) You've got to say the sounds I touch.
> 2. (Repeat *a* and *b* until firm.)

c. Again. (Repeat *b* until firm.)

d. That's how we <u>sound out</u> the word. Here's how we <u>say</u> the word. **Cars.** How do we <u>say</u> the word? (Signal.) *Cars.*

e. Now you're going to <u>sound out</u> the word. Get ready. (Touch each sound as the children say *caaarrrsss.*)

f. Now you're going to <u>say</u> the word. Get ready. (Signal.) *Cars.*

g. (Repeat *e* and *f* until firm.)

h. Yes, this word is **cars. Cars** can go fast.

EXERCISE 20

Individual test

(Call on individual children to do *e* and *f* in exercise 19.)

of

cars

READING VOCABULARY
EXERCISE 7

Children read the fast way

a. Get ready to read these words the fast way.

b. (Touch the ball for **where.** Pause three seconds.) Get ready. (Signal.) *Where.*

c. (Repeat *b* for the remaining words on the page.)

EXERCISE 8

Children read the fast way again

a. Get ready to do these words again. Watch where I point.

b. (Point to a word. Pause one second. Say:) Get ready. (Signal.) *The children respond.*

• (Point to the words in this order: **there, when, where, whȳ.**)

c. (Repeat *b* until firm.)

EXERCISE 9

Individual test

(Call on individual children to read one word the fast way.)

STORYBOOK

STORY 115
EXERCISE 21

Teacher introduces the title

a. (Pass out Storybook.)

b. Open your book to page 56. ✔

c. (Hold up your reader. Point to the title.) These words are called the title of the story. These words tell what the story is about. I'll read the title the fast way.

d. (Point to the words as you read:) Lots of cars.

e. Everybody, what is this story about? (Signal.) *Lots of cars.* Yes, **lots of cars.**

• This story is going to tell something about **lots of cars.**

EXERCISE 22

First reading—children read the story the fast way

(Have the children reread any sentences containing words that give them trouble. Keep a list of these words.)

a. Everybody, touch the title of the story and get ready to read the words in the title the fast way.

b. First word. ✔

• (Pause three seconds.) Get ready. (Tap.) *Lots.*

c. Next word. ✔

• (Pause three seconds.) Get ready. (Tap.) *Of.*

d. (Repeat c for the word **cars.**)

e. (After the children have read the title, ask:) What's this story about? (Signal.) *Lots of cars.* Yes, **lots of cars.**

f. Everybody, touch the first word of the <u>story</u>. ✔

g. Get ready to read this story the fast way.

h. First word. (Pause three seconds.) Get ready. (Tap.) *A.*

i. Next word. ✔

• (Pause three seconds.) Get ready. (Tap.) *Man.*

j. (Repeat i for the remaining words in the first sentence. Pause at least three seconds between taps. The children are to identify each word without sounding it out.)

k. (Repeat h through j for the next two sentences. Have the children reread the first three sentences until firm.)

l. (The children are to read the remainder of the story the fast way, stopping at the end of each sentence.)

m. (After the first reading of the story, print on the board the words that the children missed more than one time. Have the children sound out each word one time and tell what word.)

n. (After the group's responses are firm, call on individual children to read the words.)

EXERCISE 23

Individual test

a. Look at page 56. I'm going to call on individual children to read a whole sentence the fast way.

b. (Call on individual children to read a sentence. Do not tap for each word.)

EXERCISE 24

Second reading—children read the story the fast way and answer questions

a. You're going to read the story again the fast way and I'll ask questions.

b. Starting with the first word of the title. ✔

• Get ready. (Tap.) *Lots.*

c. (Tap for each remaining word. Pause at least three seconds between taps. Pause longer before words that gave the children trouble during the first reading.)

d. (Ask the comprehension questions below as the children read.)

After the children read:	You say:
Lots of cars.	What's this story about? (Signal.) *Lots of cars.*
A man on a farm has lots of cars.	What does he have? (Signal.) *Lots of cars.*
He has little cars.	What kind of cars does he have? (Signal.) *Old cars and little cars.*
Are his cars for goats?	What do you think? *The children respond.* Let's read and find out.
No.	Are they for goats? (Signal.) *No.*
He has lots of cop cars.	What kind of cars does he have? (Signal.) *Cop cars.*

SOUNDS

EXERCISE 1

Teaching **z** as in **zoo**

a. (Point to **z**.) Here's a new sound.

b. My turn. (Pause. Touch **z** and say:) zzz.

c. Again. (Touch **z** for a longer time.) zzzzz.
- (Lift your finger.)

d. (Point to **z**.) Your turn. When I touch it, you say it. (Pause.) Get ready. (Touch **z**.) zzz.
- (Lift your finger.)

e. Again. (Touch **z**.) zzzzzz.
- (Lift your finger.)

f. (Repeat **e** until firm.)

EXERCISE 2

Individual test

(Call on individual children to identify **z**.)

EXERCISE 3

Sounds firm-up

a. Get ready to say the sounds when I touch them.

b. (Alternate touching **z** and **s**. Point to the sound. Pause one second. Say:) Get ready. (Touch the sound.) *The children respond.*

c. (When **z** and **s** are firm, alternate touching **z, s, x,** and **th** until all four sounds are firm.)

EXERCISE 4

Individual test

(Have children identify **z, s, x,** or **th.**)

EXERCISE 5

Sounds firm-up

a. (Point to **z**.) When I touch the sound, you say it.

b. (Pause.) Get ready. (Touch **z**.) zzz.

c. Again. (Repeat **b** until firm.)

d. Get ready to say all the sounds when I touch them.

e. (Alternate touching **z, qu, ȳ, wh, j, er, b,** and **y** three or four times. Point to the sound. Pause one second. Say:) Get ready. (Touch the sound.) *The children respond.*

EXERCISE 6

Individual test

(Call on individual children to identify one or more sounds in exercise 5.)

EXERCISE 25

Picture comprehension

a. What do you think you'll see in the picture? *The children respond.*

b. Turn the page and look at the picture.

c. (Ask these questions:)

   1. Do you see lots of cop cars? *Yes.*

   2. What would you do if you had all those cop cars?
     The children respond.

   3. How do you know he lives on a farm?
     The children respond.

PAIR RELATIONS

The children will need pencils.

EXERCISE 26

Children draw a line through the incorrect words

a. (Pass out sides 1 and 2 of Worksheet 115 to each child.)

b. Everybody, do a good job on your worksheet today and I'll give you a bonus worksheet.

c. (Hold up side 2 of your worksheet. Point to the picture of the car in the pair-relations exercise.) Everybody, what does this picture show? (Signal.) *A car.*

d. (Point to the words next to the picture.) Let's find the word that tells about this picture. Reading the fast way.

e. (Point to the word **man.** Pause.) Everybody, what word? (Signal.) *Man.*

• Does that word tell about this picture? (Signal.) *No.*

• It's wrong. So I'll draw a line through it. (Do it.)

f. (Point to the word **cat.** Pause.) Everybody, what word? (Signal.) *Cat.*

• Does that word tell about this picture? (Signal.) *No.*

• It's wrong. So I'll draw a line through it. (Do it.)

g. (Point to the word **tāil.** Pause.) Everybody, what word? (Signal.) *Tail.*

• Does that word tell about this picture? (Signal.) *No.*

• So what do I do? (Signal.) *Draw a line through it.*
   Yes, I'll draw a line through it.

• (Do it.)

h. (Point to the word **car.** Pause.) Everybody, what word? (Signal.) *Car.*

• Does that word tell about this picture? (Signal.) *Yes.*

• It's right. So I won't draw a line through it.

i. (Point to the picture of the car.) Everybody, draw a line through the words that do not tell about this picture. ✔

j. (Hold up your worksheet. Point to the picture of the rat.) Everybody, what does this picture show? (Signal.) *A rat.* Yes, a rat.

• Draw a line through the words that do not tell about this picture. ✔

k. You'll do the rest of the boxes later.

MASTERY TEST 30 — after lesson 155, before lesson 156

(Tell child:) Read this story the fast way. (Do not tap for the words. Let children read at their own pace.)

Total number of test items: **18**
A group is weak if more than one-third of the children missed two or more words on the test.

some girls went to the

moon in a moon ship.

a girl said, "I will

find some fun."

If the group is firm on Mastery Test 30 and was firm on Mastery Test 29:

Present lesson 156, skip lesson 157, present lesson 158, and skip lessons 159 and 160. If more than one child missed two or more words on the test, present the firming procedures specified in the next column to those children.

If the group is firm on Mastery Test 30 but was weak on Mastery Test 29:

Present lesson 156 to the group during the next reading period. If more than one child missed two or more words on the test, present the firming procedures specified below to those children.

If the group is weak on Mastery Test 30:

A. Present these firming procedures to the group during the next reading period. Present each story until the children make no more than three mistakes. Then proceed to the next story.
   1. Lesson 153, Story, page 288, exercises 26, 27.
   2. Lesson 154, Story, page 296, exercises 24, 25.
   3. Lesson 155, Story, page 304, exercises 27, 28.
B. After presenting the above exercises, again give Mastery Test 30 individually to members of the group who failed the test.
C. If the group is firm (less than one-third of the total group missed two or more words in the story on the retest), present lesson 156 to the group during the next reading period.
D. If the group is still weak (more than one-third of the total group missed two or more words in the story on the retest), repeat A and B during the next reading period.

SUMMARY OF INDEPENDENT ACTIVITY
EXERCISE 27

Introduction to independent activity

a. (Hold up Worksheet 115.)

b. You're going to finish this worksheet on your own. (Tell the children when they will work the remaining items.)

• Let's go over the things you're going to do.

Sentence copying

a. (Point to the first line in the sentence-copying exercise.)

b. Everybody, here's the sentence you're going to write on the lines below.

c. Reading the fast way. First word. ✔

• Get ready. (Tap.) *He.*

d. Next word. ✔

• Get ready. (Tap.) *Has.*

e. (Repeat *d* for the remaining words.)

f. After you finish your worksheet, you get to draw a picture about the sentence, **hē has lots of cars.**

Sound writing

a. (Point to the sound-writing exercise.) Here are the sounds you're going to write today. I'll touch the sounds. You say them.

b. (Touch each sound.) *The children respond.*

c. (Repeat the series until firm.)

Matching

a. (Point to the column of words in the Matching Game.)

b. Everybody, you're going to follow the lines and write these words.

c. Reading the fast way.

d. (Point to the first word. Pause.) Get ready. (Signal.) *The children respond.*

e. (Repeat *d* for the remaining words.)

f. (Repeat *d* and *e* until firm.)

Cross-out game

(Point to the boxed word in the Cross-out Game.) Everybody, here's the word you're going to cross out today. What word? (Signal.) *Fish.* Yes, **fish.**

Pair relations

a. (Point to the pair-relations exercise on side 2.) Remember—you're going to draw a line through the words in each box that do not tell about the picture.

b. (Point to the space at the top of the page.) After you finish, remember to draw a picture that shows **hē has lots of cars.**

INDIVIDUAL CHECKOUT: STORYBOOK
EXERCISE 33

2-minute individual fluency checkout: rate/accuracy—whole story from title

a. As you are doing your worksheet, I'll call on children one at a time to read the **whole story.** Remember, you get two stars if you read the story in less than two minutes and make no more than three errors.

b. (Call on a child. Tell the child:) Start with the title and read the story carefully the fast way. Go. (Time the child. Tell the child any words the child misses. Stop the child as soon as the child makes the fourth error or exceeds the time limit.)

c. (If the child meets the rate-accuracy criterion, record two stars on your chart for lesson 115. Congratulate the child. Give children who do not earn two stars a chance to read the story again before the next lesson is presented.)

49 words/**2 min** = 25 wpm [**3 errors**]

EXERCISE 34

Bonus worksheet: sides 3 and 4

(After the children have completed their worksheet exercises, give them sides 3 and 4 of Worksheet 115. Tell them they may keep the stories and read them.)

END OF LESSON 115

Before presenting lesson 116, give Mastery Test 22 to each child. Do not present lesson 116 to any groups that are not firm on this test.

EXERCISE 30

Picture comprehension

a. What do you think you'll see in the picture? *The children respond.*

b. Turn the page and look at the picture.

c. (Ask these questions:)

  1. Who's the girl talking to in the picture? *The children respond.*

    • Her mother.

  2. What's the girl saying? *The children respond.*

    • Yes, I need my red tooth brush.

  3. Do you have a tooth brush? *The children respond.*

    • What color is it? *The children respond.*

WORKSHEET 155

SUMMARY OF INDEPENDENT ACTIVITY

EXERCISE 31

Introduction to independent activity

a. (Pass out sides 1 and 2 of Worksheet 155 to each child.)

b. Everybody, do a good job on your worksheet today and I'll give you a bonus worksheet.

c. (Hold up side 1 of your worksheet.) You're going to do this worksheet on your own. (Tell the children when they will work the items.)

  • Let's go over some of the things you're going to do.

Reading comprehension

a. (Point to the reading-comprehension exercise on side 2.)

b. Everybody, get ready to read the sentences in the box the fast way.

c. First word. ✔

  • Get ready. (Tap for each word as the children read the sentences *Bill had a brush. It was not a tooth brush.*)

d. (Point to items 1 and 2.) These items tell about the story in the box. You're going to read each item and circle the right answer.

Sentence copying

a. (Point to the dotted sentence in the sentence-copying exercise.)

b. You're going to trace the words in this sentence. Then you're going to write the sentence on the other lines.

c. Reading the fast way. First word. ✔

  • Get ready. (Tap for each word.)

d. After you finish your worksheet, you get to draw a picture about the sentence, **I nēēd a tooth brush.** You'll draw your picture on a piece of plain paper. (When the children finish their worksheets, give them sheets of plain paper.)

Other independent activity: sides 1, 2, 3, 4

Remember to do all the parts of the worksheet and to read all the parts carefully. After you draw your picture, I'll give you a bonus worksheet.

INDIVIDUAL CHECKOUT: STORYBOOK

EXERCISE 32

2½-minute individual fluency checkout: rate/accuracy

a. As you are doing your worksheet, I'll call on children one at a time to read the **whole story.** Remember, you get two stars if you read the story in less than two and a half minutes and make no more than three errors.

b. (Call on a child. Tell the child:) Start with the title and read the story carefully the fast way. Go. (Time the child. Tell the child any words the child misses. Stop the child as soon as the child makes the fourth error or exceeds the time limit.)

c. (If the child meets the rate-accuracy criterion, record two stars on your chart for lesson 155. Congratulate the child. Give children who do not earn two stars a chance to read the story again before the next lesson is presented.)

100 words/**2.5 min** = 40 wpm [**3 errors**]

END OF LESSON 155

Before presenting lesson 156, give Mastery Test 30 to each child. **Do not present lesson 156 to any groups that are not firm on this test.**

Mastery Tests—General Instructions

All children are to be given each test individually.

The test is NOT to be administered during the period allotted for reading.

A child should neither see nor hear another child working on the test.

MASTERY TEST 22—after lesson 115, before lesson 116

a. You're going to read this story the fast way.
b. Touch the first word. *The child responds.*
c. (test item) (Pause three seconds.) Get ready. (Tap.) *A.*
d. (test item) Next word. (Pause three seconds.) Get ready. (Tap.) *Dog.*
e. (test item) Next word. (Pause three seconds.) Get ready. (Tap.) *Sat.*
f. (11 test items) (Repeat *e* for the remaining eleven words in the story.)

Total number of test items: **14**
A group is weak if more than one-third of the children missed two or more words on the test.

WHAT TO DO

If the group is firm on Mastery Test 22 and was firm on Mastery Test 21:

Skip lesson 116 and present lesson 117 to the group during the next reading period. If more than one child missed two or more words on the test, present the firming procedures specified in the next column to those children.

If the group is firm on Mastery Test 22 but was weak on Mastery Test 21:

Present lesson 116 to the group during the next reading period. If more than one child missed two or more words on the test, present the firming procedures specified below to those children.

If the group is weak on Mastery Test 22:

A. Present these firming procedures to the group during the next reading period. Present each story until the children make no more than three mistakes. Then proceed to the next story.
   1. Lesson 113, Story, page 32, exercises 21, 22.
   2. Lesson 114, Story, page 38, exercises 22, 23.
   3. Lesson 115, Story, page 44, exercises 22, 23.
B. After presenting the above exercises, again give Mastery Test 22 individually to members of the group who failed the test.
C. If the group is firm (less than one-third of the total group missed two or more words in the story on the retest), present lesson 116 to the group during the next reading period.
D. If the group is still weak (more than one-third of the total group missed two or more words in the story on the retest), repeat *A* and *B* during the next reading period.

a dog sat in a little car. thē dog said, "I nēēd to ēat."

STORY 155
EXERCISE 27

First reading—children read the title and first three sentences

a. You're going to read the first part of this story today.

b. Everybody, touch the title of the story and get ready to read the words in the title the fast way.

c. First word. ✔

• (Pause two seconds.) Get ready. (Tap.) *The.*

d. (Tap for each remaining word in the title.)

e. (After the children have read the title, ask:) What's this story about? (Signal.) *The red tooth brush.* Yes, **the red tooth brush.**

f. Everybody, get ready to read this story the fast way.

g. First word. ✔

• (Pause two seconds.) Get ready. (Tap.) *A.*

h. (Tap for the remaining words in the first sentence. Pause at least two seconds between taps.)

i. (Repeat *g* and *h* for the next two sentences. Have the children reread the first three sentences until firm.)

EXERCISE 28

Individual children or the group read sentences to complete the first reading

a. I'm going to call on individual children to read a sentence. Everybody, follow along and point to the words. If you hear a mistake, raise your hand.

b. (Call on a child.) Read the next sentence. (Do not tap for the words. Let children read at their own pace, but be sure they read the sentence correctly.)

> **To Correct**
> (Have the child sound out the word. Then return to the beginning of the sentence.)

c. (Repeat *b* for most of the remaining sentences in the story. Occasionally have the group read a sentence. When the group is to read, say:) Everybody, read the next sentence. (Pause two seconds.) Get ready. (Tap for each word in the sentence. Pause at least two seconds between taps.)

EXERCISE 29

Second reading—individual children or the group read each sentence; the group answer questions

a. You're going to read the story again. This time I'm going to ask questions.

b. Starting with the first word of the title. ✔

• Get ready. (Tap as the children read the title. Pause at least two seconds between taps.)

c. (Call on a child.) Read the first sentence. *The child responds.*

d. (Repeat *b* and *c* in exercise 28. Present the following comprehension questions to the entire group.)

After the children read:	You say:
The red tooth brush.	What's this story about? (Signal.) *The red tooth brush.*
She brushed her teeth six times a day.	What did she do? (Signal.) *She brushed her teeth six times a day.* What did she use to brush her teeth? (Signal.) *Her red tooth brush.*
"They are so white they shine like the moon."	What did she say? *The children respond.* She said, "My teeth are white. They are so white they shine like the moon." Why were her teeth so white? (Signal.) *She brushed them six times a day.*
But her mother said, "I do not have your red tooth brush."	What did her mother say? (Signal.) *I do not have your red tooth brush.* I wonder how she'll brush her teeth without her red tooth brush.

Groups that are firm on Mastery Tests 21 and 22 should skip this lesson and do lesson 117 today.

SOUNDS
EXERCISE 1

Teacher and children play the sounds game

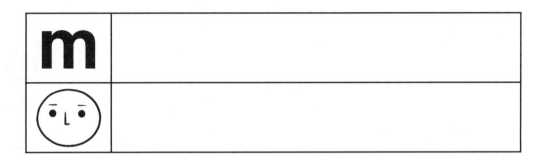

a. (Use transparency and crayon. Write the sounds in the symbol box. Keep score in the score box.)
b. I'm smart. I think I can beat you in a game.
c. Here's the rule. When I touch a sound, you say it.
d. (Play the game. Make one symbol at a time in the symbol box. Use the symbols **p, h, th,** and **d.**)
(Make each symbol quickly. Pause. Touch the symbol. Play the game for about two minutes.)
(Then ask:) Who won? (Draw a mouth on the face in the score box.)

EXERCISE 2

Sounds firm-up

a. (Point to **ch.**) When I touch the sound, you say it.
b. (Pause.) Get ready. (Touch **ch.**) *ch.*
c. Again. (Repeat *b* until firm.)
d. Get ready to say all the sounds when I touch them.
e. (Alternate touching **ō, k, o, u, n, ē, ch** and **l** three or four times. Point to the sound. Pause one second. Say:) Get ready. (Touch the sound.) *The children respond.*

EXERCISE 3

Individual test

(Call on individual children to identify one or more sounds in exercise 2.)

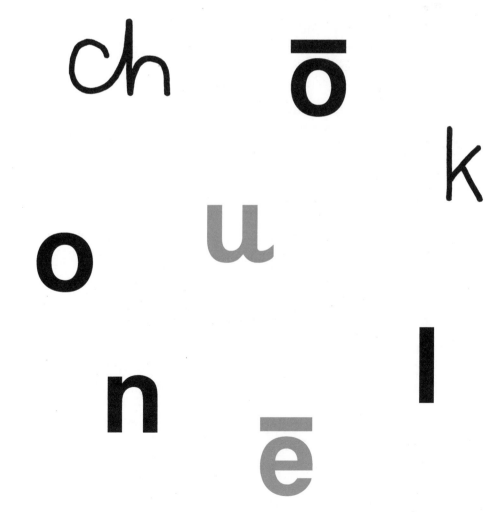

READ THE ITEMS 155

EXERCISE 24

Children read items 1 and 2

a. (Pass out Storybook.)

b. Open your book to page 174. ✔

c. Get ready to read the items and play the game.

d. Finger under the first word of the title. ✔

e. When I tap, read the title. (Pause.) Get ready. (Tap.) *Read the items.*

f. Touch item 1 and get ready to read. ✔

• First word. **(Tap for each word as the children read**
When the teacher says "Go," pat your ears.)

• (Repeat until firm.)

g. Everybody, get ready to say item 1. (Pause and signal.)
The children say the sentence.

• (Repeat four times or until firm.)

h. Touch item 2 and get ready to read. ✔

• First word. **(Tap for each word as the children read**
When the teacher says "Do it," touch your feet.)

• (Repeat until firm.)

i. Everybody, get ready to say item 2. (Pause and signal.)
The children say the sentence.

• (Repeat four times or until firm.)

EXERCISE 25

Children reread items 1 and 2 and answer questions

a. Everybody, touch item 1. ✔

b. Read item 1 to yourself. Raise your hand when you know what you're going to do and when you're going to do it.

c. (After the children raise their hands, say:) Everybody, what are you going to do when I say **"Go"?** (Signal.) *Pat my ears.*

To Correct
1. Everybody, read item 1 out loud. (Tap as the children read each word.)
2. What are you going to do when I say **"Go"?** (Signal.) *Pat my ears.*

d. Everybody, when are you going to **pat your ears?** (Signal.)
When the teacher says "Go."

To Correct
1. Everybody, read item 1 out loud. (Tap as the children read each word.)
2. When are you going to **pat your ears?** (Signal.) *When the teacher says "Go."*

e. (Repeat *c* and *d* until firm.)

f. Everybody, touch item 2. ✔

g. Read item 2 to yourself. Raise your hand when you know what you're going to do and when you're going to do it.

h. (After the children raise their hands, say:) Everybody, what are you going to do when I say **"Do it"?** (Signal.) *Touch my feet.*

To Correct
1. Everybody, read item 2 out loud. (Tap as the children read each word.)
2. What are you going to do when I say **"Do it"?** (Signal.) *Touch my feet.*

i. Everybody, when are you going to **touch your feet?** (Signal.)
When the teacher says "Do it."

To Correct
1. Everybody, read item 2 out loud. (Tap as the children read each word.)
2. When are you going to **touch your feet?** (Signal.) *When the teacher says "Do it."*

j. (Repeat *h* and *i* until firm.)

EXERCISE 26

Children play the game

a. Everybody, touch item 1. ✔

b. Read the item to yourself. Raise your hand when you know what you're going to do and when you're going to do it.

c. (After the children raise their hands, say:) Let's play the game. Think about what you're going to do (pause) and when you're going to do it.

d. (Hold out your hand. Pause.) Get ready. **Go.** (Pause. Drop your hand.) *The children pat their ears immediately.*

To Correct
1. What did I say? (Signal.) *Go.*
2. What are you supposed to do when I say **"Go"?** (Signal.) *Pat my ears.*
3. (If the children's responses are not firm, have them read item 1 aloud.)
4. (Repeat exercise 26.)

READING VOCABULARY

EXERCISE 4

Children identify, then sound out an irregular word (**to**)

a. (Touch the ball for **to**.) Everybody, you're going to read this word the fast way. (Pause three seconds.) Get ready. (Move your finger quickly along the arrow.) *To.* Yes, **to.**

b. Now you're going to sound out the word. Get ready. (Quickly touch **t, o** as the children say *tooo.*)

c. Again. (Repeat *b.*)

d. How do we say the word? (Signal.) *To.* Yes, **to.**

e. (Repeat *b* and *d* until firm.)

EXERCISE 5

Individual test

(Call on individual children to do *b* and *d* in exercise 4.)

EXERCISE 6

Children sound out the word and tell what word

a. (Touch the ball for **cāves**.) Sound it out.

b. Get ready. (Touch **c, ā, v, s** as the children say *cāāāvvvsss.*)

• (If sounding out is not firm, repeat *b.*)

c. What word? (Signal.) *Caves.* Yes, **caves.**

EXERCISE 7

Children sound out the word and tell what word

(Repeat the procedures in exercise 6 for **tēach.**)

EXERCISE 8

Children read the fast way

(Touch the ball for **will.**) Get ready to read this word the fast way. (Pause three seconds.) Get ready. (Signal.) *Will.*

EXERCISE 9

Children read the words the fast way

(Have the children read the words on this page the fast way.)

EXERCISE 10

Individual test

(Call on individual children to read one word the fast way.)

EXERCISE 21

Children read **smīle** and **smīled**

a. (Cover **s.** Point to **mīle.**) You're going to read this part of the word the fast way. (Pause three seconds.) Get ready. (Signal.) *Mīle.* Yes, **mīle.**

b. (Uncover **s.** Point to **s.**) You're going to say this first. (Move your finger quickly under **mīle.**) Then you're going to say (pause) **mīle.**

c. (Point to **s.**) What are you going to say first? (Signal.) *sss.*

• What are you going to say next? (Signal.) *Mīle.*

d. (Repeat *c* until firm.)

e. (Touch the ball for **smīle.**) Get ready. (Move to **s,** then quickly along the arrow.) *Sssmile.*

f. Say it fast. (Signal.) *Smile.*

• Yes, what word? (Signal.) *Smile.* Yes, **smile.**

• Good reading.

g. Again. (Repeat *e* and *f* until firm.)

h. (Return to the ball for **smīle.**) Yes, this word is **smile.**

i. (Touch the ball for **smīled.**) So this must be **smile . . .** (Touch **d.**) *d.*

• What word? (Signal.) *Smiled.* Yes, **smiled.**

j. Again. (Repeat *h* and *i* until firm.)

k. (Touch the ball for **smīle.**) This word is **smile.** (Touch the ball for **smīled.**) So this must be **. . . .** (Quickly run your finger under **smile** and tap **d.**) *Smiled.* Yes, **smiled.**

l. Again. (Repeat *k* until firm.)

m. Now you're going to sound out (pause) **smiled.** Get ready. (Touch **s, m, ī, l, d** as the children say *sssmmmīīīllld.*)

• Yes, what word? (Signal.) *Smiled.* Yes, **smiled.**

EXERCISE 22

Children read the words the fast way

a. Now you get to read the words on this page the fast way.

b. (Touch the ball for **smīled.** Pause three seconds.) Get ready. (Move your finger quickly along the arrow.) *Smiled.*

c. (Repeat *b* for **smīle.**)

EXERCISE 23

Individual test

(Call on individual children to read one word the fast way.)

smīle

smīled

EXERCISE 11

Children sound out an irregular word (**girl**)

a. (Touch the ball for **girl**.) Sound it out.

b. Get ready. (Quickly touch each sound as the children say *giiirrrlll*.)

To Correct
If the children do not say the sounds you touch
1. (Say:) You've got to say the sounds I touch.
2. (Repeat *a* and *b* until firm.)
---

c. Again. (Repeat *b* until firm.)

d. That's how we <u>sound out</u> the word. Here's how we <u>say</u> the word. **Girl.** How do we <u>say</u> the word? (Signal.) *Girl.*

e. Now you're going to <u>sound out</u> the word. Get ready. (Touch each sound as the children say *giiirrrlll*.)

f. Now you're going to say the word. Get ready. (Signal.) *Girl.*

g. (Repeat *e* and *f* until firm.)

h. Yes, this word is **girl.** She is a **girl.**

EXERCISE 12

Individual test

(Call on individual children to do *e* and *f* in exercise 11.)

EXERCISE 13

Children identify, then sound out an irregular word (**car**)

a. (Touch the ball for **car**.) Everybody, you're going to read this word the fast way. (Pause three seconds.) Get ready. (Move your finger quickly along the arrow.) *Car.* Yes, **car.**

b. Now you're going to sound out the word. Get ready. (Quickly touch **c, a, r** as the children say *caaarrr*.)

c. Again. (Repeat *b*.)

d. How do we say the word? (Signal.) *Car.* Yes, **car.**

e. (Repeat *b* and *d* until firm.)

EXERCISE 14

Individual test

(Call on individual children to do *b* and *d* in exercise 13.)

EXERCISE 16

Children read a word beginning with two consonants (**flȳ**)

a. (Cover **f.** Run your finger under **lȳ.**) You're going to sound out this part. Get ready. (Touch **l, ȳ** as the children say *lllȳȳȳ.*)

b. Say it fast. (Signal.) *Lȳ.* Yes, this part is **lȳ.**

c. (Uncover **f.** Point to **f.**) You're going to say this first. (Move your finger quickly under **lȳ.**) Then you're going to say (pause) **lȳ.**

d. (Point to **f.**) What are you going to say first? (Signal.) *fff.*

• What are you going to say next? (Signal.) *Lȳ.*

e. (Repeat *d* until firm.)

f. (Touch the ball for **flȳ.**) Get ready. (Move to **f,** then quickly along the arrow.) *Ffflȳ.*

g. Say it fast. (Signal.) *Fly.*

• Yes, what word? (Signal.) *Fly.* Yes, **fly.**

• Good reading.

h. Again. (Repeat *f* and *g* until firm.)

i. Now you're going to sound out (pause) **fly.** Get ready. (Touch **f, l, ȳ** as the children say *ffflllȳȳ.*)

• What word? (Signal.) *Fly.* Yes, **fly.**

EXERCISE 17

Children sound out the word and tell what word

a. (Touch the ball for **tooth.**) Sound it out.

b. Get ready. (Touch **t, oo, th** as the children say *tooooththth.*)

• (If sounding out is not firm, repeat *b.*)

c. What word? (Signal.) *Tooth.* Yes, **tooth.**

EXERCISE 18

Children sound out the word and tell what word

a. (Touch the ball for **where.**) Sound it out.

b. Get ready. (Touch **wh, e, r** as the children say *wwweeerrr.*)

• (If sounding out is not firm, repeat *b.*)

c. What word? (Signal.) *Where.* Yes, **where.**

• She didn't know **where** to go.

EXERCISE 19

Children read the words the fast way

(Have the children read the words on this page the fast way.)

EXERCISE 20

Individual test

(Call on individual children to read one word the fast way.)

EXERCISE 15

Children rhyme with **wāves**

a. (Touch the ball for **wāves**.) You're going to read this word the fast way. (Pause three seconds.) Get ready. (Move your finger quickly along the arrow.) *Waves.*

b. (Touch the ball for **sāves**.) This word rhymes with (pause) **waves.** (Move to **s,** then quickly along the arrow.) *Saves.* Yes, what word? (Signal.) *Saves.*

EXERCISE 16

Children read the words the fast way

a. Now you get to read the words on this page the fast way.

b. (Touch the ball for **sāves**. Pause three seconds.) Get ready. (Move your finger quickly along the arrow.) *Saves.*

c. (Repeat *b* for **wāves**.)

EXERCISE 17

Individual test

(Call on individual children to read one word the fast way.)

wāveS

sāveS

EXERCISE 12

Children read a word beginning with two consonants (**stand**)

a. (Cover **s**. Run your finger under **tand**.) You're going to sound out this part. Get ready. (Touch **t, a, n, d** as the children say *taaannnd*.)

b. Say it fast. (Signal.) *Tand.* Yes, this part is **tand**.

c. (Uncover **s**. Point to **s**.) You're going to say this first. (Move your finger quickly under **tand**.) Then you're going to say (pause) **tand**.

d. (Point to **s**.) What are you going to say first? (Signal.) *sss.* What are you going to say next? (Signal.) *Tand.*

e. (Repeat *d* until firm.)

f. (Touch the ball for **stand**.) Get ready. (Move to **s**, then quickly along the arrow.) *Ssstand.*

g. Say it fast. (Signal.) *Stand.*

• Yes, what word? (Signal.) *Stand.* Yes, **stand**.

• Good reading.

h. Again. (Repeat *f* and *g* until firm.)

i. Now you're going to sound out (pause) **stand**. Get ready. (Touch **s, t, a, n, d** as the children say *ssstaaannnd*.)

• What word? (Signal.) *Stand.* Yes, **stand**.

EXERCISE 13

Children rhyme with **mȳ**

a. (Touch the ball for **mȳ**.) You're going to read this word the fast way. (Pause three seconds.) Get ready. (Move your finger quickly along the arrow.) *My.*

b. (Touch the ball for **whȳ**.) This word rhymes with (pause) **my**. (Move to **wh**, then quickly along the arrow.) *Why.*

• Yes, what word? (Signal.) *Why.*

EXERCISE 14

Children read the words the fast way

a. Now you get to read the words on this page the fast way.

b. (Touch the ball for **stand**. Pause three seconds.) Get ready. (Move your finger quickly along the arrow.) *Stand.*

c. (Repeat *b* for each word on the page.)

EXERCISE 15

Individual test

(Call on individual children to read one word the fast way.)

STORYBOOK

STORY 116
EXERCISE 18

Teacher introduces the title

a. (Pass out Storybook.)

b. Open your book to page 59. ✔

c. (Hold up your reader. Point to the title.) These words are called the title of the story. These words tell what the story is about. I'll read the title the fast way.

d. (Point to the words as you read:) Thē girl and thē dog.

e. Everybody, what is this story about? (Signal.) *Thē girl and thē dog.* Yes, **thē girl and thē dog.**

• This story is going to tell something about **thē girl and thē dog.**

EXERCISE 19

First reading—children read the story the fast way

(Have the children reread any sentences containing the words that give them trouble. Keep a list of these words.)

a. Everybody, touch the title of the story and get ready to read the words in the title the fast way.

b. First word. ✔

• (Pause three seconds.) Get ready. (Tap.) *Thē.*

c. Next word. ✔

• (Pause three seconds.) Get ready. (Tap.) *Girl.*

d. (Repeat c for the words **and, thē, dog.**)

e. (After the children have read the title, ask:) What's this story about? (Signal.) *Thē girl and thē dog.* Yes, **thē girl and thē dog.**

f. Everybody, touch the first word of the <u>story</u>. ✔

g. Get ready to read this story the fast way.

h. First word. (Pause three seconds.) Get ready. (Tap.) *Thē.*

i. Next word. ✔

• (Pause three seconds.) Get ready. (Tap.) *Girl.*

j. (Repeat i for the remaining words in the first sentence. Pause at least three seconds between taps. The children are to identify each word without sounding it out.)

k. (Repeat h through j for the next two sentences. Have the children reread the first three sentences until firm.)

l. (The children are to read the remainder of the story the fast way, stopping at the end of each sentence.)

m. (After the first reading of the story, print on the board the words that the children missed more than one time. Have the children sound out each word one time and tell what word.)

n. (After the group's responses are firm, call on individual children to read the words.)

EXERCISE 20

Individual test

a. Turn back to page 59. I'm going to call on individual children to read a whole sentence the fast way.

b. (Call on individual children to read a sentence. Do not tap for each word.)

EXERCISE 21

Second reading—children read the story the fast way and answer questions

a. You're going to read the story again the fast way and I'll ask questions.

b. Starting with the first word of the title. ✔

• Get ready. (Tap.) *Thē.*

c. (Tap for each remaining word. Pause at least three seconds between taps. Pause longer before words that gave the children trouble during the first reading.)

d. (Ask the comprehension questions below as the children read.)

After the children read:	You say:
The girl and the dog.	What's this story about? (Signal.) *The girl and the dog.*
The girl said, "I can teach the dog to run."	What did she say? (Signal.) *I can teach the dog to run.*
The girl said, "I will teach the dog to run."	What did she say? (Signal.) *I will teach the dog to run.*
"Ha-ha."	What did the dog say? (Signal.) *The children respond.* Why couldn't the girl teach him to run? *The children respond.* Yes, he already knew how to run. Was this story about the girl and the dog? (Signal.) *Yes.*

READING VOCABULARY
EXERCISE 7

Children sound out an irregular word (**touch**)

a. (Touch the ball for **touch.**) Sound it out.

b. Get ready. (Quickly touch each sound as the children say *tooouuuch.*)

c. Again. (Repeat *b* until firm.)

d. That's how we <u>sound out</u> the word. Here's how we <u>say</u> the word. **Touch.** How do we <u>say</u> the word? (Signal.) *Touch.*

e. Now you're going to <u>sound out</u> the word. Get ready. (Touch each sound as the children say *tooouuuch.*)

f. Now you're going to say the word. Get ready. (Signal.) *Touch.*

g. (Repeat *e* and *f* until firm.)

h. Yes, this word is **touch.** I can **touch** my nose.

EXERCISE 8

Individual test

(Call on individual children to do *e* and *f* in exercise 7.)

EXERCISE 9

Children read the fast way

a. Get ready to read these words the fast way.

b. (Touch the ball for **six.** Pause three seconds.) Get ready. (Signal.) *Six.*

c. (Repeat *b* for the remaining words on the page.)

EXERCISE 10

Children read the fast way again

a. Get ready to do these words again. Watch where I point.

b. (Point to a word. Pause one second. Say:) Get ready. (Signal.) *The children respond.*

• (Point to the words in this order: **whīte, six, shīne, brushed.**)

c. (Repeat *b* until firm.)

EXERCISE 11

Individual test

(Call on individual children to read one word on the page the fast way.)

touch

six

shīne

whīte

brushed

EXERCISE 22

Picture comprehension

a. Everybody, look at the picture.

b. (Ask these questions:)

   1. Does that girl look happy? *No.* Why not? *The children respond.*
   2. Did the dog already know how to run?
      The children respond.
   3. Did you ever teach a dog to do tricks? *The children respond.*

WORKSHEET 116
SUMMARY OF INDEPENDENT ACTIVITY
EXERCISE 23

Introduction to independent activity

a. (Pass out Worksheet 116 to each child.)

b. Everybody, you're going to do this worksheet on your own. **(Tell the children when they will work the items.)**

• Let's go over the things you're going to do.

Sentence copying

a. (Hold up side 1 of your worksheet and point to the first line in the sentence-copying exercise.)

b. Everybody, here's the sentence you're going to write on the lines below.

c. Reading the fast way. First word. ✔

• Get ready. (Tap.) *Thē.*

d. Next word. ✔

• Get ready. (Tap.) *Dog.*

e. (Repeat *d* for the remaining words.)

f. After you finish your worksheet, you get to draw a picture about the sentence, **thē dog said, "nō."**

Sound writing

a. (Point to the sound-writing exercise.) Here are the sounds you're going to write today. I'll touch the sounds. You say them.

b. (Touch each sound.) *The children respond.*

c. (Repeat the series until firm.)

Matching

a. (Point to the column of words in the Matching Game.)

b. Everybody, you're going to follow the lines and write these words.

c. Reading the fast way.

d. (Point to the first word. Pause.) Get ready. (Signal.)
   The children respond.

e. (Repeat *d* for the remaining words.)

f. (Repeat *d* and *e* until firm.)

Cross-out game

(Point to the boxed word in the Cross-out Game.) Everybody, here's the word you're going to cross out today. What word? (Signal.) *Girl.* Yes, **girl.**

Pair relations

a. (Point to the pair-relations exercise on side 2.) Remember—you're going to draw a line through the words in each box that do not tell about the picture.

b. (Point to the space at the top of the page.) After you finish, remember to draw a picture that shows **thē dog said, "nō."**

END OF LESSON 116

SOUNDS
EXERCISE 1

Teaching **qu** as in **quick**

a. (Point to **qu**.) My turn. When I touch it, I'll say it. (Pause. Touch **qu** for an instant, saying:) qu.

b. (Point to **qu**.) Your turn. When I touch it, you say it. (Pause.) Get ready. (Touch **qu**.) qu.

c. Again. (Touch **qu**.) qu.

d. (Repeat c until firm.)

EXERCISE 2

Sounds firm-up

a. Get ready to say the sounds when I touch them.

b. (Alternate touching **qu** and **wh**. Point to the sound. Pause one second. Say:) Get ready. (Touch the sound.) *The children respond.*

c. (When **qu** and **wh** are firm, alternate touching **qu, wh, p,** and **k** until all four sounds are firm.)

EXERCISE 3

Individual test

(Call on individual children to identify **qu, wh, p,** or **k**.)

EXERCISE 4

Teacher introduces cross-out game

a. (Use transparency and crayon.)

b. I'll cross out the sounds on this part of the page when you can tell me every sound.

c. Remember—when I touch it, you say it.

d. (Go over the sounds until the children can identify all the sounds in order.)

EXERCISE 5

Individual test

(Call on individual children to identify two or more sounds in exercise 4.)

EXERCISE 6

Teacher crosses out sounds

a. You told me every sound. Get ready to do it again. This time I'll cross out each sound when you tell me what it is.

b. (Point to each sound. Pause. Say:) Get ready. (Touch the sound.) *The children respond.*

• (As you cross out the sound, say:) Goodbye, _____.

SOUNDS

EXERCISE 1

Teacher and children play the sounds game

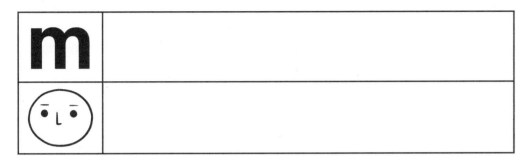

a. (Use transparency and crayon. Write the sounds in the symbol box. Keep score in the score box.)

b. I'm smart. I think I can beat you in a game.

c. Here's the rule. When I touch a sound, you say it.

d. (Play the game. Make one symbol at a time in the symbol box. Use the symbols ō, o, i, and ā.)
(Make each symbol quickly. Pause. Touch the symbol. Play the game for about two minutes.)
(Then ask:) Who won? (Draw a mouth on the face in the score box.)

EXERCISE 2

Child plays teacher

a. (Use transparency and crayon.)

b. [Child's name] is going to be the teacher.

c. [Child] is going to touch the sounds. When [child] touches a sound, you say it.

d. (The child points to and touches the sounds.) *The children respond.* (You circle any sound that is not firm.)

e. (After the child has completed the page, present all the circled sounds to the children.)

EXERCISE 3

Individual test

(Call on individual children.) If you can say the sound when I call your name, you may cross it out.

EXERCISE 27

Picture comprehension

a. Everybody, look at the picture.

b. (Ask these questions:)

1. What's happening in the picture? *The children respond.* The eagle is riding on the old horse.

2. Does the eagle look like he's having fun? *The children respond.*
   - Yes, he does.
   - What about the horse? *The children respond.* He looks happy too.

3. Which would you rather do, fly like an eagle or ride a horse? *The children respond.*

WORKSHEET 154

SUMMARY OF INDEPENDENT ACTIVITY

EXERCISE 28

Introduction to independent activity

a. (Pass out Worksheet 154 to each child.)

b. Everybody, you're going to do this worksheet on your own. **(Tell the children when they will work the items.)**
   - Let's go over the things you're going to do.

Story items

a. (Hold up side 1 of your worksheet and point to the story-items exercise.)

b. Everybody, here are items about the story we read today.

c. Think about what happened in the story and circle the right answer for each item.

Picture comprehension

a. (Point to the pictures in the picture-comprehension exercise.) Everybody, you're going to look at the picture. Then you're going to read each item and write the missing word.

b. Remember—the first sound of each missing word is already written in the blank.

Reading comprehension

a. (Point to the reading-comprehension exercise on side 2.)

b. Everybody, get ready to read the sentences in the box the fast way.

c. First word. ✔
   - Get ready. (Tap for each word as the children read the sentences *An old car did not run. The girl got mad at the car.*)

d. (Point to items 1 and 2.) These items tell about the story in the box. You're going to read each item and circle the right answer.

Sound writing

a. (Point to the sound-writing exercise.) Here are the sounds you're going to write today. I'll touch the sounds. You say them.

b. (Touch each sound.) *The children respond.*

c. (Repeat the series until firm.)

Sentence copying

a. (Point to the dotted sentence in the sentence-copying exercise.)

b. You're going to trace the words in this sentence. Then you're going to write the sentence on the other lines.

c. Reading the fast way. First word. ✔
   - Get ready. (Tap for each word.)

d. After you finish your worksheet, you get to draw a picture about the sentence, **the hōrse ran.** You'll draw your picture on a piece of plain paper. (When the children finish their worksheets, give them sheets of plain paper.)

END OF LESSON 154

READING VOCABULARY
EXERCISE 4

Children read the fast way

a. Get ready to read these words the fast way.
b. (Touch the ball for **cows.** Pause three seconds.) Get ready. (Signal.) *Cows.*
c. (Repeat *b* for the remaining words on the page.)

EXERCISE 5

Children read the fast way again

a. Get ready to do these words again. Watch where I point.
b. (Point to a word. Pause one second. Say:) Get ready. (Signal.) *The children respond.*
• (Point to the words in this order: **with, cāves, cows, will, cats.**)
c. (Repeat *b* until firm.)

EXERCISE 6

Individual test

(Call on individual children to read one word the fast way.)

cows

with

cats

will

cāveS

STORY 154
EXERCISE 24

First reading—children read the title and first three sentences

a. Now you're going to finish the story about the old horse and the eagle.

b. Everybody, touch the title of the story and get ready to read the words in the title the fast way.

c. First word. ✔

• (Pause two seconds.) Get ready. (Tap.) *An.*

d. (Tap for each remaining word in the title.)

e. (After the children have read the title, ask:) What's this story about? (Signal.) *An old horse and an eagle.* Yes, **an old horse and an eagle.**

f. Everybody, get ready to read this story the fast way.

g. First word. ✔

• (Pause two seconds.) Get ready. (Tap.) *An.*

h. (Tap for the remaining words in the first sentence. Pause at least two seconds between taps.)

i. (Repeat *g* and *h* for the next two sentences. Have the children reread the first three sentences until firm.)

EXERCISE 25

Individual children or the group read sentences to complete the first reading

a. I'm going to call on individual children to read a sentence. Everybody, follow along and point to the words. If you hear a mistake, raise your hand.

b. (Call on a child.) Read the next sentence. (Do not tap for the words. Let children read at their own pace, but be sure they read the sentence correctly.)

> **To Correct**
> (Have the child sound out the word. Then return to the beginning of the sentence.)

c. (Repeat *b* for most of the remaining sentences in the story. Occasionally have the group read a sentence. When the group is to read, say:) Everybody, read the next sentence. (Pause two seconds.) Get ready. (Tap for each word in the sentence. Pause at least two seconds between taps.)

EXERCISE 26

Second reading—individual children or the group read each sentence; the group answer questions

a. You're going to read the story again. This time I'm going to ask questions.

b. Starting with the first word of the title. ✔

• Get ready. (Tap as the children read the title. Pause at least two seconds between taps.)

c. (Call on a child.) Read the first sentence. *The child responds.*

d. (Repeat *b* and *c* in exercise 25. Present the following comprehension questions to the entire group.)

After the children read:	You say:
And he did.	Do you think the horse will fly to the top of the car? *The children respond.* Let's read and find out.
He ran into the side of the car.	Did the horse fly to the top of the car? (Signal.) *No.* What did he do? (Signal.) *He ran into the side of the car.*
"I can not fly."	What did the horse say? *The children respond.*
The horse said, "I can run with an eagle on my back, and that is fun."	What did the horse say? (Signal.) *I can run with an eagle on my back, and that is fun.* Does that sound like fun? *The children respond.*
"Yes, this is fun," they said.	What did they say? (Signal.) *Yes, this is fun.* Who said that? (Signal.) *The old horse and the eagle.*

EXERCISE 7

Children sound out an irregular word (**do**)

a. (Touch the ball for **do.**) Sound it out.

b. Get ready. (Quickly touch each sound as the children say *dooo.*)

> **To Correct**
> If the children do not say the sounds you touch
> 1. (Say:) You've got to say the sounds I touch.
> 2. (Repeat *a* and *b* until firm.)

c. Again. (Repeat *b* until firm.)

d. That's how we <u>sound</u> out the word. Here's how we <u>say</u> the word. **Do.** How do we <u>say</u> the word? (Signal.) *Do.*

e. Now you're going to <u>sound out</u> the word. Get ready. (Touch each sound as the children say *dooo.*)

f. Now you're going to say the word. Get ready. (Signal.) *Do.*

g. (Repeat *e* and *f* until firm.)

h. Yes, this word is **do. Do** you have a penny?

EXERCISE 8

Individual test

(Call on individual children to do *e* and *f* in exercise 7.)

EXERCISE 9

Children sound out an irregular word (**girl**)

a. (Touch the ball for **girl.**) Sound it out.

b. Get ready. (Quickly touch each sound as the children say *giiirrrlll.*)

c. Again. (Repeat *b* until firm.)

d. That's how we <u>sound out</u> the word. Here's how we <u>say</u> the word. **Girl.** How do we <u>say</u> the word? (Signal.) *Girl.*

e. Now you're going to <u>sound out</u> the word. Get ready. (Touch each sound as the children say *giiirrrlll.*)

f. Now you're going to say the word. Get ready. (Signal.) *Girl.*

g. (Repeat *e* and *f* until firm.)

h. Yes, this word is **girl.** Raise your hand if you're a **girl.**

EXERCISE 10

Individual test

(Call on individual children to do *e* and *f* in exercise 9.)

STORYBOOK

READ THE ITEM 154
EXERCISE 21

Children read item 1

a. (Pass out Storybook.)

b. Open your book to page 171. ✔

c. (Point to the title **rēad the ītem.**) Everybody, touch this title. ✔

d. I'll read the title. You point to the words I read. (Pause.) Get ready. **Read** (pause) **the** (pause) **item.**

e. Your turn to read the title. First word. ✔

• Get ready. (Tap for each word as the children read *read the item.*)

f. Everybody, say the title. (Pause and signal. Without looking at the words, the children say *read the item.*)

• (Repeat until firm.)

g. You're going to read the item. Touch item 1 and get ready to read. ✔

h. First word. (Tap for each word as the children read *When the teacher says "Do it," pick up your book.*)

• (Repeat three times or until firm.)

i. Everybody, get ready to say item 1 with me. (Pause and signal. Without looking at the words, you and the children say:) *When the teacher says "Do it,"* (pause one second) *pick up your book.*

• (Repeat four times or until firm.)

j. All by yourselves. Say item 1. (Signal.) *When the teacher says "Do it," pick up your book.*

• (Repeat four times or until firm.)

EXERCISE 22

Children reread item 1 and answer questions

a. Everybody, touch item 1 again. ✔

b. Read item 1 to yourself. Raise your hand when you know what you're going to do and when you're going to do it.

c. (After the children raise their hands, say:) Everybody, what are you going to do when I say **"Do it"?** (Signal.) *Pick up my book.*

To Correct
1. Everybody, read item 1 out loud. (Tap as the children read each word.)
2. What are you going to do when I say **"Do it"?** (Signal.) *Pick up my book.*

d. Everybody, when are you going to **pick up your book?** (Signal.) *When the teacher says "Do it."*

To Correct
1. Everybody, read item 1 out loud. (Tap as the children read each word.)
2. When are you going to **pick up your book?** (Signal.) *When the teacher says "Do it."*

e. (Repeat *c* and *d* until firm.)

EXERCISE 23

Children play the game

a. Everybody, touch item 1. ✔

b. Read the item to yourself. Raise your hand when you know what you're going to do and when you're going to do it.

c. (After the children raise their hands, say:) Let's play the game. Think about what you're going to do (pause) and when you're going to do it.

d. (Hold out your hand. Pause.) Get ready. **Do it.** (Pause. Drop your hand.) *The children pick up their books immediately.*

To Correct
1. What did I say? (Signal.) *Do it.*
2. What are you supposed to do when I say **"Do it"?** (Signal.) *Pick up my book.*
3. (If the children's responses are not firm, have them read item 1 aloud.)
4. (Repeat exercise 23.)

EXERCISE 11

Children identify, then sound out an irregular word (**farm**)

a. (Touch the ball for **farm.**) Everybody, you're going to read this word the fast way. (Pause three seconds.) Get ready. (Move your finger quickly along the arrow.) *Farm.* Yes, **farm.**

b. Now you're going to sound out the word. Get ready. (Quickly touch **f, a, r, m** as the children say *fffaaarrrmmm.*)

c. Again. (Repeat *b.*)

d. How do we say the word? (Signal.) *Farm.* Yes, **farm.**

e. (Repeat *b* and *d* until firm.)

EXERCISE 12

Individual test

(Call on individual children to do *b* and *d* in exercise 11.)

EXERCISE 13

Children sound out the word and tell what word

a. (Touch the ball for **pots.**) Sound it out.

b. Get ready. (Touch **p, o, t, s** as the children say *poootsss.*)

• (If sounding out is not firm, repeat *b.*)

c. What word? (Signal.) *Pots.* Yes, **pots.**

EXERCISE 14

Children sound out the word and tell what word

a. (Touch the ball for **gāme.**) Sound it out.

b. Get ready. (Touch **g, ā, m** as the children say *gāāāmmm.*)

• (If sounding out is not firm, repeat *b.*)

c. What word? (Signal.) *Game.* Yes, **game.**

EXERCISE 15

Children read the words the fast way

a. Now you get to read the words on this page the fast way.

b. (Touch the ball for **farm.** Pause three seconds.) Get ready. (Move your finger quickly along the arrow.) *Farm.*

c. (Repeat *b* for **pots** and **gāme.**)

EXERCISE 16

Individual test

(Call on individual children to read one word the fast way.)

EXERCISE 16

Children sound out an irregular word (**took**)

a. (Touch the ball for **took.**) Sound it out.

b. Get ready. (Quickly touch each sound as the children say *tooook.*)

c. Again. (Repeat *b* until firm.)

d. That's how we <u>sound out</u> the word. Here's how we <u>say</u> the word. **Took.** How do we <u>say</u> the word? (Signal.) *Took.*

e. Now you're going to <u>sound out</u> the word. Get ready. (Touch each sound as the children say *tooook.*)

f. Now you're going to say the word. Get ready. (Signal.) *Took.*

g. (Repeat *e* and *f* until firm.)

EXERCISE 17

Children rhyme with an irregular word (**took**)

a. (Touch the ball for **took.**) Everybody, you're going to read this word the fast way. Get ready. (Signal.) *Took.*

b. (Touch the ball for **look.**) This word rhymes with (pause) **took.** Get ready. (Move to **l,** then quickly along the arrow.) *Look.*

c. (Touch the ball for **book.**) This word rhymes with (pause) **took.** Get ready. (Move to **b,** then quickly along the arrow.) *Book.*

d. (Repeat *a* through *c* until firm.)

EXERCISE 18

Children sound out **look** and **book**

a. (Have the children sound out **look.**) *Lllooook.*

• How do we say the word? (Signal.) *Look.* Yes, **look.**

b. (Have the children sound out **book.**) *Booook.*

• How do we say the word? (Signal.) *Book.* Yes, **book.**

EXERCISE 19

Children read the words the fast way

a. Now you get to read the words on this page the fast way.

b. (Touch the ball for **took.** Pause three seconds.) Get ready. (Move your finger quickly along the arrow.) *Took.*

c. (Repeat *b* for each word on the page.)

took

look

book

EXERCISE 20

Individual test

(Call on individual children to read one word the fast way.)

STORY 117
EXERCISE 17

Teacher introduces the title

a. (Pass out Storybook.)

b. Open your book to page 62. ✔

c. (Hold up your reader. Point to the title.) These words are called the title of the story. These words tell what the story is about. I'll read the title the fast way.

d. (Point to the words as you read:) A girl in a cave.

e. Everybody, what is this story about? (Signal.) *A girl in a cave.* Yes, **a girl in a cave.**

• This story is going to tell something about **a girl in a cave.**

EXERCISE 18

First reading—children read the story the fast way

(Have the children reread any sentences containing words that give them trouble. Keep a list of these words.)

a. Everybody, touch the title of the story and get ready to read the words in the title the fast way.

b. First word. ✔

• (Pause three seconds.) Get ready. (Tap.) *A.*

c. Next word. ✔

• (Pause three seconds.) Get ready. (Tap.) *Girl.*

d. (Repeat *c* for the words **in, a, cāve.**)

e. (After the children have read the title, ask:) What's this story about? (Signal.) *A girl in a cave.* Yes, **a girl in a cave.**

f. Everybody, touch the first word of the story. ✔

g. Get ready to read this story the fast way.

h. First word. (Pause three seconds.) Get ready. (Tap.) *A.*

i. Next word. ✔

• (Pause three seconds.) Get ready. (Tap.) *Girl.*

j. (Repeat *i* for the remaining words in the first sentence. Pause at least three seconds between taps. The children are to identify each word without sounding it out.)

k. (Repeat *h* through *j* for the next two sentences. Have the children reread the first three sentences until firm.)

l. (The children are to read the remainder of the story the fast way, stopping at the end of each sentence.)

m. (After the first reading of the story, print on the board the words that the children missed more than one time. Have the children sound out each word one time and tell what word.)

n. (After the group's responses are firm, call on individual children to read the words.)

EXERCISE 19

Individual test

a. Look at page 62. I'm going to call on individual children to read a whole sentence the fast way.

b. (Call on individual children to read a sentence. Do not tap for each word.)

EXERCISE 20

Second reading—children read the story the fast way and answer questions

a. You're going to read the story again the fast way and I'll ask questions.

b. Starting with the first word of the title. ✔

• Get ready. (Tap.) *A.*

c. (Tap for each remaining word. Pause at least three seconds between taps. Pause longer before words that gave the children trouble during the first reading.)

d. (Ask the comprehension questions below as the children read.)

After the children read:	You say:
A girl in a cave.	What's this story about? (Signal.) *A girl in a cave.*
A girl was in a cave.	What's a cave? *The children respond.*
A wave came in the cave.	What's a wave? *The children respond.*
The girl said, "Save me, save me."	What did she say? (Signal.) *Save me, save me.*
She said, "I will save that girl."	What did the fish say? (Signal). *I will save that girl.* Do you think the fish will save her? *The children respond.* Let's read and find out.
And she did.	Did the fish save the girl? (Signal.) *Yes.*
So she gave the girl a seed and a ham.	What did the fish give her? (Signal.) *A seed and a ham.*

EXERCISE 13

Children read the fast way

a. Get ready to read these words the fast way.

b. (Touch the ball for **when.** Pause three seconds.) Get ready. (Signal.) *When.*

c. (Repeat *b* for the remaining words on the page.)

EXERCISE 14

Children read the fast way again

a. Get ready to do these words again. Watch where I point.

b. (Point to a word. Pause one second. Say:) Get ready. (Signal.) *The children respond.*

• (Point to the words in this order: **when, brush, tooth, brushing, tēēth.**)

c. (Repeat *b* until firm.)

EXERCISE 15

Individual test

(Call on individual children to read one word the fast way.)

when

brush

brushing

tooth

tēēth

EXERCISE 21

Picture comprehension

a. What do you think you'll see in the picture? *The children respond.*

b. Turn the page and look at the picture.

c. (Ask these questions:)
1. Who is in the cave? *The children respond.* The fish and the girl.
2. What is the girl eating? *The children respond.* Yes, a piece of ham.
3. Have you ever been in a cave? *The children respond.*

WORKSHEET 117

SUMMARY OF INDEPENDENT ACTIVITY
EXERCISE 22

Introduction to independent activity

a. (Pass out Worksheet 117 to each child.)

b. Everybody, you're going to do this worksheet on your own. (Tell the children when they will work the items.)

• Let's go over the things you're going to do.

Sentence copying

a. (Hold up side 1 of your worksheet and point to the first line in the sentence-copying exercise.)

b. Everybody, here's the sentence you're going to write on the lines below.

c. Reading the fast way. First word. ✔

• Get ready. (Tap.) *A.*

d. Next word. ✔

• Get ready. (Tap.) *Girl.*

e. (Repeat *d* for the remaining words.)

f. After you finish your worksheet, you get to draw a picture about the sentence, **a girl was in a cāve.**

Sound writing

a. (Point to the sound-writing exercise.) Here are the sounds you're going to write today. I'll touch the sounds. You say them.

b. (Touch each sound.) *The children respond.*

c. (Repeat the series until firm.)

Matching

a. (Point to the column of words in the Matching Game.)

b. Everybody, you're going to follow the lines and write these words.

c. Reading the fast way.

d. (Point to the first word. Pause.) Get ready. (Signal.) *The children respond.*

e. (Repeat *d* for the remaining words.)

f. (Repeat *d* and *e* until firm.)

Cross-out game

(Point to the boxed word in the Cross-out Game.) Everybody, here's the word you're going to cross out today. What word? (Signal.) *Farm.* Yes, **farm.**

Pair relations

a. (Point to the pair-relations exercise on side 2.) Remember—you're going to draw a line through the words in each box that do not tell about the picture.

b. (Point to the space at the top of the page.) After you finish, remember to draw a picture that shows **a girl was in a cāve.**

END OF LESSON 117

EXERCISE 12

Children read **slip** and **slipped**

a. (Cover **s.** Point to **lip.**) You're going to read this part of the word the fast way. (Pause three seconds.) Get ready. (Signal.) *Lip.* Yes, **lip.**

b. (Uncover **s.** Point to **s.**) You're going to say this first. (Move your finger quickly under **lip.**) Then you're going to say (pause) **lip.**

c. (Point to **s.**) What are you going to say first? (Signal.) *sss.*

• What are you going to say next? (Signal.) *Lip.*

d. (Repeat *c* until firm.)

e. (Touch the ball for **slip.**) Get ready. (Move to **s,** then quickly along the arrow.) *Ssslip.*

f. Say it fast. (Signal.) *Slip.*

• Yes, what word? (Signal.) *Slip.* Yes, **slip.**

• Good reading.

g. Again. (Repeat *e* and *f* until firm.)

h. (Return to the ball for **slip.**) Yes, this word is **slip.**

i. (Touch the ball for **slipped.**) So this must be **slip** . . . (Touch **d.**) *d.*

• What word? (Signal.) *Slipped.* Yes, **slipped.**

j. Again. (Repeat *h* and *i* until firm.)

k. (Touch the ball for **slip.**) This word is **slip.** (Touch the ball for **slipped.**) So this must be . . . . (Quickly run your finger under **slip** and tap **d.**) *Slipped.* Yes, **slipped.**

l. Again. (Repeat *k* until firm.)

m. Now you're going to sound out (pause) **slipped.** Get ready. (Touch **s, l, i,** between the **p**'s, **d** as the children say *sssllliiipd.*)

• Yes, what word? (Signal.) *Slipped.* Yes, **slipped.**

ē

e

ē

e

ē

e

SOUNDS
EXERCISE 1

Teacher firms up ē

a. (Point to **ē.**) Everybody get ready to tell me this sound. Get ready. (Touch **ē.**) *ēēē.*

b. (Point to the space over **e.**) Everybody, there's no line over this sound. This is not **ēēē.** Is it **ēēē?** (Signal.) *No.*

c. (Point to each sound and ask:) Is this **ēēē?** *The children respond.*

d. (Repeat *c* until firm.)

EXERCISE 2

Teaching **e** as in **end;** children discriminate ē—e

a. (Point to the first **e.**) Everybody, this is **eee.**

b. When I touch it, you say it. (Pause.) Get ready. (Touch **e.**) *eee.*

c. Again. (Touch **e.**) *eee.*

d. (Repeat *c* until firm.)

e. Get ready to say these sounds. When I touch the sound, you say it. (Alternate touching the sounds. Before touching each **ĕ,** point to the space over **ĕ** and say:) Remember—this is not **ēēē.**

f. (Repeat *e* until all the sounds are firm.)

e

i

ō

EXERCISE 3

Sounds firm-up

a. (Point to **e.**) When I touch the sound, you say it.

b. (Pause.) Get ready. (Touch **e.**) *ĕĕĕ.*

c. Again. (Repeat *b* until firm.)

d. Get ready to say all the sounds when I touch them.

e. (Alternate touching **ch, e, i** and **ō** three or four times. Point to the sound. Pause one second. Say:) Get ready. (Touch the sound.) *The children respond.*

EXERCISE 4

Individual test

(Call on individual children to identify one or more sounds in exercise 3.)

READING VOCABULARY

EXERCISE 7

Children read **tīme** and **tīmes**

a. (Touch the ball for **tīme**.) You're going to read this word the fast way. (Pause three seconds.) Get ready. (Move your finger quickly along the arrow.) *Time.*

b. (Return to the ball for **tīme**.) Yes, this word is **time**.

c. (Touch the ball for **tīmes**.) So this must be **time** . . . (Touch **s**.) *s.*

• What word? (Signal.) *Times.* Yes, **times**.

d. Again. (Repeat *b* and *c* until firm.)

e. (Touch the ball for **tīme**.) This word is **time**.

f. (Touch the ball for **tīmes**.) So this must be . . . . (Quickly run your finger under **tīme** and tap **s**.) *Times.* Yes, **times**.

g. Again. (Repeat *e* and *f* until firm.)

h. Now you're going to sound out (pause) **times**. Get ready. (Touch **t**, **ī**, **m**, **s** as the children say *tīīīmmmsss*.)

• Yes, what word? (Signal.) *Times.* Yes, **times**.

EXERCISE 8

Children sound out the word and tell what word

a. (Touch the ball for **where**.) Sound it out.

b. Get ready. (Touch **wh**, **e**, **r** as the children say *wwweeerrr*.)

• (If sounding out is not firm, repeat *b*.)

c. What word? (Signal.) *Where.* Yes, **where**. **Where** is my pencil?

EXERCISE 9

Children sound out the word and tell what word

(Repeat the procedures in exercise 8 for **whīte**.)

EXERCISE 10

Children read the words the fast way

(Have the children read the words on this page the fast way.)

EXERCISE 11

Individual test

(Call on individual children to read one word the fast way.)

tīme

tīmes

where

whīte

READING VOCABULARY

EXERCISE 5

Children read the fast way

a. Get ready to read these words the fast way.

b. (Touch the ball for **fish.** Pause three seconds.) Get ready. (Signal.) *Fish.*

c. (Repeat *b* for the remaining words on the page.)

EXERCISE 6

Children read the fast way again

a. Get ready to do these words again. Watch where I point.

b. (Point to a word. Pause one second. Say:) Get ready. (Signal.)
The children respond.

• (Point to the words in this order: **top, pots, with, tops, fish.**)

c. (Repeat *b* until firm.)

EXERCISE 7

Individual test

(Call on individual children to read one word the fast way.)

fish

pots

top

tops

with

SOUNDS

EXERCISE 1

Teaching **qu** as in **quick**

a. (Point to **qu**.) Here's a new sound. It's a quick sound.

b. My turn. (Pause. Touch **qu** for an instant, saying:) **qu (koo).**

c. Again. (Touch **qu** and say:) qu.

d. (Point to **qu**.) Your turn. When I touch it, you say it. (Pause.) Get ready. (Touch **qu**.) *qu.*

e. Again. (Touch **qu**.) *qu.*

f. (Repeat *e* until firm.)

EXERCISE 2

Individual test

(Call on individual children to identify **qu**.)

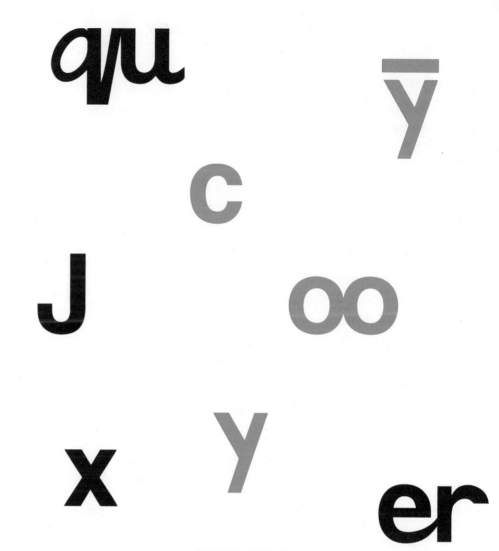

EXERCISE 3

Sounds firm-up

a. Get ready to say the sounds when I touch them.

b. (Alternate touching **qu** and **k**. Point to the sound. Pause one second. Say:) Get ready. (Touch the sound.) *The children respond.*

c. (When **qu** and **k** are firm, alternate touching **qu, k, wh,** and **ch** until all four sounds are firm.)

EXERCISE 4

Individual test

(Call on individual children to identify **qu, k, wh,** or **ch**.)

EXERCISE 5

Sounds firm-up

a. (Point to **qu**.) When I touch the sound, you say it.

b. (Pause.) Get ready. (Touch **qu**.) *qu.*

c. Again. (Repeat *b* until firm.)

d. Get ready to say all the sounds when I touch them.

e. (Alternate touching **qu, c, ȳ, j, oo, x, y,** and **er** three or four times. Point to the sound. Pause one second. Say:) Get ready. (Touch the sound.) *The children respond.*

EXERCISE 6

Individual test

(Call on individual children to identify one or more sounds in exercise 5.)

EXERCISE 8

Children identify, then sound out an irregular word (**of**)

a. (Touch the ball for **of.**) Everybody, you're going to read this word the fast way. (Pause three seconds.) Get ready. (Move your finger quickly along the arrow.) *Of.* Yes, **of.**

b. Now you're going to sound out the word. Get ready. (Quickly touch **o, f** as the children say *ooofff.*)

c. Again. (Repeat *b.*)

d. How do we say the word? (Signal.) *Of.* Yes, **of.**

e. (Repeat *b* and *d* until firm.)

f. (Call on individual children to do *b* and *d.*)

EXERCISE 9

Children sound out the word and tell what word

a. (Touch the ball for **hōme.**) Sound it out.

b. Get ready. (Touch **h, ō, m** as the children say *hōōōmmm.*)

• (If sounding out is not firm, repeat *b.*)

c. What word? (Signal.) *Home.* Yes, **home.**

EXERCISE 10

Children sound out an irregular (**do**)

a. (Touch the ball for **do.**) Sound it out.

b. Get ready. (Quickly touch each sound as the children say *dooo.*)

c. Again. (Repeat *b* until firm.)

d. That's how we <u>sound out</u> the word. Here's how we <u>say</u> the word. **Do.** How do we <u>say</u> the word? (Signal.) *Do.*

e. Now you're going to <u>sound out</u> the word. Get ready. (Touch each sound as the children say *dooo.*)

f. Now you're going to say the word. Get ready. (Signal.) *Do.*

g. (Repeat *e* and *f* until firm.)

h. Yes, this word is **do.** I **do** not run fast.

i. (Call on individual children to do *e* and *f.*)

EXERCISE 11

Children read the fast way

(Touch the ball for **fōr.**) Get ready to read this word the fast way. (Pause three seconds.) Get ready. (Signal.) *For.*

EXERCISE 12

Children read the words the fast way

(Have the children read the words on this page the fast way.)

EXERCISE 29

Picture comprehension

a. What do you think you'll see in the picture? *The children respond.*

b. Turn the page and look at the picture.

c. (Ask these questions:)
1. What's the horse doing in that picture? *The children respond.*
   Running into the side of the barn.
2. Where is the eagle? *The children respond.* Yes, on top of the barn.

WORKSHEET 153

SUMMARY OF INDEPENDENT ACTIVITY

EXERCISE 30

Introduction to independent activity

a. (Pass out Worksheet 153 to each child.)

b. Everybody, you're going to do this worksheet on your own. **(Tell the children when they will work the items.)**

• Let's go over the things you're going to do.

Story items

a. (Hold up side 1 of your worksheet and point to the story-items exercise.)

b. Everybody, here are items about the story we read today.

c. Think about what happened in the story and circle the right answer for each item.

Picture comprehension

a. (Point to the pictures in the picture-comprehension exercise.) Everybody, you're going to look at the picture. Then you're going to read each item and write the missing word.

b. Remember—the first sound of each missing word is already written in the blank.

Reading comprehension

a. (Point to the reading-comprehension exercise on side 2.)

b. Everybody, get ready to read the sentences in the box the fast way.

c. First word. ✔

• Get ready. (Tap for each word as the children read the sentences *An eagle liked to fly. He did not sit in a tree.*)

d. (Point to items 1 and 2.) These items tell about the story in the box. You're going to read each item and circle the right answer.

Sound writing

a. (Point to the sound-writing exercise.) Here are the sounds you're going to write today. I'll touch the sounds. You say them.

b. (Touch each sound.) *The children respond.*

c. (Repeat the series until firm.)

Sentence copying

a. (Point to the dotted sentence in the sentence-copying exercise.)

b. You're going to trace the words in this sentence. Then you're going to write the sentence on the other lines.

c. Reading the fast way. First word. ✔

• Get ready. (Tap for each word.)

d. After you finish your worksheet, you get to draw a picture about the sentence, **an ēagle līkes to flȳ.** You'll draw your picture on a piece of plain paper. (When the children finish their worksheets, give them sheets of plain paper.)

END OF LESSON 153

STORYBOOK

STORY 118
EXERCISE 13

Teacher introduces the title

a. (Pass out Storybook.)

b. Open your book to page 65. ✔

c. (Hold up your reader. Point to the title.) These words are called the title of the story. These words tell what the story is about. I'll read the title the fast way.

d. (Point to the words as you read:) Lots of pots.

e. Everybody, what is this story about? (Signal.) *Lots of pots.* Yes, **lots of pots.**

• This story is going to tell something about **lots of pots.**

EXERCISE 14

First reading—children read the story the fast way

(Have the children reread any sentences containing words that give them trouble. Keep a list of these words.)

a. Everybody, touch the title of the story and get ready to read the words in the title the fast way.

b. First word. ✔

• (Pause three seconds.) Get ready. (Tap.) *Lots.*

c. Next word. ✔

• (Pause three seconds.) Get ready. (Tap.) *Of.*

d. (Repeat c for the word **pots.**)

e. (After the children have read the title, ask:) What's this story about? (Signal.) *Lots of pots.* Yes, **lots of pots.**

f. Everybody, touch the first word of the <u>story</u>. ✔

g. Get ready to read this story the fast way.

h. First word. (Pause three seconds.) Get ready. (Tap.) *A.*

i. Next word. ✔

• (Pause three seconds.) Get ready. (Tap.) *Girl.*

j. (Repeat i for the remaining words in the first sentence. Pause at least three seconds between taps. The children are to identify each word without sounding it out.)

k. (Repeat h through j for the next two sentences. Have the children reread the first three sentences until firm.)

l. (The children are to read the remainder of the story the fast way, stopping at the end of each sentence.)

m. (After the first reading of the story, print on the board the words that the children missed more than one time. Have the children sound out each word one time and tell what word.)

n. (After the group's responses are firm, call on individual children to read the words.)

EXERCISE 15

Individual test

a. Turn back to page 65. I'm going to call on individual children to read a whole sentence the fast way.

b. (Call on individual children to read a sentence. Do not tap for each word.)

EXERCISE 16

Second reading—children read the story the fast way and answer questions

a. You're going to read the story again the fast way and I'll ask questions.

b. Starting with the first word of the title. ✔

• Get ready. (Tap.) *Lots.*

c. (Tap for each remaining word. Pause at least three seconds between taps. Pause longer before words that gave the children trouble during the first reading.)

d. (Ask the comprehension questions below as the children read.)

After the children read:	You say:
Lots of pots.	What's this story about? (Signal.) *Lots of pots.*
He has pots with no tops.	What kind of pots did the man have? (Signal.) *Pots with tops and pots with no tops.*
"I have fish in pots."	What did the man say? (Signal.) *I have fish in pots.*
The girl said, "Can I have a pot for a little fish?"	What did the girl want? (Signal.) *A pot for a little fish.*
The man said, "This is a pot for a little fish."	Did the man have a pot for a little fish? (Signal.) *Yes.*
And she did.	Did the girl take the pot home with her? (Signal.) *Yes.*

STORY 153
EXERCISE 26

First reading—children read the title and first three sentences

a. You're going to read the first part of this story today.
b. Everybody, touch the title of the story and get ready to read the words in the title the fast way.
c. First word. ✔
• (Pause two seconds.) Get ready. (Tap.) *An.*
d. (Tap for each remaining word in the title.)
e. (After the children have read the title, ask:) What's this story about? (Signal.) *An old horse and an eagle.* Yes, **an old horse and an eagle.**
f. Everybody, get ready to read this story the fast way.
g. First word. ✔
• (Pause two seconds.) Get ready. (Tap.) *An.*
h. (Tap for the remaining words in the first sentence. Pause at least two seconds between taps.)
i. (Repeat *g* and *h* for the next two sentences. Have the children reread the first three sentences until firm.)

EXERCISE 27

Individual children or the group read sentences to complete the first reading

a. I'm going to call on individual children to read a sentence. Everybody, follow along and point to the words. If you hear a mistake, raise your hand.
b. (Call on a child.) Read the next sentence. (Do not tap for the words. Let children read at their own pace, but be sure they read the sentence correctly.)

To Correct
(Have the child sound out the word. Then return to the beginning of the sentence.)

c. (Repeat *b* for most of the remaining sentences in the story. Occasionally have the group read a sentence. When the group is to read, say:) Everybody, read the next sentence. (Pause two seconds.) Get ready. (Tap for each word in the sentence. Pause at least two seconds between taps.)

EXERCISE 28

Second reading—individual children or the group read each sentence; the group answer questions

a. You're going to read the story again. This time I'm going to ask questions.
b. Starting with the first word of the title. ✔
• Get ready. (Tap as the children read the title. Pause at least two seconds between taps.)
c. (Call on a child.) Read the first sentence. *The child responds.*
d. (Repeat *b* and *c* in exercise 27. Present the following comprehension questions to the entire group.)

After the children read:	You say:
An old horse and an eagle.	What's this story about? (Signal.) *An old horse and an eagle.*
"And I like to fly."	Who did the eagle say likes to fly? *The children respond.*
The old horse said, "Can you teach me how to fly?"	What did the old horse say? (Signal.) *Can you teach me how to fly?* That's silly. Can horses fly? *The children respond.*
The old horse said, "I will fly to the top of the barn."	What did the old horse say? (Signal.) *I will fly to the top of the barn.* Do you think he'll do that? *The children respond.* Let's read and find out.
And he ran into the side of the barn.	Did he fly to the top of the barn? (Signal.) *No.* What did he do? (Signal.) *He ran into the side of the barn.*
He said, "You did not teach me how to fly."	What did the horse say? (Signal.) *You did not teach me how to fly.* This is a silly story. I don't think that eagle can ever teach the horse how to fly.

EXERCISE 17

Picture comprehension

a. Everybody, look at the picture.

b. (Ask these questions:)

    1. Look at all those pots. What color pot did the girl choose for her fish? *The children respond.*

    2. Have you ever had a pet fish? *The children respond.*

WORKSHEET 118

SUMMARY OF INDEPENDENT ACTIVITY
EXERCISE 18

Introduction to independent activity

a. (Pass out Worksheet 118 to each child.)

b. Everybody, you're going to do this worksheet on your own. **(Tell the children when they will work the items.)**

• Let's go over the things you're going to do.

Sentence copying

a. (Hold up side 1 of your worksheet and point to the first line in the sentence-copying exercise.)

b. Everybody, here's the sentence you're going to write on the lines below.

c. Reading the fast way. First word. ✔

• Get ready. (Tap.) *He.*

d. Next word. ✔

• Get ready. (Tap.) *Has.*

e. (Repeat *d* for the remaining words.)

f. After you finish your worksheet, you get to draw a picture about the sentence, **hē has lots of pots.**

Sound writing

a. (Point to the sound-writing exercise.) Here are the sounds you're going to write today. I'll touch the sounds. You say them.

b. (Touch each sound.) *The children respond.*

c. (Repeat the series until firm.)

Matching

a. (Point to the column of words in the Matching Game.)

b. Everybody, you're going to follow the lines and write these words.

c. Reading the fast way.

d. (Point to the first word. Pause.) Get ready. (Signal.) *The children respond.*

e. (Repeat *d* for the remaining words.)

f. (Repeat *d* and *e* until firm.)

Cross-out game

(Point to the boxed word in the Cross-out Game.) Everybody, here's the word you're going to cross out today. What word? (Signal.) *Cars.* Yes, **cars.**

Pair relations

a. (Point to the pair-relations exercise on side 2.) Remember—you're going to draw a line through the words in each box that do not tell about the picture.

b. (Point to the space at the top of the page.) After you finish, remember to draw a picture that shows **hē has lots of pots.**

END OF LESSON 118

STORYBOOK

READ THE ITEM 153
EXERCISE 23

Children read item 1

a. (Pass out Storybook.)

b. Open your book to page 168. ✔

c. (Point to the title **rēad the ītem.**) Everybody, touch this title. ✔

d. I'll read the title. You point to the words I read. (Pause.) Get ready. **Read** (pause) **the** (pause) **item.**

e. Your turn to read the title. First word. ✔

• Get ready. (Tap for each word as the children read *read the item.*)

f. Everybody, say the title. (Pause and signal. Without looking at the words, the children say *read the item.*)

• (Repeat until firm.)

g. You're going to read the item. Touch item 1 and get ready to read. ✔

h. First word. (Tap for each word as the children read *If the teacher says "Now," hold up your hands.*)

• (Repeat three times or until firm.)

i. Everybody, get ready to say item 1 with me. (Pause and signal. Without looking at the words, you and the children say:) *If the teacher says* "Now," (pause one second) *hold up your hands.*

• (Repeat four times or until firm.)

j. All by yourselves. Say item 1. (Signal.) *If the teacher says "Now," hold up your hands.*

• (Repeat four times or until firm.)

EXERCISE 24

Children reread item 1 and answer questions

a. Everybody, touch item 1 again. ✔

b. Read item 1 to yourself. Raise your hand when you know what you're going to do and when you're going to do it.

c. (After the children raise their hands, say:) Everybody, what are you going to do if I say **"Now"**? (Signal.) *Hold up my hands.*

To Correct
1. Everybody, read item 1 out loud. (Tap as the children read each word.)
2. What are you going to do if I say **"Now"**? (Signal.) *Hold up my hands.*

d. Everybody, when are you going to **hold up your hands?** (Signal.) *If the teacher says "Now."*

To Correct
1. Everybody, read item 1 out loud. (Tap as the children read each word.)
2. When are you going to **hold up your hands?** (Signal.) *If the teacher says "Now."*

e. (Repeat *c* and *d* until firm.)

EXERCISE 25

Children play the game

a. Everybody, touch item 1. ✔

b. Read the item to yourself. Raise your hand when you know what you're going to do and when you're going to do it.

c. (After the children raise their hands, say:) Let's play the game. Think about what you're going to do (pause) and when you're going to do it.

d. (Hold out your hand. Pause.) Get ready. **Now.** (Pause. Drop your hand.) *The children hold up their hands immediately.*

To Correct
1. What did I say? (Signal.) *Now.*
2. What are you supposed to do if I say **"Now"**? (Signal.) *Hold up my hands.*
3. (If the children's responses are not firm, have them read item 1 aloud.)
4. (Repeat exercise 25.)

SOUNDS

EXERCISE 1

Teaching **e** as in **end**

a. (Point to **e**.) My turn. (Pause.) (Touch **e** and say:) ĕĕĕ.

b. (Point to **e**.) Your turn. When I touch it, you say it. (Pause.) Get ready. (Touch **e**.) ĕĕĕ. (Lift your finger.)

c. Again. (Touch **e**.) ĕĕĕĕ. (Lift your finger.)

d. (Repeat *c* until firm.)

e

u

ē

o

EXERCISE 2

Sounds firm-up

a. Get ready to say the sounds when I touch them.

b. (Alternate touching **e** and **u**. Point to the sound. Pause one second. Say:) Get ready. (Touch the sound.) *The children respond.*

c. (When **e** and **u** are firm, alternate touching **ē, o, e,** and **u** until all four sounds are firm.)

EXERCISE 3

Individual test

(Call on individual children to identify **ē, o, e,** or **u**.)

EXERCISE 4

Sounds firm-up

a. (Point to **e**.) When I touch the sound, you say it.

b. (Pause.) Get ready. (Touch **e**.) *eee.*

c. Again. (Repeat *b* until firm.)

d. Get ready to say all the sounds when I touch them.

e. (Alternate touching **i, p, v, ō, w, e, k,** and **ch** three or four times. Point to the sound. Pause one second. Say:) Get ready. (Touch the sound.) *The children respond.*

EXERCISE 5

Individual test

(Call on individual children to identify one or more sounds in exercise 4.)

i

p

v

ō

k

w

ch

EXERCISE 18

Children sound out an irregular word (**look**)

a. (Touch the ball for **look.**) Sound it out.

b. Get ready. (Quickly touch each sound as the children say *lllooook.*)

c. Again. (Repeat *b* until firm.)

d. That's how we <u>sound out</u> the word. Here's how we <u>say</u> the word.
Look. How do we <u>say</u> the word? (Signal.) *Look.*

e. Now you're going to <u>sound out</u> the word. Get ready.
(Touch each sound as the children say *lllooook.*)

f. Now you're going to say the word. Get ready. (Signal.) *Look.*

g. (Repeat *e* and *f* until firm.)

EXERCISE 19

Children rhyme with an irregular word (**look**)

a. (Touch the ball for **look.**) Everybody, you're going to read this word
the fast way. Get ready. (Signal.) *Look.*

b. (Touch the ball for **book.**) This word rhymes with (pause) **look.**
Get ready. (Move to **b,** then quickly along the arrow.) *Book.*

c. (Repeat *a* and *b* until firm.)

EXERCISE 20

Children sound out **book**

(Have the children sound out **book.**) *Booook.*

• How do we say the word? (Signal.) *Book.* Yes, **book.**

EXERCISE 21

Children read the words the fast way

a. Now you get to read the words on this page the fast way.

b. (Touch the ball for **book.** Pause three seconds.) Get ready.
(Move your finger quickly along the arrow.) *Book.*

c. (Repeat *b* for **look.**)

EXERCISE 22

Individual test

(Call on individual children to read one word the fast way.)

look

book

READING VOCABULARY

EXERCISE 6

Children sound out the word and tell what word

a. (Touch the ball for **cōrn.**) Sound it out.
b. Get ready. (Touch **c, ō, r, n** as the children say *cōōōrrrnnn.*)
• (If sounding out is not firm, repeat *b.*)
c. What word? (Signal.) *Corn.* Yes, **corn.**

EXERCISE 7

Children sound out the word and tell what word

(Repeat the procedures in exercise 6 for **tāke.**)

EXERCISE 8

Children sound out the word and tell what word

(Repeat the procedures in exercise 6 for **pigs.**)

EXERCISE 9

Children sound out the word and tell what word

(Repeat the procedures in exercise 6 for **hēre.**)

EXERCISE 10

Children identify, then sound out an irregular word (**do**)

a. (Touch the ball for **do.**) Everybody, you're going to read this word the fast way. (Pause three seconds.) Get ready. (Move your finger quickly along the arrow.) *Do.* Yes, **do.**
b. Now you're going to sound out the word. Get ready. (Quickly touch **d, o** as the children say *dooo.*)
c. Again. (Repeat *b.*)
d. How do we say the word? (Signal.) *Do.* Yes, **do.**
e. (Repeat *b* and *d* until firm.)

EXERCISE 11

Individual test

(Call on individual children to do *b* and *d* in exercise 10.)

EXERCISE 12

Children read the words the fast way

(Have the children read the words on this page the fast way.)

EXERCISE 13

Individual test

(Call on individual children to read one word the fast way.)

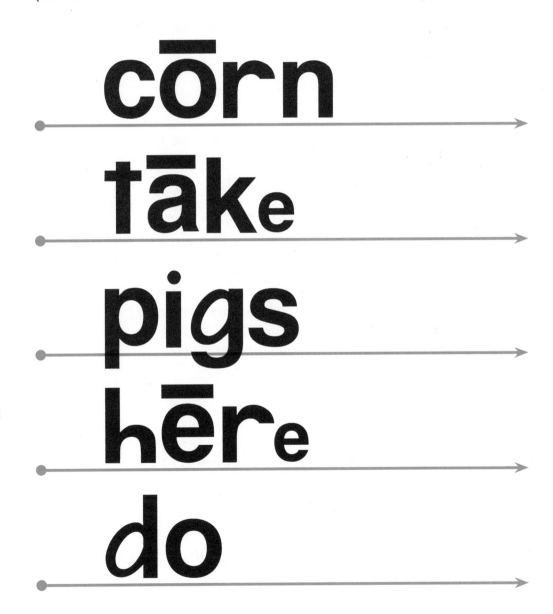

EXERCISE 12

Children identify, then sound out an irregular word (**barn**)

a. (Touch the ball for **barn.**) Everybody, you're going to read this word the fast way. (Pause three seconds.) Get ready. (Move your finger quickly along the arrow.) *Barn.* Yes, **barn.**

b. Now you're going to sound out the word. Get ready. (Quickly touch **b, a, r, n** as the children say *baaarrrnnn.*)

c. Again. (Repeat *b.*)

d. How do we say the word? (Signal.) *Barn.* Yes, **barn.**

e. (Repeat *b* and *d* until firm.)

EXERCISE 13

Individual test

(Call on individual children to do *b* and *d* in exercise 12.)

EXERCISE 14

Children identify, then sound out an irregular word (**into**)

a. (Touch the ball for **into.**) Everybody, you're going to read this word the fast way. (Pause three seconds.) Get ready. (Move your finger quickly along the arrow.) *Into.* Yes, **into.**

b. Now you're going to sound out the word. Get ready. (Quickly touch **i, n, t, o** as the children say *iiinnntooo.*)

c. Again. (Repeat *b.*)

d. How do we say the word? (Signal.) *Into.* Yes, **into.**

e. (Repeat *b* and *d* until firm.)

EXERCISE 15

Individual test

(Call on individual children to do *b* and *d* in exercise 14.)

EXERCISE 16

Children read the words the fast way

(Have the children read the words on this page the fast way.)

EXERCISE 17

Individual test

(Call on individual children to read one word the fast way.)

EXERCISE 14

Children identify, then sound out an irregular word (**car**)

a. (Touch the ball for **car.**) Everybody, you're going to read this word the fast way. (Pause three seconds.) Get ready. (Move your finger quickly along the arrow.) *Car.* Yes, **car.**

b. Now you're going to sound out the word. Get ready. (Quickly touch **c, a, r** as the children say *caaarrr.*)

c. Again. (Repeat *b.*)

d. How do we say the word? (Signal.) *Car.* Yes, **car.**

e. (Repeat *b* and *d* until firm.)

EXERCISE 15

Individual test

(Call on individual children to do *b* and *d* in exercise 14.)

EXERCISE 16

Children read the fast way

a. Get ready to read these words the fast way.

b. (Touch the ball for **for.** Pause three seconds.) Get ready. (Signal.) *For.*

c. (Repeat *b* for the remaining words on the page.)

EXERCISE 17

Children read the fast way again

a. Get ready to do these words again. Watch where I point.

b. (Point to a word. Pause one second. Say:) Get ready. (Signal.) *The children respond.*

• (Point to the words in this order: **fōr, lāke, car, ōld, mōre.**)

c. (Repeat *b* until firm.)

EXERCISE 18

Individual test

(Call on individual children to read one word the fast way.)

car

fōr

mōre

lāke

ōld

EXERCISE 11

Children read **brush** and **brushed**

a. (Cover **b.** Point to **rush.**) You're going to read this part of the word the fast way. (Pause three seconds.) Get ready. (Signal.) *Rush.* Yes, **rush.**

b. (Uncover **b.** Point to **b.**) You're going to say this first. (Move your finger quickly under **rush.**) Then you're going to say (pause) **rush.**

c. (Point to **b.**) What are you going to say first? (Signal.) *b.*

• What are you going to say next? (Signal.) *Rush.*

d. (Repeat *c* until firm.)

e. (Touch the ball for **brush.**) Get ready. (Move to **b,** then quickly along the arrow.) *Brush.*

f. Say it fast. (Signal.) *Brush.*

• Yes, what word? (Signal.) *Brush.* Yes, **brush.**

• Good reading.

g. Again. (Repeat *e* and *f* until firm.)

h. Now you're going to sound out (pause) **brush.** Get ready. (Touch **b, r, u, sh** as the children say *brrruuushshsh.*)

• What word? (Signal.) *Brush.* Yes, **brush.**

i. (Point to **brush.**) This word is **brush.**

j. (Tap under **d** in **brushed.**) So this must be . . . (Touch the ball for **brushed** and move your finger quickly along the arrow.) *Brushed.* Yes, **brushed.**

k. (Repeat *i* and *j* until firm.)

l. Now you're going to sound out (pause) **brushed.** Get ready. (Touch **b, r, u, sh, d** as the children say *brrruuushshshd.*)

• What word? (Signal.) *Brushed.* Yes, **brushed.**

brush

brushed

STORY 119
EXERCISE 19

First reading—children read the story the fast way

(Have the children reread any sentences containing words that give them trouble. Keep a list of these words.)

a. (Pass out Storybook.)

b. Open your book to page 68. ✔

c. Everybody, touch the title of the story and get ready to read the words in the title the fast way.

d. First word. ✔

• (Pause two seconds.) Get ready. (Tap.) *Al.*

e. (Tap for each remaining word in the title.)

f. (After the children have read the title, ask:) What's this story about? (Signal.) *Al and Sal.* Yes, **Al and Sal.**

g. Everybody, get ready to read this story the fast way.

h. First word. ✔

• (Pause two seconds.) Get ready. (Tap.) *Al.*

i. (Tap for the remaining words in the first sentence. Pause at least two seconds between taps.)

j. (Repeat *h* and *i* for the next two sentences. Have the children reread the first three sentences until firm.)

k. (The children are to read the remainder of the story the fast way, stopping at the end of each sentence.)

l. (After the first reading of the story, print on the board the words that the children missed more than one time. Have the children sound out each word one time and tell what word.)

m. (After the group's responses are firm, call on individual children to read the words.)

EXERCISE 20

Individual test

a. Look at page 68. I'm going to call on individual children to read a whole sentence.

b. (Call on individual children to read a sentence. Do not tap for each word.)

EXERCISE 21

Second reading—children read the story the fast way and answer questions

a. You're going to read the story again the fast way and I'll ask questions.

b. Starting with the first word of the title. ✔

• Get ready. (Tap.) *Al.*

c. (Tap for each remaining word. Pause at least two seconds between taps. Pause longer before words that gave the children trouble during the first reading.)

d. (Ask the comprehension questions below as the children read.)

After the children read:	You say:
Al and Sal.	What's this story about? (Signal.) *Al and Sal.*
Al said, "Will we go home?"	What did Al say? (Signal.) *Will we go home?*
Sal said, "No. We will go to that farm."	What did Sal say? (Signal.) *We will go to that farm.*
"We can sit in the lake."	Name the things Sal said they could do on the farm. *The children respond.* Yes, run with a cow, eat corn, feed pigs, and sit in the lake.
Al said, "I hate to sit in lakes."	What did Al say? (Signal.) *I hate to sit in lakes.*
Sal and Al had fun with the pigs.	Did Sal and Al sit in the lake? (Signal.) *No.* What did they do? (Signal.) *Had fun with the pigs.*

EXERCISE 22

Picture comprehension

a. What do you think you'll see in the picture? *The children respond.* Let's see.

b. Turn the page and look at the picture.

c. (Ask these questions:)

1. What are that boy and girl doing? *The children respond.* Yes, they're feeding the pigs.
2. Will they get dirty feeding the pigs? *The children respond.*
3. What will their grandmother say if they get dirty? *The children respond.*
4. Did you ever get dirty? *The children respond.*

READING VOCABULARY
EXERCISE 6

Children sound out an irregular word (**touch**)

a. (Touch the ball for **touch.**) Sound it out.

b. Get ready. (Quickly touch each sound as the children say *tooouuuch.*)

To Correct

If the children do not say the sounds you touch

1. (Say:) You've got to say the sounds I touch.
2. (Repeat *a* and *b* until firm.)
---

c. Again. (Repeat *b* until firm.)

d. That's how we <u>sound out</u> the word. Here's how we <u>say</u> the word. **Touch.** How do we <u>say</u> the word? (Signal.) *Touch.*

e. Now you're going to <u>sound out</u> the word. Get ready. (Touch each sound as the children say *tooouuuch.*)

f. Now you're going to say the word. Get ready. (Signal.) *Touch.*

g. (Repeat *e* and *f* until firm.)

h. Yes, this word is **touch. Touch** your ears.

EXERCISE 7

Individual test

(Call on individual children to do *e* and *f* in exercise 6.)

EXERCISE 8

Children read the fast way

a. Get ready to read these words the fast way.

b. (Touch the ball for **ēagle.** Pause three seconds.) Get ready. (Signal.) *Eagle.*

c. (Repeat *b* for the remaining words on the page.)

EXERCISE 9

Children read the fast way again

a. Get ready to do these words again. Watch where I point.

b. (Point to a word. Pause one second. Say:) Get ready. (Signal.) *The children respond.*

• (Point to the words in this order: **ēagle, six, tēach.**)

c. (Repeat *b* until firm.)

touch

ēagle

tēach

six

EXERCISE 10

Individual test

(Call on individual children to read one word on the page the fast way.)

WORKSHEET 119

SUMMARY OF INDEPENDENT ACTIVITY
EXERCISE 23

Introduction to independent activity

a. (Pass out Worksheet 119 to each child.)

b. Everybody, you're going to do this worksheet on your own. (Tell the children when they will work the items.)

• Let's go over the things you're going to do.

Sentence copying

a. (Hold up side 1 of your worksheet and point to the first line in the sentence-copying exercise.)

b. Everybody, here's the sentence you're going to write on the lines below.

c. Reading the fast way. First word. ✔

• Get ready. (Tap.) *She.*

d. Next word. ✔

• Get ready. (Tap.) *Sat.*

e. (Repeat *d* for the remaining words.)

f. After you finish your worksheet, you get to draw a picture about the sentence, **shē sat in the lāke.**

Sound writing

a. (Point to the sound-writing exercise.) Here are the sounds you're going to write today. I'll touch the sounds. You say them.

b. (Touch each sound.) *The children respond.*

c. (Repeat the series until firm.)

Matching

a. (Point to the column of words in the Matching Game.)

b. Everybody, you're going to follow the lines and write these words.

c. Reading the fast way.

d. (Point to the first word. Pause.) Get ready. (Signal.) *The children respond.*

e. (Repeat *d* for the remaining words.)

f. (Repeat *d* and *e* until firm.)

Cross-out game

(Point to the boxed word in the Cross-out Game.) Everybody, here's the word you're going to cross out today. What word? (Signal.) *Will.* Yes, **will.**

Pair relations

a. (Point to the pair-relations exercise on side 2.) Remember—you're going to draw a line through the words in each box that do not tell about the picture.

b. (Point to the space at the top of the page.) After you finish, remember to draw a picture that shows **shē sat in the lāke.**

END OF LESSON 119

Groups that are firm on Mastery Tests 28 and 29 should skip this lesson and do lesson 154 today.

SOUNDS

EXERCISE 1

Teaching **wh** as in **why**

a. (Point to **wh**.) My turn. (Pause. Touch **wh** and say:) whwhwh.

b. (Point to **wh**.) Your turn. When I touch it, you say it. (Pause.) Get ready. (Touch **wh**.) *www*.

• (Lift your finger.)

c. Again. (Touch **wh**.) *wwww*.

• (Lift your finger.)

d. (Repeat *c* until firm.)

EXERCISE 2

Sounds firm-up

a. Get ready to say the sounds when I touch them.

b. (Alternate touching **wh** and **ȳ**. Point to the sound. Pause one second. Say:) Get ready. (Touch the sound.) *The children respond*.

c. (When **wh** and **ȳ** are firm, alternate touching **wh**, **ȳ**, **w**, and **r** until all four sounds are firm.)

EXERCISE 3

Individual test

(Call on individual children to identify **wh**, **ȳ**, **w**, or **r**.)

EXERCISE 4

Sounds firm-up

a. (Point to **wh**.) When I touch the sound, you say it.

b. (Pause.) Get ready. (Touch **wh**.) *www*.

c. Again. (Repeat *b* until firm.)

d. Get ready to say all the sounds when I touch them.

e. (Alternate touching **wh, h, j, oo, x, ī, e,** and **ing** three or four times. Point to the sound. Pause one second. Say:) Get ready. (Touch the sound.) *The children respond*.

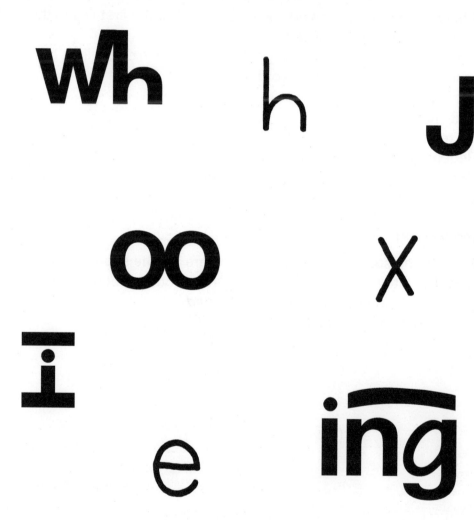

EXERCISE 5

Individual test

(Call on individual children to identify one or more sounds in exercise 4.)

SOUNDS

EXERCISE 1

Teaching **e** as in **end**

a. (Point to **e**.) My turn. (Pause.) (Touch **e** and say:) **eee.**

b. (Point to **e**.) Your turn. When I touch it, you say it. (Pause.) Get ready. (Touch **e**.) *eee.*

• (Lift your finger.)

c. Again. (Touch **e**.) *eee.*

• (Lift your finger.)

d. (Repeat *c* until firm.)

EXERCISE 2

Sounds firm-up

a. Get ready to say the sounds when I touch them.

b. (Alternate touching **i** and **e**. Point to the sound. Pause one second. Say:) Get ready. (Touch the sound.) *The children respond.*

c. (When **i** and **e** are firm, alternate touching **i, ē, o,** and **e** until all four sounds are firm.)

EXERCISE 3

Individual test

(Call on individual children to identify **i, ē, o,** or **e.**)

EXERCISE 4

Teacher introduces cross-out game

a. (Use transparency and crayon.)

b. I'll cross out the sounds on this part of the page when you can tell me every sound.

c. Remember—when I touch it, you say it.

d. (Go over the sounds until the children can identify all the sounds in order.)

EXERCISE 5

Individual test

(Call on individual children to identify two or more sounds in exercise 4.)

EXERCISE 6

Teacher crosses out sounds

a. You told me every sound. Get ready to do it again. This time I'll cross out each sound when you tell me what it is.

b. (Point to each sound. Pause. Say:) Get ready. (Touch the sound.) *The children respond.*

• (As you cross out the sound, say:) Goodbye, _____.

WORKSHEET 152

SUMMARY OF INDEPENDENT ACTIVITY
EXERCISE 30

Introduction to independent activity

a. (Pass out Worksheet 152 to each child.)

b. Everybody, you're going to do this worksheet on your own. **(Tell the children when they will work the items.)**

• Let's go over the things you're going to do.

Story items

a. (Hold up side 1 of your worksheet and point to the story-items exercise.)

b. Everybody, here are items about the story we read today.

c. Think about what happened in the story and circle the right answer for each item.

Picture comprehension

a. (Point to the pictures in the picture-comprehension exercise.) Everybody, you're going to look at the picture. Then you're going to read each item and write the missing word.

b. Remember—the first sound of each missing word is already written in the blank.

Reading comprehension

a. (Point to the reading-comprehension exercise on side 2.)

b. Everybody, get ready to read the sentences in the box the fast way.

c. First word. ✔

• Get ready. **(Tap for each word as the children read the sentences** *A man went in a sail boat. He had a lot of fun.***)**

d. (Point to items 1 and 2.) These items tell about the story in the box. You're going to read each item and circle the right answer.

Sound writing

a. (Point to the sound-writing exercise.) Here are the sounds you're going to write today. I'll touch the sounds. You say them.

b. (Touch each sound.) *The children respond.*

c. (Repeat the series until firm.)

Sentence copying

a. (Point to the dotted sentence in the sentence-copying exercise.)

b. You're going to trace the words in this sentence. Then you're going to write the sentence on the other lines.

c. Reading the fast way. First word. ✔

• Get ready. **(Tap for each word.)**

d. After you finish your worksheet, you get to draw a picture about the sentence, **"it is gōld," hē said.** You'll draw your picture on a piece of plain paper. **(When the children finish their worksheets, give them sheets of plain paper.)**

END OF LESSON 152

READING VOCABULARY
EXERCISE 7

Children identify, then sound out an irregular word (**do**)

a. (Touch the ball for **do.**) Everybody, you're going to read this word the fast way. (Pause three seconds.) Get ready. (Move your finger quickly along the arrow.) *Do.* Yes, **do.**

b. Now you're going to sound out the word. Get ready. (Quickly touch **d, o** as the children say *dooo.*)

c. Again. (Repeat *b.*)

d. How do we say the word? (Signal.) *Do.* Yes, **do.**

e. (Repeat *b* and *d* until firm.)

f. (Call on individual children to do *b* and *d.*)

EXERCISE 8

Children read the fast way

a. Get ready to read these words the fast way.

b. (Touch the ball for **cōat.** Pause three seconds.) Get ready. (Signal.) *Coat.*

c. (Repeat *b* for the remaining words on the page.)

EXERCISE 9

Children read the fast way again

a. Get ready to do these words again. Watch where I point.

b. (Point to a word. Pause one second. Say:) Get ready. (Signal.) *The children respond.*

• (Point to the words in this order: **fōr, rāin, met, cōat.**)

c. (Repeat *b* until firm.)

EXERCISE 10

Individual test

(Call on individual children to read one word the fast way.)

do

cōat

rāin

met

fōr

STORY 152
EXERCISE 26

First reading—children read the title and first three sentences

a. Now you're going to finish the story about Bill and the old box.
b. Everybody, touch the title of the story and get ready to read the words in the title the fast way.
c. First word. ✔
- (Pause two seconds.) Get ready. (Tap.) *Bill.*

d. (Tap for each remaining word in the title.)
e. (After the children have read the title, ask:) What's this story about? (Signal.) *Bill went fishing.* Yes, **Bill went fishing.**
f. Everybody, get ready to read this story the fast way.
g. First word. ✔
- (Pause two seconds.) Get ready. (Tap.) *Bill.*

h. (Tap for the remaining words in the first sentence. Pause at least two seconds between taps.)
i. (Repeat *g* and *h* for the next two sentences. Have the children reread the first three sentences until firm.)

EXERCISE 27

Individual children or the group read sentences to complete the first reading

a. I'm going to call on individual children to read a sentence. Everybody, follow along and point to the words. If you hear a mistake, raise your hand.
b. (Call on a child.) Read the next sentence. (Do not tap for the words. Let children read at their own pace, but be sure they read the sentence correctly.)

To Correct
(Have the child sound out the word. Then return to the beginning of the sentence.)

c. (Repeat *b* for most of the remaining sentences in the story. Occasionally have the group read a sentence. When the group is to read, say:) Everybody, read the next sentence. (Pause two seconds.) Get ready. (Tap for each word in the sentence. Pause at least two seconds between taps.)

EXERCISE 28

Second reading—individual children or the group read each sentence; the group answer questions

a. You're going to read the story again. This time I'm going to ask questions.
b. Starting with the first word of the title. ✔
- Get ready. (Tap as the children read the title. Pause at least two seconds between taps.)

c. (Call on a child.) Read the first sentence. *The child responds.*
d. (Repeat *b* and *c* in exercise 27. Present the following comprehension questions to the entire group.)

After the children read:	You say:
"You have an old box."	What did the other boys say? (Signal.) *You have an old box.*
And Bill said, "That box is filled with gold."	What did Bill say? (Signal.) *That box is filled with gold.* Do you think Bill will still be sad? *The children respond.* What's the title of this story? (Signal.) *Bill went fishing.* And what happened in the story? (Signal.) *Bill went fishing.* Did Bill catch fish? (Signal.) *No.* What did he catch when he went fishing? (Signal.) *An old box filled with gold.*

EXERCISE 29

Picture comprehension

a. Everybody, look at the picture.
b. (Ask these questions:)
1. What's in that box? *Gold.*
2. Are the other boys making fun of Bill now? *No.*
3. Which would you rather have, nine fish or a great big box filled with gold? *The children respond.*
4. What would you do with all that gold? *The children respond.*

EXERCISE 11

Children sound out the word and tell what word

a. (Touch the ball for **there.**) Sound it out.

b. Get ready. (Touch **th, e, r** as the children say *thththeeerrr.*)

• (If sounding out is not firm, repeat *b.*)

c. What word? (Signal.) *There.* Yes, **there. There** are swings in the yard.

EXERCISE 12

Children sound out the word and tell what word

(Repeat the procedures in exercise 11 for **wet.**)

EXERCISE 13

Children sound out the word and tell what word

(Repeat the procedures in exercise 11 for **went.**)

EXERCISE 14

Children rhyme with **let**

a. (Touch the ball for **let.**) You're going to read this word the fast way. (Pause three seconds.) Get ready. (Move your finger quickly along the arrow.) *Let.*

b. (Touch the ball for **get.**) This word rhymes with (pause) **let.** (Move to **g,** then quickly along the arrow.) *Get.*

• Yes, what word? (Signal.) *Get.*

EXERCISE 15

Children read the words the fast way

(Have the children read the words on this page the fast way.)

EXERCISE 16

Individual test

(Call on individual children to read one word the fast way.)

there

wet

went

let

get

READ THE ITEM 152
EXERCISE 23

Children read item 1

a. (Pass out Storybook.)

b. Open your book to page 165. ✔

c. (Point to the title **rēad the ītem.**) Everybody, touch this title. ✔

d. I'll read the title. You point to the words I read. (Pause.) Get ready. **Read** (pause) **the** (pause) **item.**

e. Your turn to read the title. First word. ✔

• Get ready. (Tap for each word as the children read *read the item*.)

f. Everybody, say the title. (Pause and signal. Without looking at the words, the children say *read the item*.)

• (Repeat until firm.)

g. You're going to read the item. Touch item 1 and get ready to read. ✔

h. First word. (Tap for each word as the children read *If the teacher says "Now," hold up your hand*.)

• (Repeat three times or until firm.)

i. Everybody, get ready to say item 1 with me. (Pause and signal. Without looking at the words, you and the children say:) *If the teacher says* "Now," (pause one second) *hold up your hand*.

• (Repeat four times or until firm.)

j. All by yourselves. Say item 1. (Signal.) *If the teacher says "Now," hold up your hand*. (Repeat four times or until firm.)

EXERCISE 24

Children reread item 1 and answer questions

a. Everybody, touch item 1 again. ✔

b. Read item 1 to yourself. Raise your hand when you know what you're going to do and when you're going to do it.

c. (After the children raise their hands, say:) Everybody, what are you going to do if I say **"Now"**? (Signal.) *Hold up my hand*.

┌─**To Correct**────────────────────
1. Everybody, read item 1 out loud. (Tap as the children read each word.)
2. What are you going to do if I say **"Now"**? (Signal.) *Hold up my hand.*
└──────────────────────────────

d. Everybody, when are you going to **hold up your hand?** (Signal.) *If the teacher says "Now."*

┌─**To Correct**────────────────────
1. Everybody, read item 1 out loud. (Tap as the children read each word.)
2. When are you going to **hold up your hand?** (Signal.) *If the teacher says "Now."*
└──────────────────────────────

e. (Repeat *c* and *d* until firm.)

EXERCISE 25

Children play the game

a. Everybody, touch item 1. ✔

b. Read the item to yourself. Raise your hand when you know what you're going to do and when you're going to do it.

c. (After the children raise their hands, say:) Let's play the game. Think about what you're going to do (pause) and when you're going to do it.

d. (Hold out your hand. Pause.) Get ready. **Now.** (Pause. Drop your hand.) *The children hold up their hands immediately.*

┌─**To Correct**────────────────────
1. What did I say? (Signal.) *Now.*
2. What are you supposed to do if I say **"Now"**? (Signal.) *Hold up my hand.*
3. (If the children's responses are not firm, have them read item 1 aloud.)
4. (Repeat exercise 25.)
└──────────────────────────────

EXERCISE 17

Children read the fast way

a. Get ready to read these words the fast way.
b. (Touch the ball for **the.** Pause three seconds.) Get ready. (Signal.) *The.*
c. (Repeat *b* for the remaining words on the page.)

EXERCISE 18

Children read the fast way again

a. Get ready to do these words again. Watch where I point.
b. (Point to a word. Pause one second. Say:) Get ready. (Signal.)
   The children respond.
• (Point to the words in this order: **that, the, shē, thōse.**)
c. (Repeat *b* until firm.)

EXERCISE 19

Individual test

(Call on individual children to read one word the fast way.)

the

shē

thōse

that

EXERCISE 18

Children sound out the word and tell what word

a. (Touch the ball for **filled.**) Sound it out.
b. Get ready. (Touch **f, i,** between the **l**'s, **d,** as the children say *fffiiillld.*)
• (If sounding out is not firm, repeat *b.*)
c. What word? (Signal.) *Filled.* Yes, **filled.**

EXERCISE 19

Children read the fast way

(Touch the ball for **mȳ.**) Get ready to read this word the fast way. (Pause three seconds.) Get ready. (Signal.) *My.*

EXERCISE 20

Children read a word beginning with two consonants (**flȳ**)

a. (Cover **f.** Run your finger under **lȳ.**) You're going to sound out this part. Get ready. (Touch **l, ȳ** as the children say *lllȳȳȳ.*)
b. Say it fast. (Signal.) *Lȳ.* Yes, this part is **lȳ.**
c. (Uncover **f.** Point to **f.**) You're going to say this first. (Move your finger quickly under **lȳ.**) Then you're going to say (pause) **lȳ.**
d. (Point to **f.**) What are you going to say first? (Signal.) *fff.*
• What are you going to say next? (Signal.) *Lȳ.*
e. (Repeat *d* until firm.)
f. (Touch the ball for **fly.**) Get ready. (Move to **f,** then quickly along the arrow.) *Ffflȳ.*
g. Say it fast. (Signal.) *Fly.*
• Yes, what word? (Signal.) *Fly.* Yes, **fly.**
• Good reading.
h. Again. (Repeat *f* and *g* until firm.)
i. Now you're going to sound out (pause) **fly.** Get ready. (Touch **f, l, ȳ** as the children say *ffflllȳȳȳ.*)
• What word? (Signal.) *Fly.* Yes, **fly.**

EXERCISE 21

Children read the words the fast way

a. Now you get to read the words on this page the fast way.
b. (Touch the ball for **filled.** Pause three seconds.) Get ready. (Move your finger quickly along the arrow.) *Filled.*
c. (Repeat *b* for each word on the page.)

EXERCISE 22

Individual test

(Have children read one word the fast way.)

STORY 120
EXERCISE 20

First reading—children read the story the fast way

(Have the children reread any sentences containing words that give them trouble. Keep a list of these words.)

a. (Pass out Storybook.)

b. Open your book to page 71. ✔

c. Everybody, touch the title of the story and get ready to read the words in the title the fast way.

d. First word. ✔

• (Pause two seconds.) Get ready. (Tap.) *A.*

e. (Tap for each remaining word in the title.)

f. (After the children have read the title ask:) What's this story about? (Signal.) *A fish in the rain.* Yes, **a fish in the rain.**

g. Everybody, get ready to read this story the fast way.

h. First word. ✔

• (Pause two seconds.) Get ready. (Tap.) *A.*

i. (Tap for the remaining words in the first sentence. Pause at least two seconds between taps.)

j. (Repeat *h* and *i* for the next two sentences. Have the children reread the first three sentences until firm.)

k. (The children are to read the remainder of the story the fast way, stopping at the end of each sentence.)

l. (After the first reading of the story, print on the board the words that the children missed more than one time. Have the children sound out each word one time and tell what word.)

m. (After the group's responses are firm, call on individual children to read the words.)

EXERCISE 21

Individual test

a. Turn back to page 71. I'm going to call on individual children to read a whole sentence.

b. (Call on individual children to read a sentence. Do not tap for each word.)

EXERCISE 22

Second reading—children read the story the fast way and answer questions

a. You're going to read the story again the fast way and I'll ask questions.

b. Starting with the first word of the title. ✔

• Get ready. (Tap.) *A.*

c. (Tap for each remaining word. Pause at least two seconds between taps. Pause longer before words that gave the children trouble during the first reading.)

d. (Ask the comprehension questions below as the children read.)

After the children read:	You say:
A fish in the rain.	What's this story about? (Signal.) *A fish in the rain.*
Ron said, "This is not fun."	What did Ron say? (Signal.) *This is not fun.*
Pat said, "This is fun."	Did Pat like getting wet? (Signal.) *Yes.*
So she got a fish and gave it to him.	What did she do? (Signal). *She got a fish and gave it to him.*
Ron said, "It is fun to get wet if we get fish."	What did Ron say? (Signal.) *It is fun to get wet if we get fish.*

EXERCISE 23

Picture comprehension

a. Everybody, look at the picture.

b. (Ask these questions:)

1. How do you know they are in the rain? *The children respond.*
2. What is Pat giving to Ron? *A fish.*
3. Do you like to have wet feet and walk through puddles when it's raining? *The children respond.*

EXERCISE 10

Children sound out an irregular word (**your**)

a. (Touch the ball for **your.**) Sound it out.

b. Get ready. (Quickly touch each sound as the children say *yyyooouuurrr.*)

c. Again. (Repeat *b* until firm.)

d. That's how we <u>sound out</u> the word. Here's how we <u>say</u> the word. **Your.** How do we <u>say</u> the word? (Signal.) *Your.*

e. Now you're going to <u>sound out</u> the word. Get ready. (Touch each sound as the children say *yyyooouuurrr.*)

f. Now you're going to say the word. Get ready. (Signal.) *Your.*

g. (Repeat *e* and *f* until firm.)

h. Yes, this word is **your.** I like **your** new shirt.

EXERCISE 11

Individual test

(Have children do *e* and *f* in exercise 10.)

EXERCISE 12

Children sound out an irregular word (**book**)

(Repeat the procedures in exercise 10 for **book.**)

EXERCISE 13

Individual test

(Have children sound out and say **book.**)

EXERCISE 14

Children identify, then sound out an irregular word (**says**)

a. (Touch the ball for **says.**) Everybody, you're going to read this word the fast way. (Pause three seconds.) Get ready. (Move your finger quickly along the arrow.) *Says.* Yes, **says.**

b. Now you're going to sound out the word. Get ready. (Quickly touch **s, a, y, s** as the children say *sssaaayyysss.*)

c. Again. (Repeat *b.*)

d. How do we say the word? (Signal.) *Says.* Yes, **says.**

e. (Repeat *b* and *d* until firm.)

EXERCISE 15

Individual test

(Have children do *b* and *d* in exercise 14.)

EXERCISE 16

Children read the words the fast way

(Have the children read the words on this page the fast way.)

EXERCISE 17

Individual test

(Have children read one word the fast way.)

your

book

says

WORKSHEET 120

★READING COMPREHENSION

The children will need pencils.

EXERCISE 24

Children choose the correct words to complete the sentences

---

a. (Pass out sides 1 and 2 of Worksheet 120 to each child.)

b. Everybody do a good job on your worksheet today and I'll give you a bonus worksheet.

c. (Hold up side 1 of your worksheet. Point to the sentences in the box in the reading-comprehension exercise.)

d. Everybody, touch this box on your worksheet. ✔

e. Get ready to read the words in the box the fast way. First word. ✔

• Get ready. (Tap for each word in the first sentence as the children read *ron was in the rain.*)

• (Pause at least two seconds between taps.)

f. (Have the children reread the sentence until firm.)

g. Get ready to read the next sentence. First word. ✔

• Get ready. (Tap for each word as the children read *he got wet.*)

h. (Have the children reread the sentence until firm.)

i. Listen. **Ron was in the rain.** (Pause.) **He got wet.** Everybody, get ready to tell me the answers. **Ron was in the . . .** (Signal.) *Rain.* Yes, **rain.**

• **He got . . .** (Signal.) *Wet.* Yes, **wet.**

j. (Repeat *i* until firm.)

k. Everybody, touch item 1 below the box. ✔

• This item tells about the story in the box. Everybody, get ready to read item 1 the fast way. First word. ✔

• Get ready. (Tap as the children read *ron was in the . . .*)

l. Touch the word **rat** on the next line. ✔

• Did the story say Ron was in the rat? (Signal.) *No.*

To Correct—————————————————————

(Have the children reread the first sentence in the box. Then repeat the question.)

———————————————————————————————

• Touch the word **rāin.** ✔

• Did the story say Ron was in the rain? (Signal.) *Yes.*

• Touch the word **sand.** ✔

• Did the story say Ron was in the sand? (Signal.) *No.*

m. Which word is right? (Signal.) *Rain.* Yes, **rain.** Draw a circle around it. ✔

n. I'll read the sentences in the box. **Ron was in the rain. He got wet.**

o. Everybody, get ready to read item 2. First word. ✔

• (Tap as the children read *he got . . .*)

p. Touch the word **fat** on the next line. ✔

• Did the story say he got fat? (Signal.) *No.*

• Touch the word **sick.** ✔

• Did the story say he got sick? (Signal.) *No.*

• Touch the word **wet.** ✔

• Did the story say he got wet? (Signal.) *Yes.*

q. Which word is right? (Signal.) *Wet.* Yes, **wet.**

• So what do you do with **wet?** (Signal.) *Draw a circle around it.* Yes, draw a circle around it.

• Do it. ✔

PAIR RELATIONS
EXERCISE 25

Children draw a line through the incorrect sentences

---

a. (Point to the sentences below the first picture in the pair-relations exercise on side 2.)

b. One of these sentences tells about the picture. Everybody, touch the first sentence. ✔

c. Reading the fast way.

d. First word. ✔

• Get ready. (Tap for each word as the children read *the man has a sack.*)

e. Does that sentence tell about the picture? (Signal.) *No.*

• So do you draw a line through it? (Signal.) *Yes.*

• Do it. ✔

f. Next sentence. First word. ✔

• Get ready. (Tap for each word as the children read *he has a mitt.*)

g. Does that sentence tell about the picture? (Signal.) *Yes.*

• So do you draw a line through it? (Signal.) *No.*

h. Next sentence. (Repeat *d* and *e* for the remaining sentences.)

i. Everybody, you'll do the rest of the boxes later. Remember—draw a line through the sentences that do not tell about the picture.

READING VOCABULARY
EXERCISE 7

Children read the fast way

a. Get ready to read these words the fast way.

b. (Touch the ball for **brush.** Pause three seconds.) Get ready. (Signal.) *Brush.*

c. (Repeat *b* for the remaining words on the page.)

EXERCISE 8

Children read the fast way again

a. Get ready to do these words again. Watch where I point.

b. (Point to a word. Pause one second. Say:) Get ready. (Signal.) *The children respond.*

• (Point to the words in this order: **brush, tēach, ēagle, tug, gōld.**)

c. (Repeat *b* until firm.)

EXERCISE 9

Individual test

(Call on individual children to read one word the fast way.)

brush

tug

tēach

ēagle

gōld

SUMMARY OF INDEPENDENT ACTIVITY

The children will need plain paper.

EXERCISE 26

Introduction to independent activity

a. (Hold up side 1 of Worksheet 120.)

b. Everybody, you're going to finish this worksheet on your own. (Tell the children when they will work the remaining items.)

• Let's go over the things you're going to do.

Sentence copying

---

a. (Point to the dotted sentence in the sentence-copying exercise.)

b. You're going to trace the words in this sentence. Then you're going to write the sentence on the other lines.

c. Reading the fast way. First word. ✔

• Get ready. (Tap.) *The.*

d. Next word. ✔

• Get ready. (Tap.) *Girl.*

e. (Repeat *d* for the remaining words.)

f. After you finish your worksheet, you get to draw a picture about the sentence, **the girl got wet.** You'll draw your picture on a piece of plain paper.

Cross-out game

(Point to the boxed word in the Cross-out Game.) Everybody, here's the word you're going to cross out today. What word? (Signal.) *Girl.* Yes, **girl.**

Sound writing

a. (Point to the sound-writing exercise on side 2.) Here are the sounds you're going to write today. I'll touch the sounds. You say them.

b. (Touch each sound.) *The children respond.*

c. (Repeat the series until firm.)

Pair relations

---

a. (Point to the pair-relations exercise.) Remember—you're going to draw a line through the sentences in each box that do not tell about the picture.

b. (When the children finish their worksheets, give them sheets of plain paper. Remind them to draw a picture that shows **the girl got wet.**)

INDIVIDUAL CHECKOUT: STORYBOOK
EXERCISE 31

2-minute individual fluency checkout: rate/accuracy—first page

a. As you are doing your worksheet, I'll call on children one at a time to read the **first page** of the story. Remember, you get two stars if you read the first page of the story in less than two minutes and make no more than three errors.

b. (Call on a child. Tell the child:) Start with the title and read the first page of the story carefully the fast way. Go. (Time the child. Tell the child any words the child misses. Stop the child as soon as the child makes the fourth error or exceeds the time limit.)

c. (If the child meets the rate-accuracy criterion, record two stars on your chart for lesson 120. Congratulate the child. Give children who do not earn two stars a chance to read the page again before the next lesson is presented.)

44 words/**2 min** = 22 wpm [**3 errors**]

EXERCISE 32

Bonus worksheet: sides 3 and 4

(After the children have drawn their pictures, give them sides 3 and 4 of Worksheet 120. Tell them they may keep the stories and read them.)

END OF LESSON 120

Before presenting lesson 121, give Mastery Test 23 to each child. Do not present lesson 121 to any groups that are not firm on this test.

SOUNDS

wh

EXERCISE 1

Teaching **wh** as in **why**

a. (Point to **wh.**)
Here's a new sound.

b. My turn. (Pause. Touch **wh** and say:) www.

c. Again. (Touch **wh** for a longer time.) wwwww.

• (Lift your finger.)

d. (Point to **wh.**) Your turn. When I touch it, you say it. (Pause.) Get ready. (Touch **wh.**) www.

• (Lift your finger.)

e. Again. (Touch **wh.**) wwwwww.

• (Lift your finger.)

f. (Repeat e until firm.)

w

oo

EXERCISE 2

Individual test

(Call on individual children to identify **wh.**)

r

EXERCISE 3

Sounds firm-up

a. Get ready to say the sounds when I touch them.

b. (Alternate touching **wh** and **w.** Point to the sound. Pause one second. Say:) Get ready. (Touch the sound.) *The children respond.*

c. (When **wh** and **w** are firm, alternate touching **wh, w, oo,** and **r** until all four sounds are firm.)

EXERCISE 4

Individual test

(Call on individual children to identify **wh, w, oo,** or **r.**)

EXERCISE 5

Sounds firm-up

a. (Point to **wh.**) When I touch the sound, you say it.

b. (Pause.) Get ready. (Touch **wh.**) *www.*

c. Again. (Repeat *b* until firm.)

d. Get ready to say all the sounds when I touch them.

e. (Alternate touching **wh, ch, ȳ, j, er, x, y,** and **h** three or four times. Point to the sound. Pause one second. Say:) Get ready. (Touch the sound.) *The children respond.*

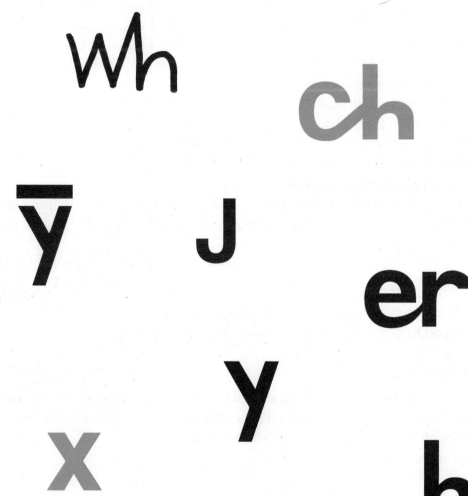

EXERCISE 6

Individual test

(Call on individual children to identify one or more sounds in exercise 5.)

●●●●●●●●●●●●●●●●●●●●●●●●●●●●●●●●●

MASTERY TEST 23—after lesson 120, before lesson 121

a. When I touch the sound, you say it.
b. (test item) (Point to ō.) Get ready. (Touch ō.) *ōōō.*
c. (test item) (Point to v.) Get ready. (Touch v.) *vvv.*
d. (test item) (Point to p.) Get ready. (Touch p.) *p.*
e. (test item) (Point to ch.) Get ready. (Touch ch.) *ch.*
f. (test item) (Point to e.) Get ready. (Touch e.) *eee.*

Total number of test items: **5**
A group is weak if more than one-third of the children missed any of the items on the test.

WHAT TO DO

If the group is firm on Mastery Test 23:

Present lesson 121 to the group during the next reading period. If more than one child missed any of the items on the test, present the firming procedures specified below to those children.

If the group is weak on Mastery Test 23:

A. Present these firming procedures to the group during the next reading period.
   1. Lesson 118, Sounds, page 60, exercises 1 through 4.
   2. Lesson 118, Reading Vocabulary, page 61, exercises 5, 6, 7.
   3. Lesson 119, Sounds, page 65, exercises 4, 5.
   4. Lesson 119, Reading Vocabulary, page 67, exercises 14 through 18.
   5. Lesson 120, Sounds, page 70, exercises 4, 5.
B. After presenting the above exercises, again give Mastery Test 23 individually to members of the group who failed the test.
C. If the group is firm (less than one-third of the total group missed any items on the retest), present lesson 121 to the group during the next reading period.
D. If the group is still weak (more than one-third of the total group missed any items on the retest), repeat *A* and *B* during the next reading period.

v

ō

p

ch

e

EXERCISE 26

Picture comprehension

a. What do you think you'll see in the picture? (The children respond.)
b. Turn the page and look at the picture.
c. Show me the boy who has five fish. (The children respond.)
d. Show me the boy who has nine fish. (The children respond.)
e. (Ask these questions:)
   1. What's Bill pulling out of the water? (The children respond.) An old box.
   2. How many fish does Bill have? *None.*

WORKSHEET 151

SUMMARY OF INDEPENDENT ACTIVITY
EXERCISE 27

Introduction to independent activity

a. (Pass out Worksheet 151 to each child.)
b. Everybody, you're going to do this worksheet on your own. (Tell the children when they will work the items.)
 • Let's go over the things you're going to do.

Story items

a. (Hold up side 1 of your worksheet and point to the story-items exercise.)
b. Everybody, here are items about the story we read today.
c. Think about what happened in the story and circle the right answer for each item.

Picture comprehension

a. (Point to the pictures in the picture-comprehension exercise.) Everybody, you're going to look at the picture. Then you're going to read each item and write the missing word.
b. Remember—the first sound of each missing word is already written in the blank.

Reading comprehension

a. (Point to the reading-comprehension exercise on side 2.)
b. Everybody, get ready to read the sentences in the box the fast way.
c. First word. ✔
 • Get ready. (Tap for each word as the children read the sentences *A girl went fishing. She got five fish.*)
d. (Point to items 1 and 2.) These items tell about the story in the box. You're going to read each item and circle the right answer.

Sound writing

a. (Point to the sound-writing exercise.) Here are the sounds you're going to write today. I'll touch the sounds. You say them.
b. (Touch each sound.) *The children respond.*
c. (Repeat the series until firm.)

Sentence copying

a. (Point to the dotted sentence in the sentence-copying exercise.)
b. You're going to trace the words in this sentence. Then you're going to write the sentence on the other lines.
c. Reading the fast way. First word. ✔
 • Get ready. (Tap for each word.)
d. After you finish your worksheet, you get to draw a picture about the sentence, **Bill did not get fish.** You'll draw your picture on a piece of plain paper. (When the children finish their worksheets, give them sheets of plain paper.)

END OF LESSON 151

Making Progress

	Since Lesson 1	Since Lesson 101
Word Reading	27 sounds 210 regular words 19 irregular words Reading words the fast way Reading stories the fast way	4 sounds 49 regular words 17 irregular words Reading stories the fast way
Comprehension	**Picture Comprehension** Predicting what the picture will show Answering questions about the picture **Story Comprehension** Answering *who, what, when, where* and *why* questions orally Making predictions about the story Finding periods, question marks, and quotation marks	

What to Use

Teacher	Students
Presentation Book C (pages 78–203)	**Storybook** (pages 74–134) Lessons 121–140 **Workbook C**
Teacher's Guide (page 62) **Answer Key** **Spelling Presentation Book**	plain paper (Sentence picture) lined paper (Spelling)

What's Ahead in Lessons 121–140

New Skills

- Story length will increase from 82 to 106 words.
- Children begin to sound out words beginning with blends.
- Beginning at Lesson 140, individuals take turns on the first reading.
- Children begin answering written comprehension questions.
- Children write a sentence from dictation during spelling lesson.

New Sounds

- Lesson 121 — **b** as in *bag* (quick sound)
- Lesson 124 — **iñg** as in *sing*
- Lesson 127 — **ī** as in *ice*
- Lesson 131 — **y** as in *yes*
- Lesson 135 — **er** as in *her*
- Lesson 139 — **x** as in *ox*

New Vocabulary

- *Regular words:*

  (121) them, red, sent
  (122) paint, men, shots, up, lift
  (123) chicks, pig, bug, duck, ducks
  (124) going, kissed
  (125) eating
  (126) be, big, bed, bit, getting, bugs
  (127) sleeping, fishing, leaf, slam, let's, but, slip
  (128) pond, back, bus
  (129) bite, tub, stop
  (130) dive, like, sliding

  (131) rabbit, sitting
  (132) having, slide, slid, time, tell
  (133) stops, rich, stopping, digging, led, boy
  (134) told, hole, yes, line, live, dig
  (135) dad, they, find
  (136) hunt, hunting, ride, gun
  (137) deer
  (138) her
  (139) beans, ever, shopping, never, toys
  (140) hop, shop

- *Irregular words:*

  (128) walk, talk
  (130) talking
  (132) doing
  (133) into, you, dark
  (134) yard

  (137) other, mother, brother, love
  (138) card
  (140) come, some

LESSONS 121–140

STORY 151

EXERCISE 23

First reading—children read the title and first three sentences

a. You're going to read the first part of this story today.

b. Everybody, touch the title of the story and get ready to read the words in the title the fast way.

c. First word. ✔

• (Pause two seconds.) Get ready. (Tap.) *Bill.*

d. (Tap for each remaining word in the title.)

e. (After the children have read the title, ask:) What's this story about? (Signal.) *Bill went fishing.* Yes, **Bill went fishing.**

f. Everybody, get ready to read this story the fast way.

g. First word. ✔

• (Pause two seconds.) Get ready. (Tap.) *Bill.*

h. (Tap for the remaining words in the first sentence. Pause at least two seconds between taps.)

i. (Repeat *g* and *h* for the next two sentences. Have the children reread the first three sentences until firm.)

EXERCISE 24

Individual children or the group read sentences to complete the first reading

a. I'm going to call on individual children to read a sentence. Everybody, follow along and point to the words. If you hear a mistake, raise your hand.

b. (Call on a child.) Read the next sentence. (Do not tap for the words. Let children read at their own pace, but be sure they read the sentence correctly.)

To Correct

(Have the child sound out the word. Then return to the beginning of the sentence.)

c. (Repeat *b* for most of the remaining sentences in the story. Occasionally have the group read a sentence. When the group is to read, say:) Everybody, read the next sentence. (Pause two seconds.) Get ready. (Tap for each word in the sentence. Pause at least two seconds between taps.)

EXERCISE 25

Second reading—individual children or the group read each sentence; the group answer questions

a. You're going to read the story again. This time I'm going to ask questions.

b. Starting with the first word of the title. ✔

• Get ready. (Tap as the children read the title. Pause at least two seconds between taps.)

c. (Call on a child.) Read the first sentence. *The child responds.*

d. (Repeat *b* and *c* in exercise 24. Present the following comprehension questions to the entire group.)

After the children read:	You say:
Bill went fishing.	What's this story about? (Signal.) *Bill went fishing.*
Bill liked to go fishing but he did not get fish.	What did Bill like to do? (Signal.) *Go fishing.* But what happened? (Signal.) *He did not get fish.*
But Bill did not get fish.	How many fish did Bill get? (Signal.) *None.* How many did the big boy get? (Signal.) *Five.* How many did the little boy get? (Signal.) *Nine.*
Then he had a tug on his line.	What happened? (Signal.) *He had a tug on his line.* What's a tug on the line? *The children respond.*
It was an old box.	I wonder if anything is in that old box. We'll find out when we read the next part of the story.

Look Ahead

Mastery Tests

Skill Tested	Implications
Test 24 (Lesson 125) Reading a story the fast way	Use these tests along with Checkouts to determine if any reading vocabulary or stories should be repeated. Beginning at Lesson 140, children begin taking turns on the first reading. Having the group read is an option; you may want to mix group and individual turns to help maintain the children's attention.
Test 25 (Lesson 130) Reading words the fast way	
Test 26 (Lesson 135) Reading the story the fast way	
Test 27 (Lesson 140) Reading words the fast way **At Lesson 140**	

Reading Checkouts (Lessons 125, 130, 135, 140)

Skills

	Lessons 121–140
Word Reading	6 sounds 73 regular words 15 irregular words Individuals take turns reading
Comprehension	**Story Comprehension** Answering written comprehension questions about the day's story and short passages

Reading Activities

Help children develop decoding and comprehension skills by using the following activities.

Beginning-Middle-End (Lessons 121–140)
After completing stories 121–140, have the children fold a piece of drawing paper lengthwise into thirds. Have children choose a story and write the title of the story across the top of the page and then draw and/or write in each section of the paper what happened in the beginning, the middle, and the end of the story. As an additional activity, have children make up a new ending for the story.

Same or Different (Lessons 124, 126, 128)
After completing a lesson, have children make a book of opposites using descriptions from a story. Children fold a piece of white drawing paper into four parts and cut on the folds. Then children draw and write a description on one side and its opposite on the other side. Direct children to make a decorated cover and title it. The contents of this activity for Lesson 124 with a title and opposite pairs is shown below. The same activity can be done with similarities for some other stories.

Paint That Nose
fat dog - little dog
red nose - black nose
clean ear - dirty ear
happy dog - sad dog

STORYBOOK

★READ THE ITEM 151
EXERCISE 20

Children read item 1

a. (Pass out Storybook.)

b. Open your book to page 162. ✔

c. (Point to the title **rēad the ītem.**) Everybody, touch this title. ✔

d. I'll read the title. You point to the words I read. (Pause.) Get ready. **Read** (pause) **the** (pause) **item.**

e. Your turn to read the title. First word. ✔
- Get ready. (Tap for each word as the children read *read the item.*)

f. Everybody, say the title. (Pause and signal. Without looking at the words, the children say *read the item.*)
- (Repeat until firm.)

g. You're going to read the item. Touch item 1 and get ready to read. ✔

h. First word. (Tap for each word as the children read *If the teacher says "Go," stand up.*)
- (Repeat three times or until firm.)

i. Everybody, get ready to say item 1 with me. (Pause and signal. Without looking at the words, you and the children say:) *If the teacher says "Go,"* (pause one second) *stand up.*
- (Repeat four times or until firm.)

j. All by yourselves. Say item 1. (Signal.) *If the teacher says "Go," stand up.*
- (Repeat four times or until firm.)

EXERCISE 21
Children reread item 1 and answer questions

a. Everybody, touch item 1 again. ✔

b. Read item 1 to yourself. Raise your hand when you know what you're going to do and when you're going to do it.

c. (After the children raise their hands, say:) Everybody, what are you going to do if I say **"Go"?** (Signal.) *Stand up.*

To Correct
1. Everybody, read item 1 out loud. (Tap as the children read each word.)
2. What are you going to do if I say **"Go"?** (Signal.) *Stand up.*

d. Everybody, when are you going to **stand up?** (Signal.) *If the teacher says "Go."*

To Correct
1. Everybody, read item 1 out loud. (Tap as the children read each word.)
2. When are you going to **stand up?** (Signal.) *If the teacher says "Go."*

e. (Repeat *c* and *d* until firm.)

EXERCISE 22
Children play the game

a. Everybody, touch item 1. ✔

b. Read the item to yourself. Raise your hand when you know what you're going to do and when you're going to do it.

c. (After the children raise their hands, say:) Let's play the game. Think about what you're going to do (pause) and when you're going to do it.

d. (Hold out your hand. Pause.) Get ready. **Go.** (Pause. Drop your hand.) *The children stand up immediately.*

To Correct
1. What did I say? (Signal.) *Go.*
2. What are you supposed to do if I say **"Go"?** (Signal.) *Stand up.*
3. (If the children's responses are not firm, have them read item 1 aloud.)
4. (Repeat exercise 22.)

SOUNDS

EXERCISE 1

Teaching b as in bag

a. (Point to **b.**) Here's a new sound. It's a quick sound.

b. My turn. (Pause. Touch **b** for an instant, saying:) b. (Do not say **buuh.**)

c. Again. (Touch **b** and say:) b.

d. (Point to **b.**) Your turn. When I touch it, you say it. (Pause.) Get ready. (Touch **b.**) *b.*

e. Again. (Touch **b.**) *b.*

f. (Repeat *e* until firm.)

EXERCISE 2

Individual test

(Call on individual children to identify **b.**)

EXERCISE 3

Sounds firm-up

a. Get ready to say the sounds when I touch them.

b. (Alternate touching **b** and **d.** Point to the sound. Pause one second. Say:) Get ready. (Touch the sound.) *The children respond.*

c. (When **b** and **d** are firm, alternate touching **b, d, p,** and **t** until all four sounds are firm.)

EXERCISE 4

Individual test

(Call on individual children to identify **b, d, p,** or **t.**)

b

v

ch

ē

ō

r

ā

EXERCISE 5

Sounds firm-up

a. (Point to **b.**) When I touch the sound, you say it.

b. (Pause.) Get ready. (Touch **b.**) *b.*

c. Again. (Repeat *b* until firm.)

d. Get ready to say all the sounds when I touch them.

e. (Alternate touching **v, e, ch, ē, ō, r, ā,** and **b** three or four times. Point to the sound. Pause one second. Say:) Get ready. (Touch the sound.) *The children respond.*

EXERCISE 6

Individual test

(Call on individual children to identify one or more sounds in exercise 5.)

EXERCISE 15

Children read **tēach** and **tēacher**

a. (Touch the ball for **tēach.**) You're going to read this word the fast way. (Pause three seconds.) Get ready. (Move your finger quickly along the arrow.) *Teach.*

b. (Return to the ball for **tēach.**) Yes, this word is **teach.**

c. (Tap under **er** in **tēacher.**) So this must be . . . (Touch the ball for **teacher** and move your finger quickly along the arrow.) *Teacher.* Yes, **teacher.**

d. (Repeat *b* and *c* until firm.)

e. Now you're going to sound out (pause) **teacher.** Get ready. (Touch **t, ē, ch, er** as the children say *tēēēcherrr.*)

• Yes, what word? (Signal.) *Teacher.* Yes, **teacher.**

EXERCISE 16

Children sound out the word and tell what word

a. (Touch the ball for **tug.**) Sound it out.

b. Get ready. (Touch **t, u, g** as the children say *tuuug.*)

• (If sounding out is not firm, repeat *b*.)

c. What word? (Signal.) *Tug.* Yes, **tug.**

EXERCISE 17

Children sound out the word and tell what word

a. (Touch the ball for **bill.**) Sound it out.

b. Get ready. (Touch **b, i,** between the **l**'s as the children say *biiilll.*)

• (If sounding out is not firm, repeat *b*.)

c. What word? (Signal.) *Bill.* Yes, **bill.**

EXERCISE 18

Children read the words the fast way

a. Now you get to read the words on this page the fast way.

b. (Touch the ball for **tēach.** Pause three seconds.) Get ready. (Move your finger quickly along the arrow.) *Teach.*

c. (Repeat *b* for each word on the page.)

EXERCISE 19

Individual test

(Call on individual children to read one word the fast way.)

tēach

tēacher

tug

bill

READING VOCABULARY

Children read the fast way

a. Get ready to read these words the fast way.
b. (Touch the ball for **red.** Pause three seconds.) Get ready. (Signal.) *Red.*
c. (Repeat *b* for the remaining words on the page.)

EXERCISE 8

Children read the fast way again

a. Get ready to do these words again. Watch where I point.
b. (Point to a word. Pause one second. Say:) Get ready. (Signal.)
   The children respond.
• (Point to the words in this order: **red, rēad, sent, let, went.**)
c. (Repeat *b* until firm.)

EXERCISE 9

Individual test

(Call on individual children to read one word the fast way.)

red

went

sent

rēad

let

EXERCISE 10

Children rhyme with **nīne** and **fīne**

a. (Touch the ball for **nīne**.) You're going to read this word the fast way. (Pause three seconds.) Get ready. (Move your finger quickly along the arrow.) *Nine.*

b. (Touch the ball for **fīne**.) This word rhymes with (pause) **nine.** (Move to **f,** then quickly along the arrow.) *Fine.*

• Yes, what word? (Signal.) *Fine.*

EXERCISE 11

Children sound out an irregular word (**your**)

a. (Touch the ball for **your.**) Sound it out.

b. Get ready. (Quickly touch each sound as the children say *yyyooouuurrr.*)

c. Again. (Repeat *b* until firm.)

d. That's how we <u>sound out</u> the word. Here's how we <u>say</u> the word. **Your.** How do we <u>say</u> the word? (Signal.) *Your.*

e. Now you're going to <u>sound out</u> the word. Get ready. (Touch each sound as the children say *yyyooouuurrr.*)

f. Now you're going to say the word. Get ready. (Signal.) *Your.*

g. (Repeat *e* and *f* until firm.)

h. Yes, this word is **your.** Touch **your** head.

i. (Call on individual children to do *e* and *f.*)

EXERCISE 12

Children identify, then sound out an irregular word (**says**)

a. (Touch the ball for **says.**) Everybody, you're going to read this word the fast way. (Pause three seconds.) Get ready. (Move your finger quickly along the arrow.) *Says.* Yes, **says.**

b. Now you're going to sound out the word. Get ready. (Quickly touch **s, a, y, s** as the children say *sssaaayyysss.*)

c. Again. (Repeat *b.*)

d. How do we say the word? (Signal.) *Says.*

e. (Repeat *b* and *d* until firm.)

f. (Call on individual children to do *b* and *d.*)

EXERCISE 13

Children read the words the fast way

(Have the children read the words on this page the fast way.)

EXERCISE 14

Individual test

(Call on individual children to read one word the fast way.)

EXERCISE 10

Children rhyme with an irregular word (**to**)

a. (Touch the ball for **to.**) Everybody, you're going to read this word the fast way. (Pause three seconds.) Get ready. (Move your finger quickly along the arrow.) *To.* Yes, **to.**

b. (Quickly touch the ball for **do.**) This word rhymes with **to.** Get ready. (Move to **d,** then quickly along the arrow.) *Do.* Yes, **do.**

c. (Repeat *a* and *b* until firm.)

EXERCISE 11

Children sound out **do**

a. (Touch the ball for **do.**) You're going to sound out this word. Get ready. (Quickly touch **d, o** as the children say *dooo.*)

b. How do we say the word? (Signal.) *Do.* Yes, **do.**

c. (If *a* and *b* are not firm, say:) Again. (Repeat *a* and *b.*)

EXERCISE 12

Individual test

(Call on individual children to do *a* and *b* in exercise 11.)

EXERCISE 13

Children sound out the word and tell what word

a. (Touch the ball for **there.**) Sound it out.

b. Get ready. (Touch **th, e, r** as the children say *thththeeerrr.*) (If sounding out is not firm, repeat *b.*)

c. What word? (Signal.) *There.* Yes, **there. There** is my desk.

EXERCISE 14

Children read the fast way

(Touch the ball for **pet.**) Get ready to read this word the fast way. (Pause three seconds.) Get ready. (Signal.) *Pet.*

EXERCISE 15

Children read the words the fast way

(Have the children read the words on this page the fast way.)

EXERCISE 16

Individual test

(Call on individual children to read one word the fast way.)

READING VOCABULARY
EXERCISE 7

Children read the fast way

a. Get ready to read these words the fast way.
b. (Touch the ball for **fill.** Pause three seconds.) Get ready. (Signal.) *Fill.*
c. (Repeat *b* for the remaining words on the page.)

EXERCISE 8

Children read the fast way again

a. Get ready to do these words again. Watch where I point.
b. (Point to a word. Pause one second. Say:) Get ready. (Signal.)
The children respond.
• (Point to the words in this order: **līked, brush, hōld, fill.**)
c. (Repeat *b* until firm.)

EXERCISE 9

Individual test

(Call on individual children to read one word the fast way.)

fill

brush

hōld

līked

EXERCISE 17

Children sound out the word and tell what word

a. (Touch the ball for **did.**) Sound it out.

b. Get ready. (Touch **d, i, d** as the children say *diiid.*)

• (If sounding out is not firm, repeat *b.*)

c. What word? (Signal.) *Did.* Yes, **did.**

EXERCISE 18

Children read the fast way

a. Get ready to read these words the fast way.

b. (Touch the ball for **the.** Pause three seconds.) Get ready. (Signal.) *The.*

c. (Repeat *b* for the remaining words on the page.)

EXERCISE 19

Children read the fast way again

a. Get ready to do these words again. Watch where I point.

b. (Point to a word. Pause one second. Say:) Get ready. (Signal.)
The children respond.

• (Point to the words in this order: **then, the, them.**)

c. (Repeat *b* until firm.)

EXERCISE 20

Individual test

(Call on individual children to read one word on the page the fast way.)

did

the

then

them

SOUNDS

EXERCISE 1

Teaching **ȳ** as in **mȳ**

a. (Point to **ȳ**.) My turn. (Pause. Touch **ȳ** and say: **ȳȳȳ (īīī).**

b. (Point to **ȳ**.) Your turn. When I touch it, you say it. (Pause.) Get ready. (Touch **ȳ**.) *ȳȳȳ.*

- (Lift your finger.)

c. Again. (Touch **ȳ**.) *ȳȳȳȳ.*

- (Lift your finger.)

d. (Repeat *c* until firm.)

EXERCISE 2

Sounds firm-up

a. Get ready to say the sounds when I touch them.

b. (Alternate touching **ȳ** and **u**. Point to the sound. Pause one second. Say:) Get ready. (Touch the sound.) *The children respond.*

c. (When **ȳ** and **u** are firm, alternate touching **ȳ, u, y,** and **i** until all four sounds are firm.)

EXERCISE 3

Individual test

(Call on individual children to identify **ȳ, u, y,** or **i.**)

EXERCISE 4

Teacher introduces cross-out game

a. (Use transparency and crayon.)

b. I'll cross out the sounds on this part of the page when you can tell me every sound.

c. Remember—when I touch it, you say it.

d. (Go over the sounds until the children can identify all the sounds in order.)

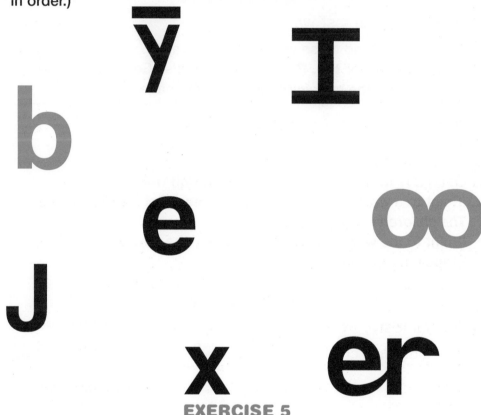

EXERCISE 5

Individual test

(Call on individual children to identify two or more sounds in exercise 4.)

EXERCISE 6

Teacher crosses out sounds

a. You told me every sound. Get ready to do it again. This time I'll cross out each sound when you tell me what it is.

b. (Point to each sound. Pause. Say:) Get ready. (Touch the sound.) *The children respond.*

- (As you cross out the sound, say:) Goodbye, _____.

STORYBOOK

STORY 121
EXERCISE 21

First reading—children read the story the fast way

(Have the children reread any sentences containing words that give them trouble. Keep a list of these words.)

a. (Pass out Storybook.)

b. Open your book to page 74. ✔

c. Everybody, touch the title of the story and get ready to read the words in the title the fast way.

d. First word. ✔

• (Pause two seconds.) Get ready. (Tap.) *The.*

e. (Tap for each remaining word in the title.)

f. (After the children have read the title, ask:) What's this story about? (Signal.) *The pet shop.* Yes, **the pet shop.**

g. Everybody, get ready to read this story the fast way.

h. First word. ✔

• (Pause two seconds.) Get ready. (Tap.) *A.*

i. (Tap for the remaining words in the first sentence. Pause at least two seconds between taps.)

j. (Repeat *h* and *i* for the next two sentences. Have the children reread the first three sentences until firm.)

k. (The children are to read the remainder of the story the fast way, stopping at the end of each sentence.)

l. (After the first reading of the story, print on the board the words that the children missed more than one time. Have the children sound out each word one time and tell what word.)

m. (After the group's responses are firm, call on individual children to read the words.)

EXERCISE 22

Individual test

a. Look at page 74. I'm going to call on individual children to read a whole sentence.

b. (Call on individual children to read a sentence. Do not tap for each word.)

EXERCISE 23

Second reading—children read the story the fast way and answer questions

a. You're going to read the story again the fast way and I'll ask questions.

b. Starting with the first word of the title. ✔

• Get ready. (Tap.) *The.*

c. (Tap for each remaining word. Pause at least two seconds between taps. Pause longer before words that gave the children trouble during the first reading.)

d. (Ask the comprehension questions below as the children read.)

After the children read:	You say:
A girl said to a man, "Let us go to the pet shop."	Who said that? (Signal.) *A girl.* Who was she talking to? (Signal.) *A man.*
The girl said to the man in the pet shop, "I need a dog."	What did she say? (Signal.) *I need a dog.* Who did she say that to? (Signal.) *The man in the pet shop.*
"Let me get that cat."	What kind of cat is he going to get? (Signal.) *A red cat.*
And the girl went home with the red cat.	What did the girl do with the cat? (Signal.) *She went home.*

EXERCISE 24

Picture comprehension

a. What do you think you'll see in the picture? *The children respond.*

b. Turn the page and look at the picture.

c. (Ask these questions:)

1. Why are those hearts all around that girl? *The children respond.*

• They mean that she loves the cat.

2. Do you think she'll take good care of that cat? *The children respond.*

3. What would you do with a red cat? *The children respond.*

MASTERY TEST 29—

a. (Tell child:) Get ready to read these words the fast way.

b. **(test item)** (Touch the ball for **jump.** Pause three seconds.)
Get ready. (Signal.) *Jump.*

c. **(test item)** (Touch the ball for **fox.** Pause three seconds.)
Get ready. (Signal.) *Fox.*

d. **(test item)** (Touch the ball for **broom.** Pause three seconds.)
Get ready. (Signal.) *Broom.*

e. **(test item)** (Touch the ball for **start.** Pause three seconds.)
Get ready. (Signal.) *Start.*

Total number of test items: **4**
A group is weak if more than one-third of the children missed any of the items on the test.

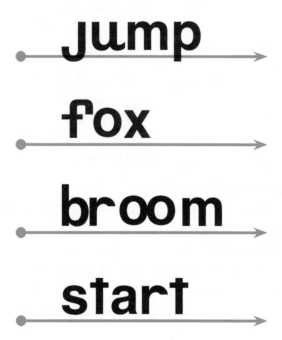

WHAT TO DO

If the group is firm on Mastery Test 29 and was firm on Mastery Test 28:

Present lesson 151 and skip lesson 153. If more than one child missed any of the items on the test, present the firming procedures specified below to those children.

If the group is firm on Mastery Test 29 but was weak on Mastery Test 28:

Present lesson 151 to the group during the next reading period. If more than one child missed any of the items on the test, present the firming procedures specified below to those children.

If the group is weak on Mastery Test 29:

A. Present these firming procedures to the group during the next reading period.
   1. Lesson 147, Reading Vocabulary, pages 243–244, exercises 6 through 15.
   2. Lesson 148, Reading Vocabulary, pages 249–251, exercises 4 through 16.
   3. Lesson 149, Reading Vocabulary, pages 255–256, exercises 5 through 11.
   4. Lesson 150, Reading Vocabulary, pages 261–264, exercises 6 through 24.
B. After presenting the above exercises, again give Mastery Test 29 individually to members of the group who failed the test.
C. If the group is firm (less than one-third of the total group missed any items in the retest), present lesson 151 to the group during the next reading period.
D. If the group is still weak (more than one-third of the total group missed any items on the retest), repeat *A* and *B* during the next reading period.

WORKSHEET 121

READING COMPREHENSION

The children will need pencils.

EXERCISE 25

Children choose the correct words to complete the sentences

a. (Pass out Worksheet 121 to each child.)

b. (Point to the sentences in the box in the reading-comprehension exercise on side 1.)

c. Everybody, touch this box on your worksheet. ✔

d. Get ready to read the words in the box the fast way. First word. ✔

• Get ready. (Tap for each word in the first sentence as the children read *the girl went to a shop.* Pause at least two seconds between taps.)

e. (Have the children reread the sentence until firm.)

f. Get ready to read the next sentence. First word. ✔

• Get ready. (Tap for each word as the children read *she got a cat.*)

g. (Have the children reread the sentence until firm.)

h. Listen. **The girl went to a shop.** (Pause.) **She got a cat.** Everybody, get ready to tell me the answers. **The girl went to a . . .** (Signal.) *Shop.* Yes, **shop.**

• **She got a . . .** (Signal.) *Cat.* Yes, **cat.**

i. (Repeat *h* until firm.)

j. Everybody, touch item 1 below the box. ✔

• This item tells about the story in the box. Everybody, get ready to read item 1 the fast way. First word. ✔

• Get ready. (Tap as the children read *the girl went to a . . .*)

k. Touch the word **ship** on the next line. ✔

• Did the story say the girl went to a ship? (Signal.) *No.*

┌─ **To Correct** ─────────────────────────────┐
│ (Have the children reread the first sentence in the box. Then repeat the question.) │
└──┘

• Touch the word **car.** ✔

• Did the story say the girl went to a car? (Signal.) *No.*

• Touch the word **shop.** ✔

• Did the story say the girl went to a shop? (Signal.) *Yes.*

l. Which word is right? (Signal.) *Shop.* Yes, **shop.** Draw a circle around it. ✔

m. I'll read the sentences in the box. **The girl went to a shop. She got a cat.**

n. Everybody, get ready to read item 2. First word. ✔ (Tap as the children read *she got a . . .*)

o. Touch the word **cat** on the next line. ✔

• Did the story say she got a cat? (Signal.) *Yes.*

• Touch the word **dog.** ✔

• Did the story say she got a dog? (Signal.) *No.*

• Touch the word **car.** ✔

• Did the story say she got a car? (Signal.) *No.*

p. Which word is right? (Signal.) *Cat.* Yes, **cat.**

• So what do you do with **cat?** (Signal.) *Draw a circle around it.* Yes, draw a circle around it.

• Do it. ✔

PAIR RELATIONS

EXERCISE 26

Children draw a line through the incorrect sentences

a. (Point to the sentences below the first picture in the pair-relations exercise on side 2.)

b. One of these sentences tells about the picture. Everybody, touch the first sentence. ✔

c. Reading the fast way.

d. First word. ✔

• Get ready. (Tap for each word as the children read *that man is mean.*)

e. Does that sentence tell about the picture? (Signal.) *No.*

• So do you draw a line through it? (Signal.) *Yes.*

• Do it. ✔

f. Next sentence. First word. ✔

• Get ready. (Tap for each word as the children read *a girl has a sack.*)

g. Does that sentence tell about the picture? (Signal.) *Yes.*

• So do you draw a line through it? (Signal.) *No.*

h. Next sentence. (Repeat *d* and *e* for the remaining sentences.)

i. Everybody, you'll do the rest of the boxes later. Remember—draw a line through the sentences that do not tell about the picture.

EXERCISE 28

Picture comprehension

a. Everybody, look at the picture.

b. (Ask these questions:)
  1. What's happening in the picture? *The children respond.* The old man is riding the horse.
  2. Does the old man look like he's having fun? *Yes.*
  3. Is the horse having fun? *Yes.*
  4. What would you do if you had a real horse? *The children respond.*

WORKSHEET 150

SUMMARY OF INDEPENDENT ACTIVITY
EXERCISE 29

Introduction to independent activity

a. (Pass out sides 1 and 2 of Worksheet 150 to each child.)

b. Everybody, do a good job on your worksheet today and I'll give you a bonus worksheet.

c. (Hold up side 1 of your worksheet.) You're going to do this worksheet on your own. **(Tell the children when they will work the items.)**

• Let's go over some of the things you're going to do.

Reading comprehension

a. (Point to the reading-comprehension exercise on side 2.)

b. Everybody, get ready to read the sentences in the box the fast way.

c. First word. ✔

• Get ready. (Tap for each word as the children read the sentences:) *A girl had a horse. She went riding on a horse.*

d. (Point to items 1 and 2.) These items tell about the story in the box. You're going to read each item and circle the right answer.

Sentence copying

a. (Point to the dotted sentence in the sentence-copying exercise.)

b. You're going to trace the words in this sentence. Then you're going to write the sentence on the other lines.

c. Reading the fast way. First word. ✔

• Get ready. (Tap for each word.)

d. After you finish your worksheet, you get to draw a picture about the sentence, **they went riding.** You'll draw your picture on a piece of plain paper. **(When the children finish their worksheets, give them sheets of plain paper.)**

Other independent activity: sides 1, 2, 3, 4

Remember to do all the parts of the worksheet and to read all the parts carefully. After you draw your picture, I'll give you a bonus worksheet.

INDIVIDUAL CHECKOUT: STORYBOOK
EXERCISE 33

3½-minute individual fluency checkout: rate skill/accuracy—4 errors

a. As you are doing your worksheet, I'll call on children one at a time to read the **whole story.** Remember, you get two stars if you read the story in less than three and a half minutes and make no more than four errors.

b. (Call on a child. Tell the child:) Start with the title and read the story carefully the fast way. Go. (Time the child. Tell the child any words the child misses. Stop the child as soon as the child makes the fifth error or exceeds the time limit.)

c. (If the child meets the rate-accuracy criterion, record two stars on your chart for lesson 150. Congratulate the child. Give children who do not earn two stars a chance to read the story again before the next lesson is presented.)

133 words/**3.5 min** = 38 wpm [**4 errors**]

END OF LESSON 150

Before presenting lesson 151, give Mastery Test 29 to each child. Do not present lesson 151 to any groups that are not firm on this test.

SUMMARY OF INDEPENDENT ACTIVITY
EXERCISE 27

Introduction to independent activity

a. (Hold up side 1 of Worksheet 121.)

b. Everybody, you're going to finish this worksheet on your own. (Tell the children when they will work the remaining items.)

• Let's go over the things you're going to do.

Sentence copying

a. (Point to the dotted sentence in the sentence-copying exercise.)

b. You're going to trace the words in this sentence. Then you're going to write the sentence on the other lines.

c. Reading the fast way. First word. ✔

• Get ready. (Tap.) *The.*

d. Next word. ✔

• Get ready. (Tap.) *Girl.*

e. (Repeat *d* for the remaining words.)

f. After you finish your worksheet, you get to draw a picture about the sentence, **the girl got a cat.** You'll draw your picture on a piece of plain paper.

Cross-out game

(Point to the boxed word in the Cross-out Game.) Everybody, here's the word you're going to cross out today. What word? (Signal.) *Went.* Yes, **went.**

Sound writing

a. (Point to the sound-writing exercise on side 2.) Here are the sounds you're going to write today. I'll touch the sounds. You say them.

b. (Touch each sound.) *The children respond.*

c. (Repeat the series until firm.)

Pair relations

a. (Point to the pair-relations exercise.) Remember—you're going to draw a line through the sentences in each box that do not tell about the picture.

b. (When the children finish their worksheets, give them sheets of plain paper. Remind them to draw a picture that shows **the girl got a cat.**)

END OF LESSON 121

STORY 150
EXERCISE 25

First reading—children read the title and first three sentences

a. (Pass out Storybook.)
b. Open your book to page 159. ✔
c. Everybody, touch the title of the story and get ready to read the words in the title the fast way.
d. First word. ✔
• (Pause two seconds.) Get ready. (Tap.) *The.*
e. (Tap for each remaining word in the title.)
f. (After the children have read the title, ask:) What's this story about? (Signal.) *The old man finds a horse.*
Yes, **the old man finds a horse.**
g. Everybody, get ready to read this story the fast way.
h. First word. ✔
• (Pause two seconds.) Get ready. (Tap.) *An.*
i. (Tap for the remaining words in the first sentence. Pause at least two seconds between taps.)
j. (Repeat *h* and *i* for the next two sentences. Have the children reread the first three sentences until firm.)

EXERCISE 26

Individual children or the group read sentences to complete the first reading

a. I'm going to call on individual children to read a sentence. Everybody, follow along and point to the words. If you hear a mistake, raise your hand.
b. (Call on a child.) Read the next sentence. (Do not tap for the words. Let children read at their own pace, but be sure they read the sentence correctly.)

To Correct
(Have the child sound out the word. Then return to the beginning of the sentence.)

c. (Repeat *b* for most of the remaining sentences in the story. Occasionally have the group read a sentence. When the group is to read, say:) Everybody, read the next sentence. (Pause two seconds.) Get ready. (Tap for each word in the sentence. Pause at least two seconds between taps.)

EXERCISE 27

Second reading—individual children or the group read each sentence; the group answer questions

a. You're going to read the story again. This time I'm going to ask questions.
b. Starting with the first word of the title. ✔
• Get ready. (Tap as the children read the title. Pause at least two seconds between taps.)
c. (Call on a child.) Read the first sentence. *The child responds.*
d. (Repeat *b* and *c* in exercise 26. Present the following comprehension questions to the entire group.)

After the children read:	You say:
The old man finds a horse.	What's this story about? (Signal.) *The old man finds a horse.*
"I can not find a man that will ride on me."	What did he say? (Signal.) *I can not find a man that will ride on me.*
	Where was the old horse? (Signal.) *In a barn.*
"Have you seen a horse that I can ride?"	What did the old man say? (Signal.) *Have you seen a horse that I can ride?*
The old man said, "Old horse, do you like to go for a ride?"	What did he say? (Signal.) *Old horse, do you like to go for a ride?*
	What do you think the horse will say? *The children respond.* Let's read and find out.
The old horse said, "Yes."	Did the horse want to go for a ride? (Signal.) *Yes.*
	Everybody, what's the title of this story? (Signal.) *The old man finds a horse.* And what happened in the story? (Signal.) *The old man found a horse.*

SOUNDS

EXERCISE 1

Teaching **b** as in **bag**

a. (Point to **b**.) My turn. When I touch it, I'll say it. (Pause. Touch **b** for an instant, saying:) b. (Do not say **buuh**.)

b. (Point to **b**.) Your turn. When I touch it, you say it. (Pause.) Get ready. (Touch **b**.) *b.*

c. Again. (Touch **b**.) *b.*

d. (Repeat *c* until firm.)

EXERCISE 2

Sounds firm-up

a. Get ready to say the sounds when I touch them.

b. (Alternate touching **b** and **p**. Point to the sound. Pause one second. Say:) Get ready. (Touch the sound.) *The children respond.*

c. (When **b** and **p** are firm, alternate touching **d, b, t,** and **p** until all four sounds are firm.)

EXERCISE 3

Individual test

(Call on individual children to identify **d, b, t,** or **p**.)

EXERCISE 4

Teacher introduces cross-out game

a. (Use transparency and crayon.)

b. I'll cross out the sounds on this part of the page when you can tell me every sound.

c. Remember—when I touch it, you say it.

d. (Go over the sounds until the children can identify all the sounds in order.)

EXERCISE 5

Individual test

(Call on individual children to identify two or more sounds in exercise 4.)

EXERCISE 6

Teacher crosses out sounds

a. You told me every sound. Get ready to do it again. This time I'll cross out each sound when you tell me what it is.

b. (Point to each sound. Pause. Say:) Get ready. (Touch the sound.) *The children respond.*

• (As you cross out the sound, say:) Goodbye, _____.

EXERCISE 19

Children sound out an irregular word (**your**)

a. (Touch the ball for **your.**) Sound it out.

b. Get ready. (Quickly touch each sound as the children say *yyyoooouuurrr.*)

c. Again. (Repeat *b* until firm.)

d. That's how we <u>sound out</u> the word. Here's how we <u>say</u> the word. **Your.** How do we <u>say</u> the word? (Signal.) *Your.*

e. Now you're going to <u>sound out</u> the word. Get ready. (Touch each sound as the children say *yyyoooouuurrr.*)

f. Now you're going to say the word. Get ready. (Signal.) *Your.*

g. (Repeat *e* and *f* until firm.)

h. Yes, this word is **your. Your** father is a man.

EXERCISE 20

Individual test

(Call on individual children to do *e* and *f* in exercise 19.)

EXERCISE 21

Children identify, then sound out an irregular word (**other**)

a. (Touch the ball for **other.**) Everybody, you're going to read this word the fast way. (Pause three seconds.) Get ready. (Move your finger quickly along the arrow.) *Other.* Yes, **other.**

b. Now you're going to sound out the word. Get ready. (Quickly touch **o, th, er** as the children say *ooothththerrr.*)

c. Again. (Repeat *b.*)

d. How do we say the word? (Signal.) *Other.* Yes, **other.**

e. (Repeat *b* and *d* until firm.)

EXERCISE 22

Individual test

(Call on individual children to do *b* and *d* in exercise 21.)

EXERCISE 23

Children read the words the fast way

(Have the children read the words on this page the fast way.)

EXERCISE 24

Individual test

(Call on individual children to read one word the fast way.)

READING VOCABULARY

EXERCISE 7

Children sound out the word and tell what word

a. (Touch the ball for **pāint.**) Sound it out.
b. Get ready. (Touch **p, ā, n, t** as the children say *pāāānnnt.*)
• (If sounding out is not firm, repeat *b.*)
c. What word? (Signal.) *Paint.* Yes, **paint.**

EXERCISE 8

Children read the fast way

a. Get ready to read these words the fast way.
b. (Touch the ball for **men.** Pause three seconds.) Get ready. (Signal.) *Men.*
c. (Repeat *b* for the remaining words on the page.)

EXERCISE 9

Children read the fast way again

a. Get ready to do these words again. Watch where I point.
b. (Point to a word. Pause one second.) Say: Get ready. (Signal.)
The children respond.
• (Point to the words in this order: **shots, men, up, pāint.**)
c. (Repeat *b* until firm.)

EXERCISE 10

Individual test

(Call on individual children to read one word the fast way.)

pāint

men

shots

up

EXERCISE 15

Children read a word beginning with two consonants (**stand**)

a. (Cover **s**. Run your finger under **tand**.) You're going to sound out this part. Get ready. (Touch **t, a, n, d** as the children say *taaannnd*.)

b. Say it fast. (Signal.) *Tand*. Yes, this part is **tand**.

c. (Uncover **s**. Point to **s**.) You're going to say this first. (Move your finger quickly under **tand**.) Then you're going to say (pause) **tand**.

d. (Point to **s**.) What are you going to say first? (Signal.) *sss*.

• What are you going to say next? (Signal.) *Tand*.

e. (Repeat **d** until firm.)

f. (Touch the ball for **stand**.) Get ready. (Move to **s,** then quickly along the arrow.) *Ssstand*.

g. Say it fast. (Signal.) *Stand*.

• Yes, what word? (Signal.) *Stand*. Yes, **stand**.

• Good reading.

h. Again. (Repeat *f* and *g* until firm.)

i. Now you're going to sound out (pause) **stand**. Get ready. (Touch **s, t, a, n, d** as the children say *ssstaaannnd*.)

• What word? (Signal.) *Stand*. Yes, **stand**.

EXERCISE 16

Children sound out an irregular word (**barn**)

a. (Touch the ball for **barn**.) Sound it out.

b. Get ready. (Quickly touch each sound as the children say *baaarrrnnn*.)

c. Again. (Repeat *b* until firm.)

d. That's how we <u>sound out</u> the word. Here's how we <u>say</u> the word. **Barn.** How do we <u>say</u> the word? (Signal.) *Barn*.

e. Now you're going to <u>sound out</u> the word. Get ready. (Touch each sound as the children say *baaarrrnnn*.)

f. Now you're going to say the word. Get ready. (Signal.) *Barn*.

g. (Repeat *e* and *f* until firm.)

h. Yes, this word is **barn**. The horse is in the **barn**.

EXERCISE 17

Individual test

(Call on individual children to do *e* and *f* in exercise 16.)

EXERCISE 18

Children read the words the fast way

(Have the children read the words on this page the fast way.)

stand

barn

EXERCISE 11

Children read the fast way

a. Get ready to read these words the fast way.
b. (Touch the ball for **lift.** Pause three seconds.) Get ready. (Signal.) *Lift.*
c. (Repeat *b* for the remaining words on the page.)

EXERCISE 12

Children read the fast way again

a. Get ready to do these words again. Watch where I point.
b. (Point to a word. Pause one second. Say:) Get ready. (Signal.)
   The children respond.
• (Point to the words in this order **with, lots, get, lift.**)
c. (Repeat *b* until firm.)

EXERCISE 13

Individual test

(Call on individual children to read one word the fast way.)

lift

lots

with

get

EXERCISE 9

Children identify, then sound out an irregular word (**talked**)

a. (Touch the ball for **talked**.) Everybody, you're going to read this word the fast way. (Pause three seconds.) Get ready. (Move your finger quickly along the arrow.) *Talked.* Yes, **talked.**

b. Now you're going to sound out the word. Get ready. (Quickly touch **t, a, l, k, d** as the children say *taaalllkd.*)

c. Again. (Repeat *b.*)

d. How do we say the word? (Signal.) *Talked.* Yes, **talked.**

e. (Repeat *b* and *d* until firm.)

EXERCISE 10

Individual test

(Call on individual children to do *b* and *d* in exercise 9.)

EXERCISE 11

Children sound out an irregular word (**says**)

a. (Touch the ball for **says**.) Sound it out.

b. Get ready. (Quickly touch each sound as the children say *sssaaayyysss.*)

c. Again. (Repeat *b* until firm.)

d. That's how we <u>sound out</u> the word. Here's how we <u>say</u> the word. **Says.** How do we <u>say</u> the word? (Signal.) *Says.*

e. Now you're going to <u>sound out</u> the word. Get ready. (Touch each sound as the children say *sssaaayyysss.*)

f. Now you're going to say the word. Get ready. (Signal.) *Says.*

g. (Repeat *e* and *f* until firm.)

h. Yes, this word is **says.** If the teacher **says** "Go," hold up a hand.

EXERCISE 12

Individual test

(Call on individual children to do *e* and *f* in exercise 11.)

EXERCISE 13

Children sound out the word and tell what word

a. (Touch the ball for **hōrse**.) Sound it out.

b. Get ready. (Touch **h, ō, r, s** as the children say *hōōōrrrsss.*)

• (If sounding out is not firm, repeat *b.*)

c. What word? (Signal.) *Horse.* Yes, **horse.**

talk͡ed

says

hōrse

EXERCISE 14

Children read the words the fast way

(Have the children read the words on this page the fast way.)

EXERCISE 14

Children identify, then sound out an irregular word (**of**)

a. (Touch the ball for **of.**) Everybody, you're going to read this word the fast way. (Pause three seconds.) Get ready. (Move your finger quickly along the arrow.) *Of.* Yes, **of.**

b. Now you're going to sound out the word. Get ready. (Quickly touch **o, f** as the children say *ooofff.*)

c. Again. (Repeat *b.*)

d. How do we say the word? (Signal.) *Of.* Yes, **of.**

e. (Repeat *b* and *d* until firm.)

EXERCISE 15

Individual test

(Call on individual children to do *b* and *d* in exercise 14.)

EXERCISE 16

Children read the fast way

a. Get ready to read these words the fast way.

b. (Touch the ball for **then.** Pause three seconds.) Get ready. (Signal.) *Then.*

c. (Repeat *b* for the remaining words on the page.)

EXERCISE 17

Children read the fast way again

a. Get ready to do these words again. Watch where I point.

b. (Point to a word. Pause one second. Say:) Get ready. (Signal.) *The children respond.*

• (Point to the words in this order: **hēre, then, of, there.**)

c. (Repeat *b* until firm.)

EXERCISE 18

Individual test

(Call on individual children to read one word the fast way.)

of

then

ther e

hēr e

READING VOCABULARY

EXERCISE 6

Children read the fast way

a. Get ready to read these words the fast way.

b. (Touch the ball for **tēacher.** Pause three seconds.)
Get ready. (Signal.) *Teacher.*

c. (Repeat *b* for the remaining words on the page.)

EXERCISE 7

Children read the fast way again

a. Get ready to do these words again. Watch where I point.

b. (Point to a word. Pause one second. Say:) Get ready. (Signal.)
The children respond.

• (Point to the words in this order: **rīding, get, sēēn, tēacher, got.**)

c. (Repeat *b* until firm.)

EXERCISE 8

Individual test

(Call on individual children to read one word the fast way.)

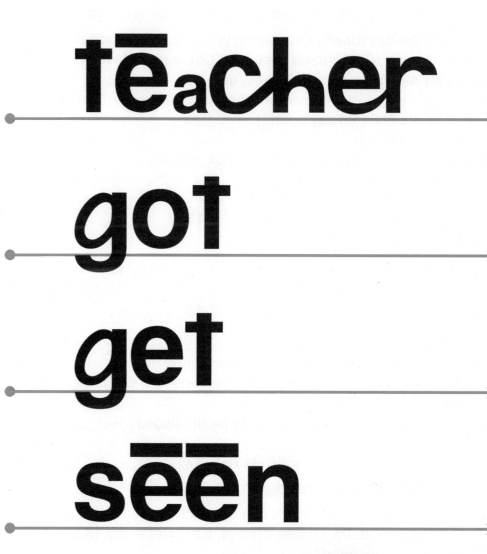

STORYBOOK

STORY 122
EXERCISE 19

First reading—children read the story the fast way

(Have the children reread any sentences containing words that give them trouble. Keep a list of these words.)

a. (Pass out Storybook.)

b. Open your book to page 77. ✔

c. Everybody, touch the title of the story and get ready to read the words in the title the fast way.

d. First word. ✔

• (Pause two seconds.) Get ready. (Tap.) *The.*

e. (Tap for each remaining word in the title.)

f. (After the children have read the title, ask:) What's this story about? (Signal.) *The cow on the road.* Yes, **the cow on the road.**

g. Everybody, get ready to read this story the fast way.

h. First word. ✔

• (Pause two seconds.) Get ready. (Tap.) *Lots.*

i. (Tap for the remaining words in the first sentence. Pause at least two seconds between taps.)

j. (Repeat *h* and *i* for the next two sentences. Have the children reread the first three sentences until firm.)

k. (The children are to read the remainder of the story the fast way, stopping at the end of each sentence.)

l. (After the first reading of the story, print on the board the words that the children missed more than one time. Have the children sound out each word one time and tell what word.)

m. (After the group's responses are firm, call on individual children to read the words.)

EXERCISE 20

Individual test

a. Turn back to page 77. I'm going to call on individual children to read a whole sentence.

b. (Call on individual children to read a sentence. Do not tap for each word.)

EXERCISE 21

Second reading—children read the story the fast way and answer questions

a. You're going to read the story again the fast way and I'll ask questions.

b. Starting with the first word of the title. ✔

• Get ready. (Tap.) *The.*

c. (Tap for each remaining word. Pause at least two seconds between taps. Pause longer before words that gave the children trouble during the first reading.)

d. (Ask the comprehension questions below as the children read.)

After the children read:	You say:
The cow on the road.	What's this story about? (Signal.) *The cow on the road.*
Lots of men went in a little car.	Who went in the little car? (Signal.) *Lots of men.*
The men said, "We will lift this cow."	What did they say? (Signal.) *We will lift this cow.* Do you think they'll lift her? *The children respond.* Let's read and find out.
The men did not lift the cow. "I can lift me."	Did they lift her? (Signal.) *No.* What did the cow say? (Signal.) *I can lift me.*
So the men sat on the road and the cow went home in the car.	What happened? (Signal.) *The men sat on the road and the cow went home in the car.*

EXERCISE 22

Picture comprehension

a. Everybody, look at the picture.

b. (Ask these questions:)

1. Do those men look happy? *No.*
2. Why couldn't they lift the cow? *The children respond.* The cow was too fat.
3. Do you think you could lift the cow? *The children respond.*

SOUNDS

EXERCISE 1

Teaching **ȳ** as in **mȳ**

a. (Point to **ȳ**.) My turn. (Pause. Touch **ȳ** and say:) **ȳȳȳ (īīī).**

b. (Point to **ȳ**.) Your turn. When I touch it, you say it. (Pause.) Get ready. (Touch **ȳ**.) *ȳȳȳ.*

• (Lift your finger.)

c. Again. (Touch **ȳ**.) *ȳȳȳȳ.*

• (Lift your finger.)

d. (Repeat *c* until firm.)

EXERCISE 2

Sounds firm-up

a. Get ready to say the sounds when I touch them.

b. (Alternate touching **ȳ** and **j.** Point to the sound. Pause one second. Say:) Get ready. (Touch the sound.) *The children respond.*

c. (When **ȳ** and **j** are firm, alternate touching **ȳ, j, e,** and **y** until all four sounds are firm.)

EXERCISE 3

Individual test

(Call on individual children to identify **ȳ, j, e,** or **y.**)

EXERCISE 4

Sounds firm-up

a. (Point to **y.**) When I touch the sound, you say it.

b. (Pause.) Get ready. (Touch **ȳ**.) *ȳȳȳ.*

c. Again. (Repeat *b* until firm.)

d. Get ready to say all the sounds when I touch them.

e. (Alternate touching **ȳ, f, ing, ch, v, x, oo,** and **er** three or four times. Point to the sound. Pause one second. Say:) Get ready. (Touch the sound.) *The children respond.*

EXERCISE 5

Individual test

(Call on individual children to identify one or more sounds in exercise 4.)

WORKSHEET 122

READING COMPREHENSION

The children will need pencils.

EXERCISE 23

Children choose the correct words to complete the sentences

a. (Pass out Worksheet 122 to each child.)

b. (Point to the sentences in the box in the reading-comprehension exercise on side 1.)

c. Everybody, touch this box on your worksheet. ✔

d. Get ready to read the words in the box the fast way. First word. ✔

- Get ready. (Tap for each word in the first sentence as the children read *the cow was on the road*.)

- (Pause at least two seconds between taps.)

e. (Have the children reread the sentence until firm.)

f. Get ready to read the next sentence. First word. ✔

- Get ready. (Tap for each word as the children read *the men got mad*.)

g. (Have the children reread the sentence until firm.)

h. Listen. **The cow was on the road.** (Pause.) **The men got mad.** Everybody, get ready to tell me the answers. **The cow was on the . . .** (Signal.) *Road.* Yes, **road. The men got . . .** (Signal.) *Mad.* Yes, **mad.**

i. (Repeat *h* until firm.)

j. Everybody, touch item 1 below the box. ✔

- This item tells about the story in the box. Everybody, get ready to read item 1 the fast way. First word. ✔

- Get ready. (Tap as the children read *the cow was on the . . .*)

k. Touch the word **car** on the next line. ✔

- Did the story say the cow was on the car? (Signal.) *No.*

To Correct
(Have the children reread the first sentence in the box. Then repeat the question.)

- Touch the word **rōad.** ✔
- Did the story say the cow was on the road? (Signal.) *Yes.*
- Touch the word **farm.** ✔
- Did the story say the cow was on the farm? (Signal.) *No.*

l. Which word is right? (Signal.) *Road.* Yes, **road.**

- Draw a circle around it. ✔

m. I'll read the sentences in the box. **The cow was on the road. The men got mad.**

n. Everybody, get ready to read item 2. First word. ✔

- (Tap as the children read *the men got . . .*)

o. Touch the word **sad** on the next line. ✔

- Did the story say the men got sad? (Signal.) *No.*
- Touch the word **māde.** ✔
- Did the story say the men got made? (Signal.) *No.*
- Touch the word **mad.** ✔
- Did the story say the men got mad? (Signal.) *Yes.*

p. Which word is right? (Signal.) *Mad.* Yes, **mad.**

- So what do you do with **mad?** (Signal.) *Draw a circle around it.* Yes, draw a circle around it.

- Do it. ✔

EXERCISE 21

Picture comprehension

a. What do you think you'll see in the picture? *The children respond.*

b. Turn the page and look at the picture.

c. (Ask these questions:)

1. Is that an old car? (Signal.) *Yes.*
2. What are those men doing? *The children respond.*
3. Do you think it would be fun to sit in an old car like that? *The children respond.*

WORKSHEET 149

SUMMARY OF INDEPENDENT ACTIVITY

EXERCISE 22

Introduction to independent activity

a. (Pass out Worksheet 149 to each child.)

b. Everybody, you're going to do this worksheet on your own. **(Tell the children when they will work the items.)**

• Let's go over the things you're going to do.

Story items

a. (Hold up side 1 of your worksheet and point to the story-items exercise.)

b. Everybody, here are items about the story we read today.

c. Think about what happened in the story and circle the right answer for each item.

Picture comprehension

a. (Point to the pictures in the picture-comprehension exercise.) Everybody, you're going to look at the picture. Then you're going to read each item and write the missing word.

b. Remember—the first sound of each missing word is already written in the blank.

Reading comprehension

a. (Point to the reading-comprehension exercise on side 2.)

b. Everybody, get ready to read the sentences in the box the fast way.

c. First word. ✔

• Get ready. (Tap for each word as the children read the sentences *A girl went riding in a car. She went to a farm.*)

d. (Point to items 1 and 2.) These items tell about the story in the box. You're going to read each item and circle the right answer.

Sound writing

a. (Point to the sound-writing exercise.) Here are the sounds you're going to write today. I'll touch the sounds. You say them.

b. (Touch each sound.) *The children respond.*

c. (Repeat the series until firm.)

Sentence copying

a. (Point to the dotted sentence in the sentence-copying exercise.)

b. You're going to trace the words in this sentence. Then you're going to write the sentence on the other lines.

c. Reading the fast way. First word. ✔

• Get ready. (Tap for each word.)

d. After you finish your worksheet, you get to draw a picture about the sentence, **the car did not start.** You'll draw your picture on a piece of plain paper. (When the children finish their worksheets give them sheets of plain paper.)

END OF LESSON 149

SUMMARY OF INDEPENDENT ACTIVITY
EXERCISE 24

Introduction to independent activity

a. (Hold up side 1 of Worksheet 122.)

b. Everybody, you're going to finish this worksheet on your own. (Tell the children when they will work the remaining items.)

• Let's go over the things you're going to do.

Sentence copying

a. (Point to the dotted sentence in the sentence-copying exercise.)

b. You're going to trace the words in this sentence. Then you're going to write the sentence on the other lines.

c. Reading the fast way. First word. ✔

• Get ready. (Tap.) *The.*

d. Next word. ✔

• Get ready. (Tap.) *Cow.*

e. (Repeat *d* for the remaining words.)

f. After you finish your worksheet, you get to draw a picture about the sentence, **the cow sat in a car.** You'll draw your picture on a piece of plain paper.

Cross-out game

(Point to the boxed word in the Cross-out Game.) Everybody, here's the word you're going to cross out today. What word? (Signal.) *Pet.* Yes, **pet.**

Sound writing

a. (Point to the sound-writing exercise on side 2.) Here are the sounds you're going to write today. I'll touch the sounds. You say them.

b. (Touch each sound.) *The children respond.*

c. (Repeat the series until firm.)

Pair relations

a. (Point to the pair-relations exercise.) Remember—you're going to draw a line through the sentences in each box that do not tell about the picture.

b. (When the children finish their worksheets, give them sheets of plain paper. Remind them to draw a picture that shows **the cow sat in a car.**)

END OF LESSON 122

STORY 149
EXERCISE 18

First reading—children read the title and first three sentences

a. (Pass out Storybook.)

b. Open your book to page 156. ✔

c. Everybody, touch the title of the story and get ready to read the words in the title the fast way.

d. First word. ✔

• (Pause two seconds.) Get ready. (Tap.) *Will.*

e. (Tap for each remaining word in the title.)

f. (After the children have read the title, ask:) What's this story about? (Signal.) *Will the old car start?* Yes, **will the old car start.**

g. Everybody, get ready to read this story the fast way.

h. First word. ✔

• (Pause two seconds.) Get ready. (Tap.) *A.*

i. (Tap for the remaining words in the first sentence. Pause at least two seconds between taps.)

j. (Repeat *h* and *i* for the next two sentences. Have the children reread the first three sentences until firm.)

EXERCISE 19

Individual children or the group read sentences to complete the first reading

a. I'm going to call on individual children to read a sentence. Everybody, follow along and point to the words. If you hear a mistake, raise your hand.

b. (Call on a child.) Read the next sentence. (Do not tap for the words. Let children read at their own pace, but be sure they read the sentence correctly.)

To Correct
(Have the child sound out the word. Then return to the beginning of the sentence.)

c. (Repeat *b* for most of the remaining sentences in the story. Occasionally have the group read a sentence. When the group is to read, say:) Everybody, read the next sentence. (Pause two seconds.) Get ready. (Tap for each word in the sentence. Pause at least two seconds between taps.)

EXERCISE 20

Second reading—individual children or the group read each sentence; the group answer questions

a. You're going to read the story again. This time I'm going to ask questions.

b. Starting with the first word of the title. ✔

• Get ready. (Tap as the children read the title. Pause at least two seconds between taps.)

c. (Call on a child.) Read the first sentence. *The child responds.*

d. (Repeat *b* and *c* in exercise 19. Present the following comprehension questions to the entire group.)

After the children read:	You say:
Will the old car start?	What are you going to find out in this story? (Signal.) *Will the old car start?*
The old car did not start.	What was wrong with the old car? (Signal.) *It did not start.*
"Rats do not have cars."	What did the rat say? (Signal.) *Rats do not have cars.* What did the man want the rat to do? (Signal.) *Start his car.*
"I can but I will not."	What did the big man say? (Signal.) *I can but I will not.* What did he say he will not do? (Signal.) *Start the car.*
"I never start cars if I am sitting."	What did the big man say? (Signal.) *I never start cars if I am sitting.*
So the big man got in the car and made the car start.	What happened? (Signal.) *The big man got in the car and made the car start.*
"So I will keep sitting in it."	Where is the big man going to keep sitting? *The children respond.* Yes, in the old car. Why does he want to sit there? *The children respond.* Yes, he likes the old car.

SOUNDS

EXERCISE 1

Teacher introduces cross-out game

a. (Use transparency and crayon.)

b. I'll cross out the sounds on this part of the page when you can tell me every sound.

c. Remember—when I touch it, you say it.

d. (Go over the sounds until the children can identify all the sounds in order.)

EXERCISE 2

Individual test

(Call on individual children to identify two or more sounds in exercise 1.)

b

r

ch

p

d

v

g

h

t

e

n

EXERCISE 3

Teacher crosses out sounds

a. You told me every sound. Get ready to do it again. This time I'll cross out each sound when you tell me what it is.

b. (Point to each sound. Pause. Say:) Get ready. (Touch the sound.) *The children respond.*

• (As you cross out the sound, say:) Goodbye, _____.

EXERCISE 4

Sounds firm-up

a. (Point to **b.**) When I touch the sound, you say it.

b. (Pause.) Get ready. (Touch **b.**) *b.*

c. Again. (Repeat *b* until firm.)

d. Get ready to say all the sounds when I touch them.

e. (Alternate touching **r, ch, b, p, d, v, e,** and **n** three or four times. Point to the sound. Pause one second. Say:) Get ready. (Touch the sound.) *The children respond.*

EXERCISE 5

Individual test

(Call on individual children to identify one or more sounds in exercise 4.)

EXERCISE 12

Children sound out an irregular word (**tart**)

a. (Touch the ball for **tart.**) Sound it out.

b. Get ready. (Quickly touch each sound as the children say *taaarrrt.*)

c. Again. (Repeat *b* until firm.)

d. That's how we <u>sound out</u> the word. Here's how we <u>say</u> the word. **Tart.** How do we <u>say</u> the word? (Signal.) *Tart.*

e. Now you're going to <u>sound out</u> the word. Get ready. (Touch each sound as the children say *taaarrrt.*)

f. Now you're going to say the word. Get ready. (Signal.) *Tart.*

g. (Repeat *e* and *f* until firm.)

h. Yes, this word is **tart.**

EXERCISE 13

Individual test

(Call on individual children to do *e* and *f* in exercise 12.)

EXERCISE 14

Children rhyme with irregular word (**tart**)

a. (Touch the ball for **tart.**) Everybody, you're going to read this word the fast way. Get ready. (Signal.) *Tart.*

b. (Touch the ball for **start.**) This word rhymes with (pause) **tart.** Get ready. (Move to **s,** then quickly along the arrow.) *Start.*

c. (Repeat *a* and *b* until firm.)

EXERCISE 15

Individual test

(Call on individual children to do *a* and *b* in exercise 14.)

EXERCISE 16

Children read the words the fast way

(Have the children read the words on this page the fast way.)

EXERCISE 17

Individual test

(Call on individual children to read one word the fast way.)

tart

start

READING VOCABULARY
EXERCISE 6

Children read the fast way

a. Get ready to read these words the fast way.

b. (Touch the ball for **there.** Pause three seconds.) Get ready. (Signal.) *There.*

c. (Repeat *b* for the remaining words on the page.)

EXERCISE 7

Children read the fast way again

a. Get ready to do these words again. Watch where I point.

b. (Point to a word. Pause one second. Say:) Get ready. (Signal.) *The children respond.*

• (Point to the words in this order: **then, there, this, the.**)

c. (Repeat *b* until firm.)

EXERCISE 8

Individual test

(Call on individual children to read one word the fast way.)

there

then

the

this

EXERCISE 10

Children read **bring** and **bringing**

a. (Cover **b**. Point to **ring**.) You're going to read this part of the word the fast way. (Pause three seconds.) Get ready. (Signal.) *Ring.* Yes, **ring**.

b. (Uncover **b**. Point to **b**.) You're going to say this first. (Move your finger quickly under **ring**.) Then you're going to say (pause) **ring**.

c. (Point to **b**.) What are you going to say first? (Signal.) *b.*
- What are you going to say next? (Signal.) *Ring.*

d. (Repeat *c* until firm.)

e. (Touch the ball for **bring**.) Get ready. (Move to **b**, then quickly along the arrow.) *Bring.*

f. Say it fast. (Signal.) *Bring.*
- Yes, what word? (Signal.) *Bring.* Yes, **bring**.
- Good reading.

g. Again. (Repeat *e* and *f* until firm.)

h. (Return to the ball for **bring**.) Yes, this word is **bring**.

i. (Touch the ball for **bringing**.) So this must be **bring** . . . (Touch **ing**.) *Ing.*
- What word? (Signal.) *Bringing.* Yes, **bringing**.

j. Again. (Repeat *h* and *i* until firm.)

k. (Touch the ball for **bring**.) This word is **bring**. (Touch the ball for **bringing**.) So this must be . . . (Quickly run your finger under **bring** and tap **ing**.) *Bringing.* Yes, **bringing**.

l. Again. (Repeat *k* until firm.)

m. Now you're going to sound out (pause) **bringing**. Get ready. (Touch **b, r, ing, ing** as the children say *brrriiingiiing*.)
- Yes, what word? (Signal.) *Bringing.* Yes, **bringing**.

EXERCISE 11

Children read **tēach** and **tēacher**

a. (Touch the ball for **tēach**.) You're going to read this word the fast way. (Pause three seconds.) Get ready. (Move your finger quickly along the arrow.) *Teach.*

b. (Return to the ball for **tēach**.) Yes, this word is **teach**.

c. (Touch the ball for **tēacher**.) So this must be **teach** . . . (Touch **er**.) *Er.*
- What word? (Signal.) *Teacher.* Yes, **teacher**.

d. Again. (Repeat *b* and *c* until firm.)

e. (Touch the ball for **tēach**.) This word is **teach**.

f. (Touch the ball for **tēacher**.) So this must be . . . (Quickly run your finger under **tēach** and tap **er**.) *Teacher.* Yes, **teacher**.

g. Again. (Repeat *e* and *f* until firm.)

h. Now you're going to sound out (pause) **teacher**. Get ready. (Touch **t, ē, ch, er** as the children say *tēēēcherrr*.)
- Yes, what word? (Signal.) *Teacher.* Yes, **teacher**.

bring

bringing

tēach

tēacher

EXERCISE 9

Children sound out the word and tell what word

a. (Touch the ball for **chicks.**) Sound it out.

b. Get ready. (Touch **ch, i, c, s** as the children say *chiiicsss.*)

• (If sounding out is not firm, repeat *b*.)

c. What word? (Signal.) *Chicks.* Yes, **chicks.**

EXERCISE 10

Children read the fast way

a. Get ready to read these words the fast way.

b. (Touch the ball for **pet.** Pause three seconds.) Get ready. (Signal.) *Pet.*

c. (Repeat *b* for the remaining words on the page.)

EXERCISE 11

Children read the fast way again

a. Get ready to do these words again. Watch where I point.

b. (Point to a word. Pause one second. Say:) Get ready. (Signal.)
The children respond.

• (Point to the words in this order: **pāint, pet, sent, pig.**)

c. (Repeat *b* until firm.)

EXERCISE 12

Individual test

(Call on individual children to read one word on the page the fast way.)

chicks

pet

sent

pig

pāint

READING VOCABULARY

EXERCISE 5

Children sound out an irregular word (**says**)

a. (Touch the ball for **says.**) Sound it out.

b. Get ready. (Quickly touch each sound as the children say *sssaaayyysss.*)

> **To Correct**
> If the children do not say the sounds you touch
> 1. (Say:) You've got to say the sounds I touch.
> 2. (Repeat *a* and *b* until firm.)

c. Again. (Repeat *b* until firm.)

d. That's how we <u>sound out</u> the word. Here's how we <u>say</u> the word. **Says.** How do we <u>say</u> the word? (Signal.) *Says.*

e. Now you're going to <u>sound out</u> the word. Get ready. (Touch each sound as the children say *sssaaayyysss.*)

f. Now you're going to say the word. Get ready. (Signal.) *Says.*

g. (Repeat *e* and *f* until firm.)

h. Yes, this word is **says.** When the teacher **says** "Go," stand up.

EXERCISE 6

Individual test

(Call on individual children to do *e* and *f* in exercise 5.)

EXERCISE 7

Children read the fast way

a. Get ready to read these words the fast way.

b. (Touch the ball for **fill.** Pause three seconds.) Get ready. (Signal.) *Fill.*

c. (Repeat *b* for the remaining words on the page.)

EXERCISE 8

Children read the fast way again

a. Get ready to do these words again. Watch where I point.

b. (Point to a word. Pause one second. Say:) Get ready. (Signal.) *The children respond.* (Point to the words in this order: **jump, fill, never, stop.**)

c. (Repeat *b* until firm.)

says

fill

stop

never

jump

EXERCISE 9

Individual test

(Call on individual children to read one word on the page the fast way.)

EXERCISE 13

Children sound out an irregular word (**park**)

a. (Touch the ball for **park.**) Sound it out.

b. Get ready. (Quickly touch each sound as the children say *paaarrrk.*)

c. Again. (Repeat *b* until firm.)

d. That's how we <u>sound out</u> the word. Here's how we <u>say</u> the word. **Park.** How do we <u>say</u> the word? (Signal.) *Park.*

e. Now you're going to <u>sound out</u> the word. Get ready. (Touch each sound as the children say *paaarrrk.*)

f. Now you're going to say the word. Get ready. (Signal.) *Park.*

g. (Repeat *e* and *f* until firm.)

h. Yes, this word is **park.** There are swings in that **park.**

i. (Call on individual children to do *e* and *f.*)

EXERCISE 14

Children sound out the word and tell what word

a. (Touch the ball for **bug.**) Sound it out.

b. Get ready. (Touch **b, u, g** as the children say *buuug.*)

• (If sounding out is not firm, repeat *b.*)

c. What word? (Signal.) *Bug.* Yes, **bug.**

EXERCISE 15

Children sound out the word and tell what word

(Repeat the procedures in exercise 14 for **duck.**)

EXERCISE 16

Children sound out an irregular word (**girl**)

a. (Touch the ball for **girl.**) Sound it out.

b. Get ready. (Quickly touch each sound as the children say *giiirrrlll.*)

c. Again. (Repeat *b* until firm.)

d. That's how we <u>sound out</u> the word. Here's how we <u>say</u> the word. **Girl.** How do we <u>say</u> the word? (Signal.) *Girl.*

e. Now you're going to <u>sound out</u> the word. Get ready. (Touch each sound as the children say *giiirrrlll.*)

f. Now you're going to say the word. Get ready. (Signal.) *Girl.*

g. (Repeat *e* and *f* until firm.)

h. Yes, this word is **girl.** The little **girl** has black hair.

i. (Call on individual children to do *e* and *f.*)

park

bug

duck

girl

EXERCISE 17

Children read the words the fast way

(Have children read the words on this page the fast way.)

SOUNDS

EXERCISE 1

Teacher firms up **y** as in **yes**

a. (Point to **y**.) Everybody, get ready to tell me this sound. Get ready. (Touch y.) *yyy.*

b. (Point to **ȳ**.) Everybody, look at the line over this sound. This is not **yyy.** Is it **yyy?** (Signal.) *No.*

c. (Point to each sound and ask:) Is this **yyy?**
The children respond.

d. (Repeat c until firm.)

EXERCISE 2

Teaching **ȳ** as in **mȳ;** children discriminate **y—ȳ**

a. (Point to the first **ȳ**.) Everybody, this is **ȳȳȳ (īīī).**

b. When I touch it, you say it. (Pause.) Get ready. (Touch ȳ.) *ȳȳȳ.*

c. Again. (Touch ȳ.) *ȳȳȳ.*

d. (Repeat c until firm.)

e. Get ready to do all these sounds. When I touch the sound, you say it. (Alternate touching the sounds. Before touching each **ȳ,** trace the line and say:) Remember— this is not **yyy.**

f. (Repeat e until all the sounds are firm.)

EXERCISE 3

Sounds firm-up

a. (Point to **ȳ**.) When I touch the sound, you say it.

b. (Pause.) Get ready. (Touch **ȳ**.) *ȳȳȳ.*

c. Again. (Repeat b until firm.)

d. Get ready to say all the sounds when I touch them.

e. (Alternate touching **ȳ, y, ī,** and **I** three or four times. Point to the sound. Pause one second. Say:) Get ready. (Touch the sound.) *The children respond.*

EXERCISE 4

Individual test

(Call on individual children to identify one or more sounds in exercise 3.)

STORYBOOK

STORY 123
EXERCISE 18

First reading—children read the story the fast way

(Have the children reread any sentences containing words that give them trouble. Keep a list of these words.)

a. (Pass out Storybook.)

b. Open your book to page 80. ✔

c. Everybody, touch the title of the story and get ready to read the words in the title the fast way.

d. First word. ✔

• (Pause two seconds.) Get ready. (Tap.) *A.*

e. (Tap for each remaining word in the title.)

f. (After the children have read the title, ask:) What's this story about? (Signal.) *A girl and a goat.* Yes, **a girl and a goat.**

g. Everybody, get ready to read this story the fast way.

h. First word. ✔

• (Pause two seconds.) Get ready. (Tap.) *A.*

i. (Tap for the remaining words in the first sentence. Pause at least two seconds between taps.)

j. (Repeat *h* and *i* for the next two sentences. Have the children reread the first three sentences until firm.)

k. (The children are to read the remainder of the story the fast way, stopping at the end of each sentence.)

l. (After the first reading of the story, print on the board the words that the children missed more than one time. Have the children sound out each word one time and tell what word.)

m. (After the group's responses are firm, call on individual children to read the words.)

EXERCISE 19

Individual test

a. Look at page 80. I'm going to call on individual children to read a whole sentence.

b. (Call on individual children to read a sentence. Do not tap for each word.)

EXERCISE 20

Second reading—children read the story the fast way and answer questions

a. You're going to read the story again the fast way and I'll ask questions.

b. Starting with the first word of the title. ✔

• Get ready. (Tap.) *A.*

c. (Tap for each remaining word. Pause at least two seconds between taps. Pause longer before words that gave the children trouble during the first reading.)

d. (Ask the comprehension questions below as the children read.)

After the children read:	You say:
A girl and a goat.	What's this story about? (Signal.) *A girl and a goat.*
She met a goat.	Who did she meet? (Signal.) *A goat.* Where was she going? (Signal.) *To a farm.*
"We will pet a pig."	What did she say? (Signal.) *We will pet a pig.*
"I do not pet pigs."	What did the goat say? (Signal.) *I do not pet pigs.*
"I will go to the park and pet a duck."	What did the goat say? (Signal.) *I will go to the park and pet a duck.* Is the goat going to the farm? (Signal.) *No.* Where's the goat going? (Signal.) *To the park.*
And the girl went to the farm to pet a pig.	What did the goat do? (Signal.) *The goat went to the park to pet a duck.* What did the girl do? (Signal.) *She went to the farm to pet a pig.*

EXERCISE 20

Picture comprehension

a. Everybody, look at the picture.

b. (Ask these questions:)

1. What's happening in the picture? *The children respond.* The girl is jumping into the pool.
2. Does that look like fun to you? *The children respond.*
3. What would you do if you had your own swimming pool? *The children respond.*

WORKSHEET 148

SUMMARY OF INDEPENDENT ACTIVITY
EXERCISE 21

Introduction to independent activity

a. (Pass out Worksheet 148 to each child.)

b. Everybody, you're going to do this worksheet on your own. (Tell the children when they will work the items.)

- Let's go over the things you're going to do.

Story items

a. (Hold up side 1 of your worksheet and point to the story-items exercise.)

b. Everybody, here are items about the story we read today.

c. Think about what happened in the story and circle the right answer for each item.

Picture comprehension

a. (Point to the pictures in the picture-comprehension exercise.) Everybody, you're going to look at the picture. Then you're going to read each item and write the missing word.

b. Remember—the first sound of each missing word is already written in the blank.

Reading comprehension

a. (Point to the reading-comprehension exercise on side 2.)

b. Everybody, get ready to read the sentences in the box the fast way.

c. First word. ✔

- Get ready. (Tap for each word as the children read the sentences *The man had a pet cow. He talked to the cow.*)

d. (Point to items 1 and 2.) These items tell about the story in the box. You're going to read each item and circle the right answer.

Sound writing

a. (Point to the sound-writing exercise.) Here are the sounds you're going to write today. I'll touch the sounds. You say them.

b. (Touch each sound.) *The children respond.*

c. (Repeat the series until firm.)

Sentence copying

a. (Point to the dotted sentence in the sentence-copying exercise.)

b. You're going to trace the words in this sentence. Then you're going to write the sentence on the other lines.

c. Reading the fast way. First word. ✔

- Get ready. (Tap for each word.)

d. After you finish your worksheet, you get to draw a picture about the sentence, **she went to the moon.** You'll draw your picture on a piece of plain paper. (When the children finish their worksheets, give them sheets of plain paper.)

END OF LESSON 148

EXERCISE 21

Picture comprehension

a. What do you think you'll see in the picture? *The children respond.*
b. Turn the page and look at the picture.
c. (Ask these questions:)
    1. Where is the girl? *The children respond.* On a farm.
    2. What is she doing? *The children respond.* Petting a pig.
    3. Did you ever pet a pig? *The children respond.*

WORKSHEET 123

READING COMPREHENSION

The children will need pencils.

EXERCISE 22

Children choose the correct words to complete the sentences

a. (Pass out Worksheet 123 to each child.)
b. (Point to the sentences in the box in the reading-comprehension exercise on side 1.)
c. Everybody, touch this box on your worksheet. ✔
d. Get ready to read the words in the box the fast way. First word. ✔
• Get ready. (Tap for each word in the first sentence as the children read *the goat went to the park*.)
• (Pause at least two seconds between taps.)
e. (Have the children reread the sentence until firm.)
f. Get ready to read the next sentence. First word. ✔
• Get ready. (Tap for each word as the children read *the girl went to the farm*.)
g. (Have the children reread the sentence until firm.)
h. Listen. **The goat went to the park.** (Pause.) **The girl went to the farm.** Everybody, get ready to tell me the answers. **The goat went . . .** (Signal.) *To the park.* Yes, **to the park.**
• **The girl went to the . . .** (Signal.) *Farm.* Yes, **farm.**
i. (Repeat *h* until firm.)
j. Everybody, touch item 1 below the box. ✔
• This item tells about the story in the box. Everybody, get ready to read item 1 the fast way. First word. ✔
• Get ready. (Tap as the children read *the goat went . . .*)
k. Touch the words **in a car** on the next line. ✔
• Did the story say the goat went in a car? (Signal.) *No.*

┌─ **To Correct** ─────────────────────────────┐
(Have the children reread the first sentence in the box. Then repeat the question.)
└──┘

• Touch the words **in the rain.** ✔
• Did the story say the goat went in the rain? (Signal.) *No.*
• Touch the words **to the park.** ✔
• Did the story say the goat went to the park? (Signal.) *Yes.*
l. What words are right? (Signal.) *To the park.* Yes, **to the park.**
• Draw a circle around them. ✔
m. I'll read the sentences in the box. **The goat went to the park. The girl went to the farm.**
n. Everybody, get ready to read item 2. First word. ✔
• (Tap as the children read *the girl went to the . . .*)
o. Touch the word **car** on the next line. ✔
• Did the story say the girl went to the car? (Signal.) *No.*
• Touch the word **farm.** ✔
• Did the story say the girl went to the farm? (Signal.) *Yes.*
• Touch the word **park.** ✔
• Did the story say the girl went to the park? (Signal.) *No.*
p. Which word is right? (Signal.) *Farm.* Yes, **farm.**
• So what do you do with **farm?** (Signal.) *Draw a circle around it.* Yes, draw a circle around it.
• Do it. ✔

STORYBOOK

STORY 148

EXERCISE 17

First reading—children read the title and first three sentences

a. (Pass out Storybook.)

b. Open your book to page 153. ✔

c. Everybody, touch the title of the story and get ready to read the words in the title the fast way.

d. First word. ✔

• (Pause two seconds.) Get ready. (Tap.) *Finding.*

e. (Tap for each remaining word in the title.)

f. (After the children have read the title, ask:) What's this story about? (Signal.) *Finding some fun on the moon.*
Yes, **finding some fun on the moon.**

g. Everybody, get ready to read this story the fast way.

h. First word. ✔

• (Pause two seconds.) Get ready. (Tap.) *Some.*

i. (Tap for the remaining words in the first sentence. Pause at least two seconds between taps.)

j. (Repeat *h* and *i* for the next two sentences. Have the children reread the first three sentences until firm.)

EXERCISE 18

Individual children or the group read sentences to complete the first reading

a. I'm going to call on individual children to read a sentence. Everybody, follow along and point to the words. If you hear a mistake, raise your hand.

b. (Call on a child.) Read the next sentence. (Do not tap for the words. Let children read at their own pace, but be sure they read the sentence correctly.)

To Correct
(Have the child sound out the word. Then return to the beginning of the sentence.)

c. (Repeat *b* for most of the remaining sentences in the story. Occasionally have the group read a sentence. When the group is to read, say:) Everybody, read the next sentence. (Pause two seconds.) Get ready. (Tap for each word in the sentence. Pause at least two seconds between taps.)

EXERCISE 19

Second reading—individual children or the group read each sentence; the group answer questions

a. You're going to read the story again. This time I'm going to ask questions.

b. Starting with the first word of the title. ✔

• Get ready. (Tap as the children read the title. Pause at least two seconds between taps.)

c. (Call on a child.) Read the first sentence. *The child responds.*

d. (Repeat *b* and *c* in exercise 18. Present the following comprehension questions to the entire group.)

After the children read:	You say:
Finding some fun on the moon.	What's this story about? (Signal.) *Finding some fun on the moon.*
A girl said, "I will find some fun."	What did she say? (Signal.) *I will find some fun.* Where was she? (Signal.) *On the moon.* How did the girls get to the moon? (Signal.) *In a moon ship.*
"Come with me."	What did the cow say? (Signal.) *We have lots of fun. Come with me.* I wonder what kind of fun they have. Let's read and find out.
She jumped into the pool.	What did the cow do? (Signal.) *She jumped into the pool.* How do they have fun on the moon? (Signal.) *Jumping into the pool.*
The girl did not tell the other girls that she went swimming with a moon cow.	I wonder why she didn't tell the other girls about the pool. *The children respond.*

SUMMARY OF INDEPENDENT ACTIVITY
EXERCISE 23

Introduction to independent activity

a. (Hold up side 1 of Worksheet 123.)

b. Everybody, you're going to finish this worksheet on your own. (Tell the children when they will work the remaining items.)

• Let's go over the things you're going to do.

Sentence copying

a. (Point to the dotted sentence in the sentence-copying exercise.)

b. You're going to trace the words in this sentence. Then you're going to write the sentence on the other lines.

c. Reading the fast way. First word. ✔

• Get ready. (Tap.) *It.*

d. Next word. ✔

• Get ready. (Tap.) *Is.*

e. (Repeat *d* for the remaining words.)

f. After you finish your worksheet, you get to draw a picture about the sentence, **it is fun to pet pigs.** You'll draw your picture on a piece of plain paper.

Cross-out game

(Point to the boxed word in the Cross-out Game.) Everybody, here's the word you're going to cross out today. What word? (Signal.) *Roads.* Yes, **roads.**

Sound writing

a. (Point to the sound-writing exercise on side 2.) Here are the sounds you're going to write today. I'll touch the sounds. You say them.

b. (Touch each sound.) *The children respond.*

c. (Repeat the series until firm.)

Pair relations

a. (Point to the pair-relations exercise.) Remember—you're going to draw a line through the sentences in each box that do not tell about the picture.

b. (When the children finish their worksheets, give them sheets of plain paper. Remind them to draw a picture that shows **it is fun to pet pigs.**)

END OF LESSON 123

EXERCISE 12

Children sound out an irregular word (**some**)

a. (Touch the ball for **some.**) Sound it out.

b. Get ready. (Quickly touch each sound as the children say *sssooommmeee.*)

> **To Correct**
> If the children do not say the sounds you touch
> 1. (Say:) You've got to say the sounds I touch.
> 2. (Repeat *a* and *b* until firm.)

c. Again. (Repeat *b* until firm.)

d. That's how we <u>sound out</u> the word. Here's how we <u>say</u> the word. **Some.** How do we <u>say</u> the word? (Signal.) *Some.*

e. Now you're going to <u>sound out</u> the word. Get ready. (Touch each sound as the children say *sssooommmeee.*)

f. Now you're going to say the word. Get ready. (Signal.) *Some.*

g. (Repeat *e* and *f* until firm.)

h. Yes, this word is **some.** Would you like to eat **some** cake?

EXERCISE 13

Individual test

(Call on individual children to do *e* and *f* in exercise 12.)

EXERCISE 14

Children sound out the word and tell what word

a. (Touch the ball for **jumped.**) Sound it out.

b. Get ready. (Touch **j, u, m, p, d** as the children say *juuummmpd.*)

• (If sounding out is not firm, repeat *b.*)

c. What word? (Signal.) *Jumped.* Yes, **jumped.**

EXERCISE 15

Children read the words the fast way

a. Now you get to read the words on this page the fast way.

b. (Touch the ball for **some.** Pause three seconds.) Get ready. (Move your finger quickly along the arrow.) *Some.*

c. (Repeat *b* for **jumped.**)

EXERCISE 16

Individual test

(Call on individual children to read one word the fast way.)

SOUNDS

EXERCISE 1

Teaching **ing** as in **sing**

a. (Point to **ing**.) Here's a new sound.

b. My turn. (Pause. Touch **ing** and say:) iiing.

c. Again. (Touch **ing** for a longer time.) iiiiing. (Lift your finger.)

d. (Point to **ing**.) Your turn. When I touch it, you say it. (Pause.) Get ready. (Touch **ing**.) *iiing.* (Lift your finger.)

e. Again. (Touch **ing**.) *iiiiiing.* (Lift your finger.)

f. (Repeat *e* until firm.)

EXERCISE 2

Individual test

(Call on individual children to identify **ing**.)

EXERCISE 3

Sounds firm-up

a. Get ready to say the sounds when I touch them.

b. (Alternate touching **n** and **ing**. Point to the sound. Pause one second. Say:) Get ready. (Touch the sound.) *The children respond.*

c. (When **n** and **ing** are firm, alternate touching **ing, g, n,** and **i** until all four sounds are firm.)

EXERCISE 4

Individual test

(Call on individual children to identify **ing, g, n,** or **i.**)

EXERCISE 5

Sounds firm-up

a. (Point to **ing**.) When I touch the sound, you say it.

b. (Pause.) Get ready. (Touch **ing**.) *ing.*

c. Again. (Repeat *b* until firm.)

d. Get ready to say all the sounds when I touch them.

e. (Alternate touching **l, u, ch, b, e, h, p,** and **ing** three or four times. Point to the sound. Pause one second. Say:) Get ready. (Touch the sound.) *The children respond.*

EXERCISE 6

Individual test

(Call on individual children to identify one or more sounds in exercise 5.)

EXERCISE 8

Children rhyme with **moon**

a. (Touch the ball for **moon.**) You're going to read this word
the fast way. (Pause three seconds.) Get ready.
(Move your finger quickly along the arrow.) *Moon.*
b. (Touch the ball for **soon.**) This word rhymes with (pause) **moon.**
(Move to **s,** then quickly along the arrow.) *Soon.*
• Yes, what word? (Signal.) *Soon.*

EXERCISE 9

Children read a word beginning with two consonants (**broke**)

a. (Cover **b.** Run your finger under **rōke.**) You're going to sound out
this part. Get ready. (Touch **r, ō, k** as the children say *rrrōōōk.*)
b. Say it fast. (Signal.) *Roke.* Yes, this part is **rōke.**
c. (Uncover **b.** Point to **b.**) You're going to say this first. (Move your
finger quickly under **rōke.**) Then you're going to say (pause) **rōke.**
d. (Point to **b.**) What are you going to say first? (Signal.) *b.*
• What are you going to say next? (Signal.) *Roke.*
e. (Repeat *d* until firm.)
f. (Touch the ball for **brōke.**) Get ready. (Move to **b,** then quickly along
the arrow.) *Broke.*
g. Say it fast. (Signal.) *Broke.*
• Yes, what word? (Signal.) *Broke.* Yes, **broke.**
• Good reading.
h. Again. (Repeat *f* and *g* until firm.)
i. Now you're going to sound out (pause) **broke.** Get ready.
(Touch **b, r, ō, k** as the children say *brrrōōōk.*)
• What word? (Signal.) *Broke.* Yes, **broke.**

EXERCISE 10

Children read the words the fast way

(Have the children read the words on this page the fast way.)

EXERCISE 11

Individual test

(Call on individual children to read one word the fast way.)

moon

soon

brōke

READING VOCABULARY

EXERCISE 7

Children read the fast way

a. Get ready to read these words the fast way.

b. (Touch the ball for **bug**. Pause three seconds.) Get ready. (Signal.) *Bug.*

c. (Repeat *b* for the remaining words on the page.)

EXERCISE 8

Children read the fast way again

a. Get ready to do these words again. Watch where I point.

b. (Point to a word. Pause one second. Say:) Get ready. (Signal.) *The children respond.*

• (Point to the words in this order: **nōse, gō, gōing, his, bug.**)

c. (Repeat *b* until firm.)

EXERCISE 9

Individual test

(Call on individual children to read one word the fast way.)

bug

his

gō

gōing

nōse

READING VOCABULARY

EXERCISE 4

Children read a word beginning with two consonants (**swimming**)

a. (Cover **s.** Run your finger under **wimming.**) You're going to sound out this part. Get ready. (Touch **w, i,** between the **m's, ing** as the children say *wwwiiimmmiiing.*)

b. Say it fast. (Signal.) *Wimming.* Yes, this part is **wimming.**

c. (Uncover **s.** Point to **s.**) You're going to say this first. (Move your finger quickly under **wimming.**) Then you're going to say (pause) **wimming.**

d. (Point to **s.**) What are you going to say first? (Signal.) *sss.*

• What are you going to say next? (Signal.) *Wimming.*

e. (Repeat *d* until firm.)

f. (Touch the ball for **swimming.**) Get ready. (Move to **s,** then quickly along the arrow.) *Ssswimming.*

g. Say it fast. (Signal.) *Swimming.*

• Yes, what word? (Signal.) *Swimming.* Yes, **swimming.**

• Good reading.

h. Again. (Repeat *f* and *g* until firm.)

i. Now you're going to sound out (pause) **swimming.** Get ready. (Touch **s, w, i,** between the **m's, ing** as the children say *ssswwwiiimmmiiing.*)

• What word? (Signal.) *Swimming.* Yes, **swimming.**

EXERCISE 5

Children read the fast way

a. Get ready to read these words the fast way.

b. (Touch the ball for **jumps.** Pause three seconds.) Get ready. (Signal.) *Jumps.*

c. (Repeat *b* for the remaining words on the page.)

EXERCISE 6

Children read the fast way again

a. Get ready to do these words again. Watch where I point.

b. (Point to a word. Pause one second. Say:) Get ready. (Signal.) *The children respond.* (Point to the words in this order: **jumps, pool, men.**)

c. (Repeat *b* until firm.)

swimming

jumps

men

pool

EXERCISE 7

Individual test

(Call on individual children to read one word on the page the fast way.)

EXERCISE 10

Children identify, then sound out an irregular word (**of**)

a. (Touch the ball for **of.**) Everybody, you're going to read this word the fast way. (Pause three seconds.) Get ready. (Move your finger quickly along the arrow.) *Of.* Yes, **of.**

b. Now you're going to sound out the word. Get ready. (Quickly touch **o, f** as the children say *ooofff.*)

c. Again. (Repeat *b.*)

d. How do we say the word? (Signal.) *Of.* Yes, **of.**

e. (Repeat *b* and *d* until firm.)

EXERCISE 11

Individual test

(Call on individual children to do *b* and *d* in exercise 10.)

EXERCISE 12

Children read the fast way

a. Get ready to read these words the fast way.

b. (Touch the ball for **pāint.** Pause three seconds.) Get ready. (Signal.) *Paint.*

c. (Repeat *b* for **get.**)

EXERCISE 13

Children read the fast way again

a. Get ready to do these words again. Watch where I point.

b. (Point to a word. Pause one second. Say:) Get ready. (Signal.) *The children respond.*

• (Point to the words in this order: **get, of, pāint.**)

c. (Repeat *b* until firm.)

EXERCISE 14

Individual test

(Call on individual children to read one word the fast way.)

SOUNDS

EXERCISE 1

Teacher and children play the sounds game

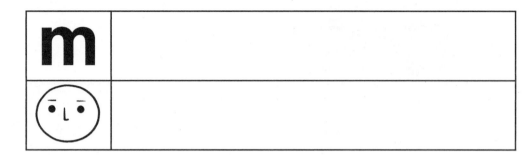

a. (Use transparency and crayon. Write the sounds in the symbol box. Keep score in the score box.)

b. I'm smart. I think I can beat you in a game.

c. Here's the rule. When I touch a sound, you say it.

d. (Play the game. Make one symbol at a time in the symbol box. Use the symbols ī, ing, b, and j.) (Make each symbol quickly. Pause. Touch the symbol. Play the game for about two minutes.) (Then ask:) Who won? (Draw a mouth on the face in the score box.)

EXERCISE 2

Child plays teacher

a. (Use transparency and crayon.)

b. [Child's name] is going to be the teacher.

c. [Child] is going to touch the sounds. When [child] touches a sound, you say it.

d. (The child points to and touches the sounds.) *The children respond.* (You circle any sound that is not firm.)

e. (After the child has completed the page, present all the circled sounds to the children.)

EXERCISE 3

Individual test

(Call on individual children.) If you can say the sound when I call your name, you may cross it out.

EXERCISE 15

Children read **kiss** and **kissed**

a. (Touch the ball for **kiss.**) You're going to read this word the fast way. (Pause three seconds.) Get ready. (Move your finger quickly along the arrow.) *Kiss.*

b. (Return to the ball for **kiss.**) Yes, this word is **kiss.**

c. (Touch the ball for **kissed.**) So this must be **kiss** . . . (Touch **d.**) *d.*

• What word? (Signal.) *Kissed.* Yes, **kissed.**

d. Again. (Repeat *b* and *c* until firm.)

e. (Touch the ball for **kiss.**) This word is **kiss.**

f. (Touch the ball for **kissed.**) So this must be . . . (Quickly run your finger under **kiss** and tap **d.**) *Kissed.* Yes, **kissed.**

g. Again. (Repeat *e* and *f* until firm.)

h. Now you're going to sound out (pause) **kissed.** Get ready. (Touch **k, i,** between the **s**'s, **d** as the children say *kiiisssd.*)

• Yes, what word? (Signal.) *Kissed.* Yes, **kissed.**

kiss

kissed

EXERCISE 24

Picture comprehension

a. What do you think you'll see in the picture? *The children respond.*

b. Turn the page and look at the picture.

c. (Ask these questions:)

1. Why does Ann look so surprised? *The children respond.* Because the cat is talking.

2. What's the cat saying? *The children respond.* Yes, **I will not go with you.**

• I think it would be a lot of fun to have a talking cat.

WORKSHEET 147

STORY ITEMS

The children will need pencils.

EXERCISE 25

Children complete sentences and answer story questions

a. (Pass out Worksheet 147 to each child.)

b. (Point to the story-items exercise on side 1.) These items are about the story you just read.

c. (Point to the blank in item 1.) Something is missing. When you get to this blank, say **"Blank."** What will you say? (Signal.) *Blank.*

d. Everybody, get ready to read item 1. Get ready. (Tap for each word as the children read *the girl said, "cats can not blank."*)

• (Repeat until firm.)

e. What goes in the blank? (Signal.) *Talk.* Yes, **talk.**

f. Everybody, read item 2 and when you come to a blank, say **"Blank."** Get ready. (Tap for each word as the children read *ann said, "can I have that blank?"*)

• (Repeat until firm.)

g. What goes in the blank? (Signal.) *Cat.* Yes, **cat.**

h. Everybody, read item 3 and when you come to a blank, say **"Blank."** Get ready. (Tap for each word as the children read *the blank said, "I will not go with you."*)

• (Repeat until firm.)

i. What goes in the blank? (Signal.) *Cat.* Yes, **cat.**

j. Everybody, read item 4 and when you come to a blank, say **"Blank."** Get ready. (Tap for each word as the children read *ann said, "I will leave this blank."*)

• (Repeat until firm.)

k. What goes in the blank? (Signal.) *Park.* Yes, **park.**

l. Now, everybody, read each item to yourself and circle the right answer. ✔

SUMMARY OF INDEPENDENT ACTIVITY
EXERCISE 26

Introduction to independent activity

(Hold up Worksheet 147.) Everybody, you're going to finish this worksheet on your own. (Tell the children when they will work the remaining items.)

• Let's go over the things you're going to do.

Picture comprehension

a. (Point to the pictures on side 1.) Everybody, you're going to look at the picture. Then you're going to read each item and write the missing word.

b. Remember—the first sound of each missing word is already written in the blank.

Reading comprehension

a. (Point to the reading-comprehension exercise on side 2.)

b. Everybody, get ready to read the sentences in the box the fast way.

c. First word. ✔

• Get ready. (Tap for each word as the children read the sentences:) *The man liked to swim. So he jumped into the lake.*

d. (Point to items 1 and 2.) These items tell about the story in the box. You're going to read each item and circle the right answer.

Sound writing

a. (Point to the sound-writing exercise.) Here are the sounds you're going to write today. I'll touch the sounds. You say them.

b. (Touch each sound.) *The children respond.* (Repeat until firm.)

Sentence copying

a. (Point to the dotted sentence in the sentence-copying exercise.)

b. You're going to trace the words in this sentence. Then you're going to write the sentence on the other lines.

c. Reading the fast way. First word. ✔

• Get ready. (Tap for each word.)

d. After you finish your worksheet, you get to draw a picture about the sentence, **cats do not talk.** You'll draw your picture on a piece of plain paper. (When the children finish their worksheets, give them sheets of plain paper.)

END OF LESSON 147

EXERCISE 16

Children read the fast way

a. Get ready to read these words the fast way.

b. (Touch the ball for **there.** Pause three seconds.) Get ready. (Signal.) *There.*

c. (Repeat *b* for the remaining words on the page.)

EXERCISE 17

Children read the fast way again

a. Get ready to do these words again. Watch where I point.

b. (Point to a word. Pause one second. Say:) Get ready. (Signal.) *The children respond.*

• (Point to the words in this order: **them, this, there, thōse.**)

c. (Repeat *b* until firm.)

EXERCISE 18

Individual test

(Call on individual children to read one word the fast way.)

ther_e

them

thōs_e

this

STORY 147
EXERCISE 21

First reading—children read the title and first three sentences

a. (Pass out Storybook.)

b. Open your book to page 150. ✔ Now you're going to finish the story about the girl and the talking cat.

c. Everybody, touch the title of the story and get ready to read the words in the title the fast way.

d. First word. ✔

• (Pause two seconds.) Get ready. (Tap.) *The.*

e. (Tap for each remaining word in the title.)

f. (After the children have read the title, ask:) What's this story about? (Signal.) *The cat that talked.* Yes, **the cat that talked.**

g. Everybody, get ready to read this story the fast way.

h. First word. ✔

• (Pause two seconds.) Get ready. (Tap.) *A.*

i. (Tap for the remaining words in the first sentence. Pause at least two seconds between taps.)

j. (Repeat *h* and *i* for the next two sentences. Have the children reread the first three sentences until firm.)

EXERCISE 22

Individual children or the group read sentences to complete the first reading

a. I'm going to call on individual children to read a sentence. Everybody, follow along and point to the words. If you hear a mistake, raise your hand.

b. (Call on a child.) Read the next sentence. (Do not tap for the words. Let children read at their own pace, but be sure they read the sentence correctly.)

To Correct

(Have the child sound out the word. Then return to the beginning of the sentence.)

c. (Repeat *b* for most of the remaining sentences in the story. Occasionally have the group read a sentence. When the group is to read, say:) Everybody, read the next sentence. (Pause two seconds.) Get ready. (Tap for each word in the sentence. Pause at least two seconds between taps.)

EXERCISE 23

Second reading—individual children or the group read each sentence; the group answer questions

a. You're going to read the story again. This time I'm going to ask questions.

b. Starting with the first word of the title. ✔

• Get ready. (Tap as the children read the title. Pause at least two seconds between taps.)

c. (Call on a child.) Read the first sentence. *The child responds.*

d. (Repeat *b* and *c* in exercise 22. Present the following comprehension questions to the entire group.)

After the children read:	You say:
"Cats can not talk."	What did the girl say? (Signal.) *Cats can not talk.* Where were the girl and the cat? (Signal.) *In the park.* Do you remember what the cat said to her? (Signal.) *I can talk to you.*
The girl gave the cat a big hug.	How do you give a cat a big hug? *The children respond.*
The cat said, "I never had a cat that talked either."	What did the cat say? (Signal.) *I never had a cat that talked either.* That's silly.
She went up to the girl and said, "Can I have that cat?"	What did she say? (Signal.) *Can I have that cat?* Who said that? (Signal.) *Ann.* What do you think will happen? *The children respond.*
The cat said, "I will not go with you."	What did the cat say? (Signal.) *I will not go with you.* What do you think Ann will do now? *The children respond.*
"I will leave this park."	What did Ann say? *The children respond.* I'll bet Ann was surprised to hear that cat talk.
And she did.	What did she do? (Signal.) *She left the park.*

STORY 124
EXERCISE 19

First reading—children read the story the fast way

(Have the children reread any sentences containing words that give them trouble. Keep a list of these words.)

a. (Pass out Storybook.)

b. Open your book to page 83. ✔

c. Everybody, touch the title of the story and get ready to read the words in the title the fast way.

d. First word. ✔

• (Pause two seconds.) Get ready. (Tap.) *Paint.*

e. (Tap for each remaining word in the title.)

f. (After the children have read the title, ask:) What's this story about? (Signal.) *Paint that nose.* Yes, **paint that nose.**

g. Everybody, get ready to read this story the fast way.

h. First word. ✔

• (Pause two seconds.) Get ready. (Tap.) *A.*

i. (Tap for the remaining words in the first sentence. Pause at least two seconds between taps.)

j. (Repeat *h* and *i* for the next two sentences. Have the children reread the first three sentences until firm.)

k. (The children are to read the remainder of the story the fast way, stopping at the end of each sentence.)

l. (After the first reading of the story, print on the board the words that the children missed more than one time. Have the children sound out each word one time and tell what word.)

m. (After the group's responses are firm, call on individual children to read the words.)

EXERCISE 20

Individual test

a. Turn back to page 83. I'm going to call on individual children to read a whole sentence.

b. (Call on individual children to read a sentence. Do not tap for each word.)

EXERCISE 21

Second reading—children read the story the fast way and answer questions

a. You're going to read the story again the fast way and I'll ask questions.

b. Starting with the first word of the title. ✔

• Get ready. (Tap.) *Paint.*

c. (Tap for each remaining word. Pause at least two seconds between taps. Pause longer before words that gave the children trouble during the first reading.)

d. (Ask the comprehension questions below as the children read.)

After the children read:	You say:
Paint that nose.	What's this story about? (Signal.) *Paint that nose.*
The fat dog had a red nose.	What did the fat dog have? (Signal.) *A red nose.*
The little dog had a red nose.	What did the little dog have? (Signal.) *A red nose.*
The little dog said, "I wish I did not have a red nose."	What did the little dog say? (Signal.) *I wish I did not have a red nose.*
He said, "Paint that nose."	What did the fat dog say? (Signal.) *Paint that nose.* Who said that? (Signal.) *The fat dog.*
Now the fat dog has paint on his ear.	Where does the fat dog have paint? (Signal.) *On his ear.* How did it get there? *The children respond.* The little dog kissed his ear.

EXERCISE 22

Picture comprehension

a. Everybody, look at the picture.

b. (Ask these questions:)

1. What is that little dog doing? *The children respond.*

• He's kissing the fat dog on the ear. I bet he'll leave a big mark on that fat dog's ear.

2. Did you ever paint your nose? *The children respond.*

EXERCISE 16

Children read a word beginning with two consonants (**stōre**)

a. (Cover **s**. Point to **tōre**.) You're going to read this part of the word the fast way. (Pause three seconds.) Get ready. (Signal.) *Tōre.* Yes, **tōre**.

b. (Uncover **s**. Point to **s**.) You're going to say this first. (Move your finger quickly under **s**.) Then you're going to say (pause) **tōre**.

c. (Point to **s**.) What are you going to say first? (Signal.) *sss.*
• What are you going to say next? (Signal.) *Tōre.*

d. (Repeat *c* until firm.)

e. (Touch the ball for **stōre**.) Remember, first you say **sss**; then you say **tōre**. Get ready. (Move to **s**, then quickly along the arrow.) *Ssstōre.*

f. Say it fast. (Signal.) *Store.*
• Yes, what word? (Signal.) *Store.* Yes, **store**.
• Good reading.

g. Again. (Repeat *e* and *f* until firm.)

h. Now you're going to sound out (pause) **store**. Get ready. (Touch **s, t, ō, r** as the children say *ssstōōōrrr.*)
• What word? (Signal.) *Store.* Yes, **store**.

stōre

EXERCISE 17

Children identify, then sound out an irregular word (**walked**)

a. (Touch the ball for **walked**.) Everybody, you're going to read this word the fast way. (Pause three seconds.) Get ready. (Move your finger quickly along the arrow.) *Walked.* Yes, **walked**.

b. Now you're going to sound out the word. Get ready. (Quickly touch **w, a, l, k, d** as the children say *wwwaaalllkd.*)

c. Again. (Repeat *b*.)

d. How do we say the word? (Signal.) *Walked.* Yes, **walked**.

e. (Repeat *b* and *d* until firm.)

walked

EXERCISE 18

Individual test

(Have children do *b* and *d* in exercise 17.)

EXERCISE 19

Children read the words the fast way

(Have the children read the words on this page the fast way.)

EXERCISE 20

Individual test

(Have children read one word the fast way.)

WORKSHEET 124

CROSS-OUT GAME

The children will need pencils.

EXERCISE 23

Children cross out **red** and circle **nōse**

a. (Pass out Worksheet 124 to each child.)

b. (Hold up side 1 of your worksheet and point to the Cross-out Game.)

c. Everybody, here's a new Cross-out Game. The words in the box show what you're going to do. (Point to the word **red**.) Look at the word **red**. It's crossed out. So you're going to cross out every word **red**.

d. (Point to the word **nōse**.) Look at the word **nose**. It's circled. So you're going to circle every word **nōse**.

e. Everybody, touch a word that you're going to cross out. ✔

f. Touch a word that you're going to circle. ✔

g. Everybody, circle every word **nōse** and cross out every word **red**. ✔

SUMMARY OF INDEPENDENT ACTIVITY

EXERCISE 24

Introduction to independent activity

a. (Hold up side 1 of Worksheet 124.)

b. Everybody, you're going to finish this worksheet on your own. (Tell the children when they will work the remaining items.)

• Let's go over the things you're going to do.

Sentence copying

a. (Point to the dotted sentence in the sentence-copying exercise.)

b. You're going to trace the words in this sentence. Then you're going to write the sentence on the other lines.

c. Reading the fast way. First word. ✔

• Get ready. (Tap.) *He.*

d. Next word. ✔

• Get ready. (Tap.) *Had.*

e. (Repeat *d* for the remaining words.)

f. After you finish your worksheet, you get to draw a picture about the sentence, **hē had a red nōse.** You'll draw your picture on a piece of plain paper.

Reading comprehension

a. (Point to the boxed sentences in the reading-comprehension exercise.)

b. Everybody, get ready to read the sentences the fast way.

c. First word. ✔

• Get ready. (Tap for each word as the children read *the little dog had a red nose.*)

d. (Have the children reread the sentence until firm.)

e. Get ready to read the next sentence. (Repeat *c* and *d* for **hē was mad.**)

f. (Point to items 1 and 2.) These items tell about the story in the box. You're going to read each item and circle the right answer.

Sound writing

a. (Point to the sound-writing exercise on side 2.) Here are the sounds you're going to write today. I'll touch the sounds. You say them.

b. (Touch each sound.) *The children respond.*

c. (Repeat the series until firm.)

Pair relations

a. (Point to the pair-relations exercise.) Remember—you're going to draw a line through the sentences in each box that do not tell about the picture.

b. (When the children finish their worksheets, give them sheets of plain paper. Remind them to draw a picture that shows **hē had a red nose.**)

END OF LESSON 124

EXERCISE 9

Children identify, then sound out an irregular word (**loved**)

a. (Touch the ball for **loved.**) Everybody, you're going to read this word the fast way. (Pause three seconds.) Get ready. (Move your finger quickly along the arrow.) *Loved.* Yes, **loved.**

b. Now you're going to sound out the word. Get ready. (Quickly touch **l, o, v, e, d** as the children say *Illooovvveeed.*)

c. Again. (Repeat *b.*)

d. How do we say the word? (Signal.) *Loved.* Yes, **loved.**

e. (Repeat *b* and *d* until firm.)

EXERCISE 10

Individual test

(Call on individual children to do *b* and *d* in exercise 9.)

EXERCISE 11

Children sound out the word and tell what word

a. (Touch the ball for **jump.**) Sound it out.

b. Get ready. (Touch **j, u, m, p** as the children say *juuummmp.*)

• (If sounding out is not firm, repeat *b.*)

c. What word? (Signal.) *Jump.* Yes, **jump.**

EXERCISE 12

Children sound out the word and tell what word

(Repeat the procedures in exercise 11 for **tōre.**)

EXERCISE 13

Children sound out the word and tell what word

(Repeat the procedures in exercise 11 for **pool.**)

EXERCISE 14

Children read the words the fast way

a. Now you get to read the words on this page the fast way.

b. (Touch the ball for **loved.** Pause three seconds.) Get ready. (Move your finger quickly along the arrow.) *Loved.*

c. (Repeat *b* for each word on the page.)

EXERCISE 15

Individual test

(Call on individual children to read one word the fast way.)

tōre

pool

SOUNDS

EXERCISE 1

Teaching **ing** as in **sing**

a. (Point to **ing**.) My turn. (Pause. Touch **ing** and say:) iiing.

b. (Point to **ing**.) Your turn. When I touch it, you say it. (Pause.) Get ready. (Touch **ing**.) *iiing.*

• (Lift your finger.)

c. Again. (Touch **ing**.) *iiing.*

• (Lift your finger.)

d. (Repeat *c* until firm.)

EXERCISE 2

Sounds firm-up

a. Get ready to say the sounds when I touch them.

b. (Alternate touching **b** and **ing**. Point to the sound. Pause one second. Say:) Get ready. (Touch the sound.) *The children respond.*

c. (When **b** and **ing** are firm, alternate touching **b, i, ing,** and **n** until all four sounds are firm.)

EXERCISE 3

Individual test

(Call on individual children to identify **b, i, ing,** or **n**.)

EXERCISE 4

Teacher introduces cross-out game

a. (Use transparency and crayon.)

b. I'll cross out the sounds on this part of the page when you can tell me every sound.

c. Remember—when I touch it, you say it.

d. (Go over the sounds until the children can identify all the sounds in order.)

EXERCISE 5

Individual test

(Call on individual children to identify two or more sounds in exercise 4.)

EXERCISE 6

Teacher crosses out sounds

a. You told me every sound. Get ready to do it again. This time I'll cross out each sound when you tell me what it is.

b. (Point to each sound. Pause. Say:) Get ready. (Touch the sound.) *The children respond.*

• (As you cross out the sound, say:) Goodbye, _____.

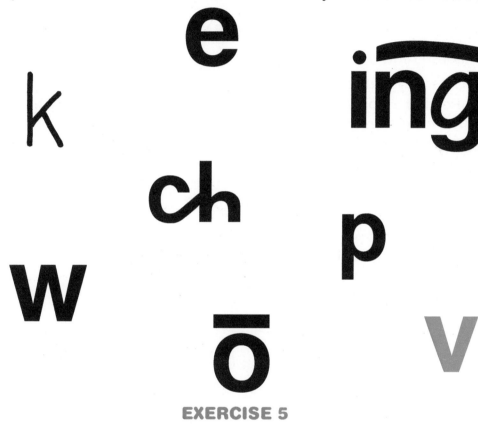

READING VOCABULARY
EXERCISE 6

Children read the fast way

a. Get ready to read these words the fast way.

b. (Touch the ball for **them.** Pause three seconds.) Get ready. (Signal.) *Them.*

c. (Repeat *b* for the remaining words on the page.)

EXERCISE 7

Children read the fast way again

a. Get ready to do these words again. Watch where I point.

b. (Point to a word. Pause one second. Say:) Get ready. (Signal.) *The children respond.*

• (Point to the words in this order: **never, they, must, them, ēither.**)

c. (Repeat *b* until firm.)

EXERCISE 8

Individual test

(Call on individual children to read one word the fast way.)

them

they

ēither

never

must

READING VOCABULARY
EXERCISE 7

Children read the fast way

a. Get ready to read these words the fast way.

b. (Touch the ball for **gōing.** Pause three seconds.) Get ready. (Signal.) *Going.*

c. (Repeat *b* for the remaining words on the page.)

EXERCISE 8

Children read the fast way again

a. Get ready to do these words again. Watch where I point.

b. (Point to a word. Pause one second. Say:) Get ready. (Signal.) *The children respond.*

• (Point to the words in this order: **bug, ēating, tāke, gōing.**)

c. (Repeat *b* until firm.)

EXERCISE 9

Individual test

(Call on individual children to read one word the fast way.)

SOUNDS

EXERCISE 1

Teaching **j** as in **jump**

a. (Point to **j**.) My turn. When I touch it, I'll say it. (Pause. Touch **j** for an instant, saying:) **j**. (Do not say **juuh**.)

b. (Point to **j**.) Your turn. When I touch it, you say it. (Pause.) Get ready. (Touch **j**.) *j*.

c. Again. (Touch **j**.) *j*.

d. (Repeat *c* until firm.)

EXERCISE 2

Sounds firm-up

a. Get ready to say the sounds when I touch them.

b. (Alternate touching **j** and **y**. Point to the sound. Pause one second. Say:) Get ready. (Touch the sound.) *The children respond.*

c. (When **j** and **y** are firm, alternate touching **j, y, g,** and **ch** until all four sounds are firm.)

J

y

g   ch

EXERCISE 3

Individual test

(Call on individual children to identify **j, y, g,** or **ch.**)

J   X

er   ī

i

EXERCISE 4

Sounds firm-up

a. (Point to **j**.) When I touch the sound, you say it.

b. (Pause.) Get ready. (Touch **j**.) *j*.

c. Again. (Repeat *b* until firm.)

d. Get ready to say all the sounds when I touch them.

e. (Alternate touching **j, x, oo, er, ī, i, e,** and **u** three or four times. Point to the sound. Pause one second. Say:) Get ready. (Touch the sound.) *The children respond.*

e

EXERCISE 5

Individual test

(Call on individual children to identify one or more sounds in exercise 4.)

u

EXERCISE 10

Children read a word beginning with two consonants **(slēēp)**

a. (Cover **s.** Run your finger under **lēēp.**) You're going to sound out this part. Get ready. (Touch **l,** between the **ē**'s, **p** as the children say *lllēēēp.*)

b. Say it fast. (Signal.) *Leep.* Yes, this part is **leep.**

c. (Uncover **s.** Point to **s.**) You're going to say this first. (Move your finger quickly under **lēēp.**) Then you're going to say (pause) **lēēp.**

d. (Point to **s.**) What are you going to say first? (Signal.) *sss.*

• What are you going to say next? (Signal.) *Leep.*

e. (Repeat *d* until firm.)

f. (Touch the ball for **slēēp.**) Remember—first you say **sss;** then you say **lēēp.** Get ready. (Move to **s,** then quickly along the arrow.) *Ssslēēp.*

g. Say it fast. (Signal.) *Sleep.*

• Yes, what word? (Signal.) *Sleep.* Yes, **sleep.**

• Good reading.

h. Again. (Repeat *f* and *g* until firm.)

i. Now you're going to sound out (pause) **sleep.** Get ready. (Touch **s, l,** between the **ē**'s, **p** as the children say *ssslllēēēp.*)

• What word? (Signal.) *Sleep.* Yes, **sleep.**

EXERCISE 11

Children read the fast way

a. Get ready to read these words the fast way.

b. (Touch the ball for **that.** Pause three seconds.) Get ready. (Signal.) *That.*

c. (Repeat *b* for the remaining words on the page.)

EXERCISE 12

Children read the fast way again

a. Get ready to do these words again. Watch where I point.

b. (Point to a word. Pause one second. Say:) Get ready. (Signal.) *The children respond.*

• (Point to the words in this order: **that, there, hat, hēre.**)

c. (Repeat *b* until firm.)

EXERCISE 13

Individual test

(Call on individual children to read one word on the page the fast way.)

slēēp

that

hat

thēre

hēre

READING COMPREHENSION
EXERCISE 25

Children choose the correct words to fill in the blanks

a. (Point to the reading-comprehension exercise on side 2.)

b. Everybody, get ready to read the sentences in the box the fast way.

c. Get ready. (Tap for each word as the children read *She had a dog. The dog did not talk.*)

• (Repeat until firm.)

d. Listen. **She had a dog.** (Pause.) **The dog did not talk.**

e. Everybody, get ready to tell me the answer. Listen. **She had a** (pause) **something.** Tell me what that something was. She had a . . . (Signal.) *Dog.* Yes, **dog.**

• She had a dog.

f. Listen. **She had a dog. The** (pause) **something did not talk.** The . . . (Signal.) *Dog.* Yes, **dog.**

• The dog did not talk.

g. (Repeat *b* through *f* until firm.)

h. Everybody, get ready to read the sentences in the box the fast way again. Get ready. (Tap for each word as the children read *She had a dog. The dog did not talk.*)

i. Everybody, read item 1 to yourself and touch the word that goes in the blank. ✔

j. What word goes in the blank? (Signal.) *Dog.*

k. Everybody, circle the word **dog** under item 1. ✔

l. Everybody, read item 2 to yourself and touch the word that goes in the blank. ✔

m. What word goes in the blank? (Signal.) *Dog.*

n. Circle the word **dog** under item 2. ✔

SUMMARY OF INDEPENDENT ACTIVITY
EXERCISE 26

Introduction to independent activity

a. (Hold up Worksheet 146.)

b. Everybody, you're going to finish this worksheet on your own. (Tell the children when they will work the remaining items.)

• Let's go over the things you're going to do.

Sound writing

a. (Point to the sound-writing exercise on side 2.) Here are the sounds you're going to write today. I'll touch the sounds. You say them.

b. (Touch each sound.) *The children respond.*

c. (Repeat the series until firm.)

Sentence copying

a. (Point to the dotted sentence in the sentence-copying exercise.)

b. You're going to trace the words in this sentence. Then you're going to write the sentence on the other lines.

c. Reading the fast way. First word. ✔

• Get ready. (Tap for each word.)

d. After you finish your worksheet, you get to draw a picture about the sentence, **I can talk to you.** You'll draw your picture on a piece of plain paper. (When the children finish their worksheets, give them sheets of plain paper.)

END OF LESSON 146

EXERCISE 14

Children read the fast way

a. Get ready to read these words the fast way.

b. (Touch the ball for **his.** Pause three seconds.) Get ready. (Signal.) *His.*

c. (Repeat *b* for the remaining words on the page.)

EXERCISE 15

Children read the fast way again

a. Get ready to do these words again. Watch where I point.

b. (Point to a word. Pause one second. Say:) Get ready. (Signal.)
The children respond.

• (Point to the words in this order: **his, give, ēach, let.**)

c. (Repeat *b* until firm.)

EXERCISE 16

Individual test

(Call on individual children to read one word the fast way.)

his

let

ēach

give

EXERCISE 22

Picture comprehension

a. Everybody, look at the picture.

b. (Ask these questions:)
1. Where are the girl and the cat in this picture? *The children respond.* In the park.
2. How do you know they're in the park? *The children respond.*
3. Why does that girl look so surprised? *The children respond.* The cat is talking to her.
4. What is the cat saying to the girl? *The children respond.* Yes, I can talk to you.
5. What would you do with a talking cat? *The children respond.*

WORKSHEET 146

STORY ITEMS

The children will need pencils.

EXERCISE 23

Children complete sentences and answer story questions

a. (Pass out Worksheet 146 to each child.)

b. (Point to the story-items exercise on side 1.) These items are about the story you just read.

c. (Point to the blank in item 1.) Something is missing. When you get to this blank, say **"Blank."** What will you say? (Signal.) *Blank.*

d. Everybody, get ready to read item 1. Get ready. (Tap for each word as the children read *a girl went to the shop with her blank.*)

• (Repeat until firm.)

e. What goes in the blank? (Signal.) *Cat.* Yes, **cat.**

f. Everybody, read item 2. Get ready. (Tap for each word as the children read *then they went to the blank.*)

• (Repeat until firm.)

g. What's the answer? (Signal.) *Park.*

h. Everybody, read item 3 and when you come to a blank, say **"Blank."** Get ready. (Tap for each word as the children read *she said, "you can not blank to me."*)

• (Repeat until firm.)

i. What goes in the blank? (Signal.) *Talk.* Yes, **talk.**

j. Everybody, read item 4. Get ready. (Tap for each word as the children read *did the cat talk?*)

• (Repeat until firm.)

k. What's the answer? (Signal.) *Yes.*

l. Now, everybody, read each item to yourself and circle the right answer. ✔

PICTURE COMPREHENSION
EXERCISE 24

Children look at the picture and complete the missing word

(Refer to sounds, not letter names, in missing words.)

a. (Point to the first picture in the picture-comprehension exercise.)

b. Everybody, touch this picture. ✔

c. Tell me what you see in this picture. (Accept reasonable responses.)

d. (Point to the sound in the blank in item 1.) Something is missing. When you get to this, say **"Blank."** What will you say? (Signal.) *Blank.*

e. Everybody, get ready to read item 1.

f. Get ready. (Tap for each word as the children read *the blank is sitting.*)

• (Repeat until firm.)

g. Look at the picture and get ready to tell me who is sitting. (Pause.) Who is sitting? (Signal.) *Cat.* Yes, **cat.**

h. I'll say the sounds in the word **cat.** c (pause) aaa (pause) t. Again. c (pause) aaa (pause) t.

i. Your turn. Say the sounds in **cat.** Get ready. (Signal for each sound as the children say:) c (pause) aaa (pause) t.

• (Repeat until firm.)

j. Look at the blank in item 1. The **c** is already written in the blank. So what sounds are you going to write next? (Signal for each sound as the children say:) aaa (pause) t.

• (The children are not to write the sounds now.)

k. (Repeat *i* and *j* until firm.)

l. Now write the missing word in the blank. Remember— the **c** is already written. ✔

m. (Repeat *e* through *l* for item 2.)

n. (Repeat *b* through *m* for the second picture.)

STORY 125
EXERCISE 17

First reading—children read the story the fast way

(Have the children reread any sentences containing words that give them trouble. Keep a list of these words.)

a. (Pass out Storybook.)

b. Open your book to page 86. ✔

c. Everybody, touch the title of the story and get ready to read the words in the title the fast way.

d. First word. ✔

• (Pause two seconds.) Get ready. (Tap.) *The.*

e. (Tap for each remaining word in the title.)

f. (After the children have read the title, ask:) What's this story about? (Signal.) *The red hat.* Yes, **the red hat.**

g. Everybody, get ready to read this story the fast way.

h. First word. ✔

• (Pause two seconds.) Get ready. (Tap.) *The.*

i. (Tap for the remaining words in the first sentence. Pause at least two seconds between taps.)

j. (Repeat *h* and *i* for the next two sentences. Have the children reread the first three sentences until firm.)

k. (The children are to read the remainder of the story the fast way, stopping at the end of each sentence.)

l. (After the first reading of the story, print on the board the words that the children missed more than one time. Have the children sound out each word one time and tell what word.)

m. (After the group's responses are firm, call on individual children to read the words.)

EXERCISE 18

Individual test

a. Look at page 86. I'm going to call on individual children to read a whole sentence.

b. (Call on individual children to read a sentence. Do not tap for each word.)

EXERCISE 19

Second reading—children read the story the fast way and answer questions

a. You're going to read the story again the fast way and I'll ask questions.

b. Starting with the first word of the title. ✔

• Get ready. (Tap.) *The.*

c. (Tap for each remaining word. Pause at least two seconds between taps. Pause longer before words that gave the children trouble during the first reading.)

d. (Ask the comprehension questions below as the children read.)

After the children read:	You say:
The red hat.	What's this story about? (Signal.) *The red hat.*
The fish had a car and no hat.	What did the fish have? (Signal.) *A car and no hat.*
"I need a red hat."	What did she say? (Signal.) *I need a red hat.*
The fish said, "Can I have that red hat?"	What did she say? (Signal.) *Can I have that red hat?* Do you think the cow will let her have the hat? *The children respond.* Let's read and find out.
The cow said, "No."	Did the cow want to give the red hat to the fish? (Signal.) *No.*
So the fish got a red hat and the cow got a car.	What did the fish get? (Signal.) *A red hat.* What did the cow get? (Signal.) *A car.* Do you think they're both happy now? *The children respond.*

EXERCISE 20

Picture comprehension

a. What do you think you'll see in the picture? *The children respond.*

b. Turn the page and look at the picture.

c. (Ask these questions:)

1. What is that fish wearing? *A red hat.*
2. What's the cow doing? *Driving a car.*
3. What would you do if you had a car? *The children respond.*
4. Would you trade it for a red hat? *The children respond.*

STORYBOOK

STORY 146

EXERCISE 19

First reading—children read the title and first three sentences

a. (Pass out Storybook.)

b. Open your book to page 148. ✔
You're going to read the first part of this story today.

c. Everybody, touch the title of the story and get ready to read the words in the title the fast way.

d. First word. ✔

• (Pause two seconds.) Get ready. (Tap.) *The.*

e. (Tap for each remaining word in the title.)

f. (After the children have read the title, ask:) What's this story about? (Signal.) *The cat that talked.* Yes, **the cat that talked.**

g. Everybody, get ready to read this story the fast way.

h. First word. ✔

• (Pause two seconds.) Get ready. (Tap.) *A.*

i. (Tap for the remaining words in the first sentence. Pause at least two seconds between taps.)

j. (Repeat *h* and *i* for the next two sentences. Have the children reread the first three sentences until firm.)

EXERCISE 20

Individual children or the group read sentences to complete the first reading

a. I'm going to call on individual children to read a sentence. Everybody, follow along and point to the words. If you hear a mistake, raise your hand.

b. (Call on a child.) Read the next sentence. (Do not tap for the words. Let children read at their own pace, but be sure they read the sentence correctly.)

To Correct

(Have the child sound out the word. Then return to the beginning of the sentence.)

c. (Repeat *b* for most of the remaining sentences in the story. Occasionally have the group read a sentence. When the group is to read, say:) Everybody, read the next sentence. (Pause two seconds.) Get ready. (Tap for each word in the sentence. Pause at least two seconds between taps.)

EXERCISE 21

Second reading—individual children or the group read each sentence; the group answer questions

a. You're going to read the story again. This time I'm going to ask questions.

b. Starting with the first word of the title. ✔

• Get ready. (Tap as the children read the title. Pause at least two seconds between taps.)

c. (Call on a child.) Read the first sentence. *The child responds.*

d. (Repeat *b* and *c* in exercise 20. Present the following comprehension questions to the entire group.)

After the children read:	You say:
The cat that talked.	What's this story about? (Signal.) *The cat that talked.*
She went to the shop with her cat.	What did she do? (Signal.) *She went to the shop with her cat.*
She went to the park with her cat.	Name two things she did with her cat. (Signal.) *She went to the shop and to the park with her cat.*
"But you can not talk to me and that makes me sad."	Why was the girl sad? (Signal.) *Because the cat couldn't talk to her.*
The cat said, "I can talk to you."	What did the cat say? (Signal.) *I can talk to you.* That cat talked to her. I wonder what will happen next. We'll find out when we read the next part of the story.

WORKSHEET 125

CROSS-OUT GAME

The children will need pencils.

EXERCISE 21

Children cross out **do** and circle **nō**

a. (Pass out sides 1 and 2 of Worksheet 125 to each child.)

b. Everybody, do a good job on your worksheet today and I'll give you a bonus worksheet.

c. (Hold up side 1 of your worksheet and point to the Cross-out Game.)

d. Everybody, here's the new Cross-out Game. The words in the box show what you're going to do. (Point to the word **do.**) Look at the word **do.** It's crossed out. So you're going to cross out every word **do.**

e. (Point to the word **nō.**) Look at the word **nō.** It's circled. So you're going to circle every word **nō.**

f. Everybody, touch a word that you're going to cross out. ✔

g. Touch a word that you're going to circle. ✔

h. Everybody, circle every word **no** and cross out every word **do.** ✔

SUMMARY OF INDEPENDENT ACTIVITY

EXERCISE 22

Sentence copying

a. (Hold up side 1 of Worksheet 125.)

b. (Point to the dotted sentence in the sentence-copying exercise.)

c. You're going to trace the words in this sentence. Then you're going to write the sentence on the other lines.

d. Reading the fast way. First word. ✔
- Get ready. (Tap.) *She.*

e. Next word. ✔
- Get ready. (Tap.) *Got.*

f. (Repeat e for the remaining words.)

g. After you finish your worksheet, you get to draw a picture about the sentence, **she got a red hat.** You'll draw your picture on a piece of plain paper.

EXERCISE 23

Reading comprehension

a. (Point to the boxed sentences in the reading-comprehension exercise.)

b. Everybody, get ready to read the sentences the fast way.

c. First word. ✔
- Get ready. (Tap for each word as the children read *the fish got a hat.*)

d. (Have the children reread the sentence until firm.)

e. Get ready to read the next sentence. (Repeat *c* and *d* for **the cow got a car.**)

f. (Point to items 1 and 2.) These items tell about the story in the box. You're going to read each item and circle the right answer.

EXERCISE 24

Other independent activity: sides 1, 2, 3, 4

Remember to do all the parts of the worksheet and to read all the parts carefully. After you draw your picture, I'll give you a bonus worksheet.

INDIVIDUAL CHECKOUT: STORYBOOK

EXERCISE 25

3-minute individual fluency checkout: rate/accuracy— whole story

a. As you are doing your worksheet, I'll call on children one at a time to read the **whole story.** Remember, you get two stars if you read the story in less than three minutes and make no more than three errors.

b. (Call on a child. Tell the child:) Start with the title and read the story carefully the fast way. Go. (Time the child. Tell the child any words the child misses. Stop the child as soon as the child makes the fourth error or exceeds the time limit.)

c. (If the child meets the rate-accuracy criterion, record two stars on your chart for lesson 125. Congratulate the child. Give children who do not earn two stars a chance to read the story again before the next lesson is presented.)
89 words/**3 min** = 30 wpm [**3 errors**]

END OF LESSON 125

Before presenting lesson 126, give Mastery Test 24 to each child. Do not present lesson 126 to any groups that are not firm on this test.

EXERCISE 16

Children identify, then sound out an irregular word

a. (Touch the ball for **walked.**) Everybody, you're going to read this word the fast way. (Pause three seconds.) Get ready. (Move your finger quickly along the arrow.) *Walked.* Yes, **walked.**

b. Now you're going to sound out the word. Get ready. (Quickly touch **w, a, l, k, d** as the children say *wwwaaalllkd.*)

c. Again. (Repeat *b.*)

d. How do we say the word? (Signal.) *Walked.* Yes, **walked.**

e. (Repeat *b* and *d* until firm.)

f. (Call on individual children to do *b* and *d.*)

walked

EXERCISE 17

Children read **rush, brush,** and **brushed**

a. (Cover **b.** Point to **rush.**) You're going to read this part of the word the fast way. (Pause three seconds.) Get ready. (Signal.) *Rush.* Yes, **rush.**

b. (Uncover **b.** Point to **b.**) You're going to say this first. (Move your finger quickly under **rush.**) Then you're going to say (pause) **rush.**

c. (Point to **b.**) What are you going to say first? (Signal.) *b.*

• What are you going to say next? (Signal.) *Rush.*

d. (Repeat *c* until firm.)

e. (Touch the ball for **brush.**) Get ready. (Move to **b,** then quickly along the arrow.) *Brush.*

f. Say it fast. (Signal.) *Brush.*

• Yes, what word? (Signal.) *Brush.* Yes, **brush.**

• Good reading.

g. Again. (Repeat *e* and *f* until firm.)

h. (Return to the ball for **brush.**) Yes, this word is **brush.**

i. (Touch the ball for **brushed.**) So this must be **brush . . .** (Touch **d.**) *d.*

• What word? (Signal.) *Brushed.* Yes, **brushed.**

j. Again. (Repeat *h* and *i* until firm.)

k. (Touch the ball for **brush.**) This word is **brush.** (Touch the ball for **brushed.**) So this must be . . . (Quickly run your finger under **brush** and tap **d.**) *Brushed.* Yes, **brushed.**

l. Again. (Repeat *k* until firm.)

m. Now you're going to sound out (pause) **brushed.** Get ready. (Touch **b, r, u, sh, d** as the children say *brrruuushshshd.*)

• Yes, what word? (Signal.) *Brushed.* Yes, **brushed.**

brush

brushed

EXERCISE 18

Children read the words the fast way

(Have the children read the words the fast way.)

Mastery Tests—General Instructions

All children are to be given each test individually.

The test is NOT to be administered during the period allotted for reading.

A child should neither see nor hear another child working on the test.

MASTERY TEST 24—after lesson 125, before lesson 126

a. (Tell child:) Get ready to read this story the fast way.
b. (test item) First word. (Pause two seconds.) Get ready. (Tap.) *A.*
c. (12 test items) (Tap one time for each remaining word in the story. Pause two seconds between taps.)

Total number of test items: **13**
A group is weak if more than one-third of the children missed two or more words on the test.

a man on a farm

has lots of cars.

hē has ōld cars.

If the group is firm on Mastery Test 24 and was firm on Mastery Test 23:

Skip lesson 126 and present lesson 127 to the group during the next reading period. If more than one child missed two or more words on the test, present the firming procedures specified in the next column to those children.

If the group is firm on Mastery Test 24 but was weak on Mastery Test 23:

Present lesson 126 to the group during the next reading period. If more than one child missed two or more words on the test, present the firming procedures specified below to those children.

If the group is weak on Mastery Test 24:

A. Present these firming procedures to the group during the next reading period. Present each story until the children make no more than three mistakes. Then proceed to the next story.
  1. Lesson 123, Story, page 96, exercises 18, 19.
  2. Lesson 124, Story, page 104, exercises 19, 20.
  3. Lesson 125, Story, page 110, exercises 17, 18.
B. After presenting the above exercises, again give Mastery Test 24 individually to members of the group who failed the test.
C. If the group is firm (less than one-third of the total group missed two or more words in the story on the retest), present lesson 126 to the group during the next reading period.
D. If the group is still weak (more than one-third of the total group missed two or more words in the story on the retest), repeat *A* and *B* during the next reading period.

EXERCISE 10

Children identify, then sound out an irregular word (**talked**)

a. (Touch the ball for **talked.**) Everybody, you're going to read this word the fast way. (Pause three seconds.) Get ready. (Move your finger quickly along the arrow.) *Talked.* Yes, **talked.**

b. Now you're going to sound out the word. Get ready. (Quickly touch **t, a, l, k, d** as the children say *taaalllkd.*)

c. Again. (Repeat *b.*)

d. How do we say the word? (Signal.) *Talked.* Yes, **talked.**

e. (Repeat *b* and *d* until firm.)

EXERCISE 11

Individual test

(Call on individual children to do *b* and *d* in exercise 10.)

EXERCISE 12

Children identify, then sound out an irregular word (**was**)

a. (Touch the ball for **was.**) Everybody, you're going to read this word the fast way. (Pause three seconds.) Get ready. (Move your finger quickly along the arrow.) *Was.* Yes, **was.**

b. Now you're going to sound out the word. Get ready. (Quickly touch **w, a, s** as the children say *wwwaaasss.*)

c. Again. (Repeat *b.*)

d. How do we say the word? (Signal.) *Was.* Yes, **was.**

e. (Repeat *b* and *d* until firm.)

EXERCISE 13

Individual test

(Call on individual children to do *b* and *d* in exercise 12.)

EXERCISE 14

Children sound out the word and tell what word

a. (Touch the ball for **dāy.**) Sound it out.

b. Get ready. (Touch **d, ā, y** as the children say *dāāāyyy.*)

• (If sounding out is not firm, repeat *b.*)

c. What word? (Signal.) *Day.* Yes, **day.**

EXERCISE 15

Children read the words the fast way

(Have the children read the words the fast way.)

Groups that are firm on Mastery Tests 23 and 24 should skip this lesson and do lesson 127 today.

SOUNDS

EXERCISE 1

Teacher introduces cross-out game

a. (Use transparency and crayon.)

b. I'll cross out the sounds on this page when you can tell me every sound.

c. Remember—when I touch it, you say it.

d. (Go over the sounds until they can identify all the sounds in order.)

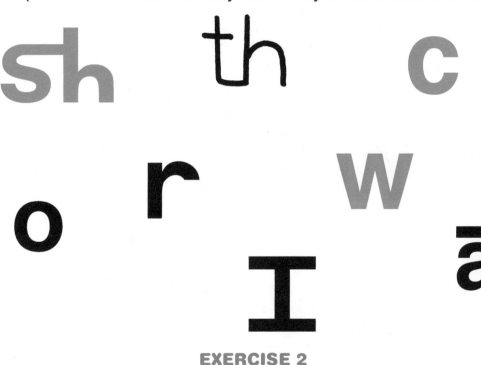

EXERCISE 2

Individual test

(Call on individual children to identify two or more sounds in exercise 1.)

EXERCISE 3

Teacher crosses out sounds

a. You told me every sound. Get ready to do it again. This time I'll cross out each sound when you tell me what it is.

b. (Point to each sound. Pause. Say:) Get ready. (Touch the sound.) *The children respond.*

• (As you cross out the sound, say:) Goodbye, _____.

EXERCISE 4

Teacher and children play the sounds game

a. (Use transparency and crayon. Write the sounds in the symbol box. Keep score in the score box.)

b. I'm smart. I think I can beat you in a game.

c. Here's the rule. When I touch a sound, you say it.

d. (Play the game. Make one symbol at a time in the symbol box. Use the symbols **b, ing, e** and **ch.**) (Make each symbol quickly. Pause. Touch the symbol. Play the game for about two minutes.) (Then ask:) Who won? (Draw a mouth on the face in the score box.)

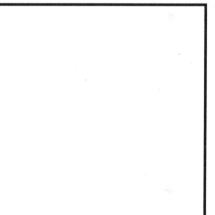

READING VOCABULARY

EXERCISE 7

Children read the fast way

a. Get ready to read these words the fast way.

b. (Touch the ball for **shop.** Pause three seconds.) Get ready. (Signal.) *Shop.*

c. (Repeat *b* for the remaining words on the page.)

EXERCISE 8

Children read the fast way again

a. Get ready to do these words again. Watch where I point.

b. (Point to a word. Pause one second. Say:) Get ready.
   (Signal.) *The children respond.*

• (Point to the words in this order: **shop, hop, never, soon, must.**)

c. (Repeat *b* until firm.)

EXERCISE 9

Individual test

(Call on individual children to read one word the fast way.)

shop

soon

must

never

hop

READING VOCABULARY
EXERCISE 5

Children sound out the word and tell what word

a. (Touch the ball for **bē**.) Sound it out.
b. Get ready. (Touch **b, ē** as the children say *bēēē*.)
• (If sounding out is not firm, repeat *b*.)
c. What word? (Signal.) *Be.* Yes, **be**.

EXERCISE 6

Children sound out the word and tell what word

a. (Touch the ball for **big**.) Sound it out.
b. Get ready. (Touch **b, i, g** as the children say *biiig*.)
• (If sounding out is not firm, repeat *b*.)
c. What word? (Signal.) *Big.* Yes, **big**.

EXERCISE 7

Children sound out the word and tell what word

(Repeat the procedures in exercise 6 for **getting.**)

EXERCISE 8

Children sound out the word and tell what word

(Repeat the procedures in exercise 6 for **bed.**)

EXERCISE 9

Children sound out the word and tell what word

(Repeat the procedures in exercise 6 for **bit.**)

EXERCISE 10

Children read the words the fast way

a. Now you get to read the words on this page the fast way.
b. (Touch the ball for **bē**. Pause three seconds.) Get ready. (Move your finger quickly along the arrow.) *Be.*
c. (Repeat *b* for each word on the page.)

EXERCISE 11

Individual test

(Call on individual children to read one word the fast way.)

Groups that are firm on Mastery Tests 27 and 28 should skip this lesson and do lesson 147 today.

SOUNDS

EXERCISE 1

Teaching **j** as in **jump**

a. (Point to **j**.) My turn. When I touch it, I'll say it. (Pause. Touch **j** for an instant, saying:) **j.** (Do not say **juuh.**)

b. (Point to **j**.) Your turn. When I touch it, you say it. (Pause.) Get ready. (Touch **j**.) *j.*

c. Again. (Touch **j**.) *j.*

d. (Repeat *c* until firm.)

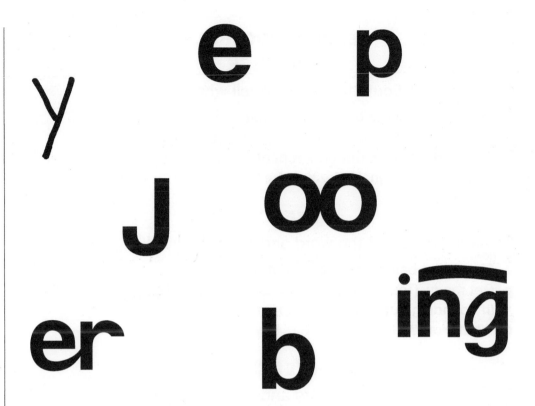

EXERCISE 2

Sounds firm-up

a. Get ready to say the sounds when I touch them.

b. (Alternate touching **j** and **ch**. Point to the sound. Pause one second. Say:) Get ready. (Touch the sound.) *The children respond.*

c. (When **j** and **ch** are firm, alternate touching **j, ch, g,** and **x** until all four sounds are firm.)

EXERCISE 3

Individual test

(Call on individual children to identify **j, ch, g,** or **x.**)

EXERCISE 4

Teacher introduces cross-out game

a. (Use transparency and crayon.)

b. I'll cross out the sounds on this part of the page when you can tell me every sound.

c. Remember—when I touch it, you say it.

d. (Go over the sounds until the children can identify all the sounds in order.)

EXERCISE 5

Individual test

(Call on individual children to identify two or more sounds in exercise 4.)

EXERCISE 6

Teacher crosses out sounds

a. You told me every sound. Get ready to do it again. This time I'll cross out each sound when you tell me what it is.

b. (Point to each sound. Pause. Say:) Get ready. (Touch the sound.) *The children respond.*

• (As you cross out the sound, say:) Goodbye, _____.

EXERCISE 12

Children read the fast way

a. Get ready to read these words the fast way.

b. (Touch the ball for **ēating.** Pause three seconds.) Get ready. (Signal.) *Eating.*

c. (Repeat *b* for the remaining words on the page.)

EXERCISE 13

Children read the fast way again

a. Get ready to do these words again. Watch where I point.

b. (Point to a word. Pause one second. Say:) Get ready. (Signal.) *The children respond.*

• (Point to the words in this order: **dog, slēēp, ēating, hit, bugs.**)

c. (Repeat *b* until firm.)

EXERCISE 14

Individual test

(Call on individual children to read one word the fast way.)

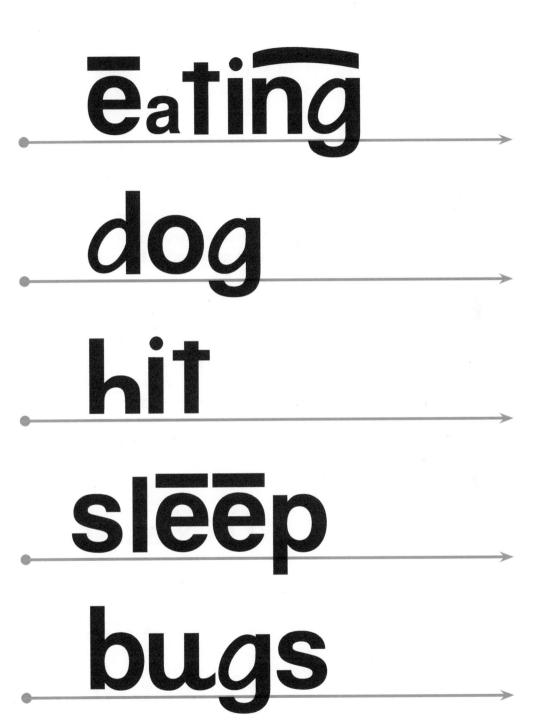

Total number of test items: **21**
A group is weak if more than one-third of the children missed two or more words on the test.

(Tell child:) Read this story the fast way. (Do not tap for the words. Let children read at their own pace.)

WHAT TO DO

If the group is firm on Mastery Test 28 and was firm on Mastery Test 27:

Skip lesson 146 and present lesson 147 to the group during the next reading period. If more than one child missed two or more words on the test, present the firming procedures specified in the next column to those children.

If the group is firm on Mastery Test 28 but was weak on Mastery Test 27:

Present lesson 146 to the group during the next reading period. If more than one child missed two or more words on the test, present the firming procedures specified below to those children.

If the group is weak on Mastery Test 28:

A. Present these firming procedures to the group during the next reading period. Present each story until the children make no more than three mistakes. Then proceed to the next story.
  1. Lesson 143, Story, page 219, exercises 18, 19.
  2. Lesson 144, Story, page 224, exercises 16, 17.
  3. Lesson 145, Story, page 231, exercises 21, 22.
B. After presenting the above exercises, again give Mastery Test 28 individually to members of the group who failed the test.
C. If the group is firm (less than one-third of the total group missed two or more words in the story on the retest), present lesson 146 to the group during the next reading period.
D. If the group is still weak (more than one-third of the total group missed two or more words in the story on the retest), repeat *A* and *B* during the next reading period.

a boy and his mother went

to a toy shop. they went

to get toys. the boy said,

"I like toys."

STORY 126

EXERCISE 15

First reading—children read the story the fast way

(Have the children reread any sentences containing words that give them trouble. Keep a list of these words.)

a. (Pass out Storybook.)

b. Open your book to page 89. ✔

c. Everybody, touch the title of the story and get ready to read the words in the title the fast way.

d. First word. ✔

• (Pause two seconds.) Get ready. (Tap.) *A.*

e. (Tap for each remaining word in the title.)

f. (After the children have read the title ask:) What's this story about? (Signal.) *A bug and a dog.* Yes, **a bug and a dog.**

g. Everybody, get ready to read this story the fast way.

h. First word. ✔

• (Pause two seconds.) Get ready. (Tap.) *A.*

i. (Tap for the remaining words in the first sentence. Pause at least two seconds between taps.)

j. (Repeat *h* and *i* for the next two sentences. Have the children reread the first three sentences until firm.)

k. (The children are to read the remainder of the story the fast way, stopping at the end of each sentence.)

l. (After the first reading of the story, print on the board the words that the children missed more than one time. Have the children sound out each word one time and tell what word.)

m. (After the group's responses are firm, call on individual children to read the words.)

EXERCISE 16

Individual test

a. Turn back to page 89. I'm going to call on individual children to read a whole sentence.

b. (Call on individual children to read a sentence. Do not tap for each word.)

EXERCISE 17

Second reading—children read the story the fast way and answer questions

a. You're going to read the story again the fast way and I'll ask questions.

b. Starting with the first word of the title. ✔

• Get ready. (Tap.) *A.*

c. (Tap for each remaining word. Pause at least two seconds between taps. Pause longer before words that gave the children trouble during the first reading.)

d. (Ask the comprehension questions below as the children read.)

After the children read:	You say:
A bug and a dog.	What's this story about? (Signal.) *A bug and a dog.*
The dog said, "That bug is so little I can not see him on the log."	What did the dog say? (Signal.) *That bug is so little I can not see him on the log.*
The bug said, "I will eat this log."	What did the bug say? (Signal.) *I will eat this log.*
He bit and bit and bit at the log.	What did the bug do? (Signal.) *He bit and bit and bit at the log.*
The dog said, "That bug can eat logs as well as a big bug can."	What did the dog say? (Signal). *That bug can eat logs as well as a big bug can.*

EXERCISE 18

Picture comprehension

a. Everybody, look at the picture.

b. (Ask these questions:)

1. What's that little bug doing with the log? *The children respond.* He is eating it.
2. Do you think a little bug can eat a log? *The children respond.*

READING COMPREHENSION
EXERCISE 27

Children choose the correct words to fill in the blanks

a. (Point to the reading-comprehension exercise on side 2.)

b. Everybody, get ready to read the sentences in the box the fast way.

c. Get ready. (Tap for each word as the children read *He liked to eat. So he ate beans and cake.*)

- (Repeat until firm.)

d. Listen. **He liked to eat.** (Pause.) **So he ate beans and cake.**

e. Everybody, get ready to tell me the answer. Listen. **He** (pause) **something to eat.** Tell me what that something was. He . . . (Signal.) *Liked.* Yes, **liked.** He liked to eat.

f. Listen. **He liked to eat. So he ate beans and something.** So he ate beans and . . . (Signal.) *Cake.* Yes, **cake.**

g. (Repeat *b* through *f* until firm.)

h. Everybody, get ready to read the sentences in the box the fast way again. Get ready. (Tap for each word as the children read *He liked to eat. So he ate beans and cake.*)

i. Everybody, read item 1 to yourself and touch the word that goes in the blank. ✔

j. What word goes in the blank? (Signal.) *Liked.*

k. Everybody, circle the word **līked** under item 1. ✔

l. Everybody, read item 2 to yourself and touch the word that goes in the blank. ✔

m. What word goes in the blank? (Signal.) *Cake.*

n. Circle the word **cāke** under item 2. ✔

SUMMARY OF INDEPENDENT ACTIVITY
EXERCISE 28

Introduction to independent activity

a. (Hold up Worksheet 145.)

b. You're going to finish this worksheet on your own. (Tell the children when they will work the remaining items.)

- Let's go over the things you're going to do.

Sound writing

a. (Point to the sound-writing exercise on side 2.) Here are the sounds you're going to write today. I'll touch the sounds. You say them.

b. (Touch each sound.) *The children respond.*

c. (Repeat the series until firm.)

Sentence copying

a. (Point to the dotted sentence in the sentence-copying exercise.)

b. You're going to trace the words in this sentence. Then you're going to write the sentence on the other lines.

c. Reading the fast way. First word. ✔

- Get ready. (Tap for each word.)

d. After you finish your worksheet, you get to draw a picture about the sentence, **"I bite," a bug said.** You'll draw your picture on a piece of plain paper. (When the children finish their worksheets, give them sheets of plain paper.)

INDIVIDUAL CHECKOUT: STORYBOOK
EXERCISE 31

3-minute individual fluency checkout: rate skill/accuracy

a. As you are doing your worksheet, I'll call on children one at a time to read the **whole story.** Remember, you get two stars if you read the story in less than three minutes and make no more than three errors.

b. (Call on a child. Tell the child:) Start with the title and read the story carefully the fast way. Go. (Time the child. Tell the child any words the child misses. Stop the child as soon as the child makes the fourth error or exceeds the time limit.)

c. (If the child meets the rate-accuracy criterion, record two stars on your chart for lesson 145. Congratulate the child. Give children who do not earn two stars a chance to read the story again before the next lesson is presented.)

107 words/**3 min** = 36 wpm [**3 errors**]

EXERCISE 32:

Bonus worksheet: sides 3 and 4

(After the children have completed their worksheet exercises, give them sides 3 and 4 of Worksheet 145. Tell them they may keep the stories and read them.)

END OF LESSON 145

Before presenting lesson 146, give Mastery Test 28 to each child. Do not present lesson 146 to any groups that are not firm on this test.

WORKSHEET 126

PAIR RELATIONS

The children will need pencils.

EXERCISE 19

Children draw a line from the word to the correct picture

a. (Pass out Worksheet 126 to each child.)

b. Point to the first set in the pair-relations exercise on side 2 **(duck, nōse, ēar).**

c. Everybody, here's a new Matching Game. In this game you match pictures with the words that tell about the picture.

d. Everybody, touch the first word. ✔

e. Get ready to read that word the fast way. (Pause.) Get ready. (Tap.) *Duck.* Yes, **duck.**

f. Everybody, touch the picture that shows a duck. ✔

g. You're going to draw a line from the word **duck** to the picture that shows a duck.

h. Read the word and draw the line. ✔

i. Everybody, touch the next word. ✔

j. Get ready to read that word the fast way. (Pause.) Get ready. (Tap.) *Nose.* Yes, **nōse.**

k. Everybody, touch the picture that shows a nose. ✔

l. You're going to draw a line from the word **nōse** to the picture that shows a nose.

m. Read the word and draw the line. ✔

n. (Repeat *i* through *m* for the word **ēar.**)

o. You'll finish drawing lines to the right pictures later.

SUMMARY OF INDEPENDENT ACTIVITY
EXERCISE 20

Introduction to independent activity

a. (Hold up side 1 of Worksheet 126.)

b. Everybody, you're going to finish this worksheet on your own. (Tell the children when they will work the remaining items.)

• Let's go over the things you're going to do.

Sentence copying

a. (Point to the dotted sentence in the sentence-copying exercise.)

b. You're going to trace the words in this sentence. Then you're going to write the sentence on the other lines.

c. Reading the fast way. First word. ✔

• Get ready. (Tap.) *The.*

d. Next word. ✔

• Get ready. (Tap.) *Bug.*

e. (Repeat *d* for the remaining words.)

f. After you finish your worksheet, you get to draw a picture about the sentence, **the bug bit the log.** You'll draw your picture on a piece of plain paper.

Cross-out game

a. (Point to the boxed words in the Cross-out Game.) Everybody, what word are you going to circle? (Signal.) *So.* Yes, **so.**

b. What word are you going to cross out? (Signal.) *On.* Yes, **on.**

Reading comprehension

a. (Point to the boxed sentences in the reading-comprehension exercise.)

b. Everybody, get ready to read the sentences the fast way.

c. First word. ✔

• Get ready. (Tap for each word as the children read *the bug got mad.*)

d. (Have the children reread the sentence until firm.)

e. Get ready to read the next sentence. (Do *c* and *d* for **sō shē bit a log.**)

f. (Point to items 1 and 2.) These items tell about the story in the box. You're going to read each item and circle the right answer.

Sound writing

a. (Point to the sound-writing exercise on side 2.) Here are the sounds you're going to write today. I'll touch the sounds. You say them.

b. (Touch each sound.) *The children respond.*

c. (Repeat the series until firm.)

Pair relations

a. (Point to the pair-relations exercise.) You're going to read each word. Then draw a line from the word to the right picture.

b. (When the children finish their worksheets, give them sheets of paper. Remind them to draw a picture that shows **the bug bit the log.**)

END OF LESSON 126

EXERCISE 24

Picture comprehension

a. Everybody, look at the picture.

b. (Ask these questions:)

1. What's the pig doing? *The children respond.* Biting his leg.
2. Why is the bug laughing? *The children respond.* Yes, she tricked the pig.

• That bug is pretty smart.

WORKSHEET 145

STORY ITEMS

The children will need pencils.

EXERCISE 25

Children complete sentences and answer story questions

a. (Pass out sides 1 and 2 of Worksheet 145 to each child.)

b. Everybody, do a good job on your worksheet today and I'll give you a bonus worksheet.

c. (Hold up side 1 of your worksheet. Point to the story-items exercise on side 1.) These items are about the story you just read.

d. (Point to the blank in item 1.) Something is missing. When you get to this blank, say **"Blank."** What will you say? (Signal.) *Blank.*

e. Everybody, get ready to read item 1. Get ready. (Tap for each word as the children read *a bug and a blank met on a road.*) (Repeat until firm.)

f. What goes in the blank? (Signal.) *Pig.* Yes, **pig.**

g. Everybody, read item 2 and when you come to a blank, say **"Blank."** Get ready. (Tap for each word as the children read *the bug bit a blank.*)

• (Repeat until firm.)

h. What goes in the blank? (Signal.) *Log.* Yes, **log.**

i. Everybody, read item 3 and when you come to a blank, say **"Blank."** Get ready. (Tap for each word as the children read *the pig bit blank.*)

• (Repeat until firm.)

j. What goes in the blank? (Signal.) *His leg.* Yes, **his leg.**

k. Everybody, read item 4. Get ready. (Tap for each word as the children read *did the pig bite better?*)

l. What's the answer? (Signal.) *Yes.*

m. Now, everybody, read each item to yourself and circle the right answer. ✔

PICTURE COMPREHENSION
EXERCISE 26

Children look at the picture and complete the missing word

(Refer to sounds, not letter names, in missing words.)

a. (Point to the first picture in the picture-comprehension exercise.)

b. Everybody, touch this picture. ✔

c. Tell me what you see in this picture. (Accept reasonable responses.)

d. (Point to the sound in the blank at the beginning of item 1.) Something is missing. When you get to this, say **"Blank."** What will you say? (Signal.) *Blank.*

e. Everybody, get ready to read item 1.

f. Get ready. (Tap for each word as the children read *blank has a cat.*)

• (Repeat until firm.)

g. Look at the picture and get ready to tell me who has a cat. (Pause.) Who has a cat? (Signal.) *She.* Yes, **she.**

h. I'll say the sounds in the word **she. shshsh** (pause) **ēēē.** Again. **shshsh** (pause) **ēēē.**

i. Your turn. Say the sounds in **she.** Get ready. (Signal for each sound as the children say:) *shshsh* (pause) *ēēē.*

• (Repeat until firm.)

j. Look at the blank in item 1. The **shshsh** is already written in the blank. So what sound are you going to write next? (Signal as the children say *ēēē.*)

• (The children are not to write the sounds now.)

k. (Repeat *i* and *j* until firm.)

l. Now write the missing word in the blank. Remember—the **shshsh** is already written. ✔

m. (Repeat *e* through *l* for item 2.)

n. (Repeat *b* through *m* for the second picture.)

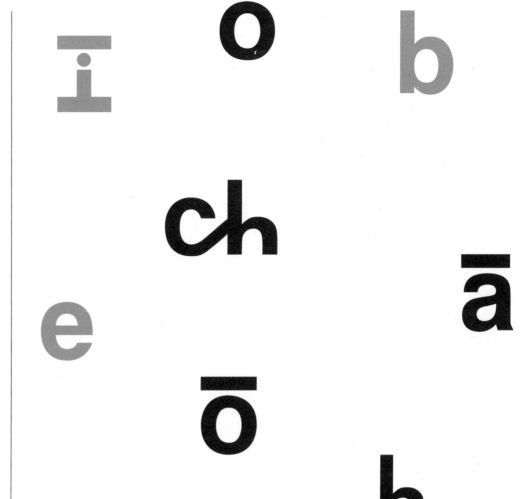

SOUNDS

EXERCISE 1

Teaching ī as in **ī**ce

a. (Point to ī.) Here's a new sound.

b. My turn. (Pause. Touch ī and say:) īīī.

c. Again. (Touch ī for a longer time.) īīīīī.

• (Lift your finger.)

d. (Point to ī.) Your turn. When I touch it, you say it. (Pause.) Get ready. (Touch. ī.) īīī.

• (Lift your finger.)

e. Again. (Touch ī.) īīīīīī.

• (Lift your finger.)

f. (Repeat e until firm.)

EXERCISE 2

Individual test

(Call on individual children to identify ī.)

EXERCISE 3

Sounds firm-up

a. Get ready to say the sounds when I touch them.

b. (Alternate touching i and ī. Point to the sound. Pause one second. Say:) Get ready. (Touch the sound.) *The children respond.*

c. (When i and ī are firm, alternate touching ī, i, I, and **ing** until all four sounds are firm.)

EXERCISE 4

Individual test

(Call on individual children to identify ī, i, I, or **ing**.)

EXERCISE 5

Sounds firm-up

a. (Point to ī.) When I touch the sound, you say it.

b. (Pause.) Get ready. (Touch ī.) īīī.

c. Again. (Repeat b until firm.)

d. Get ready to say all the sounds when I touch them.

e. (Alternate touching **o, b, ch, e, ō, ī, ā,** and **h** three or four times. Point to the sound. Pause one second. Say:) Get ready. (Touch the sound.) *The children respond.*

EXERCISE 6

Individual test

(Call on individual children to identify one or more sounds in exercise 5.)

STORY 145
EXERCISE 21

First reading—children read the title and first three sentences

a. (Pass out Storybook.)

b. Open your book to page 145. ✔

c. Everybody, touch the title of the story and get ready to read the words in the title the fast way.

d. First word. ✔

• (Pause two seconds.) Get ready. (Tap.) *The.*

e. (Tap for each remaining word in the title.)

f. (After the children have read the title, ask:) What's this story about? (Signal.) *The pig that bit his leg.* Yes, **the pig that bit his leg.**

g. Everybody, get ready to read this story the fast way.

h. First word. ✔

• (Pause two seconds.) Get ready. (Tap.) *A.*

i. (Tap for the remaining words in the first sentence. Pause at least two seconds between taps.)

j. (Repeat *h* and *i* for the next two sentences. Have the children reread the first three sentences until firm.)

EXERCISE 22

Individual children or the group read sentences to complete the first reading

a. I'm going to call on individual children to read a sentence. Everybody, follow along and point to the words. If you hear a mistake, raise your hand.

b. (Call on a child.) Read the next sentence. (Do not tap for the words. Let children read at their own pace, but be sure they read the sentence correctly.)

To Correct

(Have the child sound out the word. Then return to the beginning of the sentence.)

c. (Repeat *b* for most of the remaining sentences in the story. Occasionally have the group read a sentence. When the group is to read, say:) Everybody, read the next sentence. (Pause two seconds.) Get ready. (Tap for each word in the sentence. Pause at least two seconds between taps.)

EXERCISE 23

Second reading—individual children or the group read each sentence; the group answer questions

a. You're going to read the story again. This time I'm going to ask questions.

b. Starting with the first word of the title. ✔

• Get ready. (Tap as the children read the title. Pause at least two seconds between taps.)

c. (Call on a child.) Read the first sentence. *The child responds.*

d. (Repeat *b* and *c* in exercise 22. Present the following comprehension questions to the entire group.)

After the children read:	You say:
The pig that bit his leg.	What's this story about? (Signal.) *The pig that bit his leg.*
The pig said, "I can walk better than you."	What did the pig say? (Signal.) *I can walk better than you.* Who is he talking to? (Signal.) *A bug.*
Then she bit a log.	What did she do? (Signal.) *She bit a log.* I wonder if the pig can do that.
The pig went bite, bite, bite, and ate the log.	What did the pig do? (Signal.) *He went bite, bite, bite, and ate the log.* Who is better at eating logs? (Signal.) *The pig.*
The pig said, "I can do better than that."	What did the pig say? (Signal.) *I can do better than that.*
The pig gave his leg a big bite.	What did the pig do? (Signal.) *He gave his leg a big bite.* Whose leg did he bite? (Signal.) *His own leg.*
The bug said, "You bite pigs better than me."	What did the bug say? (Signal.) *You bite pigs better than me.* Who bites pigs better, the pig or the bug? (Signal.) *The pig.* Who is smarter? (Signal.) *The bug.* Why? *The children respond.*

READING VOCABULARY

EXERCISE 7

Children read the fast way

a. Get ready to read these words the fast way.

b. (Touch the ball for **slēēping.** Pause three seconds.) Get ready. (Signal.) *Sleeping.* Yes, **sleeping.**

c. (Repeat *b* for the remaining words on the page.)

EXERCISE 8

Children read the fast way again

a. Get ready to do these words again. Watch where I point.

b. (Point to a word. Pause one second. Say:) Get ready. (Signal.) *The children respond.*

• (Point to the words in this order: **fishing, nōse, then, slēēping, lēaf.**)

c. (Repeat *b* until firm.)

EXERCISE 9

Individual test

(Call on individual children to read one word the fast way.)

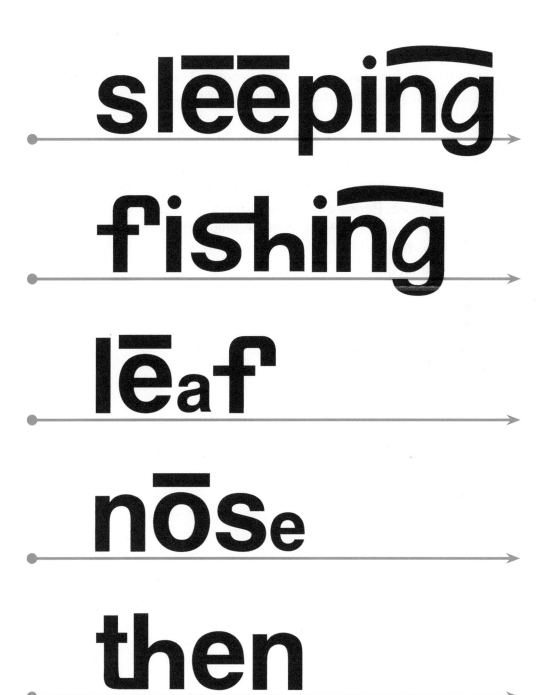

EXERCISE 18

Children read the fast way

a. Get ready to read these words the fast way.

b. (Touch the ball for **met.** Pause three seconds.) Get ready. (Signal.) *Met.*

c. (Repeat *b* for the remaining words on the page.)

EXERCISE 19

Children read the fast way again

a. Get ready to do these words again. Watch where I point.

b. (Point to a word. Pause one second. Say:) Get ready. (Signal.) *The children respond.* (Point to the words in this order: **met, let, then, ship, than.**)

c. (Repeat *b* until firm.)

EXERCISE 20

Individual test

(Call on individual children to read one word the fast way.)

met

then

ship

let

than

EXERCISE 10

Children read a word beginning with two consonants (**slam**)

a. (Cover **s.** Run your finger under **lam.**) You're going to sound out this part. Get ready. (Touch **l, a, m** as the children say *lllaaammm.*)

b. Say it fast. (Signal.) *Lam.* Yes, this part is **lam.**

c. (Uncover **s.** Point to **s.**) You're going to say this first. (Move your finger quickly under **lam.**) Then you're going to say (pause) **lam.**

d. (Point to **s.**) What are you going to say first? (Signal.) *sss.*

• What are you going to say next? (Signal.) *Lam.*

e. (Repeat *d* until firm.)

f. (Touch the ball for **slam.**) Remember—first you say **sss;** then you say **lam.** Get ready. (Move to **s,** then quickly along the arrow.) *Ssslam.*

g. Say it fast. (Signal.) *Slam.*

• Yes, what word? (Signal.) *Slam.* Yes, **slam.**

• Good reading.

h. Again. (Repeat *f* and *g* until firm.)

• Now you're going to sound out (pause) **slam.** Get ready. (Touch **s, l, a, m** as the children say *ssslllaaammm.*)

• What word? (Signal.) *Slam.* Yes, **slam.**

EXERCISE 11

Children sound out the word and tell what word

a. (Touch the ball for **let's.**) Sound it out.

b. Get ready. (Touch **l, e, t, s** as the children say *llleeetsss.*)

• (If sounding out is not firm, repeat *b.*)

c. What word? (Signal.) *Let's.* Yes, **let's.**

EXERCISE 12

Children sound out the word and tell what word

(Repeat the procedures in exercise 11 for **but.**)

EXERCISE 13

Children read the words the fast way

a. Now you get to read the words on this page the fast way.

b. (Touch the ball for **slam.** Pause three seconds.) Get ready. (Move your finger quickly along the arrow.) *Slam.*

c. (Repeat *b* for each word on the page.)

slam

let's

but

EXERCISE 14

Individual test

(Call on individual children to read one word the fast way.)

EXERCISE 12

Children read the fast way

(Touch the ball for **moon.**) Get ready to read this word the fast way. (Pause three seconds.) Get ready. (Signal.) *Moon.*

EXERCISE 13

Children sound out the word and tell what word

a. (Touch the ball for **chip.**) Sound it out.
b. Get ready. (Touch **ch, i, p** as the children say *chiiip.*)
• (If sounding out is not firm, repeat *b.*)
c. What word? (Signal.) *Chip.* Yes, **chip.**

EXERCISE 14

Children sound out the word and tell what word

a. (Touch the ball for **better.**) Sound it out.
b. Get ready. (Touch **b, e,** between the **t**'s, **er** as the children say *beeeterrr.*)
• (If sounding out is not firm, repeat *b.*)
c. What word? (Signal.) *Better.* Yes, **better.**

EXERCISE 15

Children sound out the word and tell what word

a. (Touch the ball for **pīle.**) Sound it out.
b. Get ready. (Touch **p, ī, l** as the children say *pīīīlll.*)
• (If sounding out is not firm, repeat *b.*)
c. What word? (Signal.) *Pile.* Yes, **pile.**

EXERCISE 16

Children read the words the fast way

a. Now you get to read the words on this page the fast way.
b. (Touch the ball for **moon.** Pause three seconds.) Get ready. (Move your finger quickly along the arrow.) *Moon.*
c. (Repeat *b* for each word on the page.)

EXERCISE 17

Individual test

(Call on individual children to read one word the fast way.)

moon

chip

better

pīle

EXERCISE 15

Children read a word beginning with two consonants (**slip**)

a. (Cover **s**. Point to **lip**.) You're going to read this part of the word the fast way. (Pause three seconds.) Get ready. (Signal.) *Lip.* Yes, **lip.**

b. (Uncover **s**. Point to **s**.) You're going to say this first. (Move your finger quickly under **lip**.) Then you're going to say (pause) **lip.**

c. (Point to **s**.) What are you going to say first? (Signal.) *sss.*
- What are you going to say next? (Signal.) *Lip.*

d. (Repeat *c* until firm.)

e. (Touch the ball for **slip**.) Remember—first you say **sss**; then you say **lip**. Get ready. (Move to **s,** then quickly along the arrow.) *Ssslip.*

f. Say it fast. (Signal.) *Slip.*
- Yes, what word? (Signal.) *Slip.* Yes, **slip.**
- Good reading.

g. Again. (Repeat *e* and *f* until firm.)

h. Now you're going to sound out (pause) **slip.** Get ready. (Touch **s, l, i, p** as the children say *sssllliiip.*)
- What word? (Signal.) *Slip.* Yes, **slip.**

EXERCISE 16

Children identify, then sound out an irregular word (**to**)

a. (Touch the ball for **to**.) Everybody, you're going to read this word the fast way. (Pause three seconds.) Get ready. (Move your finger quickly along the arrow.) *To.* Yes, **to.**

b. Now you're going to sound out the word. Get ready. (Quickly touch **t, o** as the children say *tooo.*)

c. Again. (Repeat *b*.)

d. How do we say the word? (Signal.) *To.* Yes, **to.**

e. (Repeat *b* and *d* until firm.)

EXERCISE 17

Individual test

(Have children do *b* and *d* in exercise 16.)

EXERCISE 18

Children read the words the fast way

Now you get to read the words on this page the fast way.

b. (Touch the ball for **slip**. Pause three seconds.) Get ready. (Move your finger quickly along the arrow.) *Slip.* Yes, **slip.**

c. (Repeat *b* for **to**.)

EXERCISE 19

Individual test

(Have individual children read one word the fast way.)

READING VOCABULARY

EXERCISE 7

Children read **walk** and **walked**

a. (Touch the ball for **walk**.) You're going to read this word the fast way. (Pause three seconds.) Get ready. (Move your finger quickly along the arrow.) *Walk.*

b. (Return to the ball for **walk**.) Yes, this word is **walk**.

c. (Touch the ball for **walked**.) So this must be **walk** . . . (Touch **d**.) *d.*

• What word? (Signal.) *Walked.* Yes, **walked**.

d. Again. (Repeat *b* and *c* until firm.)

e. (Touch the ball for **walk**.) This word is **walk**.

f. (Touch the ball for **walked**.) So this must be . . . (Quickly run your finger under **walk** and tap **d**.) *Walked.* Yes, **walked**.

g. Again. (Repeat *e* and *f* until firm.)

h. Now you're going to sound out (pause) **walked**. Get ready. (Touch **w, a, l, k, d** as the children say *wwwaaalllkd*.)

i. How do we say the word? (Signal.) *Walked.* Yes, **walked**.

EXERCISE 8

Children identify, then sound out an irregular word (**talked**)

a. (Touch the ball for **talked**.) Everybody, you're going to read this word the fast way. (Pause three seconds.) Get ready. (Move your finger quickly along the arrow.) *Talked.* Yes, **talked**.

b. Now you're going to sound out the word. Get ready. (Quickly touch **t, a, l, k, d** as the children say *taaalllkd*.)

c. Again. (Repeat *b*.)

d. How do we say the word? (Signal.) *Talked.* Yes, **talked**.

e. (Repeat *b* and *d* until firm.)

EXERCISE 9

Children identify, then sound out an irregular word (**loved**)

a. (Touch the ball for **loved**.) Everybody, you're going to read this word the fast way. (Pause three seconds.) Get ready. (Move your finger quickly along the arrow.) *Loved.* Yes, **loved**.

b. Now you're going to sound out the word. Get ready. (Quickly touch **l, o, v, e, d** as the children say *lllooovvveeed*.)

c. Again. (Repeat *b*.)

d. How do we say the word? (Signal.) *Loved.* Yes, **loved**.

e. (Repeat *b* and *d* until firm.)

walk

walked

talked

loved

EXERCISE 10

Children read the words the fast way

(Have the children read the words on this page the fast way.)

EXERCISE 11

Individual test

(Call on individual children to read one word the fast way.)

STORYBOOK

STORY 127
EXERCISE 20

First reading—children read the story the fast way

(Have the children reread any sentences containing words that give them trouble. Keep a list of these words.)

a. (Pass out Storybook.)

b. Open your book to page 92. ✔

c. Everybody, touch the title of the story and get ready to read the words in the title the fast way.

d. First word. ✔

• (Pause two seconds.) Get ready. (Tap.) *The.*

e. (Tap for the remaining word in the title.)

f. (After the children have read the title, ask:) What's this story about? (Signal.) *The bugs.* Yes, **the bugs.**

g. Everybody, get ready to read this story the fast way.

h. First word. ✔

• (Pause two seconds.) Get ready. (Tap.) *A.*

i. (Tap for the remaining words in the first sentence. Pause at least two seconds between taps.)

j. (Repeat *h* and *i* for the next two sentences. Have the children reread the first three sentences until firm.)

k. (The children are to read the remainder of the story the fast way, stopping at the end of each sentence.)

l. (After the first reading of the story, print on the board the words that the children missed more than one time. Have the children sound out each word one time and tell what word.)

m. (After the group's responses are firm, call on individual children to read the words.)

EXERCISE 21

Individual test

a. Look at page 92. I'm going to call on individual children to read a whole sentence.

b. (Call on individual children to read a sentence. Do not tap for each word.)

EXERCISE 22

Second reading—children read the story the fast way and answer questions

a. You're going to read the story again the fast way and I'll ask questions.

b. Starting with the first word of the title. ✔

• Get ready. (Tap.) *The.*

c. (Tap for each remaining word. Pause at least two seconds between taps. Pause longer before words that gave the children trouble during the first reading.)

d. (Ask the comprehension questions below as the children read.)

After the children read:	You say:
The bugs.	What's this story about? (Signal.) *The bugs.*
The big bug said, "Let's go eat."	Did the big bug want to eat? (Signal.) *Yes.*
So the big bug ate a leaf and a nut and a rock.	What did the big bug eat? (Signal.) *A leaf, a nut, and a rock.*
So the little bug ate a leaf and a nut and a rock.	What did the little bug eat? (Signal.) *A leaf, a nut, and a rock.*
She ate the log.	Did she eat the log? (Signal.) *Yes.*
Then she ate ten more logs.	Then what did she eat? (Signal.) *Ten more logs.*
The little bug said, "Now let's eat more."	What did the little bug say? (Signal.) *Now let's eat more.*

EXERCISE 23

Picture comprehension

a. What do you think you'll see in the picture? *The children respond.*

b. Look at the picture.

c. (Ask these questions:)

  1. What is the little bug eating? *The children respond.* A log.

  2. Do you think the big bug is surprised to see what the little bug can eat? *The children respond.*

J

SOUNDS

EXERCISE 1

Teaching **j** as in **jump**

a. (Point to **j**.) Here's a new sound. It's a quick sound.

b. My turn. (Pause. Touch **j** for an instant, saying:) **j**. (Do not say **juuh**.)

c. Again. (Touch **j** and say:) *j*.

d. (Point to **j**.) Your turn. When I touch it, you say it. (Pause.) Get ready. (Touch **j**.) *j*.

e. Again. (Touch **j**.) *j*.

f. (Repeat *e* until firm.)

EXERCISE 2

Individual test

(Call on individual children to identify **j**.)

EXERCISE 3

Sounds firm-up

a. Get ready to say the sounds when I touch them.

b. (Alternate touching **j** and **g**. Point to the sound. Pause one second. Say:) Get ready. (Touch the sound.) *The children respond.*

c. (When **j** and **g** are firm, alternate touching **j, g, sh,** and **ch** until all four sounds are firm.)

EXERCISE 4

Individual test

(Call on individual children to identify **j, g, sh,** or **ch.**)

EXERCISE 5

Sounds firm-up

a. (Point to **j**.) When I touch the sound, you say it.

b. (Pause.) Get ready. (Touch **j**.) *j*.

c. Again. (Repeat *b* until firm.)

d. Get ready to say all the sound when I touch them.

e. (Alternate touching **oo, y, j, er, ī, c, x,** and **ō** three or four times. Point to the sound. Pause one second. Say:) Get ready. (Touch the sound.) *The children respond.*

EXERCISE 6

Individual test

(Call on individual children to identify one or more sounds in exercise 5.)

WORKSHEET 127

PAIR RELATIONS

The children will need pencils.

EXERCISE 24

Children draw a line from the word to the correct picture

a. (Pass out Worksheet 127 to each child.)

b. Point to the first set in the pair-relations exercise on side 2 **(dog, gāte, rōad)**.

c. Everybody, here's the new Matching Game. In this game you match pictures with the words that tell about the picture.

d. Everybody, touch the first word. ✔

e. Get ready to read that word the fast way. (Pause.) Get ready. (Tap.) *Dog.* Yes, **dog.**

f. Everybody, touch the picture that shows a dog. ✔

g. You're going to draw a line from the word **dog** to the picture that shows a dog.

h. Read the word and draw the line. ✔

i. Everybody, touch the next word. ✔

j. Get ready to read that word the fast way. (Pause.) Get ready. (Tap.) *Gate.* Yes, **gate.**

k. Everybody, touch the picture that shows a gate. ✔

l. You're going to draw a line from the word **gate** to the picture that shows a gate.

m. Read the word and draw the line. ✔

n. (Repeat *i* through *m* for the word **rōad.**)

o. You'll finish drawing lines to the right pictures later.

SUMMARY OF INDEPENDENT ACTIVITY
EXERCISE 25

Introduction to independent activity

a. (Hold up side 1 of Worksheet 127.)

b. Everybody, you're going to finish this worksheet on your own. (Tell the children when they will work the remaining items.)

• Let's go over the things you're going to do.

Sentence copying

a. (Point to the dotted sentence in the sentence-copying exercise.)

b. You're going to trace the words in this sentence. Then you're going to write the sentence on the other lines.

c. Reading the fast way. First word. ✔

• Get ready. (Tap.) *She.*

d. Next word. ✔

• Get ready. (Tap.) *Ate.*

e. (Repeat *d* for the remaining words.)

f. After you finish your worksheet, you get to draw a picture about the sentence, **shē āte the log.** You'll draw your picture on a piece of plain paper.

Cross-out game

a. (Point to the boxed words in the Cross-out Game.) Everybody, what word are you going to circle? (Signal.) *Bug.* Yes, **bug.**

b. What word are you going to cross out? (Signal.) *Big.* Yes, **big.**

Reading comprehension

a. (Point to the boxed sentences in the reading-comprehension exercise.)

b. Everybody, get ready to read the sentences the fast way.

c. First word. ✔

• Get ready. (Tap for each word as the children read *a big bug met a little bug.*)

d. (Have the children reread the sentence until firm.)

e. Get ready to read the next sentence. (Repeat *c* and *d* for **hē said, "let's gō ēat."**)

f. (Point to items 1 and 2.) These items tell about the story in the box. You're going to read each item and circle the right answer.

Sound writing

a. (Point to the sound-writing exercise on side 2.) Here are the sounds you're going to write today. I'll touch the sounds. You say them.

b. (Touch each sound.) *The children respond.*

• (Repeat until firm.)

Pair relations

a. (Point to the pair-relations exercise.) You're going to read each word. Then draw a line from the word to the right picture.

b. (When the children finish their worksheets, give them sheets of plain paper. Remind them to draw a picture that shows **shē āte the log.**)

END OF LESSON 127

123 Lesson 127

READING COMPREHENSION
EXERCISE 22

Children choose the correct words to fill in the blanks

a. (Point to the reading-comprehension exercise on side 2.)

b. Everybody, get ready to read the sentences in the box the fast way.

c. Get ready. (Tap for each word as the children read *A little bug bit a big bug. The little bug was mad.*)

• (Repeat until firm.)

d. Listen. **A little bug bit a big bug.** (Pause.) **The little bug was mad.**

e. Everybody, get ready to tell me the answer. Listen. **A little** (pause) **something bit a big bug.** Tell me what that something was. A little . . . (Signal.) *Bug.* Yes, **bug.**

• A little bug bit a big bug.

f. Listen. **A little bug bit a big bug. The little bug was** (pause) **something.** The little bug was . . . (Signal.) *Mad.* Yes, **mad.**

g. (Repeat *b* through *f* until firm.)

h. Everybody, get ready to read the sentences in the box the fast way again. Get ready. (Tap for each word as the children read *A little bug bit a big bug. The little bug was mad.*)

i. Everybody, read item 1 to yourself and touch the word that goes in the blank. ✔

j. What word goes in the blank? (Signal.) *Bug.*

k. Everybody, circle the word **bug** under item 1. ✔

l. Everybody, read item 2 to yourself and touch the word that goes in the blank. ✔

m. What word goes in the blank? (Signal.) *Mad.*

n. Circle the word **mad** under item 2. ✔

SUMMARY OF INDEPENDENT ACTIVITY
EXERCISE 23

Introduction to independent activity

a. (Hold up Worksheet 144.)

b. Everybody, you're going to finish this worksheet on your own. (Tell the children when they will work the remaining items.)

• Let's go over the things you're going to do.

Sound writing

a. (Point to the sound-writing exercise on side 2.) Here are the sounds you're going to write today. I'll touch the sounds. You say them.

b. (Touch each sound.) *The children respond.*

c. (Repeat the series until firm.)

Sentence copying

a. (Point to the dotted sentence in the sentence-copying exercise.)

b. You're going to trace the words in this sentence. Then you're going to write the sentence on the other lines.

c. Reading the fast way. First word. ✔

• Get ready. (Tap for each word.)

d. After you finish your worksheet, you get to draw a picture about the sentence, **he sat on the shōre.** You'll draw your picture on a piece of plain paper. (When the children finish their worksheets, give them sheets of plain paper.)

END OF LESSON 144

SOUNDS

EXERCISE 1

Teaching ī as in **īce**

a. (Point to **ī.**) My turn. (Pause. Touch **ī** and say:) ī̄ī̄ī̄.

b. (Point to **ī.**) Your turn. When I touch it, you say it. (Pause.) Get ready. (Touch **ī.**) *ī̄ī̄ī̄.*

• (Lift your finger.)

c. Again. (Touch **ī.**) *ī̄ī̄ī̄ī̄.*

• (Lift your finger.)

d. (Repeat *c* until firm.)

EXERCISE 2

Sounds firm-up

a. Get ready to say the sounds when I touch them.

b. (Alternate touching **ī** and **e.** Point to the sound. Pause one second. Say:) Get ready. (Touch the sound.) *The children respond.*

c. (When **i** and **e** are firm, alternate touching **e, ī, i,** and **ing** until all four sounds are firm.)

EXERCISE 3

Individual test

(Call on individual children to identify **e, ī, i,** or **ing.**)

EXERCISE 4

Sounds firm-up

a. (Point to **ī.**) When I touch the sound, you say it.

b. (Pause.) Get ready. (Touch **ī.**) *ī̄ī̄ī̄.*

c. Again. (Repeat *b* until firm.)

d. Get ready to say all the sounds when I touch them.

e. (Alternate touching **ī, ō, ch, v, w, k, p,** and **b** three or four times. Point to the sound. Pause one second. Say:) Get ready. (Touch the sound.) *The children respond.*

EXERCISE 5

Individual test

(Call on individual children to identify one or more sounds in exercise 4.)

EXERCISE 19

Picture comprehension

a. What do you think you'll see in the picture? *The children respond.*
b. Turn the page and look at the picture.
c. (Ask these questions:)
  1. What's happening in the picture? *The children respond.* The bug is giving the eagle a dime.
  2. Would you give the eagle a dime? *The children respond.*

WORKSHEET 144

STORY ITEMS

The children will need pencils.

EXERCISE 20

Children complete sentences and answer story questions

a. (Pass out Worksheet 144 to each child.)
b. (Point to the story-items exercise on side 1.) These items are about the story you just read.
c. (Point to the blank in item 1.) Something is missing. When you get to this blank, say **"Blank."** What will you say? (Signal.) *Blank.*
d. Everybody, get ready to read item 1. Get ready. (Tap for each word as the children read *a big blank came and sat on the shore.* Repeat until firm.)
e. What goes in the blank? (Signal.) *Eagle.* Yes, **eagle.**
f. Everybody, read item 2 and when you come to a blank, say **"Blank."**
g. Get ready. (Tap for each word as the children read)
  the eagle said, "give me a blank.")
• (Repeat until firm.)
h. What goes in the blank? (Signal.) *Dime.* Yes, **dime.**
i. Everybody, read item 3. Get ready. (Tap for each word as the children read *did the bug give the eagle a dime?*)
• (Repeat until firm.)
j. What's the answer? (Signal.) *Yes.*
k. Everybody, get ready to read item 4. Get ready. (Tap for each word as the children read *did the bug go to the other side?*)
• What's the answer? (Signal.) *Yes.*
l. Now, everybody, read each item to yourself and circle the right answer. ✔

PICTURE COMPREHENSION

EXERCISE 21

Children look at the picture and complete the missing word

(Refer to sounds, not letter names, in missing words.)
a. (Point to the first picture in the picture-comprehension exercise.)
b. Everybody, touch this picture. ✔
c. Tell me what you see in this picture. (Accept reasonable responses.)
d. (Point to the sound in the blank in item 1.) Something is missing. When you get to this, say **"Blank."** What will you say? (Signal.) *Blank.*
e. Everybody, get ready to read item 1.
f. Get ready. (Tap for each word as the children read *the blank is fat.*)
• (Repeat until firm.)
g. Look at the picture and get ready to tell me what is fat. (Pause.) The . . . (Signal.) *man . . .* is fat. Yes, **man.**
h. I'll say the sounds in the word **man. mmm** (pause) **aaa** (pause) **nnn.**
i. Your turn. Say the sounds in **man.** Get ready. (Signal for each sound as the children say:) *mmm* (pause) *aaa* (pause) *nnn.*
• (Repeat until firm.)
j. Look at the blank in item 1. The **mmm** is already written in the blank. So what sounds are you going to write next? (Signal for each sound as the children say:) *aaa* (pause) *nnn.*
• (The children are not to write the sounds now.)
k. (Repeat *i* and *j* until firm.)
l. Now write the missing word in the blank. Remember—the **mmm** is already written. ✔
m. (Repeat *e* through *l* for item 2.)
n. (Repeat *b* through *m* for the second picture.)

READING VOCABULARY
EXERCISE 6

Children sound out the word and tell what word

a. (Touch the ball for **pond.**) Sound it out.
b. Get ready. (Touch **p, o, n, d** as the children say *pooonnnd.*)
• (If sounding out is not firm, repeat *b.*)
c. What word? (Signal.) *Pond.* Yes, **pond.**

EXERCISE 7

Children sound out the word and tell what word

a. (Touch the ball for **back.**) Sound it out.
b. Get ready. (Touch **b, a, c** as the children say *baaac.*)
• (If sounding out is not firm, repeat *b.*)
c. What word? (Signal.) *Back.* Yes, **back.**

EXERCISE 8

Children sound out the word and tell what word

a. (Touch the ball for **bed.**) Sound it out.
b. Get ready. (Touch **b, e, d** as the children say *beeed.*)
• (If sounding out is not firm, repeat *b.*)
c. What word? (Signal.) *Bed.* Yes, **bed.**

EXERCISE 9

Children sound out the word and tell what word

a. (Touch the ball for **bus.**) Sound it out.
b. Get ready. (Touch **b, u, s** as the children say *buuusss.*)
• (If sounding out is not firm, repeat *b.*)
c. What word? (Signal.) *Bus.* Yes, **bus.**

EXERCISE 10

Children read the words the fast way

a. Now you get to read the words on this page the fast way.
b. (Touch the ball for **pond.** Pause three seconds.) Get ready.
(Move your finger quickly along the arrow.) *Pond.*
c. (Repeat *b* for each word on the page.)

pond

back

bed

bus

EXERCISE 11

Individual test

(Call on individual children to read one word the fast way.)

STORY 144
EXERCISE 16

First reading—children read the title and first three sentences

a. (Pass out Storybook.)

b. Open your book to page 142. ✔ Now you're going to finish the story about the bug that wanted to get to the other side of the lake.

c. Everybody, touch the title of the story and get ready to read the words in the title the fast way.

d. First word. ✔

• (Pause two seconds.) Get ready. (Tap.) *The.*

e. (Tap for each remaining word in the title.)

f. (After the children have read the title, ask:) What's this story about? (Signal.) *The other side of the lake.* Yes, **the other side of the lake.**

g. Everybody, get ready to read this story the fast way.

h. First word. ✔

• (Pause two seconds.) Get ready. (Tap.) *A.*

i. (Tap for the remaining words in the first sentence. Pause at least two seconds between taps.)

j. (Repeat *h* and *i* for the next two sentences. Have the children reread the first three sentences until firm.)

EXERCISE 17

Individual children or the group read sentences to complete the first reading

a. I'm going to call on individual children to read a sentence. Everybody, follow along and point to the words. If you hear a mistake, raise your hand.

b. (Call on a child.) Read the next sentence. (Do not tap for the words. Let children read at their own pace, but be sure they read the sentence correctly.)

To Correct
(Have the child sound out the word. Then return to the beginning of the sentence.)

c. (Repeat *b* for most of the remaining sentences in the story. Occasionally have the group read a sentence. When the group is to read, say:) Everybody, read the next sentence. (Pause two seconds.) Get ready. (Tap for each word in the sentence. Pause at least two seconds between taps.)

EXERCISE 18

Second reading—individual children or the group read each sentence; the group answer questions

a. You're going to read the story again. This time I'm going to ask questions.

b. Starting with the first word of the title. ✔

• Get ready. (Tap as the children read the title. Pause at least two seconds between taps.)

c. (Call on a child.) Read the first sentence. *The child responds.*

d. (Repeat *b* and *c* in exercise 17. Present the following comprehension questions to the entire group.)

After the children read:	You say:
Then a big eagle came and sat down on the shore.	What happened? (Signal.) *A big eagle came and sat down on the shore.* Do you think the eagle can help the bug get to the other side? *The children respond.* How? *The children respond.* Let's read and find out.
"Give me a dime and I will take you to the other side."	What did the eagle say? (Signal.) *Give me a dime and I will take you to the other side.* Do you think the bug will do that? *The children respond.* Let's read and find out.
So the bug gave the eagle a dime and got on the eagle.	Did the bug give the eagle a dime? (Signal.) *Yes.* Then what did the bug do? (Signal.) *He got on the eagle.*
They went over the lake.	Did the bug get to the other side of the lake? (Signal.) *Yes.* How? *The children respond.* Yes, the eagle took him over.

EXERCISE 12

Children sound out an irregular word (**walk**)

a. (Touch the ball for **walk.**) Sound it out.

b. Get ready. (Quickly touch each sound as the children say *wwwaaalllk.*)

c. Again. (Repeat *b* until firm.)

d. That's how we <u>sound out</u> the word. Here's how we <u>say</u> the word. **Walk.** How do we <u>say</u> the word? (Signal.) *Walk.*

e. Now you're going to <u>sound out</u> the word. Get ready. (Touch each sound as the children say *wwwaaalllk.*)

f. Now you're going to <u>say</u> the word. Get ready. (Signal.) *Walk.*

g. (Repeat *e* and *f* until firm.)

walk

EXERCISE 13

Children rhyme with an irregular word (**walk**)

a. (Touch the ball for **walk.**) Everybody, you're going to read this word the fast way. Get ready. (Signal.) *Walk.*

b. (Touch the ball for **talk.**) This word rhymes with (pause) **walk.** Get ready. (Move to **t,** then quickly along the arrow.) *Talk.*

c. (Repeat *a* and *b* until firm.)

talk

EXERCISE 14

Children sound out **talk**

(Have the children sound out **talk.**) *Taaalllk.*

- How do we say the word? (Signal.) *Talk.* Yes, **talk.**
- A baby can not **talk.**

EXERCISE 15

Children read the words the fast way

a. Now you get to read the words on this page the fast way.

b. (Touch the ball for **talk.** Pause three seconds.) Get ready. (Move your finger quickly along the arrow.) *Talk.*

c. (Repeat *b* for **walk.**)

EXERCISE 16

Individual test

(Call on individual children to read one word the fast way.)

EXERCISE 9

Children read a word beginning with two consonants

a. (Cover **b.** Point to **room.**) You're going to read this part of the word the fast way. (Pause three seconds.) Get ready. (Signal.) *Room.* Yes, **room.**

b. (Uncover **b.** Point to **b.**) You're going to say this first. (Move your finger quickly under **b.**) Then you're going to say (pause) **room.**

c. (Point to **b.**) What are you going to say first? (Signal.) *b.* What are you going to say next? (Signal.) *Room.* (Repeat until firm.)

d. (Touch the ball for **broom.**) Remember, first you say **b;** then you say **room.** Get ready. (Move to **b,** then quickly along the arrow.) *Broom.*

e. Say it fast. (Signal.) *Broom.*

• Yes, what word? (Signal.) *Broom.* Yes, **broom.**

• Good reading.

f. Again. (Repeat *d* and *e* until firm.)

g. Now you're going to sound out (pause) **broom.** Get ready. (Touch **b, r, oo, m** as the children say *brrroooommm.*)

• What word? (Signal.) *Broom.* Yes, **broom.**

EXERCISE 10

Children sound out the word and tell what word

a. (Touch the ball for **dīme.**) Sound it out.

b. Get ready. (Touch **d, ī, m** as the children say *dīīīmmm.*)

c. What word? (Signal.) *Dime.* Yes, **dime.**

EXERCISE 11

Children sound out the word and tell what word

(Repeat the procedures in exercise 10 for **chōre.**)

EXERCISE 12

Children identify, then sound out an irregular word (**you**)

a. (Touch the ball for **you.**) Everybody, you're going to read this word the fast way. (Pause three seconds.) Get ready. (Move your finger quickly along the arrow.) *You.* Yes, **you.**

b. Now you're going to sound out the word. Get ready. (Quickly touch **y, o, u** as the children say *yyyooouuu.*)

• (Repeat until firm.)

c. How do we say the word? (Signal.) *You.* Yes, **you.**

d. (Repeat *b* and *c* until firm.)

EXERCISE 13

Individual test

(Have children do *b* and *c* in exercise 12.)

EXERCISE 14

Children read the words the fast way

(Have the children read the words on this page the fast way.)

EXERCISE 15

Individual test

(Have children read one word the fast way.)

broom

dīme

chōre

you

EXERCISE 17

Children read the fast way

a. Get ready to read these words the fast way.
b. (Touch the ball for **get.** Pause three seconds.) Get ready. (Signal.) *Get.*
c. (Repeat *b* for the remaining words on the page.)

EXERCISE 18

Children read the fast way again

a. Get ready to do these words again. Watch where I point.
b. (Point to a word. Pause one second. Say:) Get ready. (Signal.)
   The children respond.
• (Point to the words in this order: **bit, down, get.**)
c. (Repeat *b* until firm.)

EXERCISE 19

Individual test

(Call on individual children to read one word the fast way.)

get

bit

down

READING VOCABULARY

EXERCISE 6

Children read the fast way

a. Get ready to read these words the fast way.

b. (Touch the ball for **room.** Pause three seconds.) Get ready. (Signal.) *Room.*

c. (Repeat *b* for the remaining words on the page.)

EXERCISE 7

Children read the fast way again

a. Get ready to do these words again. Watch where I point.

b. (Point to a word. Pause one second. Say:) Get ready. (Signal.) *The children respond.*

• (Point to the words in this order: **room, shōre, ēagle, sitting, yes.**)

c. (Repeat *b* until firm.)

EXERCISE 8

Individual test

(Call on individual children to read one word the fast way.)

STORY 128
EXERCISE 20

First reading—children read the story the fast way

(Have the children reread any sentences containing words that give them trouble. Keep a list of these words.)

a. (Pass out Storybook.)

b. Open your book to page 95. ✔

c. Everybody, touch the title of the story and get ready to read the words in the title the fast way.

d. First word. ✔

• (Pause two seconds.) Get ready. (Tap.) *The*

e. (Tap for each remaining word in the title.)

f. (After the children have read the title, ask:) What's this story about? (Signal.) *The bug bus.* Yes, the **bug bus.**

g. Everybody, get ready to read this story the fast way.

h. First word. ✔

• (Pause two seconds.) Get ready. (Tap.) *A.*

i. (Tap for the remaining words in the first sentence. Pause at least two seconds between taps.)

j. (Repeat *h* and *i* for the next two sentences. Have the children reread the first three sentences until firm.)

k. (The children are to read the remainder of the story the fast way, stopping at the end of each sentence.)

l. (After the first reading of the story, print on the board the words that the children missed more than one time. Have the children sound out each word one time and tell what word.)

m. (After the group's responses are firm, call on individual children to read the words.)

EXERCISE 21

Individual test

a. Turn back to page 95. I'm going to call on individual children to read a whole sentence.

b. (Call on individual children to read a sentence. Do not tap for each word.)

EXERCISE 22

Second reading—children read the story the fast way and answer questions

a. You're going to read the story again the fast way and I'll ask questions.

b. Starting with the first word of the title. ✔

• Get ready. (Tap.) *The.*

c. (Tap for each remaining word. Pause at least two seconds between taps. Pause longer before words that gave the children trouble during the first reading.)

d. (Ask the comprehension questions below as the children read.)

After the children read:	You say:
The bug bus.	What's this story about? (Signal.) *The bug bus.*
A little bug sat on the back of a big dog.	What did the little bug do? (Signal.) *Sat on the back of a big dog.*
"I am not a bus."	What did the dog say? (Signal.) *I am not a bus.*
She went to sleep.	Did the bug get down? (Signal.) *No.* What did she do? (Signal.) *She went to sleep.*
The dog said, "I am not a bed."	What did the dog say? (Signal.) *I am not a bed.* Do you think the bug will get down? *The children respond.* Let's read and find out.
The dog ran to the pond and went in.	What did the dog do? (Signal). *The dog ran to the pond and went in.*
"Take me back to the sand."	What did the bug say? (Signal.) *Take me back to the sand.*
"No," the dog said.	Did the dog go back to the sand? (Signal.) *No.*
Ten bugs came and got on the dog.	What happened? (Signal.) *Ten bugs came and got on the dog.*
The dog said, "I feel like a bug bus."	What did the dog say? (Signal.) *I feel like a bug bus.*

oo

r

x

w

SOUNDS

EXERCISE 1

Sounds firm-up

a. Get ready to say the sounds when I touch them.

b. (Alternate touching **oo** and **r.** Point to the sound. Pause one second. Say:) Get ready. (Touch the sound.) *The children respond.*

c. (When **oo** and **r** are firm, alternate touching **oo, r, x,** and **w** until all four sounds are firm.)

EXERCISE 2

Individual test

(Call on individual children to identify **oo, r, x,** or **w.**)

EXERCISE 3

Teacher introduces cross-out game

a. (Use transparency and crayon.)

b. I'll cross out the sounds on this part of the page when you can tell me every sound.

c. Remember—when I touch it, you say it.

d. (Go over the sounds until the children can identify all the sounds in order.)

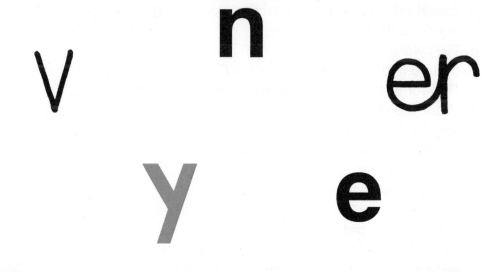

EXERCISE 4

Individual test

(Call on individual children to identify two or more sounds in exercise 4.)

EXERCISE 5

Teacher crosses out sounds

a. You told me every sound. Get ready to do it again. This time I'll cross out each sound when you tell me what it is.

b. (Point to each sound. Pause. Say:) Get ready. (Touch the sound.) *The children respond.*

• (As you cross out the sound, say:) Goodbye, _____.

EXERCISE 23

Picture comprehension

a. Everybody, look at the picture.

b. (Ask these questions:)

1. What are those little bugs doing? *The children respond.* They're riding on a bug bus.
2. Does the dog like having the bugs on his back? *No.*

WORKSHEET 128

SUMMARY OF INDEPENDENT ACTIVITY

EXERCISE 24

Introduction to independent activity

a. (Pass out Worksheet 128 to each child.)

b. Everybody, you're going to do this worksheet on your own. (Tell the children when they will work the items.)

• Let's go over the things you're going to do.

Sentence copying

a. (Hold up side 1 of your worksheet and point to the dotted sentence in the sentence-copying exercise.)

b. You're going to trace the words in this sentence. Then you're going to write the sentence on the other lines.

c. Reading the fast way. First word. ✔

• Get ready. (Tap.) *The.*

d. Next word. ✔

• Get ready. (Tap.) *Bug.*

e. (Repeat *d* for the remaining words.)

f. After you finish your worksheet, you get to draw a picture about the sentence, **the bug was on a dog.** You'll draw your picture on a piece of plain paper.

Cross-out game

a. (Point to the boxed words in the Cross-out Game.) Everybody, what word are you going to circle? (Signal.) *Pet.* Yes, pet.

b. What word are you going to cross out? (Signal.) *Get.* Yes, **get.**

Reading comprehension

a. (Point to the boxed sentences in the reading-comprehension exercise.)

b. Everybody, get ready to read the sentences the fast way.

c. First word. ✔

• Get ready. (Tap for each word as the children read *the dog said, "I am a dog."*)

d. (Have the children reread the sentence until firm.)

e. Get ready to read the next sentence. (Repeat *c* and *d* for **"I am not a bus."**)

f. (Point to items 1 and 2.) These items tell about the story in the box. You're going to read each item and circle the right answer.

Sound writing

a. (Point to the sound-writing exercise on side 2.) Here are the sounds you're going to write today. I'll touch the sounds. You say them.

b. (Touch each sound.) *The children respond.*

c. (Repeat the series until firm.)

Pair relations

a. (Point to the pair-relations exercise.) You're going to read each word. Then draw a line from the word to the right picture.

b. (When the children finish their worksheets, give them sheets of plain paper. Remind them to draw a picture that shows **the bug was on a dog.**)

END OF LESSON 128

EXERCISE 21

Picture comprehension

a. Everybody, look at the picture.

b. (Ask these questions:)

1. What is that bug doing? *The children respond.*
   Sitting on the shore.

2. I wonder why he doesn't swim across that lake. *The children respond.* He doesn't want to get wet.

3. I wonder why he doesn't take his car to the other side. *The children respond.* He doesn't have one.

4. What would you do if you were that bug? *The children respond.*

WORKSHEET 143

SUMMARY OF INDEPENDENT ACTIVITY
EXERCISE 22

Introduction to independent activity

a. (Pass out Worksheet 143 to each child.)

b. Everybody, you're going to do this worksheet on your own. (Tell the children when they will work the items.)

• Let's go over the things you're going to do.

Story items

a. (Hold up side 1 of your worksheet and point to the story-items exercise.)

b. Everybody, read item 1 about the story the fast way. First word. ✔

• Get ready. (Tap for each word as the children read *the bug sat on the shore of . . .*)

c. Everybody, what's the answer? (Signal.) *A lake.*

d. Think about what happened in the story and circle the right answer for each item.

Sound writing

a. (Point to the sound-writing exercise.) Here are the sounds you're going to write today. I'll touch the sounds. You say them.

b. (Touch each sound.) *The children respond.*

c. (Repeat the series until firm.)

Reading comprehension

a. (Point to the boxed sentences in the reading-comprehension exercise.)

b. Everybody, get ready to read the sentences the fast way.

c. First word. ✔

• Get ready. (Tap for each word as the children read *a boy had a box.*)

d. (Have the children reread the sentence until firm.)

e. Get ready to read the next sentence. (Repeat *c* and *d* for **a fox went in the box.**)

f. (Point to items 1 and 2.) These items tell about the story in the box. You're going to read each item and circle the right answer.

Sentence copying

a. (Hold up side 2 of your worksheet and point to the dotted sentence in the sentence-copying exercise.)

b. You're going to trace the words in this sentence. Then you're going to write the sentence on the other lines.

c. Reading the fast way. First word. ✔

• Get ready. (Tap for each word.)

d. After you finish your worksheet, you get to draw a picture about the sentence, **a bug sat at the lāke.** You'll draw your picture on a piece of plain paper.

Pair relations

a. (Point to the pair-relations exercise.) You're going to read each sentence. Then draw a line from the sentence to the right picture.

b. (When the children finish their worksheets, give them sheets of plain paper. Remind them to draw a picture that shows **a bug sat at the lāke.**)

END OF LESSON 143

SOUNDS

EXERCISE 1

Child plays teacher

a. (Use transparency and crayon.)

b. [Child's name] is going to be the teacher.

c. [Child] is going to touch the sounds. When [child] touches a sound, you say it.

d. (The child points to and touches the sounds.) *The children respond.* (You circle any sound that is not firm.)

e. (After the child has completed the page, present all the circled sounds to the children.)

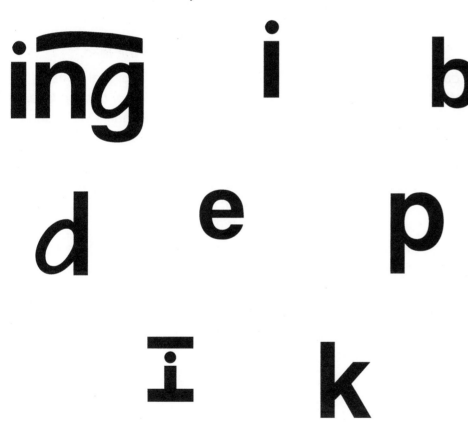

EXERCISE 2

Individual test

(Call on individual children.) If you can say the sound when I call your name, you may cross it out.

EXERCISE 3

Sounds firm-up

a. (Point to **l**.) When I touch the sound, you say it.

b. (Pause.) Get ready. (Touch **l**.) *lll.*

c. Again. (Repeat *b* until firm.)

d. Get ready to say all the sounds when I touch them.

e. (Alternate touching **ch, c, e, o, l, u, ō,** and **I** three or four times. Point to the sound. Pause one second. Say:) Get ready. (Touch the sound.) *The children respond.*

EXERCISE 4

Individual test

(Call on individual children to identify one or more sounds in exercise 3.)

STORY 143
EXERCISE 18

First reading—children read the title and first three sentences

a. (Pass out Storybook.)

b. Open your book to page 140. ✔
You're going to read the first part of this story today.

c. Everybody, touch the title of the story and get ready to read the words in the title the fast way.

d. First word. ✔

• (Pause two seconds.) Get ready. (Tap.) *The.*

e. (Tap for each remaining word in the title.)

f. (After the children have read the title, ask:) What's this story about? (Signal.) *The other side of the lake.* Yes, **the other side of the lake.**

g. Everybody, get ready to read this story the fast way.

h. First word. ✔

• (Pause two seconds.) Get ready. (Tap.) *A.*

i. (Tap for the remaining words in the first sentence. Pause at least two seconds between taps.)

j. (Repeat *h* and *i* for the next two sentences. Have the children reread the first three sentences until firm.)

EXERCISE 19

Individual children or the group read sentences to complete the first reading

a. I'm going to call on individual children to read a sentence. Everybody, follow along and point to the words. If you hear a mistake, raise your hand.

b. (Call on a child.) Read the next sentence. (Do not tap for the words. Let children read at their own pace, but be sure they read the sentence correctly.)

To Correct
(Have the child sound out the word. Then return to the beginning of the sentence.)

c. (Repeat *b* for most of the remaining sentences in the story. Occasionally have the group read a sentence. When the group is to read, say:) Everybody, read the next sentence. (Pause two seconds.) Get ready. (Tap for each word in the sentence. Pause at least two seconds between taps.)

EXERCISE 20

Second reading—individual children or the group read each sentence; the group answer questions

a. You're going to read the story again. This time I'm going to ask questions.

b. Starting with the first word of the title. ✔

• Get ready. (Tap as the children read the title. Pause at least two seconds between taps.)

c. (Call on a child.) Read the first sentence. *The child responds.*

d. (Repeat *b* and *c* in exercise 19. Present the following comprehension questions to the entire group.)

After the children read:	You say:
The other side of the lake.	What's this story about? (Signal.) *The other side of the lake.*
The bug said, "I need to get to the other side of this big lake."	What did he say? (Signal.) *I need to get to the other side of this big lake.* Where was he? (Signal.) *On the shore.*
"But I do not like to get wet."	What did the bug say? *The children respond.* He said, "I like to sleep and I like to ride in a car. But I do not like to get wet."
So he sat and sat on the shore of the lake.	What did he do? (Signal.) *He sat and sat on the shore of the lake.* I wonder how he'll get to the other side of the lake. We'll find out when we read the next part of the story.

READING VOCABULARY

EXERCISE 5

Children read the fast way

a. Get ready to read these words the fast way.

b. (Touch the ball for **slēēp.** Pause three seconds.) Get ready. (Signal.) *Sleep.*

c. (Repeat *b* for the remaining words on the page.)

EXERCISE 6

Children read the fast way again

a. Get ready to do these words again. Watch where I point.

b. (Point to a word. Pause one second. Say:) Get ready. (Signal.) *The children respond.*

• (Point to the words in this order: **big, bit, but, slēēp.**)

c. (Repeat *b* until firm.)

EXERCISE 7

Individual test

(Call on individual children to read one word the fast way.)

slēēp

bit

but

big

EXERCISE 12

Children identify, then sound out an irregular word (**other**)

a. (Touch the ball for **other**.) Everybody, you're going to read this word the fast way. (Pause three seconds.) Get ready. (Move your finger quickly along the arrow.) *Other.* Yes, **other.**

b. Now you're going to sound out the word. Get ready. (Quickly touch **o, th, er** as the children say *ooothththerrr.*)

c. Again. (Repeat *b.*)

d. How do we say the word? (Signal.) *Other.* Yes, **other.**

e. (Repeat *b* and *d* until firm.)

EXERCISE 13

Individual test

(Call on individual children to do *b* and *d* in exercise 12.)

EXERCISE 14

Children identify, then sound out an irregular word (**you**)

a. (Touch the ball for **you**.) Everybody, you're going to read this word the fast way. (Pause three seconds.) Get ready. (Move your finger quickly along the arrow.) *You.* Yes, **you.**

b. Now you're going to sound out the word. Get ready. (Quickly touch **y, o, u** as the children say *yyyooouuu.*)

c. Again. (Repeat *b.*)

d. How do we say the word? (Signal.) *You.* Yes, **you.**

e. (Repeat *b* and *d* until firm.)

EXERCISE 15

Individual test

(Call on individual children to do *b* and *d* in exercise 14.)

EXERCISE 16

Children identify, then sound out an irregular word (**are**)

a. (Touch the ball for **are**.) Everybody, you're going to read this word the fast way. (Pause three seconds.) Get ready. (Move your finger quickly along the arrow.) *Are.* Yes, **are.**

b. Now you're going to sound out the word. Get ready. (Quickly touch **a, r** as the children say *aaarrr.*)

c. Again. (Repeat *b.*)

d. How do we say the word? (Signal.) *Are.* Yes, **are.**

e. (Repeat *b* and *d* until firm.)

EXERCISE 17

Individual test

(Call on individual children to do *b* and *d* in exercise 16.)

EXERCISE 8

Children sound out the word and tell what word

a. (Touch the ball for **bīte.**) Sound it out.

b. Get ready. (Touch **b, ī, t,** as the children say *bīīit.*)

• (If sounding out is not firm, repeat *b.*)

c. What word? (Signal.) *Bite.* Yes, **bite.**

EXERCISE 9

Children sound out the word and tell what word

a. (Touch the ball for **tub.**) Sound it out.

b. Get ready. (Touch **t, u, b** as the children say *tuuub.*)

• (If sounding out is not firm, repeat *b.*)

c. What word? (Signal.) *Tub.* Yes, **tub.**

EXERCISE 10

Children sound out an irregular word (**walk**)

a. (Touch the ball for **walk.**) Sound it out.

b. Get ready. (Quickly touch each sound as the children say *wwwaaalllk.*)

To Correct

If the children do not say the sounds you touch

1. (Say:) You've got to say the sounds I touch.
2. (Repeat *a* and *b* until firm.)

c. Again. (Repeat *b* until firm.)

d. That's how we <u>sound out</u> the word. Here's how we <u>say</u> the word. **Walk.** How do we <u>say</u> the word? (Signal.) *Walk.*

e. Now you're going to <u>sound out</u> the word. Get ready. (Touch each sound as the children say *wwwaaalllk.*)

f. Now you're going to say the word. Get ready. (Signal.) *Walk.*

g. (Repeat *e* and *f* until firm.)

h. Yes, this word is **walk.** Let's go for a walk.

EXERCISE 11

Individual test

(Call on individual children to do *e* and *f* in exercise 10.)

bīte

tub

walk

EXERCISE 12

Children read the words the fast way

(Have the children read the words on this page the fast way.)

EXERCISE 13

Individual test

(Call on individual children to read one word the fast way.)

EXERCISE 9

Children read **slide** and **slider**

a. (Cover **s.** Run your finger under **līde.**) You're going to sound out this part. Get ready. (Touch **l, ī, d** as the children say *lllīīīd.*)

b. Say it fast. (Signal.) *Līde.* Yes, this part is **līde.**

c. (Uncover **s.** Point to **s.**) You're going to say this first. (Move your finger quickly under **līde.**) Then you're going to say (pause) **līde.**

d. (Point to **s.**) What are you going to say first? (Signal.) *sss.*

• What are you going to say next? (Signal.) *Līde.*

e. (Repeat *d* until firm.)

f. (Touch the ball for **slide.**) Get ready. (Move to **s,** then quickly along the arrow.) *Ssslide.*

g. Say it fast. (Signal.) *Slide.*

• Yes, what word? (Signal.) *Slide.* Yes, **slide.**

• Good reading.

h. Again. (Repeat *f* and *g* until firm.)

i. Now you're going to sound out (pause) **slide.** Get ready. (Touch **s, l, ī, d** as the children say *ssslllīīīd.*)

• What word? (Signal.) *Slide.* Yes, **slide.**

j. (Point to **slīde.**) This word is slide.

k. (Tap under **er** in **slīder.**) So this must be . . . (Touch the ball for **slīder** and move your finger quickly along the arrow.) *Slider.* Yes, **slider.**

l. (Repeat *j* and *k* until firm.)

m. Now you're going to sound out (pause) **slider.** Get ready. (Touch **s, l, ī, d, er** as the children say *ssslllīīīderrr.*)

• What word? (Signal.) *Slider.* Yes, **slider.**

EXERCISE 10

Children identify, then sound out an irregular word (**car**)

a. (Touch the ball for **car.**) Everybody, you're going to read this word the fast way. (Pause three seconds.) Get ready. (Move your finger quickly along the arrow.) *Car.* Yes, **car.**

b. Now you're going to sound out the word. Get ready. (Quickly touch **c, a, r** as the children say *caaarrr.*)

c. Again. (Repeat *b.*)

d. How do we say the word? (Signal.) *Car.* Yes, **car.**

e. (Repeat *b* and *d* until firm.)

slīde

slīder

car

EXERCISE 11

Individual test

(Call on individual children to do *b* and *d* in exercise 10.)

EXERCISE 14

Children sound out an irregular word (**talk**)

a. (Touch the ball for **talk.**) Sound it out.

b. Get ready. (Quickly touch each sound as the children say *taaalllk.*)

c. Again. (Repeat *b* until firm.)

d. That's how we <u>sound out</u> the word. Here's how we <u>say</u> the word. **Talk.** How do we <u>say</u> the word? (Signal.) *Talk.*

e. Now you're going to <u>sound out</u> the word. Get ready. (Touch each sound as the children say *taaalllk.*)

f. Now you're going to say the word. Get ready. (Signal.) *Talk.*

g. (Repeat *e* and *f* until firm.)

h. Yes, this word is **talk.** I am **talking** to you now.

i. (Call on individual children to do *e* and *f* in exercise 14.)

talk

EXERCISE 15

Children read a word beginning with two consonants (**stop**)

a. (Cover **s.** Point to **top.**) You're going to read this part of the word the fast way. (Pause three seconds.) Get ready. (Signal.) *Top.* Yes, **top.**

b. (Uncover **s.** Point to **s.**) You're going to say this first. (Move your finger quickly under **top.**) Then you're going to say (pause) **top.**

c. (Point to **s.**) What are you going to say first? (Signal.) *sss.*

• What are you going to say next? (Signal.) *Top.*

d. (Repeat *c* until firm.)

e. (Touch the ball for **stop.**) Remember—first you say **sss;** then you say **top.** Get ready. (Move to **s,** then quickly along the arrow.) *Ssstop.*

f. Say it fast. (Signal.) *Stop.*

• Yes, what word? (Signal.) *Stop.* Yes, **stop.**

• Good reading.

g. Again. (Repeat *e* and *f* until firm.)

h. Now you're going to sound out (pause) **stop.** Get ready. (Touch **s, t, o, p** as the children say *ssstooop.*)

• What word? (Signal.) *Stop.*

• Yes, stop.

stop

EXERCISE 16

Children read the words the fast way

(Have the children read the words on this page the fast way.)

EXERCISE 17

Individual test

(Call on individual children to read one word the fast way.)

READING VOCABULARY

EXERCISE 6

Children sound out the word and tell what word

a. (Touch the ball for **shōre.**) Sound it out.

b. Get ready. (Touch **sh, ō, r** as the children say *shshshōōōrrr.*)

• (If sounding out is not firm, repeat *b.*)

c. What word? (Signal.) *Shore.* Yes, **shore.**

EXERCISE 7

Children read the fast way

a. Get ready to read these words the fast way.

b. (Touch the ball for **tāke.** Pause three seconds.) Get ready. (Signal.) *Take.*

c. (Repeat *b* for the remaining words on the page.)

EXERCISE 8

Children read the fast way again

a. Get ready to do these words again. Watch where I point.

b. (Point to a word. Pause one second. Say:) Get ready. (Signal.) *The children respond.*

• (Point to the words in this order: **shōre, tāke, lāke, ēagle, wet.**)

c. (Repeat *b* until firm.)

Individual test

(Call on individual children to read one word the fast way.)

shōre

tāke

ēagle

wet

lāke

STORY 129

EXERCISE 18

First reading—children read the story the fast way

(Have the children reread any sentences containing words that give them trouble. Keep a list of these words.)

a. (Pass out Storybook.)

b. Open your book to page 98. ✔

c. Everybody, touch the title of the story and get ready to read the words in the title the fast way.

d. First word. ✔

- (Pause two seconds.) Get ready. (Tap.) *The.*

e. (Tap for each remaining word in the title.)

f. (After the children have read the title, ask:) What's this story about? (Signal.) *The man and his bed.* Yes, the man and his bed.

g. Everybody, get ready to read this story the fast way.

h. First word. ✔

- (Pause two seconds.) Get ready. (Tap.) *A.*

i. (Tap for the remaining words in the first sentence. Pause at least two seconds between taps.)

j. (Repeat *h* and *i* for the next two sentences. Have the children reread the first three sentences until firm.)

k. (The children are to read the remainder of the story the fast way, stopping at the end of each sentence.)

l. (After the first reading of the story, print on the board the words that the children missed more than one time. Have the children sound out each word one time and tell what word.)

m. (After the group's responses are firm, call on individual children to read the words.)

EXERCISE 19

Individual test

a. Look at page 98. I'm going to call on individual children to read a whole sentence.

b. (Call on individual children to read a sentence. Do not tap for each word.)

EXERCISE 20

Second reading—children read the story the fast way and answer questions

a. You're going to read the story again the fast way and I'll ask questions.

b. Starting with the first word of the title. ✔

- Get ready. (Tap.) *The.*

c. (Tap for each remaining word. Pause at least two seconds between taps. Pause longer before words that gave the children trouble during the first reading.)

d. (Ask the comprehension questions below as the children read.)

After the children read:	You say:
The man and his bed.	What's this story about? (Signal.) *The man and his bed.*
He said, "I like to sit in the tub and rub, rub, rub."	What did the man say? (Signal.) *I like to sit in the tub and rub, rub, rub.*
Then the man said, "Now I will sleep in this bed."	What did the man say? (Signal.) *Now I will sleep in this bed.*
But a dog was in his bed.	What was in his bed? (Signal.) *A dog.*
"So he can sleep with me."	Will the man let the dog sleep in the bed? (Signal.) *Yes.*
And the dog did not bite the man.	Does the dog like to bite? (Signal.) *No.* Did he bite the man? (Signal.) *No.*

EXERCISE 21

Picture comprehension

a. What do you think you'll see in the picture? *The children respond.*

b. Turn the page and look at the picture.

c. (Ask these questions:)

1. What is in the man's bed? *A dog.*
2. What would you do if a dog wanted to sleep in your bed? *The children respond.*

Groups that are firm on Mastery Tests 26 and 27 should skip this lesson and do lesson 144 today.

SOUNDS

EXERCISE 1

Teaching **oo** as in **moon** (not **look**)

a. (Point to **oo**.) My turn. (Pause. Touch **oo** and say:) **oo**oo.

b. (Point to **oo**.) Your turn. When I touch it, you say it. (Pause.) Get ready. (Touch **oo**.) *oooo.*

• (Lift your finger.)

c. Again. (Touch **oo**.) *ooooooo.*

• (Lift your finger.)

d. (Repeat *c* until firm.)

EXERCISE 2

Sounds firm-up

a. Get ready to say the sounds when I touch them.

b. (Alternate touching **oo** and **w**. Point to the sound. Pause one second. Say:) Get ready. (Touch the sound.) *The children respond.*

c. (When **oo** and **w** are firm, alternate touching **oo, w, o,** and **ō** until all four sounds are firm.)

EXERCISE 3

Individual test

(Call on individual children to identify **oo, w, o,** or **ō**.)

EXERCISE 4

Sounds firm-up

a. (Point to **oo**.) When I touch the sound, you say it.

b. (Pause.) Get ready. (Touch **oo**.) *oooo.*

c. Again. (Repeat *b* until firm.)

d. Get ready to say all the sounds when I touch them.

e. (Alternate touching **oo, er, ī, x, b, e, ā,** and **y** three or four times. Point to the sound. Pause one second. Say:) Get ready. (Touch the sound.) *The children respond.*

EXERCISE 5

Individual test

(Call on individual children to identify one or more sounds in exercise 4.)

WORKSHEET 129

SUMMARY OF INDEPENDENT ACTIVITY
EXERCISE 22

Introduction to independent activity

a. (Pass out Worksheet 129 to each child.)

b. Everybody, you're going to do this worksheet on your own. (Tell the children when they will work the items.)

• Let's go over the things you're going to do.

Sentence copying

a. (Hold up side 1 of your worksheet and point to the dotted sentence in the sentence-copying exercise.)

b. You're going to trace the words in this sentence. Then you're going to write the sentence on the other lines.

c. Reading the fast way. First word. ✔

• Get ready. (Tap.) *A.*

d. Next word. ✔

• Get ready. (Tap.) *Man.*

e. (Repeat *d* for the remaining words.)

f. After you finish your worksheet, you get to draw a picture about the sentence **a man had a tub.** You'll draw your picture on a piece of plain paper.

Cross-out game

a. (Point to the boxed words in the Cross-out Game.) Everybody, what word are you going to circle? (Signal.) *Hat.* Yes, **hat.**

b. What word are you going to cross out? (Signal.) *Hate.* Yes, **hate.**

Reading comprehension

a. (Point to the boxed sentences in the reading-comprehension exercise.)

b. Everybody, get ready to read the sentences the fast way.

c. First word. ✔

• Get ready. (Tap for each word as the children read *the man had a tub.*)

d. (Have the children reread the sentence until firm.)

e. Get ready to read the next sentence. (Repeat *c* and *d* for **hē said, "I līke to rub, rub."**)

f. (Point to items 1 and 2.) These items tell about the story in the box. You're going to read each item and circle the right answer.

Sound writing

a. (Point to the sound-writing exercise on side 2.) Here are the sounds you're going to write today. I'll touch the sounds. You say them.

b. (Touch each sound.) *The children respond.*

c. (Repeat the series until firm.)

Pair relations

a. (Point to the pair-relations exercise.) You're going to read each word. Then draw a line from the word to the picture.

b. (When the children finish their worksheets, give them sheets of plain paper. Remind them to draw a picture that shows **a man had a tub.**)

END OF LESSON 129

EXERCISE 21

Picture comprehension

a. Everybody, look at the picture.

b. (Ask these questions:)

1. What do you see in the box? *The children respond.* The fat fox and his brother.

2. I wonder which is the fat fox and which is his brother? *The children respond.*

• I can see why it got hot in that box with two foxes hitting it.

WORKSHEET 142

SUMMARY OF INDEPENDENT ACTIVITY

EXERCISE 22

Introduction to independent activity

a. (Pass out Worksheet 142 to each child.)

b. Everybody, you're going to do this worksheet on your own. (Tell the children when they will work the items.)

• Let's go over the things you're going to do.

Story items

a. (Hold up side 1 of your worksheet and point to the story-items exercise.)

b. Everybody, read item 1 about the story the fast way. First word. ✔

• Get ready. (Tap for each word as the children read *a fat fox went in . . .*)

c. Everybody, what's the answer? (Signal.) *A box.*

d. Think about what happened in the story and circle the right answer for each item.

Sound writing

a. (Point to the sound-writing exercise.) Here are the sounds you're going to write today. I'll touch the sounds. You say them.

b. (Touch each sound.) *The children respond.*

c. (Repeat the series until firm.)

Reading comprehension

a. (Point to the boxed sentences in the reading-comprehension exercise.)

b. Everybody, get ready to read the sentences the fast way.

c. First word. ✔

• Get ready. (Tap for each word as the children read *a boy had a toy.*)

d. (Have the children reread the sentence until firm.)

e. Get ready to read the next sentence. (Repeat *c* and *d* for **the toy was red.**)

f. (Point to items 1 and 2.) These items tell about the story in the box. You're going to read each item and circle the right answer.

Sentence copying

a. (Hold up side 2 of your worksheet and point to the dotted sentence in the sentence-copying exercise.)

b. You're going to trace the words in this sentence. Then you're going to write the sentence on the other lines.

c. Reading the fast way. First word. ✔

• Get ready. (Tap for each word.)

d. After you finish your worksheet, you get to draw a picture about the sentence, **I love to hit a box.** You'll draw your picture on a piece of plain paper.

Pair relations

a. (Point to the pair-relations exercise.) You're going to read each sentence. Then draw a line from the sentence to the right picture.

b. (When the children finish their worksheets, give them sheets of plain paper. Remind them to draw a picture that shows **I love to hit a box.**)

END OF LESSON 142

SOUNDS

EXERCISE 1

Teacher and children play the sounds game

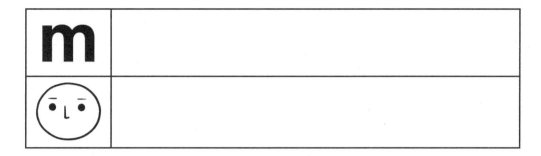

a. (Use transparency and crayon. Write the sounds in the symbol box. Keep score in the score box.)

b. I'm smart. I think I can beat you in a game.

c. Here's the rule. When I touch a sound, you say it.

d. (Play the game. Make one symbol at a time in the symbol box. Use the symbols **b, ing, e,** and **e.**) (Make each symbol quickly. Pause. Touch the symbol. Play the game for about two minutes.)
(Then ask:) Who won? (Draw a mouth on the face in the score box.)

EXERCISE 2

Child plays teacher

a. (Use transparency and crayon.)

b. [Child's name] is going to be the teacher.

c. [Child] is going to touch the sounds. When [child] touches a sound, you say it.

d. (The child points to and touches the sounds.) *The children respond.* (You circle any sound that is not firm.)

e. (After the child has completed the page, present all the circled sounds to the children.)

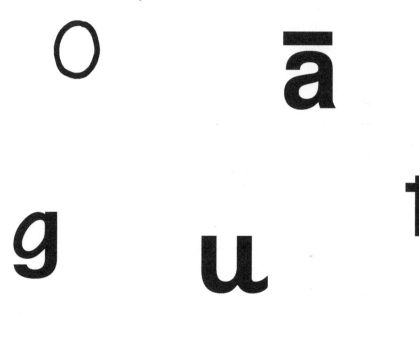

EXERCISE 3

Individual test

(Call on individual children.) If you can say the sound when I call your name, you may cross it out.

STORY 142
EXERCISE 18

First reading—children read the title and first three sentences

a. (Pass out Storybook.)

b. Open your book to page 137. ✔

c. Everybody, touch the title of the story and get ready to read the words in the title the fast way.

d. First word. ✔

• (Pause two seconds.) Get ready. (Tap.) *The.*

e. (Tap for each remaining word in the title.)

f. (After the children have read the title, ask:) What's this story about? (Signal.) *The fat fox and his brother.*
Yes, **the fat fox and his brother.**

g. Everybody, get ready to read this story the fast way.

h. First word. ✔

• (Pause two seconds.) Get ready. (Tap.) *A.*

i. (Tap for the remaining words in the first sentence. Pause at least two seconds between taps.)

j. (Repeat *h* and *i* for the next two sentences. Have the children reread the first three sentences until firm.)

EXERCISE 19

Individual children or the group read sentences to complete the first reading

a. I'm going to call on individual children to read a sentence. Everybody, follow along and point to the words. If you hear a mistake, raise your hand.

b. (Call on a child.) Read the next sentence. (Do not tap for the words. Let children read at their own pace, but be sure they read the sentence correctly.)

To Correct
(Have the child sound out the word. Then return to the beginning of the sentence.)

c. (Repeat *b* for most of the remaining sentences in the story. Occasionally have the group read a sentence. When the group is to read, say:) Everybody, read the next sentence. (Pause two seconds.) Get ready. (Tap for each word in the sentence. Pause at least two seconds between taps.)

EXERCISE 20

Second reading—individual children or the group read each sentence; the group answer questions

a. You're going to read the story again. This time I'm going to ask questions.

b. Starting with the first word of the title. ✔

• Get ready. (Tap as the children read the title. Pause at least two seconds between taps.)

c. (Call on a child.) Read the first sentence. *The child responds.*

d. (Repeat *b* and *c* in exercise 19. Present the following comprehension questions to the entire group.)

After the children read:	You say:
The fat fox and his brother.	What's this story about? (Signal.) *The fat fox and his brother.*
His brother said, "Sitting in a box is not a lot of fun."	What did his brother say? (Signal.) *Sitting in a box is not a lot of fun.* Where were the fat fox and his brother? (Signal.) *In a big box.* Did the fat fox like to sit in a box? (Signal.) *No.*
So he hit and hit.	What happened? *The children respond.* He hit the box with his hand, nose, and tail.
"Let's stop hitting."	What did the fat fox say? (Signal.) *Let's stop hitting.*
"Sleeping in a box is fun."	What did his brother say? (Signal.) *Sleeping in a box is fun.* Why are the foxes tired? *The children respond.* From hitting the box.

READING VOCABULARY

EXERCISE 4

Children read the fast way

a. Get ready to read these words the fast way.

b. (Touch the ball for **them.** Pause three seconds.) Get ready. (Signal.) *Them.*

c. (Repeat *b* for the remaining words on the page.)

EXERCISE 5

Children read the fast way again

a. Get ready to do these words again. Watch where I point.

b. (Point to a word. Pause one second. Say:) Get ready. (Signal.) *The children respond.*

• (Point to the words in this order: **cats, bed, fishing, gōing, them.**)

c. (Repeat *b* until firm.)

EXERCISE 6

Individual test

(Call on individual children to read one word the fast way.)

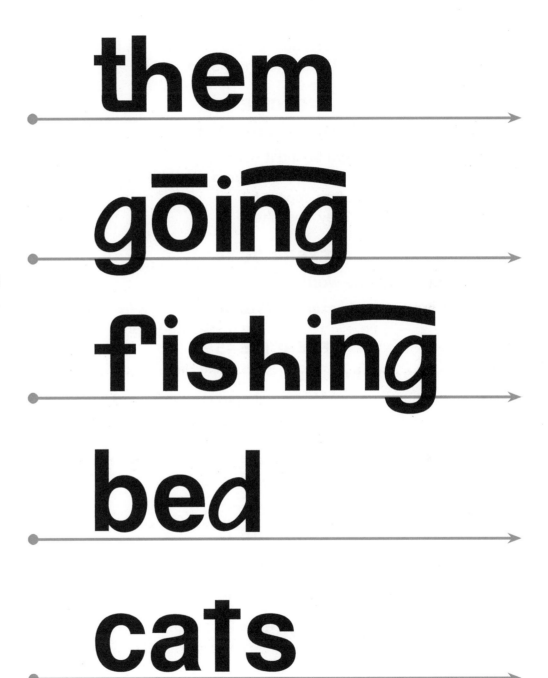

EXERCISE 12

Children read the fast way

(Touch the ball for **stop.**) Get ready to read this word the fast way. (Pause three seconds.) Get ready. (Signal.) *Stop.*

EXERCISE 13

Children sound out the word and tell what word

a. (Touch the ball for **they.**) Sound it out.
b. Get ready. (Touch **th, e, y** as the children say *thththeeeyyy.*)
• (If sounding out is not firm, repeat *b.*)
c. What word? (Signal.) *They.* Yes, **they.**

EXERCISE 14

Children sound out the word and tell what word

(Repeat the procedures in exercise 13 for **ever.**)

EXERCISE 15

Children rhyme with **box**

a. (Touch the ball for **box.**) You're going to read this word the fast way. (Pause three seconds.) Get ready. (Move your finger quickly along the arrow.) *Box.*
b. (Touch the ball for **fox.**) This word rhymes with (pause) **box.** (Move to **f,** then quickly along the arrow.) *Fffox.*
• Yes, what word? (Signal.) *Fox.*

EXERCISE 16

Children read the words the fast way

(Have the children read the words on this page the fast way.)

EXERCISE 17

Individual test

(Call on individual children to read one word the fast way.)

stop

they

ever

box

fox

EXERCISE 7

Children identify, then sound out an irregular word (**walk**)

a. (Touch the ball for **walk.**) Everybody, you're going to read this word the fast way. (Pause three seconds.) Get ready. (Move your finger quickly along the arrow.) *Walk.* Yes, **walk.**

b. Now you're going to sound out the word. Get ready. (Quickly touch **w, a, l, k** as the children say *wwwaaalllk.*)

c. Again. (Repeat *b.*)

d. How do we say the word? (Signal.) *Walk.* Yes, **walk.**

e. (Repeat *b* and *d* until firm.)

EXERCISE 8

Individual test

(Call on individual children to do *b* and *d* in exercise 7.)

EXERCISE 9

Children identify, then sound out an irregular word (**talking**)

a. (Touch the ball for **talking.**) Everybody, you're going to read this word the fast way. (Pause three seconds.) Get ready. (Move your finger quickly along the arrow.) *Talking.* Yes, **talking.**

b. Now you're going to sound out the word. Get ready. (Quickly touch **t, a, l, k, ing** as the children say *taaalllkiiing.*)

c. Again. (Repeat *b.*)

d. How do we say the word? (Signal.) *Talking.* Yes, **talking.**

e. (Repeat *b* and *d* until firm.)

EXERCISE 10

Individual test

(Call on individual children to do *b* and *d* in exercise 9.)

EXERCISE 11

Children read the words the fast way

a. Now you get to read the words on this page the fast way.

b. (Touch the ball for **talking.** Pause three seconds.) Get ready. (Move your finger quickly along the arrow.) *Talking.*

c. (Repeat *b* for **walk.**)

EXERCISE 12

Individual test

(Call on individual children to read one word the fast way.)

READING VOCABULARY

EXERCISE 7

Children sound out the word and tell what word

a. (Touch the ball for **ōver.**) Sound it out.
b. Get ready. (Touch **ō, v, er** as the children say *ōōōvvverrr.*)
•   (If sounding out is not firm, repeat *b.*)
c. What word? (Signal.) *Over.* Yes, **over.**

EXERCISE 8

Children sound out the word and tell what word

(Repeat the procedures in exercise 7 for **ēagle.**)

EXERCISE 9

Children read the fast way

a. Get ready to read these words the fast way.
b. (Touch the ball for **sitting.** Pause three seconds.) Get ready. (Signal.) *Sitting.*
c. (Repeat *b* for the remaining words on the page.)

EXERCISE 10

Children read the words the fast way

(Have the children read the words on this page the fast way.)

EXERCISE 11

Individual test

(Call on individual children to read one word the fast way.)

ōver

ēagle

sitting

hitting

sleeping

EXERCISE 13

Children sound out the word and tell what word

a. (Touch the ball for **dīve.**) Sound it out.
b. Get ready. (Touch **d, ī, v,** as the children say *dīīīvvv.*)
• (If sounding out is not firm, repeat *b.*)
c. What word? (Signal.) *Dive.* Yes, **dive.**

EXERCISE 14

Children sound out the word and tell what word

a. (Touch the ball for **līke.**) Sound it out.
b. Get ready. (Touch **l, ī, k** as the children say *lllīīīk.*)
• (If sounding out is not firm, repeat *b.*)
c. What word? (Signal.) *Like.* Yes, **like.**

EXERCISE 15

Children read a word beginning with two consonants (**sliding**)

a. (Cover **s.** Run your finger under **līding.**) You're going to sound out this part. Get ready. (Touch **l, ī, d, ing** as the children say *lllīīīdiiing.*)
b. Say it fast. (Signal.) *Liding.* Yes, this part is **liding.**
c. (Uncover **s.** Point to **s.**) You're going to say this first. (Move your finger quickly under **liding.**) Then you're going to say (pause) **liding.**
d. (Point to **s.**) What are you going to say first? (Signal.) *sss.*
• What are you going to say next? (Signal.) *Liding.*
e. (Repeat *d* until firm.)
f. (Touch the ball for **slīding.**) Remember—first you say **sss;** then you say **līding.** Get ready.
(Move to **s,** then quickly along the arrow.) *Sssliding.*
g. Say it fast. (Signal.) *Sliding.*
• Yes, what word? (Signal.) *Sliding.* Yes, **sliding.**
• Good reading.
h. Again. (Repeat *f* and *g* until firm.)
i. Now you're going to sound out (pause) **sliding.** Get ready.
(Touch **s, l, ī, d, ing** as the children say *ssslllīīīdiiing.*)
• What word? (Signal.) *Sliding.* Yes, **sliding.**

EXERCISE 16

Children read the words the fast way

a. Now you get to read the words on this page the fast way.
b. (Touch the ball for **sliding.** Pause three seconds.) Get ready. (Move your finger quickly along the arrow.) *Sliding.*
c. (Repeat *b* for **dive.**)

EXERCISE 17

Individual test

(Call on individual children to read one word the fast way.)

oo

r

o

w

SOUNDS

EXERCISE 1

Teaching **oo** as in **moon** (not **look**)

a. (Point to **oo.**) Here's a new sound.
b. My turn. (Pause. Touch **oo** and say:) *oo*oo.
c. Again. (Touch **oo** for a longer time.) *ooooooo*o.
• (Lift your finger.)
d. (Point to **oo.**) Your turn. When I touch it, you say it. (Pause.) Get ready. (Touch **oo.**) *oooo.*
• (Lift your finger.)
e. Again. (Touch **oo.**) *ooooooo.*
• (Lift your finger.)
f. (Repeat *e* until firm.)

EXERCISE 2

Individual test

(Call on individual children to identify **oo.**)

EXERCISE 3

Sounds firm-up

a. Get ready to say the sounds when I touch them.
b. (Alternate touching **oo** and **r.** Point to the sound. Pause one second. Say:) Get ready. (Touch the sound.) *The children respond.*
c. (When **oo** and **r** are firm, alternate touching **oo, r, o,** and **w** until all four sounds are firm.)

EXERCISE 4

Individual test

(Call on individual children to identify **oo, r, o,** or **w.**)

oo   ō
       e
   ī   er
x   y
ing

EXERCISE 5

Sounds firm-up

a. (Point to **oo.**) When I touch the sound, you say it.
b. (Pause.) Get ready. (Touch **oo.**) *oooo.*
c. Again. (Repeat *b* until firm.)
d. Get ready to say all the sounds when I touch them.
e. (Alternate touching **oo, ō, e, ī, er, x, y,** and **ing** three or four times. Point to the sound. Pause one second. Say:) Get ready. (Touch the sound.) *The children respond.*

EXERCISE 6

Individual test

(Call on individual children to identify one or more sounds in exercise 5.)

STORY 130
EXERCISE 18

First reading—children read the story the fast way

(Have the children reread any sentences containing words that give them trouble. Keep a list of these words.)

a. (Pass out Storybook.)

b. Open your book to page 101. ✔

c. Everybody, touch the title of the story and get ready to read the words in the title the fast way.

d. First word. ✔

● (Pause two seconds.) Get ready. (Tap.) *The.*

e. (Tap for each remaining word in the title.)

f. (After the children have read the title, ask:) What's this story about? (Signal.) *The talking cat.* Yes, **the talking cat.**

g. Everybody, get ready to read this story the fast way.

h. First word. ✔

● (Pause two seconds.) Get ready. (Tap.) *The.*

i. (Tap for the remaining words in the first sentence. Pause at least two seconds between taps.)

j. (Repeat *h* and *i* for the next two sentences. Have the children reread the first three sentences until firm.)

k. (The children are to read the remainder of the story the fast way, stopping at the end of each sentence.)

l. (After the first reading of the story, print on the board the words that the children missed more than one time. Have the children sound out each word one time and tell what word.)

m. (After the group's responses are firm, call on individual children to read the words.)

EXERCISE 19

Individual test

a. Turn back to page 101. I'm going to call on individual children to read a whole sentence.

b. (Call on individual children to read a sentence. Do not tap for each word.)

EXERCISE 20

Second reading—children read the story the fast way and answer questions

a. You're going to read the story again the fast way and I'll ask questions.

b. Starting with the first word of the title. ✔

● Get ready. (Tap.) *The.*

c. (Tap for each remaining word. Pause at least two seconds between taps. Pause longer before words that gave the children trouble during the first reading.)

d. (Ask the comprehension questions below as the children read.)

After the children read:	You say:
The talking cat.	What's this story about? (Signal.) *The talking cat.*
She met a fat cat.	What did she meet? (Signal.) *A fat cat.* Where was the girl going when she met the cat? (Signal.) *For a walk.*
"But I do not talk to girls."	What did the cat say? (Signal.) *But I do not talk to girls.* Who is the cat talking to? (Signal.) *The girl.* That cat is silly.
The cat said, "I will not talk to girls."	What did the cat say? (Signal.) *I will not talk to girls.* Who is that cat talking to? (Signal.) *The girl.* That cat is silly.
"And I do not give fish to cats I do not like."	What did the girl say? (Signal.) *And I do not give fish to cats I do not like.* What do you think the cat will do now? *The children respond.* Let's read and find out.
The cat said, "I like fish so I will talk to this girl."	What did the cat say? (Signal.) *I like fish, so I will talk to this girl.* Why is the cat talking to her? (Signal.) *Because the cat likes fish.*
So the girl and the cat ate fish.	What did the girl and the cat do? (Signal). *They ate fish.*

SUMMARY OF INDEPENDENT ACTIVITY
EXERCISE 26

Introduction to independent activity

a. (Pass out Worksheet 141 to each child.)

b. Everybody, you're going to do this worksheet on your own. (Tell the children when they will work the items.)

• Let's go over the things you're going to do.

Story items

a. (Hold up side 1 of your worksheet and point to the story-items exercise.)

b. Everybody, read item 1 about the story the fast way. First word. ✔

• Get ready. (Tap for each word as the children read *his mother liked . . .*)

c. Everybody, what's the answer? (Signal.) *Little toys.*

d. Think about what happened in the story and circle the right answer for each item.

Sound writing

a. (Point to the sound-writing exercise.) Here are the sounds you're going to write today. I'll touch the sounds. You say them.

b. (Touch each sound.) *The children respond.*

c. (Repeat the series until firm.)

Reading comprehension

a. (Point to the boxed sentences in the reading-comprehension exercise.)

b. Everybody, get ready to read the sentences the fast way.

c. First word. ✔

• Get ready. (Tap for each word as the children read *a duck did not like to walk.*)

d. (Have the children reread the sentence until firm.)

e. Get ready to read the next sentence. (Repeat *c* and *d* for **sō the duck went in the lāke.**)

f. (Point to items 1 and 2.) These items tell about the story in the box. You're going to read each item and circle the right answer.

Sentence copying

a. (Hold up side 2 of your worksheet and point to the dotted sentence in the sentence-copying exercise.)

b. You're going to trace the words in this sentence. Then you're going to write the sentence on the other lines.

c. Reading the fast way. First word. ✔

• Get ready. (Tap for each word.)

d. After you finish your worksheet, you get to draw a picture about the sentence, **hē māde a duck big.** You'll draw your picture on a piece of plain paper.

Pair relations

a. (Point to the pair-relations exercise.) You're going to read each sentence. Then draw a line from the sentence to the right picture.

b. (When the children finish their worksheets, give them sheets of plain paper. Remind them to draw a picture that shows **hē māde a duck big.**)

END OF LESSON 141

EXERCISE 21

Picture comprehension

a. Everybody, look at the picture.

b. (Ask these questions:)

1. What are the girl and the cat doing? *The children respond.* Eating.
2. Does that cat look happy now? (Signal.) *Yes.*
3. Do you think she'll talk to the girl after she eats? *The children respond.*
4. She's such a silly cat. What would you do if you had a talking cat? *The children respond.*

WORKSHEET 130
SUMMARY OF INDEPENDENT ACTIVITY
EXERCISE 22

Introduction to independent activity

a. (Pass out sides 1 and 2 of Worksheet 130 to each child.)

b. Everybody, do a good job on your worksheet today and I'll give you a bonus worksheet.

c. (Hold up side 1 of your worksheet.) You're going to do this worksheet on your own. (Tell the children when they will work the items.)

• Let's go over some of the things you're going to do.

Sentence copying

a. (Point to the dotted sentence in the sentence-copying exercise.)

b. You're going to trace the words in this sentence. Then you're going to write the sentence on the other lines.

c. Reading the fast way. First word. ✔

• Get ready. (Tap.) *She.*

d. Next word. ✔

• Get ready. (Tap.) *Met.*

e. (Repeat *d* for the remaining words.)

f. After you finish your worksheet, you get to draw a picture about the sentence, **shē met a fat cat.** You'll draw your picture on a piece of plain paper.

Reading comprehension

a. (Point to the boxed sentences in the reading-comprehension exercise.)

b. Everybody, get ready to read the sentences the fast way.

c. First word. ✔

• Get ready. (Tap for each word as the children read *"can cats talk?" the girl said.*)

d. (Have the children reread the sentence until firm.)

e. Get ready to read the next sentence. (Repeat *c* and *d* for **the cat said, "I can talk."**)

f. (Point to items 1 and 2.) These items tell about the story in the box. You're going to read each item and circle the right answer.

Other independent activity: sides 1, 2, 3, 4

Remember to do all the parts of the worksheet and to read all the parts carefully. After you draw your picture, I'll give you a bonus worksheet.

INDIVIDUAL CHECKOUT: STORYBOOK

3-minute individual fluency checkout: rate/accuracy

a. As you are doing your worksheet, I'll call on children one at a time to read **the whole story.** Remember, you get two stars if you read the story in less than three minutes and make no more than three errors.

b. (Call on a child. Tell the child:) Start with the title and read the story carefully the fast way. Go. (Time the child. Tell the child any words the child misses. Stop the child as soon as the child makes the fourth error or exceeds the time limit.)

c. (If the child meets the rate-accuracy criterion, record two stars on your chart for lesson 130. Congratulate the child. Give children who do not earn two stars a chance to read the story again before the next lesson is presented.)

107 words/**3 min** = 36 wpm [**3 errors**]

END OF LESSON 130

Before presenting lesson 131, give Mastery Test 25 to each child. Do not present lesson 131 to any groups that are not firm on this test.

STORYBOOK

STORY 141

EXERCISE 22

First reading—children read the title and first three sentences

a. (Pass out Storybook.)

b. Open your book to page 135. ✔ Now you're going to finish the story about the boy who liked big toys.

c. Everybody, touch the title of the story and get ready to read the words in the title the fast way.

d. First word. ✔

• (Pause two seconds.) Get ready. (Tap.) *Going.*

e. (Tap for each remaining word in the title.)

f. (After the children have read the title, ask:) What's this story about? (Signal.) *Going to the toy shop.* Yes, **going to the toy shop.**

g. Everybody, get ready to read this story the fast way.

h. First word. ✔

• (Pause two seconds.) Get ready. (Tap.) *A.*

i. (Tap for the remaining words in the first sentence. Pause at least two seconds between taps.)

j. (Repeat *h* and *i* for the next two sentences. Have the children reread the first three sentences until firm.)

EXERCISE 23

Individual children or the group read sentences to complete the first reading

a. I'm going to call on individual children to read a sentence. Everybody, follow along and point to the words. If you hear a mistake, raise your hand.

b. (Call on a child.) Read the next sentence. (Do not tap for the words. Let children read at their own pace, but be sure they read the sentence correctly.)

To Correct

(Have the child sound out the word. Then return to the beginning of the sentence.)

c. (Repeat *b* for most of the remaining sentences in the story.) (Occasionally have the group read a sentence. When the group is to read, say:) Everybody, read the next sentence. (Pause two seconds.) Get ready. (Tap for each word in the sentence. Pause at least two seconds between taps.)

EXERCISE 24

Second reading—individual children or the group read each sentence; the group answer questions

a. You're going to read the story again. This time I'm going to ask questions.

b. Starting with the first word of the title. ✔

• Get ready. (Tap as the children read the title. Pause at least two seconds between taps.)

c. (Call on a child.) Read the first sentence. *The child responds.*

d. (Repeat *b* and *c* in exercise 23. Present the following comprehension questions to the entire group.)

After the children read:	You say:
"They are big and little."	What did the man say? *The children respond.* He said, "I have toys that you will like. They are big and little." I wonder how toys can be big <u>and</u> little. Let's read and find out.
He got a little toy duck and he made it big.	I wonder how he did that. *The children respond.*

EXERCISE 25

Picture comprehension

a. Everybody, look at the picture.

b. (Ask these questions:)

1. Now I see how he made the little duck big. How did he do that? *The children respond.* Yes, he blew it up.
2. Is that duck big <u>and little</u>? *Yes.*
3. When is it big? *The children respond.* After it's blown up.
4. When is it little? *The children respond.* Before it's blown up.
5. Did you ever have a toy that you could blow up and make big? *The children respond.*

Mastery Tests—General Instructions

All children are to be given each test individually.

The test is NOT to be administered during the period allotted for reading.

A child should neither see nor hear another child working on the test.

MASTERY TEST 25—after lesson 130, before lesson 131

a. (Tell child:) Get ready to read these words the fast way.

b. (test item) (Touch the ball for **sent.** Pause three seconds.) Get ready. (Signal.) *Sent.*

c. (test item) (Touch the ball for **gōing.** Pause three seconds.) Get ready. (Signal.) *Going.*

d. (test item) (Touch the ball for **bugs.** Pause three seconds.) Get ready. (Signal.) *Bugs.*

e. (test item) (Touch the ball for **walk.** Pause three seconds.) Get ready. (Signal.) *Walk.*

Total number of test items: **4**
A group is weak if more than one-third of the children missed any of the items on the test.

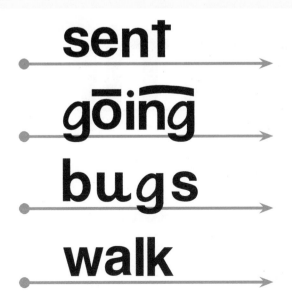

WHAT TO DO

If the group is firm on Mastery Test 25 and was firm on Mastery Test 24:

Present lessons 131 and 132, and then skip lesson 133. If more than one child missed any of the items on the test, present the firming procedures specified below to those children.

If the group is firm on Mastery Test 25 but was weak on Mastery Test 24:

Present lesson 131 to the group during the next reading period. If more than one child missed any of the items on the test, present the firming procedures specified below to those children.

If the group is weak on Mastery Test 25:

A. Present these firming procedures to the group during the next reading period.
  1. Lesson 127, Reading Vocabulary, pages 119–120, exercises 7 through 14.
  2. Lesson 128, Reading Vocabulary, page 126, exercises 12 through 16.
  3. Lesson 129, Reading Vocabulary, page 131–132, exercises 5 through 13.
  4. Lesson 130, Reading Vocabulary, pages 137–138, exercises 4 through 12.
B. After presenting the above exercises, again give Mastery Test 25 individually to members of the group who failed the test.
C. If the group is firm (less than one-third of the total group missed any items on the retest), present lesson 131 to the group during the next reading period.
D. If the group is still weak (more than one-third of the total group missed any items on the retest), repeat *A* and *B* during the next reading period.

EXERCISE 17

Children sound out an irregular word (**come**)

a. (Touch the ball for **come.**) Sound it out.

b. Get ready. (Quickly touch each sound as the children say *cooommmeee.*)

To Correct
If the children do not say the sounds you touch
1. (Say:) You've got to say the sounds I touch.
2. (Repeat *a* and *b* until firm.)

c. Again. (Repeat *b* until firm.)

d. That's how we <u>sound out</u> the word. Here's how we <u>say</u> the word. **Come.** How do we <u>say</u> the word? (Signal.) *Come.*

e. Now you're going to <u>sound out</u> the word. Get ready. (Touch each sound as the children say *cooommmeee.*)

f. Now you're going to say the word. Get ready. (Signal.) *Come.*

g. (Repeat *e* and *f* until firm.)

h. Yes, this word is **come. Come** with me to the store.

EXERCISE 18

Individual test

(Call on individual children to do *e* and *f* in exercise 17.)

EXERCISE 19

Children read the fast way

a. Get ready to read these words the fast way.

b. (Touch the ball for **līke.** Pause three seconds.) Get ready. (Signal.) *Like.*

c. (Repeat *b* for the remaining words on the page.)

EXERCISE 20

Children read the fast way again

a. Get ready to do these words again. Watch where I point.

b. (Point to a word. Pause one second. Say:) Get ready. (Signal.) *The children respond.*

• (Point to the words in this order: **līke, getting, fox.**)

c. (Repeat *b* until firm.)

EXERCISE 21

Individual test

(Call on individual children to read one word on the page the fast way.)

y

v

w

SOUNDS

EXERCISE 1

Teaching **y** as in **yes**

a. (Point to **y**.) Here's a new sound.

b. My turn. (Pause. Touch **y** and say:) yyy.

c. Again. (Touch **y** for a longer time.) yyyyyy.

- (Lift your finger.)

d. (Point to **y**.) Your turn. When I touch it, you say it. (Pause.) Get ready. (Touch **y**.) *yyy.*

- (Lift your finger.)

e. Again. (Touch **y**.) *yyyyyy.*

- (Lift your finger.)

f. (Repeat e until firm.)

EXERCISE 2

Individual test

(Call on individual children to identify **y**.)

EXERCISE 3

Sounds firm-up

a. Get ready to say the sounds when I touch them.

b. (Alternate touching **y** and **v**. Point to the sound. Pause one second. Say:) Get ready. (Touch the sound.) *The children respond.*

c. (When **y** and **v** are firm, alternate touching **y, v, w,** and **i** until all four sounds are firm.)

EXERCISE 4

Individual test

(Call on individual children to identify **y, v, w,** or **i**.)

y

o

n

e

ō

ī

EXERCISE 5

Sounds firm-up

a. (Point to **y**.) When I touch the sound, you say it.

b. (Pause.) Get ready. (Touch **y**.) *yyy.*

c. Again. (Repeat b until firm.)

d. Get ready to say all the sounds when I touch them.

e. (Alternate touching **y, n, o, ō, e, ī, ing,** and **b** three or four times. Point to the sound. Pause one second. Say:) Get ready. (Touch the sound.) *The children respond.*

EXERCISE 6

Individual test

(Call on individual children to identify one or more sounds in exercise 5.)

EXERCISE 13

Children sound out the word and tell what word

a. (Touch the ball for **topper.**) Sound it out.
b. Get ready. (Touch **t, o,** between the **p**'s, **er** as the children say *toooperrr.*)
• (If sounding out is not firm, repeat *b.*)
c. What word? (Signal.) *Topper.* Yes, **topper.**

EXERCISE 14

Children read a word beginning with two consonants (**stopper**)

a. (Cover **s.** Run your finger under **topper.**) You're going to sound out this part. Get ready. (Touch **t, o,** between the **p**'s, **er** as the children say *toooperrr.*)
b. Say it fast. (Signal.) *Topper.* Yes, this part is **topper.**
c. (Uncover **s.** Point to **s.**) You're going to say this first. (Move your finger quickly under **topper.**) Then you're going to say (pause) **topper.**
d. (Point to **s.**) What are you going to say first? (Signal.) *sss.*
• What are you going to say next? (Signal.) *Topper.*
e. (Repeat *d* until firm.)
f. (Touch the ball for **stopper.**) Remember, first you say **sss;** then you say **topper.** Get ready. (Move to **s,** then quickly along the arrow.) *Ssstopper.*
g. Say it fast. (Signal.) *Stopper.*
• Yes, what word? (Signal.) *Stopper.* Yes, **stopper.**
• Good reading.
h. Again. (Repeat *f* and *g* until firm.)
i. Now you're going to sound out (pause) **stopper.** Get ready. (Touch **s, t, o,** between the **p**'s, **er** as the children say *ssstoooperrr.*)
• What word? (Signal.) *Stopper.* Yes, **stopper.**

EXERCISE 15

Children read the words the fast way

a. Now you get to read the words on this page the fast way.
b. (Touch the ball for **topper.** Pause three seconds.) Get ready. (Move your finger quickly along the arrow.) *Topper.*
c. (Repeat *b* for **stopper.**)

EXERCISE 16

Individual test

(Call on individual children to read one word the fast way.)

topper

stopper

READING VOCABULARY

EXERCISE 7

Children sound out the word and tell what word

a. (Touch the ball for **rabbit**.) Sound it out.

b. Get ready. (Touch **r, a,** between the **b**'s, **i, t** as the children say *rrraaabiiit*.)

• (If sounding out is not firm, repeat *b*.)

c. What word? (Signal.) *Rabbit*. Yes, **rabbit**.

EXERCISE 8

Children read the fast way

a. Get ready to read these words the fast way.

b. (Touch the ball for **fishing**. Pause three seconds.) Get ready. (Signal.) *Fishing*.

c. (Repeat *b* for the remaining words on the page.)

EXERCISE 9

Children read the fast way again

a. Get ready to do these words again. Watch where I point.

b. (Point to a word. Pause one second. Say:) Get ready. (Signal.) *The children respond.* (Point to the words in this order: **slēēping, mōre, sitting, fishing**.)

c. (Repeat *b* until firm.)

EXERCISE 10

Individual test

(Call on individual children to read one word the fast way.)

rabbit

fishing

sitting

slēēping

mōre

READING VOCABULARY

EXERCISE 7

Children sound out the word and tell what word

a. (Touch the ball for **box.**) Sound it out.
b. Get ready. (Touch **b, o, x** as the children say *booox.*)
• (If sounding out is not firm, repeat *b.*)
c. What word? (Signal.) *Box.* Yes, **box.**

EXERCISE 8

Children sound out the word and tell what word

a. (Touch the ball for **hand.**) Sound it out.
b. Get ready. (Touch **h, a, n, d** as the children say *haaannnd.*)
• (If sounding out is not firm, repeat *b.*)
c. What word? (Signal.) *Hand.* Yes, **hand.**

EXERCISE 9

Children sound out the word and tell what word

a. (Touch the ball for **bīke.**) Sound it out.
b. Get ready. (Touch **b, ī, k** as the children say *bīīīk.*)
• (If sounding out is not firm, repeat *b.*)
c. What word? (Signal.) *Bike.* Yes, **bike.**

EXERCISE 10

Children sound out the word and tell what word

a. (Touch the ball for **thēse.**) Sound it out.
b. Get ready. (Touch **th, ē, s** as the children say *thththēēēsss.*)
• (If sounding out is not firm, repeat *b.*)
c. What word? (Signal.) *These.* Yes, **these.**

EXERCISE 11

Children read the words the fast way

a. Now you get to read the words on this page the fast way.
b. (Touch the ball for **box.** Pause three seconds.) Get ready. (Move your finger quickly along the arrow.) *Box.*
c. (Repeat *b* for each word on the page.)

box

hand

bīke

thēse

EXERCISE 12

Individual test

(Call on individual children to read one word the fast way.)

EXERCISE 11

Children read the fast way

a. Get ready to read these words the fast way.

b. (Touch the ball for **slēēps.** Pause three seconds.) Get ready. (Signal.) *Sleeps.*

c. (Repeat *b* for the remaining words on the page.)

EXERCISE 12

Children read the fast way again

a. Get ready to do these words again. Watch where I point.

b. (Point to a word. Pause one second. Say:) Get ready. (Signal.) *The children respond.*

• (Point to the words in this order: **ōr, dīve, slēēps, them, with.**)

c. (Repeat *b* until firm.)

EXERCISE 13

Individual test

(Call on individual children to read one word the fast way.)

slēēps

ōr

with

dīve

them

LESSON 141

Groups that are firm on Mastery Tests 26 and 27 should skip this lesson and do lesson 142 today.

SOUNDS

EXERCISE 1

Teaching **x** as in **ox**

a. (Point to **x**.) My turn. When I touch it, I'll say it. (Pause. Touch **x** for an instant, saying:) *ks.* (Do not say **ecks**.)

b. (Point to **x**.) Your turn. When I touch it, you say it. (Pause.) Get ready. (Touch **x**.) *ks.*

c. Again. (Touch **x**.) *ks.*

d. (Repeat *c* until firm.)

EXERCISE 2

Sounds firm-up

a. Get ready to say the sounds when I touch them.

b. (Alternate touching **x** and **k**. Point to the sound. Pause one second. Say:) Get ready. (Touch the sound.) *The children respond.*

c. (When **x** and **k** are firm, alternate touching **x, k, s,** and **ch** until all four sounds are firm.)

EXERCISE 3

Individual test

(Call on individual children to identify **x, k, s,** or **ch**.)

EXERCISE 4

Teacher introduces cross-out game

a. (Use transparency and crayon.)

b. I'll cross out the sounds on this part of the page when you can tell me every sound.

c. Remember—when I touch it, you say it.

d. (Go over the sounds until the children can identify all the sounds in order.)

EXERCISE 5

Individual test

(Call on individual children to identify two or more sounds in exercise 4.)

EXERCISE 6

Teacher crosses out sounds

a. You told me every sound. Get ready to do it again. This time I'll cross out each sound when you tell me what it is.

b. (Point to each sound. Pause. Say:) Get ready. (Touch the sound.) *The children respond.*

• (As you cross out the sound, say:) Goodbye, _____.

STORY 131
EXERCISE 14

First reading—children read the story the fast way

(Have the children reread any sentences containing words that give them trouble. Keep a list of these words.)

a. (Pass out Storybook.)

b. Open your book to page 104. ✔

c. Everybody, touch the title of the story and get ready to read the words in the title the fast way.

d. First word. ✔

• (Pause two seconds.) Get ready. (Tap.) *The.*

e. (Tap for each remaining word in the title.)

f. (After the children have read the title, ask:) What's this story about? (Signal.) *The dog that ate fish.* Yes, **the dog that ate fish.**

g. Everybody, get ready to read this story the fast way.

h. First word. ✔

• (Pause two seconds.) Get ready. (Tap.) *A.*

i. (Tap for the remaining words in the first sentence. Pause at least two seconds between taps.)

j. (Repeat *h* and *i* for the next two sentences. Have the children reread the first three sentences until firm.)

k. (The children are to read the remainder of the story the fast way, stopping at the end of each sentence.)

l. (After the first reading of the story, print on the board the words that the children missed more than one time. Have the children sound out each word one time and tell what word.)

m. (After the group's responses are firm, call on individual children to read the words.)

EXERCISE 15

Individual test

a. Look at page 104. I'm going to call on individual children to read a whole sentence.

b. (Call on individual children to read a sentence. Do not tap for each word.)

EXERCISE 16

Second reading—children read the story the fast way and answer questions

a. You're going to read the story again the fast way and I'll ask questions.

b. Starting with the first word of the title. ✔

• Get ready. (Tap.) *The.*

c. (Tap for each remaining word. Pause at least two seconds between taps. Pause longer before words that gave the children trouble during the first reading.)

d. (Ask the comprehension questions below as the children read.)

After the children read:	You say:
The dog that ate fish.	What's this story about? (Signal.) *The dog that ate fish.*
The girl did not like the dog to eat fish.	Who went fishing? (Signal.) *The girl and the dog.* Did the dog eat fish? (Signal.) *Yes.* How did the girl feel about the dog eating fish? *The children respond.* She did not like the dog to eat fish.
"Give me the five fish," the dog said.	What did the dog say? (Signal.) *Give me the five fish.* How many fish did the girl catch? (Signal.) *Five.* Do you think the girl will give the fish to the dog? *The children respond.*
"No," the girl said.	What did the girl say? (Signal.) *No.* Did she want to give the fish to the dog? (Signal.) *No.*
"Dive in and get them."	What did the girl say? *The children respond.* She said, "More fish are in the lake. Dive in and get them." Do you think the dog will do that? *The children respond.*
And the girl went to sleep.	Did the dog go in the lake? (Signal.) *Yes.* What did the girl do? (Signal.) *Sleep.*

Look Ahead

Mastery Tests

Skill Tested	Implications
Test 28 (Lesson 135) Reading the story the fast way; children set pace	During these last 20 lessons, be sure that children are firm on sounds and vocabulary, and that they are able to meet criterion on the Checkouts.
Test 29 (Lesson 150) Reading words the fast way	
Test 30 (Lesson 155) Reading the story the fast way; children set pace	

Reading Checkouts

Lessons 145, 150, 155, 160

Read the Items

- Read the Items activities (Lessons 151–160) allow for practice in comprehension and following directions in a game-like format. Children respond well to the challenge of "This one's tough! I bet you can't do it!" followed by praise when they do succeed.

Reading Activities

Help children develop comprehension skills by using the following activities.

Story Maps (Lessons 141–160)

Reinforce the story grammars by having children make maps or illustrations of the headings: Where, Who, Problem, Ending. Children work with partners or in small groups. To illustrate *where,* children would make a map of the places visited in the story. To illustrate *who,* children would make a picture of the main characters. With different groups making pictures of different headings of the story, the class makes an illustrated story grammar.

Ready to Write (Lessons 157–158)

Help students establish the story grammar for Lessons 157 and 158 by completing a story grammar chart. On the chart, list the following elements: Title, Where, Who, Problem, Events, Ending. First help children complete the chart using the fat eagle and tiger stories. Then show children how to create a new story by changing the characters, the problem, the events, the setting, and the title of the story. Write a group story or have children write their own. Extend the activity to include editing, revising, and publishing.

Poetry Corner (Lesson 145)

After children have finished reading story 145, have them write a cinquain to help capture the main idea of a story. A cinquain is an unrhymed, five-line poem in which the thought is stressed. The cinquain specifications and an example are shown below.

Specifications:

Line 1   One word describing the title

Line 2   Two words describing the character

Line 3   Three words expressing an action

Line 4   Four words expressing a feeling or an opinion

Line 5   One word, a synonym for the title

The Pig That Bit His Leg

Pig

Very silly

Bit his leg

The bug tricked him

Oink

WORSHEET 131

EXERCISE 17

Picture comprehension

a. What do you think you'll see in the picture? *The children respond.*

b. Turn the page and look at the picture.

c. (Ask these questions:)

1. How many fish does the girl have? *Five.*
2. What do you think she's saying to that dog? *The children respond.*
3. I wonder what's in that can near the girl. *The children respond.* Yes, worms.
4. Did you ever go fishing and catch five fish? *The children respond.*

★STORY ITEMS

The children will need pencils.

EXERCISE 18

Children complete sentences and answer story questions

a. (Pass out Worksheet 131 to each child.)

b. (Point to the story-items exercise on side 1.) These items are about the story you just read.

c. Everybody, read item 1 the fast way. First word. ✔

• Get ready. (Tap for each word as the children read *the girl got . . .*)

d. The story told that the girl went fishing, and the girl got . . . Everybody, what did the girl get? (Signal.) *Five fish.* Yes, **five fish.**

e. Touch the right words in item 1. ✔

• Circle the words. ✔

> **To Correct**
>
> (Have the children read the appropriate sentence in the story. Then repeat *d* and *e*.)

f. Everybody, read item 2 the fast way. First word. ✔

• Get ready. (Tap for each word as the children read *did she give fish to the dog?*)

g. Everybody, did she give fish to the dog? (Signal.) *No.*

h. Touch the right word in item 2. ✔

• Circle the word. ✔

i. Everybody, read item 3 the fast way. First word. ✔

• Get ready. (Tap for each word as the children read *the dog went . . . .*)

j. Everybody, where did the dog go? (Signal.) *In the lake.* Yes, **in the lake.**

k. Touch the right words in item 3. ✔

• Circle the words. ✔

Making Progress

	Since Lesson 1	Since Lesson 121
Word Reading	33 sounds	6 sounds
	283 regular words	73 regular words
	34 irregular words	15 irregular words
	Reading words the fast way	Individuals taking turns reading
	Reading stories the fast way	
	Individuals taking turns reading	
Comprehension	**Picture Comprehension**	**Story Comprehension**
	Predicting what the picture will show	
	Answering comprehension questions about the picture	Answering written comprehension questions about the day's story and short passages
	Story Comprehension	
	Answering *who, what, when, where* and *why* questions about the story	
	Finding periods, question marks, and quotation marks	
	Answering written comprehension questions about the day's story and short passages	

What to Use

Teacher	Students
Presentation Book C (pages 204–344)	**Storybook**
	Lessons 141–160 (pages 135–192)
	Workbook C
Teacher's Guide (page 58–59)	plain paper (Sentence picture)
Answer Key	lined paper (Spelling)
Spelling Presentation Book	

What's Ahead in Lessons 141–160

New Skills

- Story length will increase from 106 to 136 words.
- Children will begin reading two-part stories.
- Children will do "Read the Item" activities involving both comprehension and following directions.
- Children will do picture completion items which involve both comprehension and spelling.

New Sounds

- Lesson 142 — **oo** as in *moon*
- Lesson 145 — **J** as in *jump* (quick sound)
- Lesson 149 — **ȳ** as in *my*
- Lesson 152 — **wh** as in *why*
- Lesson 154 — **qu** as in *quick*
- Lesson 156 — **z** as in *zap*
- Lesson 158 — **ū** as in *use*

New Vocabulary

- *Regular words:*

  (141) bike, box, fox, stopper, these, topper
  (142) eagle, hitting, over
  (143) shore, slider
  (144) broom, chore, dime, room
  (145) better, chip, moon, pile, than
  (146) brush, brushed, day, must, soon
  (147) either, jump, pool, store, tore
  (148) broke, jumped, jumps, swimming
  (149) bring, bringing, fill, teacher

  (150) horse, riding, stand
  (151) bill, fine, liked, nine
  (152) filled, fly, gold, my
  (153) six
  (154) rushing, slipped, times, tooth, when, where, white
  (155) shine, smile, smiled, why
  (156) after, fatter, from, tiger, tree, under, yelled
  (157) even, fast, slow, stands, steps, things
  (158) head, life, picks, show, thing, wife

- *Irregular words:*

  (145) talked, walked
  (147) loved
  (149) start, tart
  (150) your

  (152) book
  (153) look, touch
  (154) took
  (156) looked

LESSONS 141–160

SUMMARY OF INDEPENDENT ACTIVITY
EXERCISE 19

Introduction to independent activity

a. (Hold up Worksheet 131.)

b. Everybody, you're going to finish this worksheet on your own. (Tell the children when they will work the remaining items.)

• Let's go over the things you're going to do.

Sound writing

a. (Point to the sound-writing exercise on side 1.) Here are the sounds you're going to write today. I'll touch the sounds. You say them.

b. (Touch each sound.) *The children respond.*

c. (Repeat the series until firm.)

Reading comprehension

a. (Point to the boxed sentences in the reading-comprehension exercise.)

b. Everybody, get ready to read the sentences the fast way.

c. First word. ✔

• Get ready. (Tap for each word as the children read *a man had a car.*)

d. (Have the children reread the sentence until firm.)

e. Get ready to read the next sentence. (Repeat *c* and *d* for **the car was red.**)

f. (Point to items 1 and 2.) These items tell about the story in the box. You're going to read each item and circle the right answer.

Sentence copying

a. (Hold up side 2 of your worksheet and point to the dotted sentence in the sentence-copying exercise.)

b. You're going to trace the words in this sentence. Then you're going to write the sentence on the other lines.

c. Reading the fast way. First word. ✔

• Get ready. (Tap for each word.)

d. After you finish your worksheet, you get to draw a picture about the sentence, **shē got fīve fish.** You'll draw your picture on a piece of plain paper.

Pair relations

a. (Point to the pair-relations exercise.) You're going to read each sentence. Then draw a line from the sentence to the right picture.

b. (When the children finish their worksheets, give them sheets of plain paper. Remind them to draw a picture that shows **shē got fīve fish.**)

END OF LESSON 131

a. (Tell child:) Get ready to read these words the fast way.

b. (test item) (Touch the ball for **went.** Pause three seconds.)
Get ready. (Signal.) *Went.*

c. (test item) (Touch the ball for **other.** Pause three seconds.)
Get ready. (Signal.) *Other.*

d. (test item) (Touch the ball for **you.** Pause three seconds.)
Get ready. (Signal.) *You.*

e. (test item) (Touch the ball for **card.** Pause three seconds.)
Get ready. (Signal.) *Card.*

Total number of test items: **4**
A group is weak if more than one-third of the children missed any of the items on the test.

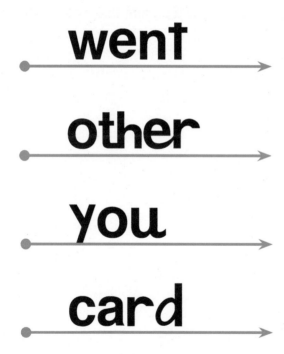

WHAT TO DO

If the group is firm on Mastery Test 27 and was firm on Mastery Test 26:

Skip lesson 141, present lesson 142, then skip lesson 143. If more than one child missed any of the items on the test, present the firming procedures specified below to those children.

If the group is firm on Mastery Test 27 but was weak on Mastery Test 26:

Present lesson 141 to the group during the next reading period. If more than one child missed any of the items on the test, present the firming procedures specified below to those children.

If the group is weak on Mastery Test 27:

A. Present these firming procedures to the group during the next reading period.
   1. Lesson 137, Reading Vocabulary, pages 180–181, exercises 4 through 13.
   2. Lesson 138, Reading Vocabulary, pages 187–188, exercises 9 through 17.
   3. Lesson 140, Reading Vocabulary, pages 198–199, exercises 6 through 16.
B. After presenting the above exercises, again give Mastery Test 27 individually to members of the group who failed the test.
C. If the group is firm (less than one-third of the total group missed any items on the retest), present lesson 141 to the group during the next reading period.
D. If the group is still weak (more than one-third of the total group missed any items on the retest), repeat *A* and *B* during the next reading period.

SOUNDS
EXERCISE 1

Teaching **y** as in **yes**

a. (Point to **y**.) My turn. (Pause. Touch **y** and say:) yyy.

b. (Point to **y**.) Your turn. When I touch it, you say it. (Pause.) Get ready. (Touch **y**.) *yyy.*

• (Lift your finger.)

c. Again. (Touch **y**.) *yyyy.*

• (Lift your finger.)

d. (Repeat *c* until firm.)

y

i

k

e

EXERCISE 2

Sounds firm-up

a. Get ready to say the sounds when I touch them.

b. (Alternate touching **y** and **i**. Point to the sound. Pause one second. Say:) Get ready. (Touch the sound.) *The children respond.*

c. (When **y** and **i** are firm, alternate touching **y, i, k,** and **e** until all four sounds are firm.)

EXERCISE 3

Individual test

(Call on individual children to identify **y, i, k,** or **e**.)

EXERCISE 4

Sounds firm-up

a. (Point to **y**.) When I touch the sound, you say it.

b. (Pause.) Get ready. (Touch **y**.) *yyy.*

c. Again. (Repeat *b* until firm.)

d. Get ready to say all the sounds when I touch them.

e. (Alternate touching **y, ing, u, sh, I, ch, ī,** and **b** three or four times. Point to the sound. Pause one second. Say:) Get ready. (Touch the sound.) *The children respond.*

EXERCISE 5

Individual test

(Call on individual children to identify one or more sounds in exercise 4.)

y

ing

u

sh

I

ch

b

i

EXERCISE 23

Picture comprehension

a. What do you think you'll see in the picture? *The children respond.*

b. (Ask these questions:)
1. Where are the boy and his mother in this picture? *The children respond.* In a toy shop.
2. What kind of toys do you see? *The children respond.*
3. Which toy would you like the best? *The children respond.*
4. Are big toys more fun than little toys? *The children respond.*

WORKSHEET 140

SUMMARY OF INDEPENDENT ACTIVITY

EXERCISE 24

Introduction to independent activity

a. (Pass out sides 1 and 2 of Worksheet 140 to each child.)

b. Everybody, do a good job on your worksheet today and I'll give you a bonus worksheet.

c. (Hold up side 1 of your worksheet.) You're going to do this worksheet on your own. (Tell the children when they will work the items.)

• Let's go over some of the things you're going to do.

Story items

a. (Point to the story-items exercise.)

b. Everybody, read item 1 about the story the fast way. First word. ✔

• Get ready. (Tap for each word as the children read, *A boy went to a . . .*)

c. Everybody, what's the answer? (Signal.) *Toy shop.*

d. Think about what happened in the story and circle the right answer for each item.

Reading comprehension

a. (Point to the boxed sentences in the reading-comprehension exercise.)

b. Everybody, get ready to read the sentences the fast way.

c. First word. ✔

• Get ready. (Tap for each word as the children read *his mother got a card.*)

d. (Have the children reread the sentence until firm.)

e. Get ready to read the next sentence. (Repeat c and d for **it said, "I love you."**)

f. (Point to items 1 and 2.) These items tell about the story in the box. You're going to read each item and circle the right answer.

Sentence copying

a. (Hold up side 2 of your worksheet and point to the dotted sentence in the sentence-copying exercise.)

b. You're going to trace the words in this sentence. Then you're going to write the sentence on the other lines.

c. Reading the fast way. First word. ✔

• Get ready. (Tap for each word.)

d. After you finish your worksheet, you get to draw a picture about the sentence, **hē is in a tōy shop.** You'll draw your picture on a piece of plain paper.

Other independent activity: sides 1, 2, 3, 4

Remember to do all the parts of the worksheet and to read all the parts carefully. After you draw your picture, I'll give you a bonus worksheet.

INDIVIDUAL CHECKOUT: STORYBOOK

EXERCISE 29

2½-minute individual fluency checkout: rate skill/accuracy

a. As you are doing your worksheet, I'll call on children one at a time to read the **whole story.** Remember, you get two stars if you read the story in less than two and a half minutes and make no more than three errors.

b. (Call on a child. Tell the child:) Start with the title and read the story carefully the fast way. Go. (Time the child. Tell the child any words the child misses. Stop the child as soon as the child makes the fourth error or exceeds the time limit.)

c. (If the child meets the rate-accuracy criterion, record two stars on your chart for lesson 140. Congratulate the child. Give children who do not earn two stars a chance to read the story again before the next lesson is presented.)
92 words/**2.5 min** = 37 wpm [**3 errors**]

END OF LESSON 140

Before presenting lesson 141, give Mastery Test 27 to each child. Do not present lesson 141 to any groups that are not firm on this test.

READING VOCABULARY
EXERCISE 6

Children read the fast way

a. Get ready to read these words the fast way.
b. (Touch the ball for **having.** Pause three seconds.)
Get ready. (Signal.) *Having.*
c. (Repeat *b* for the remaining words on the page.)

EXERCISE 7

Children read the fast way again

a. Get ready to do these words again. Watch where I point.
b. (Point to a word. Pause one second. Say:) Get ready. (Signal.)
The children respond.
• (Point to the words in this order: **top, gōing, having, sāme.**)
c. (Repeat *b* until firm.)

EXERCISE 8

Individual test

(Call on individual children to read one word the fast way.)

STORY 140

EXERCISE 20

First reading—children read the title and first three sentences

a. (Pass out Storybook.)

b. Open your book to page 132. ✔
You're going to read the first part of this story today.

c. Everybody, touch the title of the story and get ready to read the words in the title the fast way.

d. First word. ✔

- (Pause two seconds.) Get ready. (Tap.) *Going.*

e. (Tap for each remaining word in the title.)

f. (After the children have read the title, ask:) What's this story about? (Signal.) *Going to the toy shop.* Yes, **going to the toy shop.**

g. Everybody, get ready to read this story the fast way.

h. First word. ✔

- (Pause two seconds.) Get ready. (Tap.) *A.*

i. (Tap for the remaining words in the first sentence. Pause at least two seconds between taps.)

j. (Repeat *h* and *i* for the next two sentences. Have the children reread the first three sentences until firm.)

EXERCISE 21

Individual children or the group read sentences to complete the first reading

a. I'm going to call on individual children to read a sentence. Everybody, follow along and point to the words. If you hear a mistake, raise your hand.

b. (Call on a child.) Read the next sentence. (Do not tap for the words. Let children read at their own pace, but be sure they read the sentence correctly.)

To Correct
(Have the child sound out the word. Then return to the beginning of the sentence.)

c. (Repeat *b* for most of the remaining sentences in the story. Occasionally have the group read a sentence. When the group is to read, say:) Everybody, read the next sentence. (Pause two seconds.) Get ready. (Tap for each word in the sentence. Pause at least two seconds between taps.)

EXERCISE 22

Second reading—individual children or the group read each sentence; the group answers questions

a. You're going to read the story again. This time I'm going to ask questions.

b. Starting with the first word of the title. ✔

- Get ready. (Tap as the children read the title. Pause at least two seconds between taps.)

c. (Call on a child.) Read the first sentence. *The child responds.*

d. (Repeat *b* and *c* in exercise 21. Present the following comprehension questions to the entire group.)

After the children read:	You say:
Going to the toy shop.	What's this story about? (Signal.) *Going to a toy shop.*
"I like big toys."	What did the boy say? (Signal.) *I like big toys.* Where was the boy? (Signal.) *In a toy shop.* Who went with him to get toys? (Signal.) *His mother.*
"So we will get little toys."	Did his mother like big toys? (Signal.) *No.* What kind of toys did she like? (Signal.) *Little toys.*
"And I like big toys."	What did the boy say? *The children respond.* He said, "I am not a dog. I am a boy. And I like big toys." I wonder how he's going to get a big toy if his mother doesn't like big toys. *The children respond.* We'll find out in the next part of the story.

EXERCISE 9

Children read a word beginning with two consonants (**slīde**)

a. (Cover **s.** Run your finger under **līde.**) You're going to sound out this part. Get ready. (Touch **l, ī, d** as the children say *lllīīīd.*)

b. Say it fast. (Signal.) *Līde.* Yes, this part is **līde.**

c. (Uncover **s.** Point to **s.**) You're going to say this first. (Move your finger quickly under **līde.**) Then you're going to say (pause) **līde.**

d. (Point to **s.**) What are you going to say first? (Signal.) *sss.*

• What are you going to say next? (Signal.) *Līde.*

e. (Repeat *d* until firm.)

f. (Touch the ball for **slīde.**) Remember—first you say **sss;** then you say **līde.** Get ready. (Move to **s,** then quickly along the arrow.) *Ssslīde.*

g. Say it fast. (Signal.) *Slide.*

• Yes, what word? (Signal.) *Slide.* Yes, **slide.**

• Good reading.

h. Again. (Repeat *f* and *g* until firm.)

i. Now you're going to sound out (pause) **slide.** Get ready. (Touch **s, l, ī, d** as the children say *ssslllīīīd.*)

• What word? (Signal.) *Slide.* Yes, **slide.**

slīde

EXERCISE 10

Children read a word beginning with two consonants (**slid**)

a. (Cover **s.** Run your finger under **lid.**) You're going to sound out this part. Get ready. (Touch **l, i, d** as the children say *llliiid.*)

b. Say it fast. (Signal.) *Lid.* Yes, this part is **lid.**

c. (Uncover **s.** Point to **s.**) You're going to say this first. (Move your finger quickly under **lid.**) Then you're going to say (pause) **lid.**

d. (Point to **s.**) What are you going to say first? (Signal.) *sss.*

• What are you going to say next? (Signal.) *Lid.*

e. (Repeat *d* until firm.)

f. (Touch ball for **slid.**) Remember—first you say **sss;** then you say **lid.** Get ready. (Move to **s,** then quickly along the arrow.) *Ssslid.*

g. Say it fast. (Signal.) *Slid.*

• Yes, what word? (Signal.) *Slid.* Yes, **slid.**

• Good reading.

h. Again. (Repeat *f* and *g* until firm.)

i. Now you're going to sound out (pause) **slid.** Get ready. (Touch **s, l, i, d** as the children say *sssllliiid.*)

• What word? (Signal.) *Slid.* Yes, **slid.**

slid

EXERCISE 11

Individual test

(Have children read one word the fast way.)

EXERCISE 17

Children read **shop** and **shopping**

a. (Touch the ball for **shop.**) You're going to read this word the fast way. (Pause three seconds.) Get ready. (Move your finger quickly along the arrow.) *Shop.*

b. (Return to the ball for **shop.**) Yes, this word is **shop.**

c. (Touch the ball for **shopping.**) So this must be **shop . . .** (Touch **ing.**) *Ing.*

• What word? (Signal.) *Shopping.* Yes, **shopping.**

d. Again. (Repeat *b* and *c* until firm.)

e. (Touch the ball for **shop.**) This word is **shop.**

f. (Touch the ball for **shopping.**) So this must be . . . (Quickly run your finger under **shop** and tap **ing.**) *Shopping.* Yes, **shopping.**

g. Again. (Repeat *e* and *f* until firm.)

h. Now you're going to sound out (pause) **shopping.** Get ready. (Touch **sh, o,** between the **p**'s, **ing** as the children say *shshshooopiiing.*)

• Yes, what word? (Signal.) *Shopping.* Yes, **shopping.**

EXERCISE 18

Children read the word the fast way

a. Get ready to read this word the fast way.

b. (Touch the ball for **bōy.** Pause three seconds.) Get ready. (Signal.) *Boy.* Yes, **boy.**

c. (Repeat *b* for **ever** and **never.**)

EXERCISE 19

Children read the fast way again

a. Get ready to do these words again. Watch where I point.

b. (Point to a word. Pause one second. Say:) Get ready. (Signal.) *The children respond.*

• (Point to the words in this order: **bōy, shopping, ever, never, shop.**)

shop

shopping

bōy

ever

never

EXERCISE 12

Children sound out the word and tell what word

a. (Touch the ball for **rabbit.**) Sound it out.
b. Get ready. (Touch **r, a,** between the **b**'s, **i, t** as the children say *rrraaabiiit.*)
• (If sounding out is not firm, repeat *b*.)
c. What word? (Signal.) *Rabbit.* Yes, **rabbit.**

EXERCISE 13

Children sound out the word and tell what word

(Repeat the procedures in exercise 12 for **time.**)

EXERCISE 14

Children sound out the word and tell what word

(Repeat the procedures in exercise 12 for **tell.**)

EXERCISE 15

Children read **do** and **doing**

a. (Touch the ball for **do.**) You're going to read this word the fast way. (Pause three seconds.) Get ready. (Move your finger quickly along the arrow.) *Do.*
b. (Return to the ball for **do.**) Yes, this word is **do.**
c. (Touch the ball for **doing.**) So this must be **do . . .** (Touch **ing.**) *Ing.*
• What word? (Signal.) *Doing.* Yes, **doing.**
d. Again. (Repeat *b* and *c* until firm.)
e. (Touch the ball for **do.**) This word is **do.**
f. (Touch the ball for **doing.**) So this must be . . . (Quickly run your finger under **do** and tap **ing.**) *Doing.* Yes, **doing.**
g. Again. (Repeat *e* and *f* until firm.)
h. Now you're going to sound out (pause) **doing.** Get ready. (Touch **d, o, ing** as the children say *doooiiing.*)
i. How do we say the word? (Signal.) *Doing.* Yes, **doing.**

EXERCISE 16

Children read the words the fast way

(Have the children read the words on this page the fast way.)

EXERCISE 17

Individual test

(Call on individual children to read one word the fast way.)

EXERCISE 12

Children read the word the fast way

a. Get ready to read this word the fast way.

b. (Touch the ball for **tōy.** Pause three seconds.) Get ready. (Signal.) *Toy.* Yes, **toy.**

• That is a very nice (pause) **toy.**

c. (Repeat *b* until firm.)

EXERCISE 13

Individual test

(Call on individual children to do *b* in exercise 12.)

EXERCISE 14

Children read the fast way

a. Get ready to read these words the fast way.

b. (Touch the ball for **līke.** Pause three seconds.) Get ready. (Signal.) *Like.*

c. (Repeat *b* for the remaining words on the page.)

EXERCISE 15

Children read the fast way again

a. Get ready to do these words again. Watch where I point.

b. (Point to a word. Pause one second. Say:) Get ready. (Signal.) *The children respond.*

• (Point to the words in this order: **went, stop, līke.**)

c. (Repeat *b* until firm.)

EXERCISE 16

Individual test

(Call on individual children to read one word on the page the fast way.)

tōy

līke

stop

went

STORY 132
EXERCISE 18

First reading—children read the story the fast way

(Have the children reread any sentences containing words that give them trouble. Keep a list of these words.)

a. (Pass out Storybook.)

b. Open your book to page 107. ✔

c. Everybody, touch the title of the story and get ready to read.

d. First word. ✔

• (Pause two seconds.) Get ready. (Tap.) *The.*

e. (Tap for each remaining word in the title.)

f. (After the children have read the title, ask:) What's this story about? (Signal.) *The rat got a sore nose.* Yes, **the rat got a sore nose.**

g. Everybody, get ready to read this story the fast way.

h. First word. ✔

• (Pause two seconds.) Get ready. (Tap.) *A.*

i. (Tap for the remaining words in the first sentence. Pause at least two seconds between taps.)

j. (Repeat *h* and *i* for the next two sentences. Have the children reread the first three sentences until firm.)

k. (The children are to read the remainder of the story the fast way, stopping at the end of each sentence.)

l. (After the first reading of the story, print on the board the words that the children missed more than one time. Have the children sound out each word one time and tell what word.)

m. (After the group's responses are firm, call on individual children to read the words.)

EXERCISE 19

Individual test

a. Turn back to page 107. I'm going to call on individual children to read a whole sentence.

b. (Call on individual children to read a sentence. Do not tap for each word.)

EXERCISE 20

Second reading—children read the story the fast way and answer questions

a. You're going to read the story again the fast way and I'll ask questions.

b. Starting with the first word of the title. ✔

• Get ready. (Tap.) *The.*

c. (Tap for each remaining word. Pause at least two seconds between taps. Pause longer before words that gave the children trouble during the first reading.)

d. (Ask the comprehension questions below as the children read.)

After the children read:	You say:
The rat got a sore nose.	What's this story about? (Signal.) *A rat got a sore nose.*
The rabbit went down on his tail.	Who went down the slide? (Signal.) *A rat and a rabbit.* How did the rabbit go down the slide? (Signal.) *On his tail.*
The rat went up to the top of the slide and slid down on his nose.	How did the rat go down the slide? (Signal.) *On his nose.*
But he came down on his nose.	How did the rat come down the slide this time? (Signal.) *On his nose.*
The rabbit said, "That rat can not tell if he is on his nose or his tail."	What did the rabbit say? (Signal.) *The rat can not tell if he is on his nose or his tail.*

EXERCISE 21

Picture comprehension

a. Everybody, look at the picture.

b. (Ask these questions:)

1. Who's going down the slide? *The rat.*

2. What do you think the rabbit is saying? *The children respond.*

3. How did the rabbit go down the slide? *The children respond.* On his tail.

READING VOCABULARY
EXERCISE 6

Children sound out an irregular word (**come**)

a. (Touch the ball for **come.**) Sound it out.
b. Get ready. (Quickly touch each sound as the children say *cooommmeee.*)
c. Again. (Repeat *b* until firm.)
d. That's how we <u>sound out</u> the word. Here's how we <u>say</u> the word. **Come.** How do we <u>say</u> the word? (Signal.) *Come.*
e. Now you're going to <u>sound out</u> the word. Get ready. (Touch each sound as the children say *cooommmeee.*)
f. Now you're going to say the word. Get ready. (Signal.) *Come.*
g. (Repeat *e* and *f* until firm.)

EXERCISE 7

Children rhyme with an irregular word (**come**)

a. (Touch the ball for **come.**) Everybody, you're going to read this word the fast way. Get ready. (Signal.) *Come.*
b. (Touch the ball for **some.**) This word rhymes with (pause) **come.** Get ready. (Move to **s,** then quickly along the arrow.) *Some.*
c. (Repeat *a* and *b* until firm.)

EXERCISE 8

Children sound out **some**

(Have the children sound out **some.**) *Sssooommmeee.*
• How do we say the word? (Signal.) *Some.* Yes, **some.**
• **Some** dogs are mean.

EXERCISE 9

Children sound out the word and tell what word

a. (Touch the ball for **hop.**) Sound it out.
b. Get ready. (Touch **h, o, p** as the children say *hooop.*)
• (If sounding out is not firm, repeat *b.*)
c. What word? (Signal.) *Hop.* Yes, **hop.**

EXERCISE 10

Children read the words the fast way

(Have the children read the words on this page the fast way.)

EXERCISE 11

Individual test

(Call on individual children to read one word the fast way.)

hop

WORKSHEET 132

STORY ITEMS

The children will need pencils.

EXERCISE 22

Children complete sentences and answer questions

a. (Pass out Worksheet 132 to each child.)

b. (Point to the story-items exercise on side 1.) These items are about the story you just read.

c. Everybody, read item 1 the fast way. First word. ✔

• Get ready. (Tap for each word as the children read *the rabbit went down on his . . .*)

d. The story told that a rat and a rabbit went down a slide. The rabbit went down on his . . . Everybody, what did the rabbit go down the slide on? (Signal.) *His tail.* Yes, his **tail.**

e. Touch the right word in item 1. ✔

• Circle the word. ✔

To Correct

(Have the children read the appropriate sentence in the story. Then repeat *d* and *e*.)

f. Everybody, read item 2 the fast way. First word. ✔

• Get ready. (Tap for each word as the children read *the rat slid down on his . . . .*)

g. Everybody, what did the rat go down the slide on? (Signal.) *His nose.* Yes, his **nose.**

h. Touch the right word in item 2. ✔

• Circle the word. ✔

i. (Repeat *f* through *h* for item 3.)

SUMMARY OF INDEPENDENT ACTIVITY

EXERCISE 23

Introduction to independent activity

a. (Hold up Worksheet 132.)

b. Everybody, you're going to finish this worksheet on your own. (Tell the children when they will work the remaining items.)

• Let's go over the things you're going to do.

Sound writing

a. (Point to the sound-writing exercise on side 1.) Here are the sounds you're going to write today. I'll touch the sounds. You say them.

b. (Touch each sound.) *The children respond.*

c. (Repeat the series until firm.)

Reading comprehension

a. (Point to the boxed sentences in the reading-comprehension exercise.)

b. Everybody, get ready to read the sentences the fast way.

c. First word. ✔

• Get ready. (Tap for each word as the children read *the girl went for a walk.*)

d. (Have the children reread the sentence until firm.)

e. Get ready to read the next sentence. (Repeat *c* and *d* for **shē met a fat pig.**)

f. (Point to items 1 and 2.) These items tell about the story in the box. You're going to read each item and circle the right answer.

Sentence copying

a. (Hold up side 2 of your worksheet and point to the dotted sentence in the sentence-copying exercise.)

b. You're going to trace the words in this sentence. Then you're going to write the sentence on the other lines.

c. Reading the fast way. First word. ✔

• Get ready. (Tap for each word.)

d. After you finish your worksheet, you get to draw a picture about the sentence, **hē slid on his nōse.** You'll draw your picture on a piece of plain paper.

Pair relations

a. (Point to the pair-relations exercise.) You're going to read each sentence. Then draw a line from the sentence to the right picture.

b. (When the children finish their worksheets, give them sheets of plain paper. Remind them to draw a picture that shows **hē slid on his nōse.**)

END OF LESSON 132

SOUNDS

EXERCISE 1

Teaching **x** as in **ox**

a. (Point to **x**.) My turn. When I touch it, I'll say it. (Pause. Touch **x** for an instant, saying:) ks. (Do not say **ecks**.)

b. (Point to **x**.) Your turn. When I touch it, you say it. (Pause.) Get ready. (Touch **x**.) *ks.*

c. Again. (Touch **x**.) *ks.*

d. (Repeat *c* until firm.)

EXERCISE 2

Sounds firm-up

a. Get ready to say the sounds when I touch them.

b. (Alternate touching **x** and **s.** Point to the sound. Pause one second. Say:) Get ready. (Touch the sound.) *The children respond.*

c. (When **x** and **s** are firm, alternate touching **x, s, k,** and **er** until all four sounds are firm.)

EXERCISE 3

Individual test

(Call on individual children to identify **x, s, k,** or **er**.)

EXERCISE 4

Sounds firm-up.

a. (Point to **x**.) When I touch the sound, you say it.

b. (Pause.) Get ready. (Touch **x**.) *ks.*

c. Again. (Repeat *b* until firm.)

d. Get ready to say all the sounds when I touch them.

e. (Alternate touching **x, l, sh, y, b, v, I,** and **e** three or four times. Point to the sound. Pause one second. Say:) Get ready. (Touch the sound.) *The children respond.*

EXERCISE 5

Individual test

(Call on individual children to identify one or more sounds in exercise 4.)

Groups that are firm on Mastery Tests 23 and 24 should skip this lesson and do lesson 134 today.

SOUNDS
EXERCISE 1

Teaching **y** as in **yes**

a. (Point to **y**.) My turn. (Pause. Touch **y** and say:) yyy.

b. (Point to **y**.) Your turn. When I touch it, you say it. (Pause.) Get ready.

• (Touch **y**.) *yyy.*

• (Lift your finger.)

c. Again. (Touch **y**.) *yyyy.*

• (Lift your finger.)

d. (Repeat *c* until firm.)

EXERCISE 2

Sounds firm-up

a. Get ready to say the sounds when I touch them.

b. (Alternate touching **y** and **i**. Point to the sound. Pause one second. Say:) Get ready. (Touch the sound.) *The children respond.*

c. (When **y** and **i** are firm, alternate touching **y**, **i**, **ē**, and **ī** until all four sounds are firm.)

EXERCISE 3

Individual test

(Call on individual children to identify **y**, **i**, **ē**, or **ī**.)

EXERCISE 4

Teacher introduces cross-out game

a. (Use transparency and crayon.)

b. I'll cross out the sounds on this part of the page when you can tell me every sound.

c. Remember—when I touch it, you say it.

d. (Go over the sounds until the children can identify all the sounds in order.)

EXERCISE 5

Individual test

(Call on individual children to identify two or more sounds in exercise 4.)

EXERCISE 6

Teacher crosses out sounds

a. You told me every sound. Get ready to do it again. This time I'll cross out each sound when you tell me what it is.

b. (Point to each sound. Pause. Say:) Get ready. (Touch the sound.) *The children respond.*

• (As you cross out the sound, say:) Goodbye, _____.

EXERCISE 26

Picture comprehension

a. Everybody, look at the picture.

b. (Ask these questions:)

1. What's happening in the picture? *The children respond.*

2. What do you think that mother duck is saying to the pig? *The children respond.*

• I think that pig picked on the wrong mother duck.

3. Did you ever see a real duck? *The children respond.*

• Was that duck mean? *The children respond.*

WORKSHEET 139

SUMMARY OF INDEPENDENT ACTIVITY

EXERCISE 27

Introduction to independent activity

a. (Pass out Worksheet 139 to each child.)

b. Everybody, you're going to do this worksheet on your own. (Tell the children when they will work the items.)

• Let's go over the things you're going to do.

Story items

a. (Hold up side 1 of your worksheet and point to the story-items exercise.)

b. Everybody, read item 1 about the story the fast way. First word. ✔

• Get ready. (Tap for each word as the children read *the ducks went for a . . .*)

c. Everybody, what's the answer? (Signal.) *Walk.*

d. Think about what happened in the story and circle the right answer for each item.

Sound writing

a. (Point to the sound-writing exercise.) Here are the sounds you're going to write today. I'll touch the sounds. You say them.

b. (Touch each sound.) *The children respond.*

c. (Repeat the series until firm.)

Reading comprehension

a. (Point to the boxed sentences in the reading-comprehension exercise.)

b. Everybody, get ready to read the sentences the fast way.

c. First word. ✔

• Get ready. (Tap for each word as the children read *a deer came up to them.*)

d. (Have the children reread the sentence until firm.)

e. Get ready to read the next sentence. (Repeat *c* and *d* for **ann said, "are you a pet?"**)

f. (Point to items 1 and 2.) These items tell about the story in the box. You're going to read each item and circle the right answer.

Sentence copying

a. (Hold up side 2 of your worksheet and point to the dotted sentence in the sentence-copying exercise.)

b. You're going to trace the words in this sentence. Then you're going to write the sentence on the other lines.

c. Reading the fast way. First word. ✔

• Get ready. (Tap for each word.)

d. After you finish your worksheet, you get to draw a picture about the sentence, **the ducks met a pig.** You'll draw your picture on a piece of plain paper.

Pair relations

a. (Point to the pair-relations exercise.) You're going to read each sentence. Then draw a line from the sentence to the right picture.

b. (When the children finish their worksheets, give them sheets of plain paper. Remind them to draw a picture that shows **the ducks met a pig.**)

END OF LESSON 139

READING VOCABULARY

EXERCISE 7

Children sound out an irregular word (**into**)

a. (Touch the ball for **into.**) Sound it out.

b. Get ready. (Quickly touch each sound as the children say *iiinnntooo.*)

> **To Correct**
> If the children do not say the sounds you touch
> 1. (Say:) You've got to say the sounds I touch.
> 2. (Repeat *a* and *b* until firm.)

c. Again. (Repeat *b* until firm.)

d. That's how we <u>sound out</u> the word. Here's how we <u>say</u> the word. **Into.** How do we <u>say</u> the word? (Signal.) *Into.*

e. Now you're going to <u>sound out</u> the word. Get ready. (Touch each sound as the children say *iiinnntooo.*)

f. Now you're going to say the word. Get ready. (Signal.) *Into.*

g. (Repeat *e* and *f* until firm.)

h. Yes, this word is **into.** He went **into** the store.

EXERCISE 8

Individual test

(Call on individual children to do *e* and *f* in exercise 7.)

EXERCISE 9

Children read the fast way

a. Get ready to read these words the fast way.

b. (Touch the ball for **stops.** Pause three seconds.) Get ready. (Signal.) *Stops.*

c. (Repeat *b* for the remaining words on the page.)

EXERCISE 10

Children read the fast way again

a. Get ready to do these words again. Watch where I point.

b. (Point to a word. Pause one second. Say:) Get ready. (Signal.) *The children respond.*

• (Point to the words in this order: **stopping, stops, līke, rich.**)

c. (Repeat *b* until firm.)

into

stops

rich

līke

stopping

EXERCISE 11

Individual test

(Call on individual children to read one word on the page the fast way.)

STORY 139
EXERCISE 23

First reading—children read the story the fast way

(Have the children reread any sentences containing words that give them trouble. Keep a list of these words.)

a. (Pass out Storybook.)

b. Open your book to page 129. ✔

c. Everybody, touch the title of the story and get ready to read the words in the title the fast way.

d. First word. ✔

• (Pause two seconds.) Get ready. (Tap.) *The.*

e. (Tap for each remaining word in the title.)

f. (After the children have read the title, ask:) What's this story about? (Signal.) *The duck and the mean pig.* Yes, **the duck and the mean pig.**

g. Everybody, get ready to read this story the fast way.

h. First word. ✔

• (Pause two seconds.) Get ready. (Tap.) *A.*

i. (Tap for the remaining words in the first sentence. Pause at least two seconds between taps.)

j. (Repeat *h* and *i* for the next two sentences. Have the children reread the first three sentences until firm.)

k. (The children are to read the remainder of the story the fast way, stopping at the end of each sentence.)

l. (After the first reading of the story, print on the board the words that the children missed more than one time. Have the children sound out each word one time and tell what word.)

m. (After the group's responses are firm, call on individual children to read the words.)

EXERCISE 24

Individual test

a. Turn back to page 129. I'm going to call on individual children to read a whole sentence.

b. (Call on individual children to read a sentence. Do not tap for each word.)

EXERCISE 25

Second reading—children read the story the fast way and answer questions

a. You're going to read the story again the fast way and I'll ask questions.

b. Starting with the first word of the title. ✔

• Get ready. (Tap.) *The.*

c. (Tap for each remaining word. Pause at least two seconds between taps. Pause longer before words that gave the children trouble during the first reading.)

d. (Ask the comprehension questions below as the children read.)

After the children read:	You say:
The duck and the mean pig.	What's this story about? (Signal.) *The duck and the mean pig.*
A big mean pig met them on the road.	Who met them? (Signal.) *A big mean pig.* How many little ducks were walking with the mother duck? (Signal.) *Nine.* I wonder what that pig will do. *The children respond.* Let's read and find out.
"I eat beds and I eat bugs."	Oh, oh. I wonder what that mother duck will do.
"And I bite pigs that are mean."	Was the mother duck afraid of the pig? (Signal.) *No.* What do you think the pig will do? *The children respond.*
So the pig ran.	What did the pig do? (Signal.) *The pig ran.*

EXERCISE 12

Children rhyme with an irregular word (**park**)

a. (Touch the ball for **park**.) Everybody, you're going to read this word the fast way. (Pause three seconds.) Get ready. (Move your finger quickly along the arrow.) *Park.* Yes, **park.**

b. (Quickly touch the ball for **dark**.) This word rhymes with (pause) **park.** (Move to **d,** then quickly along the arrow.) *Dark.* Yes, **dark.**

c. (Repeat *a* and *b* until firm.)

EXERCISE 13

Children sound out **dark**

a. (Touch the ball for **dark**.) You're going to sound out this word. Get ready. (Quickly touch **d, a, r, k** as the children say *daaarrrk.*)

b. How do we say the word? (Signal.) *Dark.* Yes, **dark.**

• At night it is **dark** outside.

c. (If *a* and *b* are not firm, say:) Again. (Repeat *a* and *b.*)

EXERCISE 14

Individual test

(Have children do *a* and *b* in exercise 13.)

EXERCISE 15

Children sound out the word and tell what word

a. (Touch the ball for **digging**.) Sound it out.

b. Get ready. (Touch **d, i,** between the **g**'s, **ing** as the children say *diiigiiing.*)

• (If sounding out is not firm, repeat *b.*)

c. What word? (Signal.) *Digging.* Yes, **digging.**

EXERCISE 16

Children rhyme with **red**

a. (Touch the ball for **red.**) You're going to read this word the fast way. (Pause three seconds.) Get ready. (Move your finger quickly along the arrow.) *Red.*

b. (Touch the ball for **led.**) This word rhymes with (pause) **red.** (Move to **l,** then quickly along the arrow.) *Led.*

• Yes, what word? (Signal.) *Led.*

EXERCISE 17

Children read the words the fast way

(Have the children read the words on this page the fast way.)

EXERCISE 18

Individual test

(Have children read one word the fast way.)

park

dark

digging

red

led

EXERCISE 17

Children sound out the word and tell what word

a. (Touch the ball for **tōys.**) Sound it out.

b. Get ready. (Touch **t, ō, y, s** as the children say *tōōōyyysss.*)

• (If sounding out is not firm, repeat *b.*)

c. What word? (Signal.) *Toys.* Yes, **toys.**

• **Toys** are fun to play with.

EXERCISE 18

Individual test

(Call on individual children to do *b* and *c* in exercise 17.)

EXERCISE 19

Children identify, then sound out an irregular word (**other**)

a. (Touch the ball for **other.**) Everybody, you're going to read this word the fast way. (Pause three seconds.) Get ready. (Move your finger quickly along the arrow.) *Other.* Yes, **other.**

b. Now you're going to sound out the word. Get ready. (Quickly touch **o, th, er** as the children say *ooothththerrr.*)

c. Again. (Repeat *b.*)

d. How do we say the word? (Signal.) *Other.* Yes, **other.**

e. (Repeat *b* and *d* until firm.)

EXERCISE 20

Individual test

(Have children do *b* and *d* in exercise 19.)

EXERCISE 21

Children read the words the fast way

a. Now you get to read the words on this page the fast way.

b. (Touch the ball for **other.** Pause three seconds.) Get ready. (Move your finger quickly along the arrow.) *Other.*

c. (Repeat *b* for **tōys.**)

EXERCISE 22

Individual test

(Call on individual children to read one word the fast way.)

tōys

other

EXERCISE 19

Children sound out an irregular word (**you**)

a. (Touch the ball for **you.**) Sound it out.

b. Get ready. (Quickly touch each sound as the children say *yyyooouuu.*)

c. Again. (Repeat *b* until firm.)

d. That's how we <u>sound out</u> the word. Here's how we <u>say</u> the word. **You.** How do we <u>say</u> the word? (Signal.) *You.*

e. Now you're going to <u>sound out</u> the word. Get ready. (Touch each sound as the children say *yyyooouuu.*)

f. Now you're going to say the word. Get ready. (Signal.) *You.*

g. (Repeat *e* and *f* until firm.)

h. Yes, this word is **you. You** are working hard today.

EXERCISE 20

Individual test

(Call on individual children to do *e* and *f* in exercise 19.)

EXERCISE 21

Children sound out the word and tell what word

a. (Touch the ball for **bōy.**) Sound it out.

b. Get ready. (Touch **b, ō, y** as the children say *bōōōyyy.*)

• (If sounding out is not firm, repeat *b*.)

c. What word? (Signal.) *Boy.* Yes, **boy.**

EXERCISE 22

Individual test

(Call on individual children to do *a* through *c* in exercise 21.)

EXERCISE 23

Children read the words the fast way

(Have the children read the words on this page the fast way.)

EXERCISE 24

Individual test

(Call on individual children to read one word the fast way.)

EXERCISE 11

Children read the word the fast way

a. Get ready to read this word the fast way.

b. (Touch the ball for **bōys.** Pause three seconds.) Get ready.
(Signal.) *Boys.* Yes, **boys.**

c. (Repeat *b* until firm.)

EXERCISE 12

Individual test

(Call on individual children to do *c* in exercise 11.)

EXERCISE 13

Children identify, then sound out an irregular word (**mother**)

a. (Touch the ball for **mother.**) Everybody, you're going to read this
word the fast way. (Pause three seconds.) Get ready. (Move your
finger quickly along the arrow.) *Mother.* Yes, **mother.**

b. Now you're going to sound out the word. Get ready. (Quickly touch
m, o, th, er as the children say *mmmoooothththerrr.*)

c. Again. (Repeat *b.*)

d. How do we say the word? (Signal.) *Mother.* Yes, **mother.**

e. (Repeat *b* and *d* until firm.)

EXERCISE 14

Individual test

(Call on individual children to do *b* and *d* in exercise 13.)

EXERCISE 15

Children read the words the fast way

a. Now you get to read the words on this page the fast way.

b. (Touch the ball for **bōys.** Pause three seconds.) Get ready.
(Move your finger quickly along the arrow.) *Boys.*

c. (Repeat *b* for **mother.**)

EXERCISE 16

Individual test

(Call on individual children to read one word the fast way.)

bōys

mother

STORY 133
EXERCISE 25

First reading—children read the story the fast way

(Have the children reread any sentences containing words that give them trouble. Keep a list of these words.)

a. (Pass out Storybook.)

b. Open your book to page 110. ✔

c. Everybody, touch the title of the story and get ready to read the words in the title the fast way.

d. First word. ✔

• (Pause two seconds.) Get ready. (Tap.) *The.*

e. (Tap for each remaining word in the title.)

f. (After the children have read the title, ask:) What's this story about? (Signal.) *The rich pig.* Yes, **the rich pig.**

g. Everybody, get ready to read this story the fast way.

h. First word. ✔

• (Pause two seconds.) Get ready. (Tap.) *A.*

i. (Tap for the remaining words in the first sentence. Pause at least two seconds between taps.)

j. (Repeat *h* and *i* for the next two sentences. Have the children reread the first three sentences until firm.)

k. (The children are to read the remainder of the story the fast way, stopping at the end of each sentence.)

l. (After the first reading of the story, print on the board the words that the children missed more than one time. Have the children sound out each word one time and tell what word.)

m. (After the group's responses are firm, call on individual children to read the words.)

EXERCISE 26

Individual test

a. Look at page 110. I'm going to call on individual children to read a whole sentence.

b. (Call on individual children to read a sentence. Do not tap for each word.)

EXERCISE 27

Second reading—children read the story the fast way and answer questions

a. You're going to read the story again the fast way and I'll ask questions.

b. Starting with the first word of the title. ✔

• Get ready. (Tap.) *The.*

c. (Tap for each remaining word. Pause at least two seconds between taps. Pause longer before words that gave the children trouble during the first reading.)

d. (Ask the comprehension questions below as the children read.)

After the children read:	You say:
The rich pig.	What's this story about? (Signal.) *The rich pig.*
It was dark in the park.	Where was the dog? (Signal.) *In the park.* What was it like in the park? (Signal.) *Dark.*
"Pigs live on farms."	What did the dog say? (Signal.) *Pigs live on farms.* Who did the dog run into? (Signal.) *A pig.*
"I am a rich pig."	What did the pig say? (Signal.) *I am a rich pig.*
But the waves made the ship rock.	What happened to the ship? (Signal.) *The ship rocked.*
And the dog got sick.	What happened to the dog? (Signal.) *She got sick.* Why? (Signal.) *The ship rocked.*

EXERCISE 28

Picture comprehension

a. What do you think you'll see in the picture? *The children respond.*

b. Turn the page and look at the picture.

c. (Ask these questions:)

1. Who's on that ship? *The children respond.* A pig and a dog.
2. What is the ship doing? *The children respond.* Rocking.
3. What's making the ship rock? *The children respond.* The waves.

READING VOCABULARY

EXERCISE 7

Children sound out the word and tell what word

a. (Touch the ball for **bēans.**) Sound it out.

b. Get ready. (Touch **b, ē, n, s** as the children say *bēēēnnnsss.*)

• (If sounding out is not firm, repeat *b.*)

c. What word? (Signal.) *Beans.* Yes, **beans.**

EXERCISE 8

Children read the fast way

a. Get ready to read these words the fast way.

b. (Touch the ball for **ever.** Pause three seconds.) Get ready. (Signal.) *Ever.*

c. (Repeat *b* for the remaining words on the page.)

EXERCISE 9

Children read the fast way again

a. Get ready to do these words again. Watch where I point.

b. (Point to a word. Pause one second. Say:) Get ready. (Signal.) *The children respond.*

• (Point to the words in this order: **never, ever, shopping.**)

c. (Repeat *b* until firm.)

EXERCISE 10

Individual test

(Call on individual children to read one word on the page the fast way.)

bēans

ever

shopping

never

WORKSHEET 133

STORY ITEMS

The children will need pencils.

EXERCISE 29

Children complete sentences and answer questions

a. (Pass out Worksheet 133 to each child.)

b. (Point to the story-items exercise on side 1.) These items are about the story you just read.

c. Everybody, read item 1 the fast way. First word. ✔

• Get ready. (Tap for each word as the children read *the dog said, "pigs live . . ."*)

d. The story told that **the dog said, "pigs live . . ."** Everybody, where did the dog say pigs live? (Signal.) *On farms.* Yes, **on farms.**

e. Touch the right words in item 1. ✔

• Circle the words. ✔

To Correct
(Have the children read the appropriate sentence in the story. Then repeat *d* and *e*.)

f. Everybody, read item 2 the fast way. First word. ✔

• Get ready. (Tap for each word as the children read *the pig said, "I am a . . ."*)

g. Everybody, the pig said, "I am a . . ." (Signal.) *Rich pig.*

h. Touch the right words in item 2. ✔

• Circle the words. ✔

i. Everybody, read item 3 the fast way. First word. ✔

• Get ready. (Tap for each word as the children read *the ship rocked and the dog . . .*)

j. Everybody, the ship rocked and the dog . . . (Signal.) *Got sick.* Yes, **got sick.**

k. Touch the right words in item 3. ✔

• Circle the words. ✔

SUMMARY OF INDEPENDENT ACTIVITY
EXERCISE 30

Introduction to independent activity

a. (Hold up Worksheet 133.)

b. Everybody, you're going to finish this worksheet on your own. (Tell the children when they will work the remaining items.) Let's go over the things you're going to do.

Sound writing

a. (Point to the sound-writing exercise on side 1.) Here are the sounds you're going to write today. I'll touch the sounds. You say them.

b. (Touch each sound.) *The children respond.*

c. (Repeat the series until firm.)

Reading comprehension

a. (Point to the boxed sentences in the reading-comprehension exercise.)

b. Everybody, get ready to read the sentences the fast way.

c. First word. ✔

• Get ready. (Tap for each word as the children read *a girl went fishing.*)

d. (Have the children reread the sentence until firm.)

e. Get ready to read the next sentence. (Repeat *c* and *d* for **shē did not get fish.**)

f. (Point to items 1 and 2.) These items tell about the story in the box. You're going to read each item and circle the right answer.

Sentence copying

a. (Hold up side 2 of your worksheet and point to the dotted sentence in the sentence-copying exercise.)

b. You're going to trace the words in this sentence. Then you're going to write the sentence on the other lines.

c. Reading the fast way. First word. ✔

• Get ready. (Tap for each word.)

d. After you finish your worksheet, you get to draw a picture about the sentence, **I live on a ship.** You'll draw your picture on a piece of plain paper.

Pair relations

a. (Point to the pair-relations exercise.) You're going to read each sentence. Then draw a line from the sentence to the right picture.

b. (When the children finish their worksheets, give them sheets of plain paper. Remind them to draw a picture that shows **I live on a ship.**)

END OF LESSON 133

SOUNDS

EXERCISE 1

Teaching **x** as in **ox**

a. (Point to **x.**) Here's a new sound. It's a quick sound.

b. My turn. (Pause. Touch **x** for an instant, saying:) **ks.**
(Do not say **ecks.**)

c. Again. (Touch **x** and say:) **ks.**

d. (Point to **x.**) Your turn. When I touch it, you say it. (Pause.) Get ready. (Touch **x.**) *ks.*

e. Again. (Touch **x.**) *ks.*

f. (Repeat *e* until firm.)

EXERCISE 2

Individual test

(Call on individual children to identify **x.**)

EXERCISE 3

Sounds firm-up

a. Get ready to say the sounds when I touch them.

b. (Alternate touching **x** and **k.** Point to the sound. Pause one second. Say:) Get ready. (Touch the sound.) *The children respond.*

c. (When **x** and **k** are firm, alternate touching **x, k, s,** and **ch** until all four sounds are firm.)

EXERCISE 4

Individual test

(Call on individual children to identify **x, k, s,** or **ch.**)

EXERCISE 5

Sounds firm-up

a. (Point to **x.**) When I touch the sound, you say it.

b. (Pause.) Get ready. (Touch **x.**) *ks.*

c. Again. (Repeat *b* until firm.)

d. Get ready to say all the sounds when I touch them.

e. (Alternate touching **x, ī, y, ē, ō, u, ing,** and **er** three or four times. Point to the sound. Pause one second. Say:) Get ready. (Touch the sound.) *The children respond.*

EXERCISE 6

Individual test

(Call on individual children to identify one or more sounds in exercise 5.)

SOUNDS

EXERCISE 1

Teacher and children play the sounds game

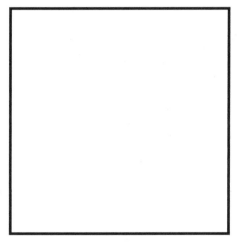

a. (Use transparency and crayon. Write the sounds in the symbol box. Keep score in the score box.)

b. I'm smart. I think I can beat you in a game.

c. Here's the rule. When I touch a sound, you say it.

d. (Play the game. Make one symbol at a time in the symbol box. Use the symbols **r, w, e,** and **b.**) (Make each symbol quickly. Pause. Touch the symbol. Play the game for about two minutes.)
(Then ask:) Who won? (Draw a mouth on the face in the score box.)

EXERCISE 2

Child plays teacher

a. (Use transparency and crayon.)

b. [Child's name] is going to be the teacher.

c. [Child] is going to touch the sounds. When [child] touches a sound, you say it.

d. (The child points to and touches the sounds.) *The children respond.* (You circle any sound that is not firm.)

e. (After the child has completed the page, present all the circled sounds to the children.)

EXERCISE 3

Individual test

(Call on individual children.) If you can say the sound when I call your name, you may cross it out.

EXERCISE 21

Picture comprehension

a. Everybody, look at the picture.

b. (Ask these questions:)

1. Who is that in the picture? *The children respond.* The boy and his mother.

2. What do you think the card says? *The children respond.* Mother, I love you.

3. Did you ever send a pretty card to your mother? *The children respond.*

WORKSHEET 138

SUMMARY OF INDEPENDENT ACTIVITY
EXERCISE 22

Introduction to independent activity

a. (Pass out Worksheet 138 to each child.)

b. Everybody, you're going to do this worksheet on your own. (Tell the children when they will work the items.)

• Let's go over the things you're going to do.

Story items

a. (Hold up side 1 of your worksheet and point to the story-items exercise.)

b. Everybody, read item 1 about the story the fast way. First word. ✔

• Get ready. (Tap for each word as the children read *a boy sent a card to his . . .*)

c. Everybody, what's the answer? (Signal.) *Mother.*

d. Think about what happened in the story and circle the right answer for each item.

Sound writing

a. (Point to the sound-writing exercise.) Here are the sounds you're going to write today. I'll touch the sounds. You say them.

b. (Touch each sound.) *The children respond.*

c. (Repeat the series until firm.)

Reading comprehension

a. (Point to the boxed sentences in the reading-comprehension exercise.)

b. Everybody, get ready to read the sentences the fast way.

c. First word. ✔

• Get ready. (Tap for each word as the children read *a girl met a boy.*)

d. (Have the children reread the sentence until firm.)

e. Get ready to read the next sentence. (Repeat *c* and *d* for **shē said, "let's dig a hōle."**)

f. (Point to items 1 and 2.) These items tell about the story in the box. You're going to read each item and circle the right answer.

Sentence copying

a. (Hold up side 2 of your worksheet and point to the dotted sentence in the sentence-copying exercise.)

b. You're going to trace the words in this sentence. Then you're going to write the sentence on the other lines.

c. Reading the fast way. First word. ✔

• Get ready. (Tap for each word.)

d. After you finish your worksheet, you get to draw a picture about the sentence, **hē gāve mom a card.** You'll draw your picture on a piece of plain paper.

Pair relations

a. (Point to the pair-relations exercise.) You're going to read each sentence. Then draw a line from the sentence to the right picture.

b. (When the children finish their worksheets, give them sheets of plain paper. Remind them to draw a picture that shows **hē gāve mom a card.**)

END OF LESSON 138

134

READING VOCABULARY

EXERCISE 4

Children sound out the word and tell what word

a. (Touch the ball for **tōld.**) Sound it out.

b. Get ready. (Touch **t, ō, l, d** as the children say *tōōōllld.*)

• (If sounding out is not firm, repeat *b.*)

c. What word? (Signal.) *Told.* Yes, **told.**

EXERCISE 5

Children sound out the word and tell what word

(Repeat the procedures in exercise 4 for **hōle.**)

EXERCISE 6

Children sound out the word and tell what word

(Repeat the procedures in exercise 4 for **yes.**)

EXERCISE 7

Children sound out an irregular word (**you**)

a. (Touch the ball for **you.**) Sound it out.

b. Get ready. (Quickly touch each sound as the children say *yyyooouuu.*)

c. Again. (Repeat *b* until firm.)

d. That's how we <u>sound out</u> the word. Here's how we <u>say</u> the word. **You.** How do we <u>say</u> the word? (Signal.) *You.*

e. Now you're going to <u>sound out</u> the word. Get ready. (Touch each sound as the children say *yyyooouuu.*)

f. Now you're going to say the word. Get ready. (Signal.) *You.*

g. (Repeat *e* and *f* until firm.)

h. Yes, this word is **you.** I like **you.**

EXERCISE 8

Individual test

(Call on individual children to do *e* and *f* in exercise 7.)

EXERCISE 9

Children read the words the fast way

(Have the children read the words on this page the fast way.)

EXERCISE 10

Individual test

(Call on individual children to read one word the fast way.)

STORY 138
EXERCISE 18

First reading—children read the story the fast way

(Have the children reread any sentences containing words that give them trouble. Keep a list of these words.)

a. (Pass out Storybook.)

b. Open your book to page 126. ✔

c. Everybody, touch the title of the story and get ready to read the words in the title the fast way.

d. First word. ✔

• (Pause two seconds.) Get ready. (Tap.) *A.*

e. (Tap for each remaining word in the title.)

f. (After the children have read the title, ask:) What's this story about? (Signal.) *A card for mother.* Yes, **a card for mother.**

g. Everybody, get ready to read this story the fast way.

h. First word. ✔

• (Pause two seconds.) Get ready. (Tap.) *A.*

i. (Tap for the remaining words in the first sentence. Pause at least two seconds between taps.)

j. (Repeat *h* and *i* for the next two sentences. Have the children reread the first three sentences until firm.)

k. (The children are to read the remainder of the story the fast way, stopping at the end of each sentence.)

l. (After the first reading of the story, print on the board the words that the children missed more than one time. Have the children sound out each word one time and tell what word.)

m. (After the group's responses are firm, call on individual children to read the words.)

EXERCISE 19

Individual test

a. Turn back to page 126. I'm going to call on individual children to read a whole sentence.

b. (Call on individual children to read a sentence. Do not tap for each word.)

EXERCISE 20

Second reading—children read the story the fast way and answer questions

a. You're going to read the story again the fast way and I'll ask questions.

b. Starting with the first word of the title. ✔

• Get ready. (Tap.) *A.*

c. (Tap for each remaining word. Pause at least two seconds between taps. Pause longer before words that gave the children trouble during the first reading.)

d. (Ask the comprehension questions below as the children read.)

After the children read:	You say:
A card for mother.	What's this story about? (Signal.) *A card for mother.*
But his mother did not get the card.	Who sent the card? (Signal.) *A boy.* Who did he send the card to? (Signal.) *His mother.* What did the card say? (Signal.) *Mother, I love you.* Did his mother get the card? (Signal.) *No.*
A cop got the card.	Who got the card? (Signal.) *A cop.*
They met the boy.	Who did they meet? (Signal.) *The boy.* Who were they looking for? (Signal.) *Mother.*
"Give me that card."	What did the boy say? (Signal.) *Give me that card.* Do you think the cop and her brother will give the boy the card? *The children respond.* Let's read and find out.
So they gave him the card.	Did they give the boy the card? (Signal.) *Yes.*
And he gave the card to his mother.	What did the boy do? (Signal.) *He gave the card to his mother.*

EXERCISE 11

Children sound out an irregular word (**yard**)

a. (Touch the ball for **yard.**) Sound it out.

b. Get ready. (Quickly touch each sound as the children say *yyyaaarrrd.*)

> **To Correct**
> If the children do not say the sounds you touch
> 1. (Say:) You've got to say the sounds I touch.
> 2. (Repeat *a* and *b* until firm.)

c. Again. (Repeat *b* until firm.)

d. That's how we <u>sound out</u> the word. Here's how we <u>say</u> the word. **Yard.** How do we <u>say</u> the word? (Signal.) *Yard.*

e. Now you're going to <u>sound out</u> the word. Get ready. (Touch each sound as the children say *yyyaaarrrd.*)

f. Now you're going to say the word. Get ready. (Signal.) *Yard.*

g. (Repeat *e* and *f* until firm.)

h. Yes, this word is **yard.**

EXERCISE 12

Individual test

(Call on individual children to do *e* and *f* in exercise 11.)

EXERCISE 13

Children read the fast way

a. Get ready to read these words the fast way.

b. (Touch the ball for **dug.** Pause three seconds.) Get ready. (Signal.) *Dug.*

c. (Repeat *b* for the remaining words on the page.)

EXERCISE 14

Children read the fast way again

a. Get ready to do these words again. Watch where I point.

b. (Point to a word. Pause one second. Say:) Get ready. (Signal.) *The children respond.*

• (Point to the words in this order: **lived, dug, līne.**)

c. (Repeat *b* until firm.)

EXERCISE 15

Individual test

(Call on individual children to read one word on the page the fast way.)

EXERCISE 14

Children sound out an irregular word (**mother**)

a. (Touch the ball for **mother.**) Sound it out.

b. Get ready. (Quickly touch each sound as the children say *mmmooothththerrr.*)

c. Again. (Repeat *b* until firm.)

d. That's how we <u>sound out</u> the word. Here's how we <u>say</u> the word. **Mother.** How do we <u>say</u> the word? (Signal.) *Mother.*

e. Now you're going to <u>sound out</u> the word. Get ready. (Touch each sound as the children say *mmmooothththerrr.*)

f. Now you're going to say the word. Get ready. (Signal.) *Mother.*

g. (Repeat *e* and *f* until firm.)

h. Yes, this word is **mother.** His **mother** took him to school.

i. (Call on individual children to do *e* and *f*.)

EXERCISE 15

Children read the word the fast way

a. Get ready to read this word the fast way.

b. (Touch the ball for **bōy.** Pause three seconds.) Get ready. (Signal.) *Boy.* Yes, **boy.**

c. (Repeat *b* until firm.)

EXERCISE 16

Children sound out an irregular word (**other**)

a. (Touch the ball for **other.**) Sound it out.

b. Get ready. (Quickly touch each sound as the children say *ooothththerrr.*)

c. Again. (Repeat *b* until firm.)

d. That's how we <u>sound out</u> the word. Here's how we <u>say</u> the word. **Other.** How do we <u>say</u> the word? (Signal.) *Other.*

e. Now you're going to <u>sound out</u> the word. Get ready. (Touch each sound as the children say *ooothththerrr.*)

f. Now you're going to say the word. Get ready. (Signal.) *Other.*

g. (Repeat *e* and *f* until firm.)

h. Yes, this word is **other.** The **other** day we went to a show.

i. (Call on individual children to do *e* and *f*.)

mother

bōy

other

EXERCISE 17

Children read the words the fast way

(Have the children read the words on this page the fast way.)

EXERCISE 16

Children read **dig** and **digging**

a. (Touch the ball for **dig.**) You're going to read this word the fast way. (Pause three seconds.) Get ready. (Move your finger quickly along the arrow.) *Dig.*

b. (Return to the ball for **dig.**) Yes, this word is **dig.**

c. (Touch the ball for **digging.**) So this must be **dig** . . . (Touch **ing.**) *Ing.*

• What word? (Signal.) *Digging.* Yes, **digging.**

d. Again. (Repeat *b* and *c* until firm.)

e. (Touch the ball for **dig.**) This word is **dig.**

f. (Touch the ball for **digging.**) So this must be . . . (Quickly run your finger under **dig** and tap **ing.**) *Digging.* Yes, **digging.**

g. Again. (Repeat *e* and *f* until firm.)

h. Now you're going to sound out (pause) **digging.** Get ready. (Touch **d, i,** between the **g**'s, **ing** as the children say *diiigiiing.*)

• Yes, what word? (Signal.) *Digging.* Yes, **digging.**

EXERCISE 17

Individual test

(Call on individual children to read one word the fast way.)

EXERCISE 9

Children sound out the word and tell what word

a. (Touch the ball for **her.**) Sound it out.

b. Get ready. (Touch **h, er** as the children say *herrr.*)

• (If sounding out is not firm, repeat *b.*)

c. What word? (Signal.) *Her.* Yes, **her.**

EXERCISE 10

Children sound out an irregular word (**card**)

a. (Touch the ball for **card.**) Sound it out.

b. Get ready. (Quickly touch each sound as the children say *caaarrrd.*)

c. Again. (Repeat *b* until firm.)

d. That's how we <u>sound out</u> the word. Here's how we <u>say</u> the word. **Card.** How do we <u>say</u> the word? (Signal.) *Card.*

e. Now you're going to <u>sound out</u> the word. Get ready. (Touch each sound as the children say *caaarrrd.*)

f. Now you're going to say the word. Get ready. (Signal.) *Card.*

g. (Repeat *e* and *f* until firm.)

h. Yes, this word is **card.** She got a birthday **card.**

i. (Call on individual children to do *e* and *f.*)

EXERCISE 11

Children sound out an irregular word (**love**)

a. (Touch the ball for **love.**) Sound it out.

b. Get ready. (Quickly touch each sound as the children say *lllooovvveee.*)

c. Again. (Repeat *b* until firm.)

d. That's how we <u>sound out</u> the word. Here's how we <u>say</u> the word. **Love.** How do we <u>say</u> the word? (Signal.) *Love.*

e. Now you're going to <u>sound out</u> the word. Get ready. (Touch each sound as the children say *lllooovvveee.*)

f. Now you're going to say the word. Get ready. (Signal.) *Love.*

g. (Repeat *e* and *f* until firm.)

h. Yes, this word is **love.** I **love** to eat cookies.

i. (Call on individual children to do *e* and *f.*)

EXERCISE 12

Children read the words the fast way

(Have the children read the words on this page the fast way.)

EXERCISE 13

Individual test

(Call on individual children to read one word the fast way.)

her

card

love

STORY 134
EXERCISE 18

First reading—children read the story the fast way

(Have the children reread any sentences containing words that give them trouble. Keep a list of these words.)

a. (Pass out Storybook.)

b. Open your book to page 113. ✔

c. Everybody, touch the title of the story and get ready to read the words in the title the fast way.

d. First word. ✔

• (Pause two seconds.) Get ready. (Tap.) *Digging.*

e. (Tap for each remaining word in the title.)

f. (After the children have read the title, ask:) What's this story about? (Signal.) *Digging in the yard.* Yes, **digging in the yard.**

g. Everybody, get ready to read this story the fast way.

h. First word. ✔

• (Pause two seconds.) Get ready. (Tap.) *A.*

i. (Tap for the remaining words in the first sentence. Pause at least two seconds between taps.)

j. (Repeat *h* and *i* for the next two sentences. Have the children reread the first three sentences until firm.)

k. (The children are to read the remainder of the story the fast way, stopping at the end of each sentence.)

l. (After the first reading of the story, print on the board the words that the children missed more than one time. Have the children sound out each word one time and tell what word.)

m. (After the group's responses are firm, call on individual children to read the words.)

EXERCISE 19

Individual test

a. Look at page 113. I'm going to call on individual children to read a whole sentence.

b. (Call on individual children to read a sentence. Do not tap for each word.)

EXERCISE 20

Second reading—children read the story the fast way and answer questions

a. You're going to read the story again the fast way and I'll ask questions.

b. Starting with the first word of the title. ✔

• Get ready. (Tap.) *Digging.*

c. (Tap for each remaining word. Pause at least two seconds between taps. Pause longer before words that gave the children trouble during the first reading.)

d. (Ask the comprehension questions below as the children read.)

After the children read:	You say:
Digging in the yard.	What's this story about? (Signal.) *Digging in the yard.*
The dog dug a hole in the yard.	Where did the dog live? (Signal.) *In the yard.* What did the dog do? (Signal.) *Dug a hole.* Do you think the man will like that? *The children respond.* Let's read and find out.
The little man got mad.	Did the man like the dog to dig? (Signal.) *No.*
The man got a cop.	Who did the man get? (Signal.) *A cop.*
The cop said, "Dogs can not dig in this yard."	What did the cop say? (Signal.) *Dogs can not dig in this yard.*
"Can I be a cop dog?"	What did the dog ask? (Signal.) *Can I be a cop dog?*
"I need a cop dog."	What did the cop say? (Signal.) *Yes. I need a cop dog.*

READING VOCABULARY
EXERCISE 4

Children sound out an irregular word (**brother**)

a. (Touch the ball for **brother.**) Sound it out.

b. Get ready. (Quickly touch each sound as the children say *brrrooothththerrr.*)

c. Again. (Repeat **b** until firm.)

d. That's how we <u>sound out</u> the word. Here's how we <u>say</u> the word. **Brother.** How do we <u>say</u> the word? (Signal.) *Brother.*

e. Now you're going to <u>sound out</u> the word. Get ready. (Touch each sound as the children say *brrrooothththerrr.*)

f. Now you're going to say the word. Get ready. (Signal.) *Brother.*

g. (Repeat *e* and *f* until firm.)

h. Yes, this word is **brother.** Do you have a **brother?**

EXERCISE 5

Individual test

(Call on individual children to do *e* and *f* in exercise 4.)

EXERCISE 6

Children read the fast way

a. Get ready to read these words the fast way.

b. (Touch the ball for **give.** Pause three seconds.) Get ready. (Signal.) *Give.*

c. (Repeat *b* for the remaining words on the page.)

EXERCISE 7

Children read the fast way again

a. Get ready to do these words again. Watch where I point.

b. (Point to a word. Pause one second. Say:) Get ready. (Signal.) *The children respond.*

• (Point to the words in this order: **gāve, sent, give.**)

c. (Repeat *b* until firm.)

EXERCISE 8

Individual test

(Call on individual children to read one word on the page the fast way.)

brother

gīve

gāve

sent

EXERCISE 21

Picture comprehension

a. Everybody, look at the picture.

b. (Ask these questions:)

1. What is the dog doing? *The children respond.* Digging a hole.
2. What is he using to dig? *A shovel.*
3. Do dogs really use shovels? *The children respond.*
4. Did you ever dig a hole with a shovel? *The children respond.*

WORKSHEET 134

SUMMARY OF INDEPENDENT ACTIVITY

EXERCISE 22

Introduction to independent activity

a. (Pass out Worksheet 134 to each child.)

b. Everybody, you're going to do this worksheet on your own. (Tell the children when they will work the items.)

• Let's go over the things you're going to do.

Story items

a. (Hold up side 1 of your worksheet and point to the story-items exercise.)

b. Everybody, read item 1 about the story the fast way. First word. ✔

• Get ready. (Tap for each word as the children read *the dog dug a hole in the . . .*)

c. Everybody, what's the answer? (Signal.) *Yard.*

d. Think about what happened in the story and circle the right answer for each item.

Sound writing

a. (Point to the sound-writing exercise.) Here are the sounds you're going to write today. I'll touch the sounds. You say them.

b. (Touch each sound.) *The children respond.*

c. (Repeat the series until firm.)

Reading comprehension

a. (Point to the boxed sentences in the reading-comprehension exercise.)

b. Everybody, get ready to read the sentences the fast way.

c. First word. ✔

• Get ready. (Tap for each word as the children read *a rat likes to eat.*)

d. (Have the children reread the sentence until firm.)

e. Get ready to read the next sentence. (Repeat *c* and *d* for **hē ēats a red lēaf.**)

f. (Point to items 1 and 2.) These items tell about the story in the box. You're going to read each item and circle the right answer.

Sentence-copying

a. (Hold up side 2 of your worksheet and point to the dotted sentence in the sentence-copying exercise.)

b. You're going to trace the words in this sentence. Then you're going to write the sentence on the other lines.

c. Reading the fast way. First word. ✔

• Get ready. (Tap for each word.)

d. After you finish your worksheet, you get to draw a picture about the sentence, **the dog dug a hōle.** You'll draw your picture on a piece of plain paper.

Pair relations

a. (Point to the pair-relations exercise.) You're going to read each sentence. Then draw a line from the sentence to the right picture.

b. (When the children finish their worksheets, give them sheets of plain paper. Remind them to draw a picture that shows **the dog dug a hōle.**)

END OF LESSON 134

Groups that are firm on Mastery Tests 25 and 26 should skip this lesson and do lesson 139 today.

SOUNDS

EXERCISE 1

Teacher and children play the sounds game

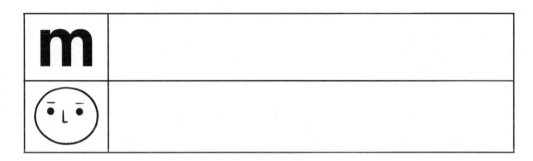

a. (Use transparency and crayon. Write the sounds in the symbol box. Keep score in the score box.)

b. I'm smart. I think I can beat you in a game.

c. Here's the rule. When I touch a sound, you say it.

d. (Play the game. Make one symbol at a time in the symbol box. Use the symbols **y, i, b,** and **t.**)
(Make each symbol quickly. Pause. Touch the symbol. Play the game for about two minutes.)
(Then ask:) Who won? (Draw a mouth on the face in the score box.)

er   k

e

ing   th

v

h   l

EXERCISE 2

Child plays teacher

a. (Use transparency and crayon.)

b. [Child's name] is going to be the teacher.

c. [Child] is going to touch the sounds. When [child] touches a sound, you say it.

d. (The child points to and touches the sounds.) *The children respond.* (You circle any sound that is not firm.)

e. (After the child has completed the page, present all the circled sounds to the children.)

EXERCISE 3

Individual test

(Call on individual children.) If you can say the sound when I call your name, you may cross it out.

SOUNDS

EXERCISE 1

Teaching **er** as in **brother**

a. (Point to **er.**) Here's a new sound.

b. My turn. (Pause. Touch **er** and say:) **errr (urrr).**

c. Again. (Touch **er** for a longer time.) **errrrrr.**

- (Lift your finger.)

d. (Point to **er.**) Your turn. When I touch it, you say it. (Pause.) Get ready. (Touch **er.**) *errr.*

- (Lift your finger.)

e. Again. (Touch **er.**) *errrrrr.*

- (Lift your finger.)

f. (Repeat *e* until firm.)

EXERCISE 2

Individual test

(Call on individual children to identify **er.**)

EXERCISE 3

Sounds firm-up

a. Get ready to say the sounds when I touch them.

b. (Alternate touching **er** and **r.** Point to the sound. Pause one second. Say:) Get ready. (Touch the sound.) *The children respond.*

c. (When **er** and **r** are firm, alternate touching **er, r, y,** and **e** until all four sounds are firm.)

EXERCISE 4

Individual test

(Call on individual children to identify **er, r, y,** or **e.**)

EXERCISE 5

Sounds firm-up

a. (Point to **er.**) When I touch the sound, you say it.

b. (Pause.) Get ready. (Touch **er.**) *errr.*

c. Again. (Repeat *b* until firm.)

d. Get ready to say all the sounds when I touch them.

e. (Alternate touching **ing, ī, er, i, v, p, b,** and **w** three or four times. Point to the sound.) Pause one second. Say: Get ready. (Touch the sound.) *The children respond.*

EXERCISE 6

Individual test

(Call on individual children to identify one or more sounds in exercise 5.)

EXERCISE 23

Picture comprehension

a. Everybody, look at the picture.

b. (Ask these questions:)

1. What is Ann doing? *The children respond.* Petting a deer.
2. Where do you think they are? *The children respond.*
3. Have you ever seen a deer? *The children respond.*

WORKSHEET 137

SUMMARY OF INDEPENDENT ACTIVITY

EXERCISE 24

Introduction to independent activity

a. (Pass out Worksheet 137 to each child.)

b. Everybody, you're going to do this worksheet on your own. (Tell the children when they will work the items.)

• Let's go over the things you're going to do.

Story items

a. (Hold up side 1 of your worksheet and point to the story-items exercise.)

b. Everybody, read item 1 about the story the fast way. First word. ✔

• Get ready. (Tap for each word as the children read *ann and her dad went hunting for . . .*)

c. Everybody, what's the answer? (Signal.) *Deer.*

d. Think about what happened in the story and circle the right answer for each item.

Sound writing

a. (Point to the sound-writing exercise.) Here are the sounds you're going to write today. I'll touch the sounds. You say them.

b. (Touch each sound.) *The children respond.*

c. (Repeat the series until firm.)

Reading comprehension

a. (Point to the boxed sentences in the reading-comprehension exercise.)

b. Everybody, get ready to read the sentences the fast way.

c. First word. ✔

• Get ready. (Tap for each word as the children read *a boy had red paint.*)

d. (Have the children reread the sentence until firm.)

e. Get ready to read the next sentence. (Repeat *c* and *d* for **sō hē māde a car red.**)

f. (Point to items 1 and 2.) These items tell about the story in the box. You're going to read each item and circle the right answer.

Sentence copying

a. (Hold up side 2 of your worksheet and point to the dotted sentence in the sentence-copying exercise.)

b. You're going to trace the words in this sentence. Then you're going to write the sentence on the other lines.

c. Reading the fast way. First word. ✔

• Get ready. (Tap for each word.)

d. After you finish your worksheet, you get to draw a picture about the sentence, **the girl has pets.** You'll draw your picture on a piece of plain paper.

Pair relations

a. (Point to the pair-relations exercise.) You're going to read each sentence. Then draw a line from the sentence to the right picture.

b. (When the children finish their worksheets, give them sheets of plain paper. Remind them to draw a picture that shows **the girl has pets.**)

END OF LESSON 137

READING VOCABULARY

EXERCISE 7

Children sound out the word and tell what word

a. (Touch the ball for **dad.**) Sound it out.

b. Get ready. (Touch **d, a, d** as the children say *daaad.*)

• (If sounding out is not firm, repeat *b.*)

c. What word? (Signal.) *Dad.* Yes, **dad.**

EXERCISE 8

Children sound out the word and tell what word

a. (Touch the ball for **they.**) Sound it out.

b. Get ready. (Touch **th, e, y** as the children say *thththeeeyyy.*)

• (If sounding out is not firm, repeat *b.*)

c. What word? (Signal.) *They.* Yes, **they.**

EXERCISE 9

Children read the fast way

a. Get ready to read these words the fast way.

b. (Touch the ball for **mom.** Pause three seconds.) Get ready. (Signal.) *Mom.*

c. (Repeat *b* for the remaining words on the page.)

EXERCISE 10

Children read the fast way again

a. Get ready to do these words again. Watch where I point.

b. (Point to a word. Pause one second. Say:) Get ready. (Signal.) *The children respond.*

• (Point to the words in this order: **then, bed, mom.**)

c. (Repeat *b* until firm.)

Individual test

(Call on individual children to read one word on the page the fast way.)

dad

they

mom

then

bed

STORY 137
EXERCISE 20

First reading—children read the story the fast way

(Have the children reread any sentences containing words that give them trouble. Keep a list of these words.)

a. (Pass out Storybook.)

b. Open your book to page 123. ✔

c. Everybody, touch the title of the story and get ready to read the words in the title the fast way.

d. First word. ✔

• (Pause two seconds.) Get ready. (Tap.) *Hunting.*

e. (Tap for each remaining word in the title.)

f. (After the children have read the title, ask:) What's this story about? (Signal.) *Hunting for a deer.* Yes, **hunting for a deer.**

g. Everybody, get ready to read this story the fast way.

h. First word. ✔

• (Pause two seconds.) Get ready. (Tap.) *Ann.*

i. (Tap for the remaining words in the first sentence. Pause at least two seconds between taps.)

j. (Repeat *h* and *i* for the next two sentences. Have the children reread the first three sentences until firm.)

k. (The children are to read the remainder of the story the fast way, stopping at the end of each sentence.)

l. (After the first reading of the story, print on the board the words that the children missed more than one time. Have the children sound out each word one time and tell what word.)

m. (After the group's responses are firm, call on individual children to read the words.)

EXERCISE 21

Individual test

a. Turn back to page 123. I'm going to call on individual children to read a whole sentence.

b. (Call on individual children to read a sentence. Do not tap for each word.)

EXERCISE 22

Second reading—children read the story the fast way and answer questions

a. You're going to read the story again the fast way and I'll ask questions.

b. Starting with the first word of the title. ✔

• Get ready. (Tap.) *Hunting.*

c. (Tap for each remaining word. Pause at least two seconds between taps. Pause longer before words that gave the children trouble during the first reading.)

d. (Ask the comprehension questions below as the children read.)

After the children read:	You say:
Hunting for a deer.	What's this story about? (Signal.) *Hunting for a deer.*
Ann said, "Let's go find a deer for a pet."	Why does Ann want a deer? (Signal.) *For a pet.* Who is Ann talking to? (Signal.) *Her dad.*
"And cats are pets."	Are dogs pets? (Signal.) *Yes.* And are cats pets? (Signal.) *Yes.* Are deer pets? (Signal.) *No.*
"But I will let a girl and her dad pet me."	Who is talking? (Signal.) *The deer.* I think it might be fun to pet a deer.
It was.	A deer is big. Show me how you would pet a deer. *The children respond.*
They go with her to hunt for the deer that she can pet.	Does she have pets now? (Signal.) *Yes.* What are they? *The children respond.* Yes, a pet dog and a pet cat.

EXERCISE 11

Children sound out the word and tell what word

a. (Touch the ball for **bōy.**) Sound it out.
b. Get ready. (Touch **b, ō, y** as the children say *bōōōyyy.*)
• (If sounding out is not firm, repeat *b.*)
c. What word? (Signal.) *Boy.* Yes, **boy.**

EXERCISE 12

Individual test

(Call on individual children to do *b* and *c* in exercise 11.)

EXERCISE 13

Children read the fast way

a. Get ready to read these words the fast way.
b. (Touch the ball for **yes.** Pause three seconds.) Get ready. (Signal.) *Yes.*
c. (Repeat *b* for the remaining words on the page.)

EXERCISE 14

Children read the fast way again

a. Get ready to do these words again. Watch where I point.
b. (Point to a word. Pause one second. Say:) Get ready. (Signal.)
The children respond.
• (Point to the words in this order: **yes, fīnd, red.**)
c. (Repeat *b* until firm.)

EXERCISE 15

Individual test

(Call on individual children to read one word on the page the fast way.)

bōy

yes

red

fīnd

EXERCISE 15

Children sound out an irregular word (**love**)

a. (Touch the ball for **love.**) Sound it out.

b. Get ready. (Quickly touch each sound as the children say *Illlooovvveee.*)

> **To Correct**
> If the children do not say the sounds you touch
> 1. (Say:) You've got to say the sounds I touch.
> 2. (Repeat *a* and *b* until firm.)

c. Again. (Repeat *b* until firm.)

d. That's how we <u>sound out</u> the word. Here's how we <u>say</u> the word. **Love.** How do we <u>say</u> the word? (Signal.) *Love.*

e. Now you're going to <u>sound out</u> the word. Get ready. (Touch each sound as the children say *Illlooovvveee.*)

f. Now you're going to say the word. Get ready. (Signal.) *Love.*

g. (Repeat *e* and *f* until firm.)

h. Yes, this word is **love.** I **love** you.

EXERCISE 16

Individual test

(Call on individual children to do *e* and *f* in exercise 15.)

EXERCISE 17

Children sound out the word and tell what word

a. (Touch the ball for **dēēr.**) Sound it out.

b. Get ready. (Touch **d,** between the **e**'s, **r** as the children say *dēēērrr.*)

• (If sounding out is not firm, repeat *b.*)

c. What word? (Signal.) *Deer.* Yes, **deer.**

EXERCISE 18

Children read the words the fast way

a. Now you get to read the words on this page the fast way.

b. (Touch the ball for **love.** Pause three seconds.) Get ready. (Move your finger quickly along the arrow.) *Love.*

c. (Repeat *b* for **deer.**)

EXERCISE 19

Individual test

(Call on individual children to read one word the fast way.)

STORYBOOK

STORY 135
EXERCISE 16

First reading—children read the story the fast way

(Have the children reread any sentences containing words that give them trouble. Keep a list of these words.)

a. (Pass out Storybook.)

b. Open your book to page 116. ✔

c. Everybody, touch the title of the story and get ready to read the words in the title the fast way.

d. First word. ✔

• (Pause two seconds.) Get ready. (Tap.) *Ron.*

e. (Tap for each remaining word in the title.)

f. (After the children have read the title, ask:) What's this story about? (Signal.) *Ron said, "Yes."* Yes, **Ron said, "Yes."**

g. Everybody, get ready to read this story the fast way.

h. First word. ✔

• (Pause two seconds.) Get ready. (Tap.) *Ron's.*

i. (Tap for the remaining words in the first sentence. Pause at least two seconds between taps.)

j. (Repeat *h* and *i* for the next two sentences. Have the children reread the first three sentences until firm.)

k. (The children are to read the remainder of the story the fast way, stopping at the end of each sentence.)

l. (After the first reading of the story, print on the board the words that the children missed more than one time. Have the children sound out each word one time and tell what word.)

m. (After the group's responses are firm, call on individual children to read the words.)

EXERCISE 17

Individual test

a. Turn back to page 116. I'm going to call on individual children to read a whole sentence.

b. (Call on individual children to read a sentence. Do not tap for each word.)

EXERCISE 18

Second reading—children read the story the fast way and answer questions

a. You're going to read the story again the fast way and I'll ask questions.

b. Starting with the first word of the title. ✔

• Get ready. (Tap.) *Ron.*

c. (Tap for each remaining word. Pause at least two seconds between taps. Pause longer before words that gave the children trouble during the first reading.)

d. (Ask the comprehension questions below as the children read.)

After the children read:	You say:
Ron said, "Yes."	What did Ron say? (Signal.) *Yes.*
"Yes," Ron said.	What did Ron's dad tell him to do? (Signal.) *Sleep in bed.* What did Ron say? (Signal.) *Yes.*
He got the paint and made the bed red.	What did his mom tell him to do? (Signal.) *Paint the bed red.* What did Ron say? (Signal.) *Yes.* Did he paint the bed? (Signal.) *Yes.*
And he made the car red.	What did the big boy ask? (Signal.) *Can Ron paint a car red?* What did Ron say? (Signal.) *Yes.* Did he make the car red? (Signal.) *Yes.*
Now Ron is not red.	Is Ron red now? (Signal.) *No.* Why not? *The children respond.* He went to the tub and went rub, rub, rub.

EXERCISE 9

Children identify, then sound out an irregular word (**you**)

a. (Touch the ball for **you.**) Everybody, you're going to read this word the fast way. (Pause three seconds.) Get ready. (Move your finger quickly along the arrow.) *You.* Yes, **you.**

b. Now you're going to sound out the word. Get ready. (Quickly touch **y, o, u** as the children say *yyyooouuu.*)

c. Again. (Repeat *b.*)

d. How do we say the word? (Signal.) *You.* Yes, **you.**

e. (Repeat *b* and *d* until firm.)

EXERCISE 10

Individual test

(Have children do *b* and *d* in exercise 9.)

EXERCISE 11

Children sound out an irregular word (**other**)

a. (Touch the ball for **other.**) Sound it out.

b. Get ready. (Quickly touch each sound as the children say *ooothththerrr.*)

c. Again. (Repeat *b* until firm.)

d. That's how we <u>sound out</u> the word. Here's how we <u>say</u> the word. **Other.** How do we <u>say</u> the word? (Signal.) *Other.*

e. Now you're going to <u>sound out</u> the word. Get ready. (Touch each sound as the children say *ooothththerrr.*)

f. Now you're going to <u>say</u> the word. Get ready. (Signal.) *Other.*

g. (Repeat *e* and *f* until firm.)

EXERCISE 12

Children rhyme with an irregular word (**other**)

a. (Touch the ball for **other.**) Everybody, you're going to read this word the fast way. Get ready. (Signal.) *Other.*

b. (Touch the ball for **mother.**) This word rhymes with (pause) **other.** Get ready. (Move to **m,** then quickly along the arrow.) *Mother.*

c. (Repeat *a* and *b* until firm.)

EXERCISE 13

Children sound out **mother**

(Have the children sound out **mother.**) *Mmmooothththerrr.*
- How do we say the word? (Signal.) *Mother.* Yes, **mother.**
- **Mother** is feeding the baby.

EXERCISE 14

Individual test

(Have children read one word the fast way.)

EXERCISE 19

Picture comprehension

a. Everybody, look at the picture.

b. (Ask these questions:)
   1. What's that stuff all over Ron? *The children respond.* Red paint.
   2. What's Ron doing? *The children respond.* Painting a car.
   3. Ron sure is silly. How's he going to get that red paint off himself? *The children respond.* By taking a bath.

WORKSHEET 135

SUMMARY OF INDEPENDENT ACTIVITY

EXERCISE 20

Introduction to independent activity

a. (Pass out sides 1 and 2 of Worksheet 135 to each child.)

b. Everybody, do a good job on your worksheet today and I'll give you a bonus worksheet.

c. (Hold up side 1 of your worksheet.) You're going to do this worksheet on your own. **(Tell the children when they will work the items.)**

• Let's go over some of the things you're going to do.

Story items

a. (Point to the story-items exercise.)

b. Everybody, read item 1 about the story the fast way. First word. ✔

• Get ready. (Tap for each word as the children read, *Ron said, . . .*)

c. Everybody, what's the answer? (Signal.) *Yes.*

d. Think about what happened in the story and circle the right answer for each item.

Reading comprehension

a. (Point to the boxed sentences in the reading-comprehension exercise.)

b. Everybody, get ready to read the sentences the fast way.

c. First word. ✔

• Get ready. (Tap for each word as the children read *a man went on a ship.*)

d. (Have the children reread the sentence until firm.)

e. Get ready to read the next sentence. (Repeat *c* and *d* for **the ship was big.**)

f. (Point to items 1 and 2.) These items tell about the story in the box. You're going to read each item and circle the right answer.

Sentence copying

a. (Hold up side 2 of your worksheet and point to the dotted sentence in the sentence-copying exercise.)

b. You're going to trace the words in this sentence. Then you're going to write the sentence on the other lines.

c. Reading the fast way. First word. ✔

• Get ready. (Tap for each word.)

d. After you finish your worksheet, you get to draw a picture about the sentence, **ron got the pāint.** You'll draw your picture on a piece of plain paper.

Other independent activity: sides 1, 2, 3, 4

Remember to do all the parts of the worksheet and to read all the parts carefully. After you draw your picture, I'll give you a bonus worksheet.

INDIVIDUAL CHECKOUT: STORYBOOK

EXERCISE 25

3-minute individual fluency checkout: rate skill/accuracy

a. As you are doing your worksheet, I'll call on children one at a time to read the **whole story.** Remember, you get two stars if you read the story in less than three minutes and make no more than three errors.

b. (Call on a child. Tell the child:) Start with the title and read the story carefully the fast way. Go. (Time the child. Tell the child any words the child misses. Stop the child as soon as the child makes the fourth error or exceeds the time limit.)

c. (If the child meets the rate-accuracy criterion, record two stars on your chart for lesson 135. Congratulate the child. Give children who do not earn two stars a chance to read the story again before the next lesson is presented.)
112 words/**3 min** = 37 wpm [**3 errors**]

END OF LESSON 135

Before presenting lesson 136, give Mastery Test 26 to each child. Do not present lesson 136 to any groups that are not firm on this test.

READING VOCABULARY

EXERCISE 4

Children sound out an irregular word (**brother**)

a. (Touch the ball for **brother.**) Sound it out.

b. Get ready. (Quickly touch each sound as the children say *brrrooothththerrr.*)

To Correct

If the children do not say the sounds you touch
1. (Say:) You've got to say the sounds I touch.
2. (Repeat *a* and *b* until firm.)

---

c. Again. (Repeat *b* until firm.)

d. That's how we <u>sound out</u> the word. Here's how we <u>say</u> the word. **Brother.** How do we <u>say</u> the word? (Signal.) *Brother.*

e. Now you're going to <u>sound out</u> the word. Get ready. (Touch each sound as the children say *brrrooothththerrr.*)

f. Now you're going to say the word. Get ready. (Signal.) *Brother.*

g. (Repeat *e* and *f* until firm.)

h. Yes, this word is **brother.** I have a big **brother.**

EXERCISE 5

Individual test

(Call on individual children to do *e* and *f* in exercise 4.)

EXERCISE 6

Children read the fast way

a. Get ready to read these words the fast way.

b. (Touch the ball for **hunting.** Pause three seconds.) Get ready. (Signal.) *Hunting.*

c. (Repeat *b* for the remaining words on the page.)

EXERCISE 7

Children read the fast way again

a. Get ready to do these words again. Watch where I point.

b. (Point to a word. Pause one second. Say:) Get ready. (Signal.) *The children respond.*

• (Point to the words in this order: **hunt, hunting, but, sēēn.**)

c. (Repeat *b* until firm.)

brother

hunting

sēēn

but

hunt

EXERCISE 8

Individual test

(Call on individual children to read one word on the page the fast way.)

Mastery Tests—General Instructions

All children are to be given each test individually.

The test is NOT to be administered during the period allotted for reading.

A child should neither see nor hear another child working on the test.

MASTERY TEST 26—after lesson 135, before lesson 136

a. (Tell child:) Get ready to read this story the fast way.
b. (test item) First word. (Pause two seconds.) Get ready. (Tap.) *A.*
c. (15 test items) (Tap one time for each remaining word in the story. Pause two seconds between taps.)

Total number of test items: **16**
A group is weak if more than one-third of the children missed two or more words on the test.

a rat and a rabbit

went down a slīde.

the rabbit went down

on his tāil.

If the group is firm on Mastery Test 26 and was firm on Mastery Test 25:

Skip lesson 136, and present lesson 137, and skip lesson 138. If more than one child missed two or more words on the test, present the firming procedures specified in the next column to those children.

If the group is firm on Mastery Test 26 but was weak on Mastery Test 25:

Present lesson 136 to the group during the next reading period. If more than one child missed two or more words on the test, present the firming procedures specified below to those children.

If the group is weak on Mastery Test 26:

A. Present these firming procedures to the group during the next reading period. Present each story until the children make no more than three mistakes. Then proceed to the next story.
  1. Lesson 133, Story, page 159, exercises 25, 26.
  2. Lesson 134, Story, page 165, exercises 18, 19.
  3. Lesson 135, Story, page 170, exercises 16, 17.
B. After presenting the above exercises, again give Mastery Test 26 individually to members of the group who failed the test.
C. If the group is firm (less than one-third of the total group missed two or more words in the story on the retest), present lesson 136 to the group during the next reading period.
D. If the group is still weak (more than one-third of the total group missed two or more words in the story on the retest), repeat *A* and *B* during the next reading period.

SOUNDS

EXERCISE 1

Teacher and children play the sounds game

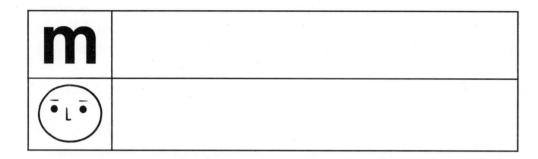

a. (Use transparency and crayon. Write the sounds in the symbol box. Keep score in the score box.)

b. I'm smart. I think I can beat you in a game.

c. Here's the rule. When I touch a sound, you say it.

d. (Play the game. Make one symbol at a time in the symbol box. Use the symbols **y, b, er,** and **c.**) (Make each symbol quickly. Pause. Touch the symbol. Play the game for about two minutes.) (Then ask:) Who won? (Draw a mouth on the face in the score box.)

EXERCISE 2

Child plays teacher

a. (Use transparency and crayon.)

b. [Child's name] is going to be the teacher.

c. [Child] is going to touch the sounds. When [child] touches a sound, you say it.

d. (The child points to and touches the sounds.) *The children respond.* (You circle any sound that is not firm.)

e. (After the child has completed the page, present all the circled sounds to the children.)

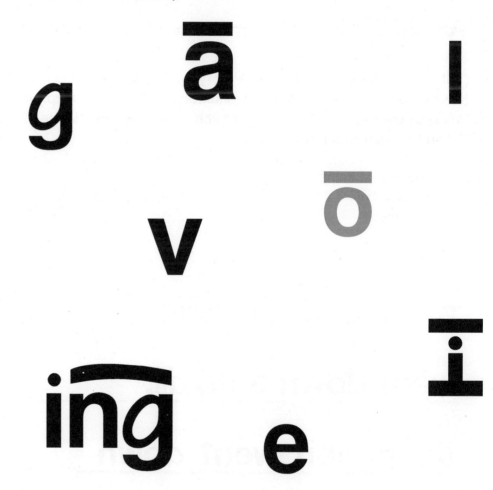

EXERCISE 3

Individual test

(Call on individual children.) If you can say the sound when I call your name, you may cross it out.

Groups that are firm on Mastery Tests 25 and 26 should skip this lesson and do lesson 137 today.

SOUNDS

EXERCISE 1

Teaching **er** as in **brother**

a. (Point to **er**.) My turn. (Pause. Touch **er** and say:) errr **(urrr).**

b. (Point to **er**.) Your turn. When I touch it, you say it. (Pause.) Get ready. (Touch **er**.) *errr.*

• (Lift your finger.)

c. Again. (Touch **er**.) *errrr.*

• (Lift your finger.)

d. (Repeat *c* until firm.)

EXERCISE 2

Sounds firm-up

a. Get ready to say the sounds when I touch them.

b. (Alternate touching **er** and **ē**. Point to the sound. Pause one second. Say:) Get ready. (Touch the sound.) *The children respond.*

c. (When **er** and **ē** are firm, alternate touching **er, ē, r,** and **e** until all four sounds are firm.)

EXERCISE 3

Individual test

(Call on individual children to identify **er, e, r,** or **ē**.)

EXERCISE 4

Teacher introduces cross-out game

a. (Use transparency and crayon.)

b. I'll cross out the sounds on this part of the page when you can tell me every sound.

c. Remember—when I touch it, you say it.

d. (Go over the sounds until the children can identify all the sounds in order.)

EXERCISE 5

Individual test

(Call on individual children to identify two or more sounds in exercise 4.)

EXERCISE 6

Teacher crosses out sounds

a. You told me every sound. Get ready to do it again. This time I'll cross out each sound when you tell me what it is.

b. (Point to each sound. Pause. Say:) Get ready. (Touch the sound.) *The children respond.*

• (As you cross out the sound, say:) Goodbye, _____.

EXERCISE 25

Picture comprehension

a. What do you think you'll see in the picture?

b. Turn the page and look at the picture.

c. (Ask these questions:)

1. What are the boy and the girls doing? *The children respond.* Running to the park.

2. Do you think they're near the park in the picture? (Signal.) *Yes.* How do you know? *The children respond.*

3. I'll bet they're tired. Did you ever run a long, long way? *The children respond.*

WORKSHEET 136

SUMMARY OF INDEPENDENT ACTIVITY

EXERCISE 26

Introduction to independent activity

a. (Pass out Worksheet 136 to each child.)

b. Everybody, you're going to do this worksheet on your own. (Tell the children when they will work the items.)

• Let's go over the things you're going to do.

Story items

a. (Hold up side 1 of your worksheet and point to the story-items exercise.)

b. Everybody, read item 1 about the story the fast way. First word. ✔

• Get ready. (Tap for each word as the children read *the boy said, "let's go to . . ."*)

c. Everybody, what's the answer? (Signal.) *The park.*

d. Think about what happened in the story and circle the right answer for each item.

Sound writing

a. (Point to the sound-writing exercise.) Here are the sounds you're going to write today. I'll touch the sounds. You say them.

b. (Touch each sound.) *The children respond.*

c. (Repeat the series until firm.)

Reading comprehension

a. (Point to the boxed sentences in the reading-comprehension exercise.)

b. Everybody, get ready to read the sentences the fast way.

c. First word. ✔

• Get ready. (Tap for each word as the children read *a dog dug a hole.*)

d. (Have the children reread the sentence until firm.)

e. Get ready to read the next sentence. (Repeat *c* and *d* for **a man fell in the hōle.**)

f. (Point to items 1 and 2.) These items tell about the story in the box. You're going to read each item and circle the right answer.

Sentence copying

a. (Hold up side 2 of your worksheet and point to the dotted sentence in the sentence-copying exercise.)

b. You're going to trace the words in this sentence. Then you're going to write the sentence on the other lines.

c. Reading the fast way. First word. ✔

• Get ready. (Tap for each word.)

d. After you finish your worksheet, you get to draw a picture about the sentence, **they ran to the park.** You'll draw your picture on a piece of plain paper.

Pair relations

a. (Point to the pair-relations exercise.) You're going to read each sentence. Then draw a line from the sentence to the right picture.

b. (When the children finish their worksheets, give them sheets of plain paper. Remind them to draw a picture that shows **they ran to the park.**)

END OF LESSON 136

READING VOCABULARY

EXERCISE 7

Children read hunt and hunting

a. (Touch the ball for **hunt.**) Sound it out.

b. Get ready. (Touch **h, u, n, t,** as the children say *huuunnnt.*)

• (If sounding out is not firm, repeat *b.*)

c. What word? (Signal.) *Hunt.* Yes, **hunt.**

d. (Return to the ball for **hunt.**) This word is **hunt.**

e. (Touch the ball for **hunting.**) So this must be **hunt . . .** (Touch **ing.**) *Ing.*

• What word? (Signal.) *Hunting.* Yes, **hunting.**

f. Again. (Repeat *d* and *e* until firm.)

g. (Touch the ball for **hunt.**) This word is **hunt.**

h. (Touch the ball for **hunting.**) So this must be . . . (Run your finger under **hunt** and tap **ing.**) *Hunting.* Yes, **hunting.**

i. Again. (Repeat *g* and *h* until firm.)

j. Now you're going to sound out (pause) **hunting.** Get ready. (Touch **h, u, n, t, ing** as the children say *huuunnntiiing.*)

• Yes, what word? (Signal.) *Hunting.* Yes, **hunting.**

EXERCISE 8

Children read the fast way

a. Get ready to read these words the fast way.

b. (Touch the ball for **nēar.** Pause three seconds.) Get ready. (Signal.) *Near.*

c. (Repeat *b* for the remaining words on the page.)

EXERCISE 9

Children read the fast way again

a. Get ready to do these words again. Watch where I point.

b. (Point to a word. Pause one second. Say:) Get ready. (Signal.) *The children respond.*

• (Point to the words in this order: **gun, nēar, rīde.**)

c. (Repeat *b* until firm.)

EXERCISE 10

Individual test

(Call on individual children to read one word on the page the fast way.)

hunt

hunting

nēar

rīde

gun

STORY 136
EXERCISE 22

First reading—children read the story the fast way

(Have the children reread any sentences containing words that give them trouble. Keep a list of these words.)

a. (Pass out Storybook.)

b. (Open your book to page 120.) ✔

c. Everybody, touch the title of the story and get ready to read the words in the title the fast way.

d. First word. ✔

• (Pause two seconds.) Get ready. (Tap.) *Going.*

e. (Tap for each remaining word in the title.)

f. (After the children have read the title, ask:) What's this story about? (Signal.) *Going to the park.* Yes, **going to the park.**

g. Everybody, get ready to read this story the fast way.

h. First word. ✔

• (Pause two seconds.) Get ready. (Tap.) *A.*

i. (Tap for the remaining words in the first sentence. Pause at least two seconds between taps.)

j. (Repeat *h* and *i* for the next two sentences. Have the children reread the first three sentences until firm.)

k. (The children are to read the remainder of the story the fast way, stopping at the end of each sentence.)

l. (After the first reading of the story, print on the board the words that the children missed more than one time. Have the children sound out each word one time and tell what word.)

m. (After the group's responses are firm, call on individual children to read the words.)

EXERCISE 23

Individual test

a. Look at page 120. I'm going to call on individual children to read a whole sentence.

b. (Call on individual children to read a sentence. Do not tap for each word.)

EXERCISE 24

Second reading—children read the story the fast way and answer questions

a. You're going to read the story again the fast way and I'll ask questions.

b. Starting with the first word of the title. ✔

• Get ready. (Tap.) *Going.*

c. (Tap for each remaining word. Pause at least two seconds between taps. Pause longer before words that gave the children trouble during the first reading.)

d. (Ask the comprehension questions below as the children read.)

After the children read:	You say:
Going to the park.	What's this story about? (Signal.) *Going to the park.*
He said, "Let's go to the park."	What did the boy say? (Signal.) *Let's go to the park.* Who is he talking to? (Signal.) *Five girls.*
"Is the park near here?"	What did a girl say to the boy? *The children respond.* She said, "We can not see the park. Is the park near here?"
"We need a car to get to the park."	What did the boy say? (Signal.) *We need a car to get to the park.*
"How will we get to the park?"	Can they ride to the park? (Signal.) *No.* Can they walk to the park? (Signal.) *No.* How do you think they'll get to the park? *The children respond.* Let's read and find out.
So the boy and the girls ran to the park.	What happened? (Signal.) *The boy and the girls ran to the park.*

EXERCISE 11

Children sound out the word and tell what word

a. (Touch the ball for **hēre.**) Sound it out.

b. Get ready. (Touch **h, ē, r** as the children say *hēēērrr.*)

• (If sounding out is not firm, repeat *b.*)

c. What word? (Signal.) *Here.* Yes, **here.**

EXERCISE 12

Children identify, then sound out an irregular word (**walk**)

a. (Touch the ball for **walk.**) Everybody, you're going to read this word the fast way. (Pause three seconds.) Get ready. (Move your finger quickly along the arrow.) *Walk.* Yes, **walk.**

b. Now you're going to sound out the word. Get ready. (Quickly touch **w, a, l, k** as the children say *wwwaaalllk.*)

c. Again. (Repeat *b.*)

d. How do we say the word? (Signal.) *Walk.* Yes, **walk.**

e. (Repeat *b* and *d* until firm.)

EXERCISE 13

Individual test

(Call on individual children to do *b* and *d* in exercise 12.)

EXERCISE 14

Children read the words the fast way

(Have the children read the words on this page the fast way.)

EXERCISE 15

Individual test

(Call on individual children to read one word the fast way.)

EXERCISE 16

Children sound out the word and tell what word

a. (Touch the ball for **bōy.**) Sound it out.
b. Get ready. (Touch **b, ō, y** as the children say *bōōōyyy.*)
• (If sounding out is not firm, repeat *b.*)
c. What word? (Signal.) *Boy.* Yes, **boy.**

EXERCISE 17

Individual test

(Call on individual children to do *b* and *c* in exercise 16.)

EXERCISE 18

Children sound out an irregular word (**you**)

a. (Touch the ball for **you.**) Sound it out.
b. Get ready. (Quickly touch each sound as the children say *yyyooouuu.*)
c. Again. (Repeat *b* until firm.)
d. That's how we <u>sound out</u> the word. Here's how we <u>say</u> the word. **You.** How do we <u>say</u> the word? (Signal.) *You.*
e. Now you're going to <u>sound out</u> the word. Get ready. (Touch each sound as the children say *yyyooouuu.*)
f. Now you're going to say the word. Get ready. (Signal.) *You.*
g. Yes, this word is **you. You** are smart today.

EXERCISE 19

Individual test

(Call on individual children to do *e* and *f* in exercise 18.)

EXERCISE 20

Children read the words the fast way

a. Now you get to read the words on this page the fast way.
b. (Touch the ball for **bōy.** Pause three seconds.) Get ready. (Move your finger quickly along the arrow.) *Boy.*
c. (Repeat *b* for **you.**)

EXERCISE 21

Individual test

(Call on individual children to read one word the fast way.)

bōy

you

Grade K Reading Curriculum Map

Key: (for Teachers) √ = informal assessment   Numbers = exercise numbers   Bold face type = first appearance

		Lesson 1	Lesson 2	Lesson 3	Lesson 4	Lesson 5
Phonemic Awareness		Introduction/Sound Pronunciation: 1 (m) Introduction/Sound Pronunciation: 2 (a) Review: 3 (m and a) Oral Blending: 8, 10, 12 Review/Individual Turns: 9, 13 √ 3, 9, 13	Sound Pronunciation: 1 (review a, m; introduction d) Oral Blending: 6, 8, 10 Review/Individual Turns: 7, 11 √ 1, 6, 7, 8, 10, 11	Sound Pronunciation: 1 (review m; introduction ē, f) Oral Blending: 6, 8, 10 Review/Individual Turns: 7 Review/Individual Turns: 11 √ 1, 7, 11	Sound Pronunciation: 1 (review m; introduction r, s) Oral Blending: 6, 8, 10, 11 Review/Individual Turns: 7, 12 √ 1, 7, 12	Sound Pronunciation: 1 (review a, r; introduction th) Oral Blending: 6, 8, 10, 11 Review/Individual Turns: 7, 12 √ 1, 7, 12
		Oral Blending: 14	Oral Blending: 12 √ 12	Oral Blending: 12 √ 12	Oral Blending: 13 √ 13	Oral Blending: 13 √ 13
Print Awareness						
		Follow Left to Right: 17 Review/Individual Turns: 18 Introduction/Letter Tracing and Writing: 19 Letter Tracing/Writing: 20 Review/Independent Work: 23 √ 18, 23 (workcheck)	Follow Left to Right: 13, 15 Review/Individual Turns: 14, 16 Letter Tracing/Writing: 17, 19 Review: 20 √ 14, 16, 20 (workcheck)	Follow Left to Right: 13, 15 Review/Individual Turns: 14, 16 Letter Tracing/Writing: 17, 19 Review: 20 √ 14, 16, 20 (workcheck)	Follow Left to Right: 14, 15 Letter Tracing/Writing: 16 Review: 17 √ 14, 15, 16, 17 (workcheck)	Follow Left to Right: 14, 15 Letter Sound Tracing/Writing: 16 Review: 17 √ 14, 15, 16, 17 (workcheck)
Letter Sound Correspondence		Introduction: 4 **(a)** Letter Sound/Picture Discrimination: 7 (a, tree, dog) Letter Sound/Picture Discrimination: 11 (a, shoe, girl, dog, cat) √ 7, 11	Review: 2 (a) Letter Sound/Picture Discrimination: 5 (a, cat, girl, shoe) Letter Sound/Picture Discrimination: 9 (a, cat, tree, car, boy) √ 2, 5, 9	Letter Sound Identification/Review: 2 (a) Letter Sound/Picture Discrimination: 5 (a, tree, boy) Letter Sound/Picture Discrimination: 9 (a, cat, shoe, girl) √ 2, 5, 9	Letter Sound Identification/Review: 2 (a) Introduction/Letter Sound Identification: 5 **(m)** Letter Sound/Picture Discrimination: 9 (a, shoe, girl) √ 2, 5, 9	Letter Sound Identification/Review: 2 **(m)** Review: 5, 9 (m, a) √ 2, 5, 9
		Sound Identification: 15 (a) Review/Individual Turns: 16 (a) Sound/Picture Discrimination: 21 √ 16	Sound Identification: 18 (a) √ 18	Sound Identification: 18 (a) √ 18		
Phonics and Word Recognition	**Irregular**					
	Regular					
Fluency		Say it Fast: 8, 10, 12	Say it Fast: 6, 8, 10	Say it Fast: 6, 8, 10	Say it Fast: 6, 8, 10, 11	Say it Fast: 6, 8, 10, 11
Comprehension		Picture Comprehension: 5 Sequencing: 6 Picture comprehension: 10 √ 5, 6	Picture Comprehension: 3 Sequencing: 4 Picture Comprehension: 8 √ 3, 4	Picture Comprehension: 3 Sequencing: 4 Picture Comprehension: 8 √ 3, 4	Picture Comprehension: 3 Sequencing: 4 Picture Comprehension: 8 √ 3, 4	Picture Comprehension: 3, 8 Sequencing: 4 √ 3, 4
		Picture Comprehension: 14, 22	Picture Comprehension: 19			

Reading Mastery Signature Edition, Grade K

Key: (for Teachers) √ = informal assessment Numbers = exercise numbers Bold face type = first appearance

	Lesson 6	Lesson 7	Lesson 8	Lesson 9	Lesson 10
Phonemic Awareness	Sound Pronunciation: 1 (review f, ē; introduction z) Oral Blending: 6, 8, 12 Review/Individual Turns: 7 Introduction: Phoneme "Stretching" to Blending: 11 √ 1, 6, 7, 8, 12	Sound Pronunciation: 1 (review d, r, z) Oral Blending: 6, 8, 12 Review/Individual Turns: 7 Phoneme "Stretching" to Blending: 11 √ 1, 6, 7, 8, 11, 12	Sound Pronunciation: 1 (review f, th, d) Oral Blending: 6, 8, 12 Review/Individual Turns: 7 Phoneme "Stretching": 10 Phoneme "Stretching" to Oral Blending: 11 √ 1, 6, 7, 8, 12, 10, 11	Sound Pronunciation: 1 (review r; introduction s, ī) Oral Blending: 6, 8, 12 Review/Individual Turns: 7 Phoneme "Stretching": 10 Phoneme "Stretching" to Oral Blending: 11 √ 1, 6, 7, 8, 10, 11, 12	Sound Pronunciation: 1 (review f, s, ē) Oral Blending: 6, 8, 12 Review/Individual Turns: 7 Phoneme "Stretching": 10 Phoneme "Stretching" to Oral Blending: 11 √ 1, 6, 7, 8, 10, 11, 12
	Oral Blending: 13 Review/Individual Turns: 14 √ 14	Oral Blending: 13 Review/Individual Turns: 14 √ 14	Oral Blending: 13 Review/Individual Turns: 14 √ 14	Oral Blending: 13 Review/Individual Turns: 14 √ 14	Oral Blending: 13 Review/Individual Turns: 14 √ 14
Print Awareness					
	Follow Left to Right: 15, 16 (review a) Letter Symbol Tracing/Writing: 17 Review: 18 √ 16, 17, 18 (workcheck)	Follow Left to Right: 15, 16 (introduction m) Letter Symbol Tracing/Writing: 17 Review: 18 √ 16, 17, 18 (workcheck)	Follow Left to Right: 15, 16 (review m) Letter Symbol Tracing/Writing: 17 (review m) Review: 18 √ 15, 16, 17, 18 (workcheck)	Follow Left to Right: 15, 16 (review m) Letter Symbol Tracing/Writing: 17 (review m) Review: 18 √ 15, 16, 17, 18 (workcheck)	Follow Left to Right: 15, 16 (review a) Letter Symbol Tracing/Writing: 17 (review a) Review: 18 √ 15, 16, 17, 18 (workcheck)
Letter Sound Correspondence	Letter Sound Discrimination/Review: 2, 5, 9, 10 (m, a) √ 2, 5, 9, 10	Letter Sound Discrimination/Review: 2, 5, 9, 10 (m, a) √ 2, 5, 9, 10	Letter Sound Discrimination/Review: 2, 5, 9 (m, a) √ 2, 5, 9	Letter Sound Discrimination/Review: 2 (a, m) Introduction/Letter Sound/Symbol Identification: 5 **(s)** Letter Sound Discrimination/Review: 9 (a, m, s) √ 2, 9	Letter Sound/Symbol Identification: 2 (review s) Letter Sound/Symbol Discrimination: 5, 9 (review s, m, a) √ 2, 5, 9
		Sound Identification: 18 (a) √ 18	Mastery Test 1 after L8		
			Letter Sound/Symbol Identification: a, m		
Phonics and Word Recognition — Irregular					
Phonics and Word Recognition — Regular					
Fluency	Say it Fast: 6, 8, 12	Say it Fast: 6, 8, 12	Say it Fast: 6, 8, 11, 12	Say it Fast: 6, 8, 11, 12	Say it Fast: 6, 8, 11, 12
Comprehension	Picture Comprehension: 3 Sequencing: 4 √ 3, 4	Picture Comprehension: 3 Sequencing: 4 √ 3, 4	Picture Comprehension: 3 Sequencing: 4 √ 3, 4	Picture Comprehension: 3 Sequencing: 4 √ 3, 4	Picture Comprehension: 3 Sequencing: 4 √ 3,4

Key: (for Teachers) √ = informal assessment   Numbers = exercise numbers   Bold face type = first appearance

		Lesson 11	Lesson 12	Lesson 13	Lesson 14	Lesson 15
Phonemic Awareness		Sound Pronunciation: 1 (review a, m, f) Oral Blending: 6, 7, 11 Phoneme "Stretching": 9 Individual Sound "Stretching" to "Saying it Fast": 10 (m, s, a) √ 1, 6, 7, 9, 10, 11	Sound Pronunciation: 1 (review th, m, i) Phoneme "Stretching" to Oral Blending: 6 Oral Blending: 7 Phoneme "Stretching": 10 Individual Sound "Stretching" to "Saying it Fast": 11 (r, s, m) √ 1, 6, 7, 10, 11	Sound Pronunciation: 1 (review a, s, r) Oral Blending: 5, 6 Review/Individual Turns: 7 Phoneme "Stretching": 8 Phoneme "Stretching" to "Say it Fast": 9 (a, m) √ 1, 5, 6, 7, 8, 9	Sound Pronunciation: 1 (d, ŏ, f) Oral Blending: 5, 6 Phoneme "Stretching": 9 Review/Phoneme "Stretching" to "Say it Fast": 10 (a, m) √ 1, 5, 6, 9, 10	Sound Pronunciation: 1 (review a, s, t) Oral Blending: 5, 6 Phoneme "Stretching" to "Say it Fast": 8 √ 1, 5, 6, 8
		Oral Blending: 12 Review/Individual Turns: 13 √ 13	Oral Blending: 12 Review/Individual Turns: 13 √ 13	Oral Blending: 10 Review/Individual Turns: 11 √ 11	Oral Blending: 11 Review/Individual Turns: 12 √ 12	Oral Blending: 10 Review/Individual Turns: 11 √ 11
						Mastery Test 2 after L15 Oral Blending: in, mad, s
Print Awareness						
		Follow Left to Right: 14, 16 (review m) Review/Individual Turns: 15, 17 (m) Letter Symbol Tracing/Writing: 18, 19 (m) Review: 20, 21, 22 √ 14, 15, 16, 17, 18, 19, 20, 21, 22 (workcheck)	Follow Left to Right: 14, 16 (review m) Review/Individual Turns: 15, 17 (m) Letter Symbol Tracing/Writing: 18 Review: 19, 20, 21 √ 14, 15, 16, 17, 18, 19, 20, 21 (workcheck)	Follow Left to Right: 12, 13 (review a) Letter Symbol Tracing/Writing: 14 (review a) Review: 15 √ 12, 13, 14, 15 (workcheck)	Follow Left to Right: 13, 14 (review a) Letter Symbol Tracing/Writing: 15 (review a) Review: 16 √ 13, 14, 15, 16 (workcheck)	Follow Left to Right: 12, 13 (review a, m) Letter Symbol Tracing/Writing: 14 (review m) Review: 15 √ 12, 13, 14, 15 (workcheck)
Letter Sound Correspondence		Letter Sound Identification: 2 (introduction m) Letter Sound Symbol Discrimination: 5, 8 (m, pictures) √ 2, 5, 8	Letter Sound Identification/Review: 2 (m) Letter Sound Identification: 5 (a) Letter Sound/Symbol Discrimination: 8, 9 (m, a) √ 2, 5, 8, 9	Letter Sound Identification: 2(a) Letter Sound Discrimination/Review: 4, 7 (a, m) √ 2, 4, 7	Letter Sound Discrimination/Review: 2, 4, 7, 8 (a, m) √ 2, 4, 7, 8	Letter Sound/Symbol Discrimination/Review: 2, 4, 7 (m, a) Introduction/Individual Sound Blending: 9 (mmm, aaa) √ 2, 4, 7, 9
Phonics and Word Recognition	Irregular					
	Regular					
Fluency		Say it Fast: 6, 7, 10, 11	Say it Fast: 6, 7, 11	Say it Fast: 5, 6, 9	Say it Fast: 5, 6, 10	Say it Fast: 5, 6, 8, 9
Comprehension		Picture Comprehension: 3 Sequencing: 4 √ 3, 4	Picture Comprehension: 3 Sequencing: 4 √ 3, 4	Sequencing: 3 √ 3	Sequencing: 3 √ 3	Sequencing: 3 √ 3

Key: (for Teachers)	√ = informal assessment	Numbers = exercise numbers	Bold face type = first appearance

		Lesson 16	Lesson 17	Lesson 18	Lesson 19	Lesson 20
Phonemic Awareness		Sound Pronunciation: 1 (review ŏ, s, m) Oral Blending: 5, 6 Introduction/Rhyming (blending initial sound to ending): 10 Review/Rhyming: 11, 12, 13, 14, 15 Individual Turns: √ 5, 6, 11, 12, 13, 14, 15, 16	Oral Blending: 4, 5 Review/Rhyming: 8, 9, 10, 11, 12, 13 Individual Turns: 14 √ 4, 5, 8, 9, 10, 11, 12, 13, 14	Oral Blending: 2, 3 Review/Rhyming: 9 √ 2, 3, 9	Sound Pronunciation: 1 (ē, r, n) Oral Blending: 3, 4 Review/Rhyming: 9 √ 1, 3, 4, 9	Oral Blending: 2, 3 Review/Rhyming: 8 √ 2, 3, 8
		Oral Blending: 16, 17 √ 16, 17	Oral Blending: 14, 15 Review/Individual Turns: 15 √ 15	Oral Blending: 10, 11 √ 11	Oral Blending: 10, 11 √ 10, 11	Oral Blending: 9, 10 √ 9, 10
						Mastery Test 3 after L20 Rhyming (mat, fun, my, see)
Print Awareness						
		Follow Left to Right: 17 (review a, m) Letter Symbol Tracing/Writing: 19 (a) Review: 20 √ 18, 19, 20	Follow Left to Right: 15, 16 (review a, introduce s) Letter Symbol Tracing/Writing: 17 (introduce s) Review: 18 √ 16, 17, 19	Follow Left to Right: 12, 13 (review s) Letter Symbol Tracing/Writing: 14 (review s) Review: 15 √ 12, 13, 14, 15	Follow Left to Right: 12, 13 (review s, ē) Letter Symbol Tracing/Writing: 16 (ē) Review: 17 √ 12, 13, 16, 17	Follow Left to Right: 11, 12 (review ē, s) Letter Symbol Tracing/Writing: 15 (review s) Review: 16 √ 11, 12, 15, 16
						Identification of m, s, a, ē
Letter Sound Correspondence		Letter Sound Discrimination/Review: 2, 9 (m, a, s) Introduction/Letter Sound Symbol Identification: 4 (s) Review/Blending Individual Sounds: 7, 8 (mmm, aaa) √ 2, 7, 8, 9	Letter Sound Identification/Review: 1 (s) Letter Sound/Symbol Discrimination: 3, 7 (m, a, s) Individual Sound Blending: 6 (s, a) √ 1, 3, 6, 7	Letter Sound Discrimination/Review: 1, 5, 7, 8 (a, m, s) Blending Sounds: 4 (m, s) Introduction/Sounding Out 2 Different Sounds: 6 (mmmaaa, aaammm) √ 1, 5, 7, 8	Letter Sound Discrimination/Review: 2, 8 (a, m, s, ē) Individual Sound Blending/Review: 5 (sss, a) Letter Sound Identification Introduction: 6 (ē) Sounding Out 2 Different Sounds: 7 (sssaaa, mmmaaa) √ 2, 5, 7, 8	Review/Letter Sound/Symbol Identification: 1(ē) Blending Individual Sounds to Saying them Fast: 4 (mmm, ss, ē, a) Review/Sounding Out 2 Different Sounds: 6 (sa) Review/ Sound Discrimination: 7 (s, ē, a, m) √ 1, 4, 6, 7
					Introduction/Sounding Out: 14 (am) Individual Turns: 15 (am) √ 15	Sounding Out: 13, 14 (ma)
Phonics and Word Recognition	Irregular					
	Regular					
Fluency		Say it Fast: 5, 6, 7, 8	Say it Fast: 4, 5, 6	Say it Fast: 2, 3, 4, 9	Say it Fast: 3, 4, 5, 9	Say it Fast: 2, 3, 4
						Curriculum-Based Assessment 20 after L20
Comprehension		Sequencing: 3 √ 3	Sequencing: 2 √ 2			

Key: (for Teachers)   √= informal assessment   Numbers = exercise numbers   Bold face type = first appearance

	Lesson 21	Lesson 22	Lesson 23	Lesson 24	Lesson 25
Phonemic Awareness	Oral Blending: 2, 3 Review/Rhyming: 6 √ 2, 3, 6	Oral Blending: 2, 3 Review/Rhyming: 6 √ 2, 3, 6	Review/Sound Pronunciation: 1 (**r**, d, f) Oral Blending: 3, 4 Review/Rhyming: 6 √ 1, 3, 4, 6	Oral Blending: 2,3 Review/Rhyming: 6 √ 2, 3, 6	Oral Blending: 2, 3 Review/Rhyming: 4 √ 2, 3, 4
Print Awareness	Introduction/Pair Relations/Phonograms Freehand: 11 (m, a) Review: 12 √ 11, 12	Follow Left to Right/Sounding Out: 10 (sa) Pair Relations/Freehand Sound Writing: 11 (m, s) Review: 12 √ 10, 11, 12	Follow Left to Right/Sounding Out: 9 (em) Pair Relations/Sound Writing: 10 (ē, a) Review: 11 √ 9, 10, 11	Follow Left to Right/Sounding Out: 9 (see) Pair Relations/Sound Writing: 10 (m, s) Review: 11 √ 9, 10, 11	Follow Left to Right/Sounding Out: 7 (rē) Review/Letter Symbol Tracing/Writing: 8 √ 7, 8
Letter Sound Correspondence	Letter Sound Discrimination/Review: 1, 4, 5, 8 (m, a, s, ē) Review/Blending Individual Sounds to "Say it Fast": 7 (m, ēēē) Blending 2 Different Sounds: 9 (sē) √ 1, 4, 5, 7, 8, 9	Letter Sound Discrimination/Review: 1, 5, 8, 9 (m, s, ē, a) Review/Sounding Out Words: 4 (me) Individual Sound Blending: 7 (s, ē) √ 1, 4, 5, 7, 8, 9	Review/Letter Sound Discrimination: 2, 5, 8 (r, s, m, ē, a) Blending Sounds: 7 (m, ē) √ 2, 5, 7, 8	Letter Sound Identification/Review: 1 (r) Review/Letter Sound Discrimination: 4, 5, 8 (r, s, m, ē, a) Blending Sounds: 7 (r, a) √ 1, 4, 5, 7, 8	Review/Letter Sound Discrimination: 1, 5 (m, ē, r, s, a) Blending Individual Sounds to Saying them Fast: 3 (rrr, ē) Review/Sounding Out 2 Different Sounds: 6 (rē) √ 1, 3, 5, 6
	Follow Left to Right/Sounding Out: 10 (mē) √ 10				Mastery Test 4 after L25 Letter Sound Identification: s, r, m, a, ē
Phonics and Word Recognition — Irregular					
Phonics and Word Recognition — Regular	Sounding Out: 10 mē			Sounding Out: 9 (see)	
Fluency	Say it Fast: 2, 3, 6, 7	Say it Fast: 2, 3, 6, 7	Say it Fast: 2, 3, 4, 6, 7	Say it Fast: 2, 3, 6, 7	
Comprehension					

Key: (for Teachers)	√ = informal assessment	Numbers = exercise numbers	Bold face type = first appearance

	Lesson 26	**Lesson 27**	**Lesson 28**	**Lesson 29**	**Lesson 30**
Phonemic Awareness	Oral Blending: 3 Review/Rhyming: 7 √ 3, 7	Review/Sound Pronunciation: 1 (f, d, ī) Oral Blending: 4 √ 1, 4, 6	Oral Blending: 3 √ 3	Oral Blending: 2 √ 2	Review/Oral Blending: 3 √ 3
Print Awareness	Review: 10 √ 10	Follow Left to Right/Sounding Out: 9 (ra) Review: 10 √ 9, 10	Follow Left to Right/Sounding Out: 8 (me) Review: 9 √ 8, 9	Follow Left to Right/Sounding Out: 9 (see) Introduction/Sound/ Symbol Matching: 10 Introduction/ Freehand Sound Writing: 11 Review: 12 √ 9, 10, 11, 12	Follow Left to Right/Sounding Out: 12 (ma) Review/Sound Matching: 13 Review/Freehand Sound Tracing/Writing: 14 Pair Relations: 15 Review: 16 √ 12, 13, 14, 15, 16

Letter Sound Correspondence	Letter Sound Discrimination/Review:
	  1, 5, 6 (r, m, a, s, ē)
	Review/Blending Individual Sounds to "Say it Fast": 2 (r, ēēē)
	Blending 2 Different Sounds: 4 (ēr)
	Introduction/Sound Identification to Rhyming: 8
	√ 1, 2, 4, 5, 6, 8
		Introduction/Sound Symbol Identification: 2 **(d)**
		Letter Sound Discrimination/Review:
		  3, 7 (r, d, m, s, ē, a)
		Review/Sound Identification to Rhyming: 5, 6
		Review/Sounding Out 2 Different Sounds: 8 (ra)
		√ 2, 3, 5, 6, 7, 8
			Review/Letter Sound Identification: 1 (d)
			Review/Letter Sound Discrimination:
			  2, 5 (r, s, m, ē, a, d)
			Review/Sound Identification to Rhyming: 4
			Sounding Out Regular Words: 6, 7 **(am, me)**
			√ 1, 2, 4, 5, 6, 7
				Review/Letter Sound Discrimination:
				  1, 5, 6 (r, s, m, ē, a, d)
				Review/Sound Identification to Rhyming: 3, 4
				Review/Sounding Out Words: 7, 8 **(see,** am)
				√ 1, 3, 4, 5, 6, 7, 8
					Review/Letter Sound Discrimination:
					  1, 7, 8 (m, ē, r, s, a, d)
					Individual Sound Blending: 2 (rrr, mmm)
					Review/Sound Identification to Rhyming: 4, 5, 6
					Introduction/Sounding Out Words:
					  9, 10 **(sad, mad)**
					Review/Sounding Out Words: 11 (me)
					√ 1, 2, 4, 5, 6, 7, 8, 9, 10, 11

	Follow Left to Right/Sounding Out: 9 (ēr) √ 9		Review/Sounding Out: 8 (me) √ 8	Review/Sounding Out Words: 9 (see) √ 9	Review/Sounding Out: 12 (ma) √ 12
					Mastery Test 5 after L30 Letter Sound Identification to Rhyming: m, r, man, ran
Phonics and Word Recognition — Irregular					
Phonics and Word Recognition — Regular			Sounding Out: 6 **am**	see	sad mad me
Fluency	Say it Fast: 2, 3, 7	Say it Fast: 4, 5, 6	Say it Fast: 3, 4	Say it Fast: 2	Say it Fast: 2, 3
Comprehension					

Key: (for Teachers) √= informal assessment Numbers = exercise numbers Bold face type = first appearance

		Lesson 31	Lesson 32	Lesson 33	Lesson 34	Lesson 35
Phonemic Awareness		Sound Pronunciation: 1 Onset Rime: 4, 5, 6 Segmentation/Blending: 8 √ 1, 4, 5, 6, 8	Onset Rime: 3, 4, 5, 6 Segmentation/Blending: 7 √ 3, 4, 5, 6, 7	Onset Rime: 2, 3, 4, 5, 6 Segmentation/Blending: 7 √ 2, 3, 4, 5, 6, 7	Sound Pronunciation: 1 Onset Rime: 4, 5, 6, 7, 8 Segmentation/Blending: 10 √ 1, 4, 5, 6, 7, 8, 10	Onset Rime: 3, 4, 5, 6, 7, Segmentation/Blending: 10 √ 3, 4, 5, 6, 7, 10
Print Awareness		Sequencing: 15, 16	Sequencing: 14	Sequencing: 13	Sequencing: 16	Sequencing: 16 Sequencing
Letter Sound Correspondence		Introduction: 2 **(f)** Review: 3 (f, d, r, s, e) Review: 7 (f, r, d,) √ 2, 3, 7	Review: 1 (f) Review: 2 (f, d, e, a, r) Review: 8, 9 (r, f, d, m) √1, 2, 8	Review: 1 (f, d, r, e, s) Review: 8 (s, f, d, a, r) √ 1	Introduction: 2 **(i)** Review: 3 (i, f, s, d, e) Review: 9: (i, m, f, a,) √ 2, 3, 9	Introduction: 1 (i) Review: 2 (i, f, m, a) Review: 8, 9 (r, i, f, e, d) √ 1, 2, 8
		Review: 13, 14, 16,	Review: 14	Review: 13	Review: 15	Review: 16 Mastery Test 6 after L35 Sound Identification Sounding Out
Phonics and Word Recognition	Irregular					
	Regular	Blending Sounds into Words: 9 (**ram**), 10, 11 √ 9, 10, 11	Blending Sounds into Words: 10 (**ear**), 11, 12, √ 10, 11. 12	Blending Sounds into Words: 9 (**seed**), 10, 11 √ 9, 10, 11	Blending Sounds into Words: 11 (**feed**), 12, 13 √ 11, 12, 13	Blending Sounds into Words: 11 (**seem**), 12, 13 √ 11, 12, 13
		Sounding Out: 12 √ 12	Sounding Out: 13 √ 13	Sounding Out: 12 √ 12	Blending Sounds into Words: 14 √ 15	Blending Sounds into Words: 14 √ 15
Fluency		Say it Fast: 8	Say it Fast: 7	Say it Fast: 7	Say it Fast: 10	Say it Fast: 10
Comprehension						

Key: (for Teachers)	√ = informal assessment	Numbers = exercise numbers	Bold face type = first appearance

		Lesson 36	Lesson 37	Lesson 38	Lesson 39	Lesson 40
Phonemic Awareness		Segmentation/Blending: 2 Onset Rime: 3 √ 2, 3	Segmentation/Blending: 2 Onset Rime: 3, 11 √ 2, 3, 11	Sound Pronunciation: 1 Segmentation/Blending: 4 Onset Rime: 5, 11 √ 2, 3, 4, 5, 6, 7, 11	Segmentation/Blending: 3 Onset Rime: 6 √ 3, 6	Segmentation/Blending: 2 Onset Rime: 8 √ 2, 8
Print Awareness						
		Sequencing: 10	Follow Left to Right: 14	Sequencing: 14	Sequencing: 14	Sequencing: 14, 15 Sequencing
Letter Sound Correspondence		Review: 1(f, d, m, s, i) Review: 4 (i, a, d, r, f, ē) √ 1, 4	Review: 1 (d, r, e, i) Review: 4, 5 (f, d, i, s, m) √ 1, 4, 5	Introduction: 2 (**th**) Review: 3 (f, th, i, m, s) Review: 6 (th, f, i, a) √ 1	Review: 1 (th) Review 2: (i, f, r, th, e) Review: 4, 5 (i, d, f, th) √ 1, 2, 4, 5	Review: 1 (i, th, r, e, d) Review: 3, 4 (r, i,f, e, s) √ 1, 3, 4
		Review: 10	Review: 14	Review: 14	Review: 14	Review: 15 Mastery Test 7 after L40 Sound Identification Sounding Out Blending Sounds into Words
Phonics and Word Recognition	Irregular					
	Regular	Blending Sounds into Words: 5 (**read**), 6, 7 √ 5, 6, 7	Blending Sounds into Words: 6 (if), 7 (**miss**), 8, 9, 11 (**sam**) √ 10, 11. 12	Blending Sounds into Words: 7, 8, 9 √ 7, 8, 9	Blending Sounds into Words: 7, 9, 10, 11 √ 7, 9, 10, 11	Blending Sounds into Words: 5 (**this**), 6, 7 √ 5, 6, 7
		Sounding Out: 8 √ 9	Sounding Out: 12 √ 13	Sounding Out: 12 √ 13	Blending Sounds into Words: 12 √ 13	Reading Stories by Sounding Out Words: 9, 10 √ 11
Fluency		Say it Fast: 2	Say it Fast: 2	Say it Fast: 4	Say it Fast: 3	Say it Fast: 2, 12
						Teacher Models Reading Connected Text: 12
						Curriculum-Based Assessment 40 after L40
Comprehension			Picture Comprehension: 10	Picture Comprehension: 10	Picture Comprehension: 8	Picture Comprehension: 13

Key: (for Teachers) √ = informal assessment Numbers = exercise numbers Bold face type = first appearance

		Lesson 41	Lesson 42	Lesson 43	Lesson 44	Lesson 45
Phonemic Awareness		Sound Pronunciation: 1 Onset Rime: 14 √ 1, 14	Onset Rime: 12, 13 √ 3, 12, 13	Onset Rime: 11, 12 √ 11, 12	Onset Rime: 12, 13 √ 12, 13	Onset Rime: 12, 13 √ 12, 13
Print Awareness		Sequencing: 20, 21	Follow Left to Right: 22, 24	Sequencing: 19	Sequencing: 20	Sequencing: 19 Sequencing
Letter Sound Correspondence		Introduction: 2 **(t)** Review: 4 (t, d, th, e) Review: 6 (i, a, t, r, f, ē, s, th) √ 3, 5, 7	Review: 1 (t) Review: 2 (t, d, i, f) Review: 4, 6 (f, t, r, th, i, m) √ 3, 5, 6	Review: 1 (t, th, d, f) Review: 3, 5 (th, f, i, a, t, r, m, e) √ 2, 4	Introduction: 1 **(n)** Review: 3 (n, m, t, r) Review: 5 (i, r, f, th, t, m, e, n) √ 2, 4, 6	Review: 1 (n) Review: 2 (n, t, i, m) Review: 4, 6 (i,f, e, s, d, th, t, n) √ 3, 5
		Review: 21	Review: 23, 24	Review: 18, 19	Review: 19, 20	Review: 19 Mastery Test 8 after L45 Sounding Out Blending Sounds into Words
Phonics and Word Recognition	*Irregular*					
	Regular	Blending Sounds into Words: 8, 9, 10, 11, 12 √ 8, 9, 10, 11, 12, 13	Blending Sounds into Words: 7, 8 **(the)**, 9 **(is)** 10, 11, 12 **(fear)**, 14 √ 11, 15	Blending Sounds into Words: 6, 7 **(sit)**, 8, 9, 11 **(that)**, 12 **(dim)** √ 10	Blending Sounds into Words: 7 **(me)**, 8 **(that)**, 9, 10, 12, 13 **(dear)** √ 11	Blending Sounds into Words: 7, 8, 9, 10, 12, 13 **(tear)** √ 11
		Reading Stories by Blending Sounds into Words: 15, 16 √ 17	Reading Stories by Blending Sounds into Words: 17, 18 √ 19	Reading Stories by Blending Sounds into Words: 13, 14 √ 15	Reading Stories by Blending Sounds into Words: 14, 15 √ 16	Reading Stories by Sounding Out Words: 14, 15 √ 16
Fluency		Say it Fast: 18	Say it Fast: 20	Say it Fast: 16	Say it Fast: 17	Say it Fast: 17
		Teacher Models Reading Connected Text: 18	Teacher Models Reading Connected Text: 20	Teacher Models Reading Connected Text: 16	Teacher Models Reading Connected Text: 17	Teacher Models Reading Connected Text: 17
Comprehension			Picture Comprehension: 16			
		Picture Comprehension: 19	Picture Comprehension: 21	Picture Comprehension: 17	Picture Comprehension: 18	Picture Comprehension: 18

Key: (for Teachers)	√ = informal assessment	Numbers = exercise numbers	Bold face type = first appearance

		Lesson 46	Lesson 47	Lesson 48	Lesson 49	Lesson 50
Phonemic Awareness		Onset Rime: 12, 13 √ 12, 13	Onset Rime: 11 (in), 12 √ 11, 12	Sound Pronunciation: 1 Onset Rime: 14, 15 √ 14, 15	Onset Rime: 12, 13 √ 12, 13	Onset Rime: 13, 14 √ 13, 14
Print Awareness		Sequencing: 19	Follow Left to Right: 18	Sequencing: 22	Sequencing: 19, 20	Sequencing: 21
Letter Sound Correspondence		Review: 1 (n) Review: 2 (t, r, n, m) Review: 4 (i, a, th, r, f, ë, s, n) √ 3, 5	Review: 1, 2, 4 (t, th, f, m, r, i, d, n) Review: 2 (t, d, i, f) Review: 4, 6 (f, t, r, th, i, m) √ 3	Introduction: 2 **(c)** Review: 4 (c, d, s, n) Review: 6 (th, f, i, a, t, n, c, e) √ 3, 5, 7	Review: 1 (c) Review: 2 (c, t, d, f) Review: 4 (i, e, s, c, th, t, s, r) √ 3, 5	Review: 1 (c) Review: 2 (c, th, n, t) Review: 4 (m, d, c, l, a, e, r, f) √ 3, 5
		Review: 19	Review: 18	Review: 22	Review: 20	Review: 20, 21 Mastery Test 9 after L50 Sound Identification (t, i, f, d)
Phonics and Word Recognition	Irregular					
	Regular	Blending Sounds into Words: 6, 7 **(eat)**, 8 **(sat)**, 9 **(meat)**, 10, 12 **(near)**, 13 **(team)** √ 11	Blending Sounds into Words: 5, 6, 7, 8, 9, 11 **(in, fin)**, 12 **(tin)** √ 10	Blending Sounds into Words: 8 **(an)**, 9, 10, 11, 12, 14 **(ran)**, 15 **(dan)** √ 13	Blending Sounds into Words: 6 **(rack)**, 7, 8, 9, 10, 12 **(mean)**, 13 **(tan)** √ 11	Blending Sounds into Words: 6, 7, 8, 9, 10 **(fan)**, 11 **(fat)**, 13, 14 **(cat)** √ 12
		Reading Stories by Blending Sounds into Words: 14, 15 √ 16	Reading Stories by Blending Sounds into Words: 13, 14 √ 15	Reading Stories by Blending Sounds into Words: 16, 17 √ 18	Reading Stories by Blending Sounds into Words: 14, 15 √ 16	Reading Stories by Sounding Out Words: 15, 16 √ 17
Fluency		Say it Fast: 17	Say it Fast: 16	Say it Fast: 19	Say it Fast: 17	Say it Fast: 18
		Teacher Models Reading Connected Text: 17	Teacher Models Reading Connected Text: 16	Teacher Models Reading Connected Text: 19	Teacher Models Reading Connected Text: 17	Teacher Models Reading Connected Text: 18
Comprehension		Picture Comprehension: 18	Picture Comprehension: 17	Picture Comprehension: 20	Picture Comprehension: 18	Picture Comprehension: 19

		Lesson 51	Lesson 52	Lesson 53	Lesson 54	Lesson 55
Phonemic Awareness						Saying Sounds in Words: 3 (it, in)
Print Awareness		Sequencing: 23 Copying Text: 24	Sequencing: 19 Copying Text: 20	Sequencing: 20 Copying Text: 21	Copying Text: 17 Sequencing: 17	Copying Text: 21 Sequencing: 21
Letter Sound Correspondence		Introduction: 1 (**ŏ**) Review: 2 (ŏ) Review: 3 (ŏ, c, a, i) Review: 5, 7 (th, n, t, ŏ, ē, c, f, a) √: 2, 4, 6	Review: 1 (ŏ) Review: 2 (ŏ, ĭ, c, a) Review: 4, 6 (t, th, ŏ, r, n, a, ē, ĭ) √: 3, 5	Review: 1 (ŏ) Review: 2 (ŏ, ē, a, ĭ) Review: 4 (ŏ, r, th, n, c, ē, ĭ, f) √: 3, 5	Review: 1 (f, th, n, m) Review: 2 (c, d, ŏ, a, i, s, r, ē) √: 3	Review: 1, 3 (ŏ, n, ĭ, d, a, f, t, m) Review: 4 (c, ē, th, a)
		Phonograms: (i, r)	Phonograms: (i, r)	Phonograms: 1 (o, ē, a, i) Review: 2	Phonograms: 1, 2	Phonograms: 1, 2
Phonics and Word Recognition	Irregular			Blending Sounds into Words: 12 (**neat**) √: 13		
	Regular	Blending Sounds into Words: 8, 9, 10, 11 (**rock**), 12 (rat), 14, 15, 17 (**can**) √: 13, 16	Blending Sounds into Words: 7, 8 (**not**), 9, 10, 12 (**sack**), 13 (**man**) √: 11	Sounding Out and Blending Words: 6, 7, 8, 9, 11, 14 √: 10, 13	Blending Sounds into Words: 4, 5, 6, 7, 8, 10, 11 √: 9	Blending Sounds into Words: 5. 6. 7 (**sock**), 8, 9, 11, 12 (**on**), 13, 15 (**tack**) √: 10, 14
		Reading Stories by Blending Sounds into Words: 18, 19 √: 20	Reading Stories by Blending Sounds into Words: 14, 15 √: 16	Reading Stories by Blending Sounds into Words: 15, 16 √: 17	Reading Stories by Blending Sounds into Words: 12, 13 √: 14	Reading Stories by Blending Sounds into Words: 16, 17 √: 18
						Mastery Test 10 after L55
Fluency		Say it Fast: 21	Say it Fast: 17	Say it Fast: 18	Say it Fast: 15	Say it Fast: 19
		Teacher Models Reading Connected Text: 21	Teacher Models Reading Connected Text: 17	Teacher Models Reading Connected Text: 18	Teacher Models Reading Connected Text: 15 Reading Words: 15	Teacher Models Reading Connected Text: 19 Reading Words: 19
		Visual Discrimination: 24	Visual Discrimination: 20	Visual Discrimination: 21	Visual Discrimination: 17	Visual Discrimination: 21
Comprehension		Picture Comprehension: 22	Picture Comprehension: 18	Note details: 19 Infer Feelings: 19	Picture Inference: 16 Note details: 16 Make predictions: 16 Prior Knowledge: 16	Note details: 20 Picture Inference: 20 Infer Character Feelings: 20 Prior Knowledge: 20

Key: (for Teachers) √= informal assessment   Numbers = exercise numbers   Bold face type = first appearance

		Lesson 56	Lesson 57	Lesson 58	Lesson 59	Lesson 60
Phonemic Awareness		Onset Rime: 14, 15 √: 14, 15	Onset Rime: 12			Onset Rime: 15
		Saying Sounds in Words: 3 (**at**, in)	Saying Sounds in Words: 3 (it, an)	Saying Sounds in Words: 3 (am, it)	Saying Sounds in Words: 2 (an, in), 3 (it)	Saying Sounds in Words: 4 (at, it)
Print Awareness		Copying Text: 21 Sequencing: 21	Copying Text: 19 Sequencing: 19	Copying Text: 20 Sequencing: 20	Copying Text: 21 Sequencing: 21	Copying Text: 23 Sequencing: 23
Letter Sound Correspondence		Review: 1 (th, t, ŏ, c, d, ĭ, r, ē) Review: 3, 5 (s, ĭ, ŏ, n, f, ē, m, a) √: 2, 4	Review: 1 (t, ŏ, a, ĭ) Review: 2 (a, r, ē, d, ĭ, th, ŏ, c) √: 3	Review: 1 (a) Introduction: 2 (**ā**) Review: 3 (ā, ŏ, c, n) √: 4	Introduction: 1 (ā) Review: 2 (ā, a, ĭ, ŏ) Review: 4 (ā, ŏ, c, ē, t, th, n) √: 3, 5	Review: 1 (ā) Review: 2 (ā, ē, d, ŏ) Review: 4, 6 (ŏ, t, c, th, ā, d, n, ĭ) √: 3, 5
		Phonograms: 1, 2 (a, i, r)	Phonograms: 1 (t, r) Phonograms: 2 (t, a, t, i)	Phonograms: 1 (t, i) Phonograms: 2 (t, r, a)	Phonograms: 1 (r, i, t, a)	Phonograms: 1 (n), 2 (t, r, n), 3 (n, a, t) Identifying Sounds
Phonics and Word Recognition	Irregular	Review: 6				
	Regular	Blending Sounds into Words: 6, 7, 8 (**feet**), 9, 11 (**fit**), 12, 14 (**sick**), 15 √: 10, 13, 14, 15	Blending Sounds into Words: 4, 5, 6, 7, 9, 10, 11 (**seat**), 12 √: 8	Blending Sounds into Words: 5, 6, 7, 8, 9, 10, 11, 12, 13 √: 9	Blending Sounds into Words: 6 (**ate**), 7, 8, 9 (**name**), 11, 12, 13, 14 √: 10	Blending Sounds into Words: 7, 8, 10, 11, 13, 14, 15, 16 (**rate**) √: 9, 12, 16
		Reading Stories by Blending Sounds into Words: 16, 17 √: 18	Reading Stories by Blending Sounds into Words: 13, 14 √: 15	Reading Stories by Blending Sounds into Words: 14, 15 √: 16	Reading Stories by Blending Sounds into Words: 15, 16 √: 17	Reading Stories by Blending Sounds into Words: 17, 18 √: 19
					V-C: 3	V-C: 5, 6 Mastery Test 11 after L60 Blending Sounds into Words
Fluency		Rhyming: 14, 15 √: 14, 15	Rhyming: 12			Rhyming: 15
		Teacher Models Reading Connected Text: 19 Reading Words: 19	Teacher Models Reading Connected Text: 16 Reading Words: 16 Word Recognition: 18	Teacher Models Reading Connected Text: 17 Reading Words: 17 Word Recognition: 19	Teacher Models Reading Connected Text: 18 Reading Words: 18 Word Recognition: 20	Teacher Models Reading Connected Text: 20 Reading Words: 20 Word Recognition: 22
		Visual Discrimination: 21	Visual Discrimination: 19	Visual Discrimination: 20	Visual Discrimination: 21	Visual Discrimination: 23 Rhyming Curriculum-Based Assessment 60 after L60
Comprehension		Note details: 20 Inference: 20 Making Predictions: 20	Note Details: 17 Make Connections: 17	Predict/Confirm Predictions: 18 Making Inferences: 18 Note Details: 18 Make Connections: 18	Predict/Confirm Predictions: 19 Note details: 19 Verification/Metacognitive Skills: 19 Make Connections: 19	Predict/Confirm Predictions: 21 Note Details: 21 Make Inferences: 21

Key: (for Teachers)   √ = informal assessment   Numbers = exercise numbers   Bold face type = first appearance

		Lesson 61	Lesson 62	Lesson 63	Lesson 64	Lesson 65
Phonemic Awareness		Onset Rime: 16	Onset Rime: 11	Onset Rime: 13, 15, 17, 19		Onset Rime: 12
		Saying Sounds in Words: 3 (in, an)				
Print Awareness		Sequencing: 18	Sequencing: 18	Sequencing: 21		
		Copying Text: 24 Sequencing: 24	Copying Text: 25 Sequencing: 25	Copying Text: 29	Copying Text: 27	Copying Text: 30
						Sequencing
Letter Sound Correspondence		Introduction: 1 **(h)** Review: 3 (h, ā, th, n) Review: 5 (h, m, r, ŏ, ē, ā, f) √: 2, 4, 6	Review: 1 (h) Review: 2 (th, h, r, n) Review: 4 (ā, c, a, h, i, ŏ, d, t), 6 √: 3, 5	Review: 1 (h) Review: 2 (h, f, ā, th) Review: 4 (h, ŏ, ē, n, ĭ, ā, a, c) √: 3, 5	Introduction: 1 **(u)** Review: 3 (ü, a, ŏ, i) Review: 5 (h, ā, ŏ, ü, n, t, d, c), 7 √: 2, 4, 6	Review: 1 (ü) Review: 2 (ü, ŏ, i, a) Review: 4 (u, ē, d, h, ŏ, f, ā, c) √: 3, 5
		Phonograms: 1 (n, i, r, t) Phonograms: 2 (t, a, n)	Phonograms: 1 (n, r, a) Phonograms: 2 (t, a, n)	Phonograms: 1 (f) Phonograms: 2 (r, f, t, a, i)	Phonograms: 1 (f, i, a, n, t)	Phonograms: 1 (f, a, n, t)
						Mastery Test 12 after L65
Phonics and Word Recognition	Irregular					
	Regular	Blending Sounds into Words: 7, 8, 9, 12, 13, 14, 17 Onset Rime: 16 √: 10, 11, 15	Blending Sounds into Words: 7, 8, 9, 11 **(mack)**, 12, 13, 14, 15 √: 10, 16, 17	Blending Sounds into Words: 6, 7, 8, 10, 13 **(hot)**, 14, 15 **(he)**, 17 **(hit)**, 19 **(his)** Onset Rime: 13, 15, 17, 19 √: 9, 11, 12, 16, 18, 20	Blending Sounds into Words: 8, 9, 11, 13, 15, 18 **(mitt)**, 19 √: 10, 12, 14, 16, 17	Blending Sounds into Words: 6, 8, 10, 12 **(had)**, 13 **(ham)**, 15, 22 √: 7, 9, 11, 14, 16, 18, 20
		Reading Stories by Blending Sounds into Words: 19, 20 √: 20	Reading Stories by Blending Sounds into Words: 19, 20 √: 21	Reading Stories by Blending Sounds into Words: 22, 23 √: 24	Reading Stories by Blending Sounds into Words: 20, 21 √: 22	Reading Stories by Blending Sounds into Words: 23, 24 √: 25
		V-C: 4, 5	V-C: 3, 4, 5	V-C: 3 (an, in, at)	V-C: 2 C-V-C: 2	V-C: 2, 3 C-V-C: 3
						Blending Sounds into Words Connected Text
Fluency		Rhyming: 16	Rhyming: 11	Rhyming: 13, 15, 17, 19	Reading Words: 9, 11 Rhyming: 13, 15, 18 √: 10, 12	Reading Words: 6, 8, 10, 15, 17, 19, 21 Rhyming: 12, 13 √: 7, 9, 11, 16, 18, 20
		Teacher Models Reading Connected Text: 21 Reading Words: 21 Word Recognition: 23	Teacher Models Reading Connected Text: 22 Reading Words: 22 Word Recognition: 24	Teacher Models Reading Connected Text: 25 Reading Words: 25 Word Recognition: 27	Teacher Models Reading Connected Text: 23 Reading Words: 23 Word Recognition: 25	Teacher Models Reading Connected Text: 26 Reading Words: 26 Word Recognition: 28
		Visual Discrimination: 24	Visual Discrimination: 25	Visual Discrimination: 28, 29	Visual Discrimination: 26, 27	Visual Discrimination: 29, 30
Comprehension		Note Details: 22 Make Connections: 22	Note Details: 23 Make Connections: 23	Literal Comprehension: 26 Note Details: 26 Make Inferences: 26 Predict/Confirm Predictions: 26 Make Connections: 26	Note Details: 24 Make Inferences: 24 Make Connections: 24	Note Details: 27 Predict/Confirm Predictions: 27 Make Connections: 27

Key: (for Teachers)   √= informal assessment   Numbers = exercise numbers   Bold face type = first appearance

		Lesson 66	Lesson 67	Lesson 68	Lesson 69	Lesson 70
Phonemic Awareness		Onset Rime: 11, 16	Onset Rime: 10	Onset Rime: 12, 23, 25		Onset Rime: 6, 16
Print Awareness		Copying Text: 30	Copying Text: 27	Copying Text: 33	Copying Text: 33	Copying Text: 31
Letter Sound Correspondence		Review: 1 (ŭ) Review: 2 (ŭ, ŏ, a, ĭ) Review: 4 (ă, th, n, ŭ, ŏ, c, h, ĕ) √: 3, 5	Review: 1 (ă, ĕ, th, h) Review: 2 (m, ŏ, c, a, t, d, ŭ, r), 4 √: 3	Introduction: 1 **(g)** Review: 3 (g, c, d, t) Review: 5 (g, ŭ, h, ĕ, n, ā, ŏ, ĭ) √: 2, 4, 6	Review: 1 (g) Review: 2 (g, d, t, c) Review: 4 (g, ŭ, h, ŏ, f, ĭ, ā, th), 6 √: 3, 5	Review: 1 (g) Review: 2 (g, ŭ, d, t) Review: 4 (g, ĭ, ā, n, ē, ŏ, a, h) √: 3, 5
		Phonograms: 1 (ŏ) Phonograms: 2 (t, ĭ, ŏ, f)	Phonograms: 1 (ŏ, ĭ, t, r)	Phonograms: 1 (n, ŏ, t, a, f)	Phonograms: 1: (a, n, t, ŏ, n)	Phonograms: 1 (m) Phonograms: 2 (a, n, m, ŏ, ĭ) Sound Identification Mastery Test 13 after L70
Phonics and Word Recognition	**Irregular**					
	Regular	Blending Sounds into Words: 6, 7, 9, 11 **(run, fun)**, 12, 14 **(sun)**, 16, 18, 20 √: 8, 10, 13, 15, 17, 19, 21, 22	Blending Sounds into Words: 5 **(nut)**, 6 **(cut)**, 7, 9, 10, 11, 13, 14, 16, 18, 19 √: 8, 12, 15, 17, 20	Blending Sounds into Words: 7, 9, 11, 12 **(dot)**, 13, 14 **(sin)**, 16, 18, 20, 22, 23 **(has)**, 25 **(hat)** √: 8, 10, 15, 17, 19, 21, 24, 26	Blending Sounds into Words: 7, 9, 11, 12 **(us)**, 14, 15 **(mud)**, 17, 18, 20, 22, 23 **(ant)**, 25 √: 8, 10, 13, 16, 19, 21, 24, 26	Blending Sounds into Words: 6, 8, 10, 12, 14 **(rag)**, 16 **(made, fade)**, 17 **(rug)**, 19, 21, 23 √: 7, 9, 11, 13, 15, 18, 20, 22
		Reading Stories by Blending Sounds into Words: 23, 24 √: 25	Reading Stories by Blending Sounds into Words: 21, 22 √: 23	Reading Stories by Blending Sounds into Words: 27, 28 √: 29	Reading Stories by Blending Sounds into Words: 27, 28 √: 29	Reading Stories by Blending Sounds into Words: 24, 25 √: 26
		V-C: 3 C-V-C: 3	V-C: 2 C-V-C: 2	V-C: 2 C-V-C: 2	V-C: 2 C-V-C: 2	V-C: 3 C-V-C: 3
Fluency		Reading Words: 7, 9, 12, 14, 18, 20, 22 Rhyming: 11, 16 √: 8, 10, 13, 15, 17, 19, 21	Reading Words: 7, 9, 14, 16, 18, 19 Rhyming: 10 √: 8, 12, 15, 17, 20	Reading Words: 7, 9, 14, 16, 18, 20, 22 Rhyming: 12, 23, 25 √: 8, 10, 15, 17, 19, 21, 24, 26	Reading Words: 7, 9, 12, 15, 18, 20, 22, 23, 25 √: 8, 10, 13, 16, 19, 21, 26	Rhyming: 6, 16 Reading Words: 8, 10, 12, 14, 17, 19, 21, 23 √: 9, 11, 13, 15, 18, 20, 22
		Teacher Models Reading Connected Text: 26 Reading Words: 26 Word Recognition: 28	Teacher Models Reading Connected Text: 24 Word Recognition: 26	Teacher Models Reading Connected Text: 30 Word Recognition: 32	Teacher Models Reading Connected Text: 30 Word Recognition: 32	Teacher Models Reading Connected Text: 27 Reading Words: 27 Word Recognition: 29
		Visual Discrimination: 29, 30	Visual Discrimination: 27	Visual Discrimination: 33	Visual Discrimination: 33	Visual Discrimination: 30, 31
Comprehension		Predict/Confirm Predictions: 27 Note Details: 27 Make Inferences: 27 Make Connections: 27	Predict/Confirm Predictions: 25 Note details: 25 Make Connections: 25	Note Details: 31 Make Connections: 31	Note Details: 31 Make Connections: 31	Note Details: 28 Make Inferences: 28 Make Connections: 28

Key: (for Teachers)   √ = informal assessment   Numbers = exercise numbers   Bold face type = first appearance

		Lesson 71	Lesson 72	Lesson 73	Lesson 74	Lesson 75
Phonemic Awareness		Onset Rime: 7, 12	Onset Rime: 17	Onset Rime: 10, 14	Onset Rime: 7, 9, 20	Onset Rime: 15, 16, 17
Print Awareness		Copying Text: 25	Copying Text: 31	Copying Text: 26	Copying Text: 28	Copying Text: 26
Letter Sound Correspondence		Review: 1 (m, ŭ, ĭ, a, s, r) Review: 2 (ā, h, ŏ, c, ē, f, g, t) √: 3	Introduction: 1 **(l)** Review: 3 (l, r, ŭ, g) Review: 5 (l, s, ŭ, g, ĭ, ŏ, ā, h) √: 2, 4, 6	Review: 1 (l) Review: 2 (l, ŭ, ŏ, ĭ) Review: 4 (l, h, c, ĭ, g, ā, ŏ, n) √: 3, 5	Review: 1 (l) Review: 2 (g, l, ŭ, r) Review: 4 (h, t, ĭ, f, l, ē, ā, ŏ), 6 √: 3, 5	Review: 1 (ĭ, c, n, t, s) Review: 2 (ŭ, g, ŏ, th, ē, h, a, l) √: 3
		Phonograms: 1 (ŏ, m, ĭ, f, t)	Phonograms: 1(ŏ, n, m a, t)	Phonograms: 1 (m, n, ŏ, r)	Phonograms: 1 (ŏ, t, m, f, r, ĭ)	Phonograms: 1 (a, m ī) Mastery Test 14 after L75
Phonics and Word Recognition	*Irregular*					
	Regular	Blending Sounds into Words: 4, 5, 6, 7, 8, 10, 13, 14 **(and)**, 15 √: 9, 11	Blending Sounds into Words: 7, 9, 11, 13, 15, 17, 19, 20, 21 √: 8, 10, 12, 14, 16, 18	Blending Sounds into Words: 6, 8, 10, 12, 14 **(came)**, 15, 16 **(fig)**, 17 √: 7, 9, 11, 13	Blending Sounds into Words: 7, 9, 11, 12, 13, 16, 17, 18 **(late)**, 20, 21 √: 8, 10, 19	Blending Sounds into Words: 4 **(sand)**, 6, 8 **(rain)**, 10, 11, 12, 15 **(lick)**, 16 **(hate)**, 17 √: 5, 7, 9, 19
		Reading Stories by Blending Sounds into Words: 18, 19 √: 20	Reading Stories by Blending Sounds into Words: 24, 25 √: 26	Reading Stories by Blending Sounds into Words: 20, 21 √: 22	Reading Stories by Blending Sounds into Words: 22, 23 √: 24	Reading Stories by Blending Sounds into Words: 20, 21 Reading Words: 24 √25
		V-C: 2, 4 C-V-C: 3, 5	V-C: 2, 4 C-V-C: 3, 5	V-C: 2 C-V-C: 3	V-C: 2, 4, 6 C-V-C: 3, 5	V-C: 2, 3, 4 C-V-C: 5 Blending Sounds into Words
Fluency		Rhyming: 7, 12 Reading Words: 16 √: 17	Rhyming: 17 Reading Words: 22 √: 23	Rhyming: 10, 14 Reading Words: 18 √: 19	Rhyming: 7, 9, 20 Reading Words: 14 √15	Reading Words: 13 Rhyming: 15, 16, 17 √: 14
		Teacher Models Reading Connected Text: 21 Reading Words: 21 Word Recognition: 23	Teacher Models Reading Connected Text: 27 Reading Words: 27 Word Recognition: 29	Teacher Models Reading Connected Text: 23 Reading Words: 23 Word Recognition: 25	Teacher Models Reading Connected Text: 25 Reading Words: 23 Word Recognition: 27	Reading Connected Text: 24
		Visual Discrimination: 25	Visual Discrimination: 31	Visual Discrimination: 26	Visual Discrimination: 28	Visual Discrimination: 26
Comprehension		Note Details: 22 Make Connections: 22	Predict/Confirm Predictions: 28	Note Details: 24 Make Connections: 24	Note Details: 26 Make Connections: 26	Literal Questions: 21 Note Details: 22 Make Inferences: 22
		Match Words to Pictures: 24, 25	Match Words to Pictures: 30, 31	Match Words to Pictures: 26	Match Words to Pictures: 28	Match Words to Pictures: 26

Key: (for Teachers) √= informal assessment Numbers = exercise numbers Bold face type = first appearance

		Lesson 76	Lesson 77	Lesson 78	Lesson 79	Lesson 80
Phonemic Awareness		Onset Rime: 7, 10, 15	Onset Rime: 13, 14	Onset Rime: 6	Onset Rime: 12	Onset Rime: 15
Print Awareness		Copying Text: 27	Copying Text: 29	Copying Text: 28	Copying Text: 26	Copying Text: 28
Letter Sound Correspondence		Introduction: 1 **(w)** Review: 3 (w, r, l, ŭ) Review: 5 (w, g, ă, ŏ, ĕ, h, f, ĭ) √: 2, 4, 6	Review: 1 (w) Review: 2 (w, l, ŭ, m) Review: 4 (a, c, d, w, ĭ, r, ŏ, g), 6 √: 3, 5	Review: 1(w) Review: 2 (w, r, l, m) Review: 4 (ĕ, g, h, ĭ, w, f, n, ă) √: 3, 5	Review: 1 (l, ĭ, ă, a, ŏ, g, ŭ, t) Review: 3 (ĕ, s, th, h, d, r, w, c), 5 √: 2, 4	Introduction: 1 **(sh)** Review: 3 (sh, th, s, h) Review: 5 (sh, ĭ, l, ĕ, ŏ, w, g, ŭ) √: 2, 4, 6
						Mastery Test 15 after L80
Phonics and Word Recognition / **Irregular**						
Phonics and Word Recognition / **Regular**		Blending Sounds into Words: 7 **(hand)**, 9 **(lock)**, 10, 11, 13, 15 **(land)**, 16, 17, 18 √: 8, 9, 10, 12, 14	Blending Sounds into Words: 7, 9, 11, 13 **(same)**, 14 **(game)**, 16, 18, 19, 20 **(mail)** √: 8, 10, 12, 15	Blending Sounds into Words: 6 **(sail, nail)**, 7, 11, 13, 15, 17 **(we)**, 18, 19 √: 8, 12, 14, 16	Blending Sounds into Words: 6, 8 **(rut)**, 9, 10 **(sag)**, 12 **(ill, mill)**, 13, 15, 16 **(will)**, 17 √: 7, 11, 14	Blending Sounds into Words: 7, 9, 11, 13, 15, 16, 17, 18, 19 √: 8, 10, 12, 14
		Reading Stories by Blending Sounds into Words: 21, 22 Reading Words: 25 √: 26	Reading Stories by Blending Sounds into Words: 23, 24 Reading Words: 27 √: 28	Reading Stories by Blending Sounds into Words: 22, 23 Reading Words: 26 √: 27	Reading Stories by Blending Sounds into Words: 20, 21 Reading Words: 24 √: 25	Reading Stories by Blending Sounds into Words: 22, 23 Reading Words: 26 √: 27
		V-C: 1, 3, 4 C-V-C: 2, 3, 4	V-C: 1, C-V-C: 1, 2	V-C: 1, 3 C-V-C: 1, 2, 3	V-C: 1 C-V-C: 1	V-C: 1 C-V-C: 1 Blending Sounds into Words
Fluency		Rhyming: 7, 10, 15 Reading Words: 19 √: 20	Rhyming: 13, 14 Reading Words: 16, 21 √: 17, 22	Rhyming: 6 Reading Words: 9, 20 √: 10, 21	Rhyming: 12 Reading Words: 18 √: 19	Rhyming: 15 Reading Words: 20 √: 21
		Word Recognition: 24 Reading Connected Text: 25	Word Recognition: 26 Reading Connected Text: 27	Word Recognition: 25 Reading Connected Text: 26	Word Recognition: 23 Reading Connected Text 24	Word Recognition: 25 Reading Connected Text: 26
		Visual Discrimination: 27	Visual Discrimination: 29	Visual Discrimination: 28	Visual Discrimination: 26	Visual Discrimination: 28
						Reading Words
						Curriculum-Based Assessment 80 after L80
Comprehension		Literal Questions: 22 Identify Items: 23 Make Inferences: 23	Literal Questions: 24 Note Details: 25 Make Connections: 25	Literal Questions: 23 Predict/Confirm Predictions: 24 Make Inferences: 24 Note Details: 24	Literal Questions: 21, 22 Identify Items: 22	Literal Questions: 23 Predict/Confirm Predictions: 24 Note Details: 24 Make Connections: 24
		Match Words to Pictures: 27	Match Words to Pictures: 29	Match Words to Pictures: 28	Match Words to Pictures: 26	Match Words to Pictures: 28

Key: (for Teachers)　　　√= informal assessment　　　Numbers = exercise numbers　　　Bold face type = first appearance

		Lesson 81	Lesson 82	Lesson 83	Lesson 84	Lesson 85
Phonemic Awareness		Onset Rime: 18, 20	Onset Rime: 7, 18	Onset Rime: 7	Onset Rime: 16, 18	Onset Rime: 14, 16
Print Awareness		Copying Text: 30	Copying Text: 27	Copying Text: 23	Copying Text: 28	Copying Text: 25
Letter Sound Correspondence		Review: 1 (sh) Review: 2 (sh, s, f, th) Review: 4 (w, ŭ, l, g, ĭ, sh, n, ā), 6 √: 3, 5	Review: 1 (sh) Review: 2 (sh, l, th, g) Review: 4 (a, r, c, sh, ŭ, w, ŏ, d), 6 √: 3, 5	Review: 1 (l, f, ē, ā) Review: 2 (w, ŭ, sh, ĭ, ŏ, t, g, a) √: 3	Review: 1 (sh, w, h, ŏ) Review: 2 (ĭ, g, ŭ, th, ā, n, a, l), 4 √: 3	Review: 1 (sh, g, ā, ŭ, c, t, ŏ) Review: 3 (a, w, m, l) √: 2
			Phonograms: 27	Phonograms: 23	Phonograms: 28	Phonograms: 25
		Phonograms: 1 (s)	Phonograms: 1 (s)		Phonograms: 1 (h)	Phonograms: 1 (h)
						Mastery Test 16 after L85
Phonics and Word Recognition	**Irregular**			V-C: 1 (is)	V-C: 3 (is)	V-C: 2 (is)
	Regular	Blending Sounds into Words: 7, 8, 9, 12 (**ron**), 13, 14, 15, 18 (**tame**), 20 √: 19, 21	Blending Sounds into Words: 7, 8 (**little**), 9 (**she**), 12, 13, 14, 15, 18 √: 19	Blending Sounds into Words: 4, 5, 6 (**got**), 7, 10, 11, 12, 13	Blending Sounds into Words: 5, 6, 7, 8 (**shack**), 11, 12, 13, 16, 18 √: 17, 19	Blending Sounds into Words: 4, 5, 6, 9, 10, 11, 14 (**did**), 16 √: 15
		Reading Stories by Blending Sounds into Words: 24, 25 Reading Words: 28 √: 29	Reading Stories by Blending Sounds into Words: 20, 21 Reading Words: 24 √: 25	Reading Stories by Blending Sounds into Words: 16, 17 Reading Words: 20 √: 21	Reading Stories by Blending Sounds into Words: 22, 23 Reading Words: 26 √: 27	Reading Stories by Blending Sounds into Words: 19, 20 Reading Words: 23 √: 24
		V-C: 2	V-C: 2 C-V-C: 2	V-C: 1 C-V-C: 1	V-C: 2, 4 C-V-C: 2	V-C: 3 C-V-C: 3 Blending Sounds into Words
Fluency		Reading Words: 10, 16, 22 Rhyming: 18, 20 √: 11, 17, 23	Rhyming: 7, 18 Reading Words: 10, 16 √: 11, 17	Rhyming: 7 Reading Words: 8, 14 √: 9, 15	Reading Words: 9, 14, 20 Rhyming: 16, 18 √: 10, 15, 21	Reading Words: 7, 12, 17 Rhyming: 14, 16 √: 8, 13, 18
		Word Recognition: 27 Reading Connected Text: 28	Word Recognition: 23 Reading Connected Text: 24	Word Recognition: 19 Reading Connected Text: 20	Word Recognition: 25 Reading Connected Text: 26	Word Recognition: 22 Reading Connected Text: 23
		Visual Discrimination: 30		Visual Discrimination: 23	Visual Discrimination: 28	Visual Discrimination: 25
Comprehension		Literal Questions: 25 Predict/Confirm Predictions: 25, 26 Note Details: 25	Literal Questions: 21 Predict/Confirm Predictions: 22 Note Details: 22	Literal Questions: 17 Predict/Confirm Predictions: 18 Note Details: 18 Make Connections: 18	Literal Questions: 23 Predict/Confirm Predictions: 24 Note Details: 24 Make Connections: 24	Literal Questions: 20 Predict/Confirm Predictions: 21 Note Details: 21 Make Connections: 21
		Match Words to Pictures: 30	Match Words to Pictures: 26, 27	Match Words to Pictures: 22, 23	Match Words to Pictures: 28	Match Words to Pictures: 25

Key: (for Teachers)	√ = informal assessment	Numbers = exercise numbers	Bold face type = first appearance

		Lesson 86	Lesson 87	Lesson 88	Lesson 89	Lesson 90
Phonemic Awareness		Onset Rime: 16, 18	Onset Rime: 7, 11, 13	Onset Rime: 10, 14, 16	Onset Rime: 14	
Print Awareness			Find Punctuation: 20	Find Punctuation: 22	Find Punctuation: 20	Find Punctuation: 21
		Copying Text: 26	Copying Text: 26	Copying Text: 27	Copying Text: 25	Copying Text: 26
Letter Sound Correspondence		Review: 1 (ă, d, ŏ, th, ŭ, ĭ, m, n) Review: 3 (w, l, sh, ŭ, ĕ, a, f, g), 5 √: 2, 4	Review: 1 (ĭ, n, h, ŭ, t, ĕ, ŏ, a) Review: 3 (ŏ, w, sh, ă) √: 2	Introduction: 1 (**l**) Review: 3 (l, ĭ, ă, t) Review: 5 (l, ŏ, sh, ĕ, w, l, ŭ, g) √: 2, 4, 6	Review: 1 (l) Review: 2 (l, h, l, ĭ) Review: 4 (l, g, a, sh, w, ŏ, ŭ, l) √: 3, 5	Review: 1 (l) Review: 2 (l, ĭ, t, l) Review: 4 (m, n, ă, h, g, l, ŭ, sh), 6 √: 3, 5
		Phonograms: 26	Phonograms: 26	Phonograms: 27	Phonograms: 25	Phonograms: 26
						Saying Sounds
						Mastery Test 17 after L90
Phonics and Word Recognition	**Irregular**				**said: 8** √: 9	said: 14 √: 15
		V-C: 5 (is)		V-C: 5 (is) C-V-C: 6 (his, has)	V-C: 5 (is) C-V-C: 5 (his), 6 (has)	V-C: 5 (is) C-V-C: 5 (his)
	Regular	Blending Sounds into Words: 6 (**ears**), 7, 8, 11 (**runs**), 12, 13, 16, 18 (**hears**) √: 17, 19	Blending Sounds into Words: 4, 5, 6 (**suns**), 7 (**tail**), 11 (**guns**), 13 √: 8, 12, 14	Blending Sounds into Words: 7, 8, 9 (**wins**), 10 (**dish**), 14, 16 √: 11, 15	Blending Sounds into Words: 6 (**hats**), 7, 12, 13, 14 (**wish**)	Blending Sounds into Words: 7, 8 (**shut**), 9 (**tacks**), 12 (**with**), 13 (**sacks**)
		Reading Stories by Blending Sounds into Words: 20, 21 Reading Words: 24 √: 25	Reading Stories by Blending Sounds into Words: 17, 18 Reading Words: 21, 22 √: 23	Reading Stories by Blending Sounds into Words: 19, 20 Reading Words: 23, 24 √: 25	Reading Stories by Blending and Sounding Out Words: 17, 18 Reading Words: 21, 22 √: 23	Reading Stories by Blending Sounds into Words: 18, 19 Reading Words: 22, 23 √: 24
		V-C: 1, 3 C-V-C: 1, 2, 3, 4	V-C: 1, 3, 5 C-V-C: 1, 2, 4, 5	V-C: 1, 3, 7 C-V-C: 2, 4	V-C: 1, 3 C-V-C: 2, 4, 7	C-V-C: 1, 2, 3, 4
Fluency		Reading Words: 9, 14 Rhyming: 16, 18 √: 10, 15	Rhyming: 7, 11, 13 Reading Words: 9, 15 √: 10, 16	Rhyming: 10, 14, 16 Reading Words: 12, 17 √: 13, 18	Reading Words: 10, 15 Rhyming: 14 √: 11, 16	Reading Words: 10, 16 √: 11, 17
		Word Recognition: 23 Reading Connected Text: 24	Reading Connected Text: 21, 22 Saying Sentences: 24	Reading Connected Text: 23, 24 Saying Sentences: 26	Reading Connected Text: 21, 22 Saying Sentences: 23	Reading Connected Text: 22, 23 Saying Sentences: 25
		Visual Discrimination: 26	Visual Discrimination: 25	Visual Discrimination: 27	Visual Discrimination: 25	Visual Discrimination: 26
Comprehension		Literal Questions: 21 Predict/Confirm Predictions: 22 Note Details: 22 Make Inferences: 22 Make Connections: 22	Literal Questions: 18 Make Inferences: 18 Predict/Confirm Predictions: 19 Note Details: 19	Literal Questions: 20 Predict/Confirm Predictions: 21 Note Details: 21 Make Connections: 21	Literal Questions: 18 Predict/Confirm Predictions: 19 Note Details: 19 Make Connections: 19	Literal Comprehension: 19 Predict/Confirm Predictions: 20 Note Details: 20 Make Connections: 20
		Match Words to Pictures: 26	Match Words to Pictures: 26	Match Words to Pictures: 27	Match Words to Pictures: 25	Match Words to Pictures: 16

Key: (for Teachers)   √= informal assessment   Numbers = exercise numbers   Bold face type = first appearance

		Lesson 91	Lesson 92	Lesson 93	Lesson 94	Lesson 95
Phonemic Awareness		Onset Rime: 4	Onset Rime: 18			Onset Rime: 11
Print Awareness					Finding Punctuation: 24	Finding Punctuation: 21
		Copying Text: 23, 25	Copying Text: 28, 30	Copying Text: 29, 30	Copying Text: 30	Copying Text: 27
Letter Sound Correspondence		Review: 1 (g, d, ŭ, ā) Review: 2 (f, th, sh, ĭ, ŏ, c, l, t) √: 3	Introduction: 1 **(k)** Review: 3 (k, g, c, l) Review: 5 (k, ŭ, sh, ĭ, w, l, ē, a) √: 2, 4, 6	Review: 1 (k) Review: 2 (k, c, t, g) Review: 4 (ŭ, sh, ā, ŏ, k, ĭ, w, r), 6 √: 3, 5	Review: 1 (k) Review: 2 (k, t, c, h) Review: 4 (l, sh, w, k, ŏ, ĭ, l, ā), 6 √: 3, 5	Review: 1 (l, l, ĭ, a, th, ā, g, d) Review: 3 (w, ŭ, sh, k, n, h, ŏ, ē) √: 2, 4
		Phonograms: 25	Phonograms: 30	Phonograms: 30	Phonograms: 30	Phonograms: 27
				Phonograms: 1 (u)	Phonograms: 1 (u)	
						Mastery Test 18 after L95
Phonics and Word Recognition	**Irregular**	said: 13 √: 14	said: 7 √: 8	said: 19 √: 20	**was:** 20 √: 21	said: 12 was: 17 √: 13, 18
		C-V-C: 3 (has)	V-C: 1 (is)			C-V-C: 3 (his)
	Regular	Blending Sounds into Words: 4 **(tears)**, 5, 6 **(win)**, 9, 10, 11 **(now)**, 12 **(licks)**	Blending Sounds into Words: 9, 10 **(rigs)**, 13, 14 **(digs)**, 15, 18 **(names)**, 19 **(games)**	Blending Sounds into Words: 7 **(cow)**, 8, 9, 10, 13, 14 **(how)**, 15, 16 **(mom)**, 18	Blending Sounds into Words: 7, 8 **(shot)**, 9, 10, 13, 14, 15, 18, 19	Blending Sounds into Words: 5 **(gates)**, 6, 7 **(feel)**, 8, 11, 16 **(gate)**
		Reading Stories by Blending Sounds into Words: 17, 18 Reading Connected Text: 20 √: 21	Reading Stories by Blending Sounds into Words: 22, 23 Reading Connected Text: 25 √: 26	Reading Stories by Blending Sounds into Words: 23, 24 Reading Connected Text: 26 √: 27	Reading Stories by Blending Sounds into Words: 25 Reading Connected Text: 26 √: 28	Reading Stories by Blending Sounds into Words: 22 Reading Connected Text: 23 √: 25
		Reading Connected Text: 23				
		C-V-C: 1, 2, 4	V-C: 1 C-V-C: 2, 3, 4	V-C: 4 C-V-C: 2, 3, 4	V-C: 8 C-V-C: 2, 3, 4, 5, 6, 7	V-C: 2 C-V-C: 1, 2, 4, 5
						Blending Sounds into Words
Fluency		Rhyming: 4 Reading Words: 7, 15 √: 8, 16	Reading Words: 11, 16, 20 Rhyming: 18 √: 12, 17, 21	Reading Words: 11, 17, 21 √: 12, 17, 22	Reading Words: 11, 16, 22 √: 12, 17, 23	Reading Words: 9, 14, 19 Rhyming: 11 √: 10, 15, 20
		Reading Connected Text: 20 Saying Sentences: 22	Reading Connected Text: 25 Saying Sentences: 27	Reading Connected Text: 26 Saying Sentences: 28	Reading Connected Text: 26 Saying Sentences: 29	Reading Connected Text: 23 Saying Sentences: 26
		Visual Discrimination: 24, 25	Visual Discrimination: 29, 30	Visual Discrimination: 30	Visual Discrimination: 30	Visual Discrimination: 27
Comprehension		Literal Questions: 18 Predict/Confirm Predictions: 19 Make Inferences: 19 Make Connections: 19	Literal Questions: 23 Predict/Confirm Predictions: 24 Note Details: 24 Make Connections: 24	Literal Questions: 24 Predict/Confirm Predictions: 25 Note Details: 25 Make Connections: 25	Literal Questions: 26 Predict/Confirm Predictions: 27 Make Connections: 27 Note Details: 27	Literal Questions: 23 Predict/Confirm Predictions: 24 Note Details: 24 Make Inferences: 24 Make Connections: 24
		Match Words to Pictures: 25	Match Words to Pictures: 30	Matching Words to Pictures: 30	Matching Words to Pictures: 30	Match Words to Pictures: 27

		Lesson 96	Lesson 97	Lesson 98	Lesson 99	Lesson 100
Phonemic Awareness					Onset Rime: 8	
Print Awareness		Finding Punctuation: 18	Finding Punctuation: 18	Finding Punctuation: 18	Finding Punctuation: 15	Finding Punctuation: 14
		Copying Text: 24	Copying Text: 24	Copying Text: 23	Copying Text: 21	Copying Text: 19
Letter Sound Correspondence		Review: 1 (l, k, sh, w, ŭ, ŏ, ā, ĭ) Review: 3 (l, g, c, r) √: 2	Review: 1 (ŭ, k, r, th, f, ā, ŏ, n), 3 Review: 4 (ē, ā, ĭ, ŏ) √: 2	Review: 1 (o) Introduction: 2 (**ō**) Review: 3 (ŏ, ā, ē, k) √: 4	Review: 1 (ŏ) Review: 2 (ŏ, ĭ, ā, ŏ) Review: 4 (ŏ, ĭ, k, ē, ŭ, a, w, sh) √: 3, 5	Review: 1 (ŏ) Review: 2 (ŏ, ŏ, ĭ, ā) Review: 4 (g, ŏ, w, t, s, ŭ, ā, k) √: 3
		Phonograms: 24	Phonograms: 24	Phonograms: 23	Phonograms: 21	Phonograms: 19
						Identifying Sounds
						Mastery Test 19 after L100
Phonics and Word Recognition	**Irregular**	said: 7 was: 16 √: 8, 17	his: 5 was: 11 √: 12	was: 9 √: 10		
			C-V-C: 3 (has)	C-V-C: 1 (has)	V-C: 1 (is)	
	Regular	Reading Words: 4, 10, 13 Blending Sounds into Words: 9	Reading Words: 5 (**nod**), 15 Blending Sounds into Words: 8 (**hits**), 9 (**kicks**), 10 (**him**)	Reading Words: 5 (**rats, no**), 11 (**hug**), 15 Blending Sounds into Words: 8 (**kiss**), 14 (**those**)	Blending Sounds into Words: 6 (**cakes**), 7 (**go**), 8 (**or, for**), 9 Reading Words: 12 (**so**)	Reading Words: 7 (**rocks, nose, socks**), 10 Blending Sounds into Words: 13 (**teeth**)
		Reading Stories by Blending Sounds into Words: 19 Reading Connected Text: 20 √: 22	Reading Stories by Blending Sounds into Words: 19 Reading Connected Text: 20 √: 22	Reading Stories by Blending Sounds into Words: 18 Reading Connected Text: 19 √: 21	Reading Stories by Blending Sounds into Words: 16 Reading Connected Text: 17 √: 16, 19	Reading Stories by Blending Sounds into Words: 14 Reading Connected Text: 15 √: 17
		C-V-C: 1, 2, 3, 4, 5	V-C: 4 C-V-C: 1, 2, 4	V-C: 1 C-V-C: 1	C-V-C: 1	V-C: 1 C-V-C: 1
Fluency		Reading Words: 5, 11, 14 √: 6, 12, 15	Reading Words: 6, 13, 16 √: 7, 14, 17	Reading Words: 6, 12, 16 Rhyming: 11 √: 7, 13, 17	Rhyming: 8 Reading Words: 10, 13 √: 11, 14	Reading Words: 8, 11 √: 9, 12
		Reading Connected Text: 20 Saying Sentences: 23	Reading Connected Text: 20 Saying Sentences: 23	Reading Connected Text: 19 Saying Sentences: 22	Reading Connected Text: 17 Saying Sentences: 20	Reading Connected Text: 15 Saying Sentences: 18
		Visual Discrimination: 24	Visual Discrimination: 24	Visual Discrimination: 23	Visual Discrimination: 21	Visual Discrimination: 19
						Curriculum-Based Assessment 100 after L100
Comprehension		Literal Comprehension: 20 Predict/Confirm Predictions: 21 Make Connections: 21	Literal Questions: 20 Predict/Confirm Predictions: 21	Literal Questions: 19 Predict/Confirm Predictions: 19, 20	Literal Questions: 16, 17 Note Details: 18	Literal Questions: 14 Recall Details: 15 Predict/Confirm Predictions: 15 Note Details: 16 Make Connections: 16
		Match Words to Pictures: 24	Match Words to Pictures: 24	Match Words to Pictures: 23	Match Words to Pictures: 21	Match Words to Pictures: 19

Key: (for Teachers) √ = informal assessment   Numbers = exercise numbers   Bold face type = first appearance

		Lesson 101	Lesson 102	Lesson 103	Lesson 104	Lesson 105
Phonemic Awareness						
Print Awareness		Finding Punctuation: 16	Finding Punctuation: 16	Finding Punctuation: 20		Finding Punctuation: 18
		Copying Text: 21	Copying Text: 21	Copying Text: 25	Copying Text: 20	Copying Text: 24
Letter Sound Correspondence		Review: 1 (ŭ, ŏ, ō, ē, sh, th, l, r) Review: 3 (c, g, k, d) √: 2	Introduction: 1 **(v)** Review: 3 (f, v, w, th) Review: 5 (v, ō, k, ī, sh, ā, n, u) √: 2, 4, 6	Review: 1 (v) Review: 2 (v, th, sh, f) Review: 4 (v, k, ō, ā, ŏ, c, ĭ, g) √: 3, 5	Review: 1 (v) Review: 2 (v, w, f, l) Review: 4 (l, ŭ, v, sh, ē, t, sh, k, ō), 6 √: 3, 5	Review: 1 (r, h, c, w, k, v, ō, ŏ) Review: 3 (n, ē, sh, g) √: 2
		Phonograms: 21	Phonograms: 21	Phonograms: 25	Phonograms: 20	Phonograms: 24
					Phonograms: 1 (d)	Phonograms: 1 (d)
						Mastery Test 20 after L105
Phonics and Word Recognition	**Irregular**	**of:** 7 √: 8	now: 7 of: 14 √: 15	of: 9 was: 15 √: 10, 16		**to:** 4 said: 10 √: 5, 11
		C-V-C: 1 (has)			V-C: 2 (is)	C-V-C: 2 (has)
	Regular	Reading Words: 4, 9, 13 Blending Sounds into Words: 11 **(kitten)**, 12	Reading Words: 7, 10 Blending Sounds into Words: 13 **(have)**	Reading Words: 6, 12, 17 Blending Sounds into Words: 11 **(hold)**	Reading Words: 7, 10 Blending Sounds into Words: 13 **(give)**, 14 **(save, gave)**	Reading Words: 6, 12, 15 **(shave, rugs)** Blending Sounds into Words: 7 **(hugs)**
		Reading Stories by Blending Sounds into Words: 16 Reading Connected Text: 17 √: 19	Reading Stories by Blending Sounds into Words: 16 Reading Connected Text: 17 √: 19	Reading Stories by Blending Sounds into Words: 20 Reading Connected Text: 21 √: 23	Reading Stories by Blending Sounds into Words: 15 Reading Connected Text: 16 √: 18	Reading Stories by Blending Sounds into Words: 19 Reading Connected Text: 20 √: 19, 22
		C-V-C: 1	V-C: 1 C-V-C: 1	V-C: 1 C-V-C: 1	V-C: 2 C-V-C: 2	V-C: 4 C-V-C: 2, 3, 5, 6, 7
						Blending Sounds into Words Reading Words
Fluency		Reading Words: 5, 10, 14 √: 6, 15	Reading Words: 8, 11 √: 9, 12	Reading Words: 7, 13, 18 √: 8, 14, 19	Reading Words: 8, 11 Rhyming: 14 √: 9, 12	Reading Words: 8, 13, 16 √: 9, 14, 17
		Reading Connected Text: 17 Saying Sentences: 20	Reading Connected Text: 17 Saying Sentences: 20	Reading Connected Text; 21 Saying Sentences: 24	Reading Connected Text: 16 Saying Sentences: 19	Reading Connected Text: 20 Saying Sentences: 23
		Visual Discrimination: 21	Visual Discrimination: 21	Visual Discrimination: 25	Visual Discrimination: 20	Visual Discrimination: 24
Comprehension		Literal Questions: 16, 17 Make Inferences: 18 Make Connections: 18	Literal Questions: 17 Note Details: 18 Make Connections: 18r	Literal Questions: 21 Make Connections: 21	Literal Questions: 16 Note Details: 17 Make Connections: 17	Literal Questions: 19 Make Inferences: 20 Predict/Confirm Predictions: 21 Note Details: 21 Make Connections: 21
		Match Words to Pictures: 21	Match Words to Pictures: 21	Match Words to Pictures: 25	Match Words to Pictures: 20	Match Words to Pictures: 24

Reading Mastery Signature Edition, Grade K

		Lesson 106	Lesson 107	Lesson 108	Lesson 109	Lesson 110
Phonemic Awareness			Onset Rime: 6			
Print Awareness		Finding Punctuation: 13				
		Copying Text: 19	Copying Text: 24	Copying Text: 24	Copying Text: 20	Copying Text: 18
Letter Sound Correspondence		Review: 1 (ă, l, ŭ, g, h, ŏ, s, c) Review: 3 (v, k, th, ō) √: 2	Review: 1 (ē, ĭ, l, sh, n, t, d), 3 Review: 4 (ā, k, v, ŭ, g, ō, ŏ, w) √: 2, 5	Introduction: 1 (p) Review: 3 (p, d, g, t) Review: 5 (p, k, v, ŭ, ō, sh, h, n) √: 2, 4, 6	Review: 1 (p) Review: 2 (p, d, k, g) Review: 4 (l, l, p, v, w, ā, ō, k), 6 √: 3, 5	Review: 1 (p, t, g, v) Review: 3 (p, k, n, sh, ŏ, c, ō, ŭ) √: 2, 4
		Phonograms: 19	Phonograms: 24	Phonograms: 24	Phonograms: 22	Phonograms: 18
						Mastery Test 21 after L110
Phonics and Word Recognition	**Irregular**	to: 8 √: 9	to: 7 was: 11 now: 14 said: 17 √: 8, 12, 18	was: 8 of: 13 to: 14 √: 9	said: 10 of: 14	to: 8 √: 9
			C-V-C: 2 (his, has)			C-V-C: 3 (his)
	Regular	Reading Words: 4 Blending Sounds into Words: 7 (**goat**), 10	Reading Words: 6 (**oats, goats, coats**), 9, 13, 14 Blending Sounds into Words: 19 (**cold**) √: 10	Reading Words: 7 (**mop, cop, top**), 10, 15 Blending Sounds into Words: 16, 17	Reading Words: 7 (**ship**) Blending Sounds into Words: 11, 12 (**dip**), 13 (**down**)	Reading Words: 5 (**fog, log**) Blending Sounds into Words: 10 (**dog**), 11
		Reading Stories by Blending Sounds into Words: 14 Reading Connected Text: 15 √: 14, 17	Reading Connected Text: 20 √: 21	Reading Connected Text: 20 √: 21	Reading Connected Text: 16 √: 17	Reading Connected Text: 14 √: 15
		V-C: 2 C-V-C: 1, 2, 3, 4	C-V-C: 1, 2, 3	V-C: 3 C-V-C: 1, 2, 3	V-C: 1 C-V-C: 1, 2, 3	C-V-C: 1, 2, 3
						Reading Words
Fluency		Reading Words: 5, 11 Rhyming: 10 √: 6	Rhyming: 6 Reading Words: 15 √: 16	Rhyming: 7 Reading Words: 11, 18 √: 12, 19	Reading Words: 8, 15 √: 9	Reading Words: 6, 12 √: 7, 13
		Reading Connected Text: 15 Saying Sentences: 18	Reading Connected Text: 22	Reading Connected Text: 22	Reading Connected Text: 18	Reading Connected Text: 16
		Visual Discrimination: 19	Visual Discrimination: 24	Visual Discrimination: 24 Individual Checkout: 30 (16 wpm/3 errors)	Visual Discrimination: 20 Individual Checkout: 26 (18 wpm/3 errors)	Visual Discrimination: 18
						Individual Checkout: 24 (22 wpm/3 errors)
Comprehension		Literal Questions: 14 Predict/Confirm Predictions: 16 Note Details: 16	Literal Questions: 22 Predict/Confirm Predictions: 23 Note Details: 23 Make Connections: 23	Literal Questions: 22 Predict/Confirm Predictions: 23 Make Inferences: 23 Make Connections: 23	Literal Questions: 18 Note Details: 19 Make Inferences: 19 Make Connections: 19	Literal Questions: 16 Predict/Confirm Predictions: 17 Note Details: 17 Make Connections: 17
		Match Words to Pictures: 19	Match Words to Pictures: 24	Match Words to Pictures: 24	Match Words to Pictures: 20	Match Words to Pictures: 18

Key: (for Teachers) √= informal assessment   Numbers = exercise numbers   Bold face type = first appearance

		Lesson 111	Lesson 112	Lesson 113	Lesson 114	Lesson 115
Phonemic Awareness				Onset Rime: 19		Onset Rime: 12
Print Awareness		Copying Text: 17	Copying Text: 22	Copying Text: 25	Copying Text: 27	Copying Text: 26
Letter Sound Correspondence		Review: 1 (l, w, l, h) Review: 2 (â, k, ŏ, p, v, ŏ, f, s), 4 √: 3	Review: 1 (ē, ĭ, n, ā) Review: 2 (th, p, sh, k, c, ŏ, ŏ, ü) √: 3	Introduction: 1 **(ch)** Review: 3 (ch, sh, c, th) Review: 5 (ch, p, v, ŏ, l, w, k, r) √: 2, 4, 6	Review: 1 (ch) Review: 2 (g, ch, th, sh) Review: 4 (ch, v, ā, ŏ, n, p, d, k) √: 3, 5	Review: 1 (ch, c, h, v) Review: 3 (p, w, k, ŏ, r, ch, ĭ, ü), 5 √: 2, 4
		Phonograms: 17	Phonograms: 22	Phonograms: 25	Phonograms: 27	Phonograms: 26
		Phonograms: 1 (ē)	Phonograms: 1 (ē)		Phonograms: 1 (w)	Phonograms: 1
						Mastery Test 22 after L115
Phonics and Word Recognition	**Irregular**	of: 9 √: 10	**are:** 4 **car:** 5 **tar:** 6 of: 7 to: 14 √: 8, 15	car: 7 are: 13 **art:** 18 **part:** 20 √: 8, 14	car: 6 **far:** 9 **farm:** 16 are: 18 √: 7, 10, 17, 19	are: 6 **arm:** 11 farm: 12 of: 17 **cars:** 19 √: 7, 18, 20
		C-V-C: 6 (his)			C-V-C: 7	
	Regular	Reading Words: 5, 8	Blending Sounds into Words: 9, 10 **(pot)** Reading Words: 13, 16	Blending Sounds into Words: 9, 10 **(chops)** Reading Words: 15 **(shops)**	Blending Sounds into Words: 8 **(chips)** Reading Words: 13 **(road)**	Reading Words: 8 **(each)** Blending Sounds into Words: 13, 14 **(teach)**
		Reading Connected Text: 13 √: 14	Reading Connected Text: 18 √: 19	Reading Connected Text: 21 √: 22	Reading Connected Text: 22 √: 23	Reading Connected Text: 22 √: 23
		V-C: 2 C-V-C: 2, 3, 4, 5, 6	V-C: 2, 3 C-V-C: 4, 5, 7 C-V-C-C: 6	C-V-C: 3, 6 C-V: 1, 2 C-V-C-C: 5 V-C-C: 4	V-C: 5 C-V-C: 5, 6 C-V: 2, 4 C-V-C-C: 3	V-C: 5 C-V-C: 2, 4, 5 C-V: 2, 3
						Reading Connected Text
Fluency		Reading Words: 6, 11 Rhyming: 8 √: 7, 12	Reading Words: 11 √: 12, 17	Reading Words: 11, 16 Rhyming: 19 √: 12, 17	Reading Words: 11, 14, 20 √: 12, 15, 21	Reading Words: 9, 15 Rhyming: 12 √: 10, 16
		Reading Connected Text: 15	Reading Connected Text: 20	Reading Connected Text: 23	Reading Connected Text: 24	Reading Connected Text: 24
		Visual Discrimination: 17	Visual Discrimination: 22	Visual Discrimination: 25	Visual Discrimination: 27	Visual Discrimination: 26
						Individual Checkout: 33 (25 wpm/3 errors)
Comprehension		Literal Questions: 15 Make Inferences: 16 Make Connections: 16	Literal Questions: 20, 21 Predict/Confirm Predictions: 20, 21	Literal Questions: 23 Predict/Confirm Predictions: 24 Make Connections: 24	Literal Questions: 24 Note Details: 25 Make Connections: 25	Story Grammar: 21 Literal Comprehension: 24 Predict/Confirm Predictions: 24, 25 Note Details: 25 Make Connections; 25
		Match Words to Pictures: 17	Match Words to Pictures: 22	Match Words to Pictures: 25	Match Words to Pictures: 26, 27	Match Words to Pictures: 26

Key: (for Teachers) √ = informal assessment   Numbers = exercise numbers   Bold face type = first appearance

		Lesson 116	Lesson 117	Lesson 118	Lesson 119	Lesson 120
Phonemic Awareness						
Print Awareness		Copying Text: 23	Copying Text: 22	Copying Text: 18	Copying Text: 23	Copying Text: 24
Letter Sound Correspondence		Review: 1 (p, h, th, d) Review: 2 (ch, ö, ŏ, k, n, ē, l) √: 3	Review: 1 (ö, ŏ, ĭ, ā) Review: 2 (ē, p, ŭ, sh, l, ch, f, v) √: 3	Review: 1 (ē) Introduction: 2 **(e)** Review: 2 (ē, ě) Review: 3 (ē, ch, ĭ, ö) √: 4	Review: 1 (ē) Review: 2 (ē, ŭ, ŏ, ě) Review: 4 (ē, ĭ, v, p, ö, w, k, ch) √: 3, 5	Review: 1 (ē) Review: 2 (ē, ĭ, ŏ, ě) Review: 4 (p, c, v, ě, ö, a, ch, d), 6 √: 3, 5
		Phonograms: 23	Phonograms: 22		Phonograms: 23 Phonograms: 1 (l)	Phonograms: 24 Identify Sounds Mastery Test 23 after L120
Phonics and Word Recognition	Irregular	to: 4 **girl:** 11 car: 13 √: 5, 12, 14	**do:** 7 girl: 9 farm: 11 √: 8, 10, 12	of: 8 do: 10	do: 10 car: 14 √: 11, 15	do: 7
	Regular	Blending Sounds into Words: 6 **(caves)**, 7 Reading Words: 8, 15 **(waves, saves)**	Reading Words: 4 **(cows, cats)** Blending Sounds into Words: 13 **(pots)**, 14	Reading Words: 5 **(tops)**, 11 Blending Sounds into Words: 9 **(home)**	Blending Sounds into Words: 6 **(corn, take, pigs, here)** Reading Words: 16 **(more, lake)**	Reading Words: 8 **(met)**, 14 **(let, get)**, 17 Blending Sounds into Words: 11 **(there)**, 12 **(wet)**, 13 **(went)**
		Reading Connected Text: 19 √: 20	Reading Connected Text: 18 √: 19	Reading Connected Text: 14 √: 15	Reading Connected Text: 19 √: 20	Reading Connected Text: 20 √: 21
		V-C: 1, 3 C-V-C: 1, 3 C-V: 2, 3	V-C: 1 C-V-C: 1 C-V: 1 V-C-C: 1	C-V-C : 2, 4 C-V: 2 C-V-C-C: 3	V-C: 5 C-V-C: 2, 4 C-V-C-C: 3 V-C-C: 3	C-V-C: 1, 2, 3 C-V: 1 C-V-C-C: 1
Fluency		Reading Words: 9, 16 Rhyming: 15 √: 10, 17	Reading Words: 5, 15 √: 6, 16	Reading Words: 6, 12 √: 7	Reading Words: 12, 17 √: 13, 18	Reading Words: 9, 15, 18 Rhyming: 14 √: 10, 16, 19
		Reading Connected Text: 21	Reading Connected Text: 20	Reading Connected Text: 16	Reading Connected Text: 21	Reading Connected Text: 22
		Visual Discrimination: 23	Visual Discrimination: 22	Visual Discrimination: 18	Visual Discrimination: 23	Visual Discrimination: 24
						Individual Checkout: 30 (22 wpm/3 errors)
						Curriculum-Based Assessment 120 after L120
Comprehension		Story Grammar: 18 Literal Questions: 21 Make Inferences: 21, 22 Note Details: 22 Make Connections: 22	Story Grammar: 17 Literal Questions: 20 Predict/Confirm Predictions: 20, 21 Note Details: 21 Make Connections: 21	Story Grammar: 13 Literal Questions: 16 Make Inferences: 17 Make Connections: 17	Literal Questions: 21 Predict/Confirm Predictions: 22 Note Details: 22 Make Connections: 22	Literal Questions: 22 Note Details: 23 Make Connections: 23
		Match Words to Pictures: 23	Match Words to Pictures: 22	Match Words to Pictures: 18	Match Words to Pictures: 23	**Modified Cloze: 24** Match Sentences with Pictures: 24

Key: (for Teachers)	√= informal assessment	Numbers = exercise numbers	Bold face type = first appearance

		Lesson 121	Lesson 122	Lesson 123	Lesson 124	Lesson 125
Phonemic Awareness						Onset Rime: 10
Print Awareness		Copying Text: 27	Copying Text: 24	Copying Text: 23	Copying Text: 24	Copying Text: 22
Letter Sound Correspondence		Introduction: 1 **(b)** Review: 3 (d, p, b, t) Review: 5 (b, c, ĕ, ch, ē, ō, r, ā) √: 2, 4, 6	Review: 1 (b) Review: 2 (p, d, b, t) Review: 4 (ĕ, ch, b, c, ō, sh, v, l), 6 √: 3, 5	Review: 1 (g, b, h, t), 3 Review: 4 (b, p, r, d, ch, v, ĕ, n) √: 2, 5	Introduction: 1 **(ing)** Review: 3 (ing, g, n, ĭ) Review: 5 (ing, l, ŭ, ch, b, ĕ, h, p) √: 2, 4, 6	Review: 1 (ing) Review: 2 (ing, b, ĭ, n) Review: 4 (k, ĕ, ing, w, ch, p, ō, v), 6 √: 3, 5
		Phonograms: 27	Phonograms: 24	Phonograms: 23	Phonograms: 24	Phonograms: 22
						Mastery Test 24 after L125
Phonics and Word Recognition	**Irregular**	to: 10 do: 11 √: 12	of: 14 √: 15	park: 13 girl: 16	his: 7 of: 10 √: 11	his: 14
	Regular	Reading Words: 7 **(red, sent)**, 14, 18 **(them)** Blending Sounds into Words: 13, 17	Blending Sounds into Words: 7 **(paint)** Reading Words: 8 **(men, shots, up)**, 11 **(lift)**, 16	Reading Words: 6, 10 **(pig)** Blending Sounds into Words: 9 **(chicks)**, 14 **(bug)**, 15 **(duck)** √: 17	Reading Words: 7 **(going)**, 12, 15 **(kissed)**, 16 Inflectional Ending: 15 (_ed, kissed)	Reading Words: 7 **(eating)**, 11, 14 Blending Sounds into Words: 10 Consonant Blend: 10
		Reading Connected Text: 21 √: 22	Reading Connected Text: 19 √: 20	Reading Connected Text: 18 √: 19	Reading Connected Text: 19 √: 20	Reading Connected Text: 17 √: 48
		V-C: 1 C-V-C: 1 C-V-C-C: 1	C-V-C: 1	C-V-C: 1, 2 C-V-C-C: 2, 3	C-V-C: 1, 2, 4 C-V: 4 C-V-C-C: 3	C-V-C: 1, 2, 3 C-V: 1
						Reading Connected Text
Fluency		Reading Words: 8, 15, 19 √: 9, 16, 20	Reading Words: 9, 12, 17 √: 10, 13, 18	Reading Words: 7, 11 √: 8, 12	Reading Words: 8, 13, 17 √: 9, 14, 18	Reading Words: 8, 12, 15 √: 9, 13, 16
		Reading Connected Text: 23	Reading Connected Text: 21	Reading Connected Text: 20	Reading Connected Text: 21	Reading Connected Text: 19
		Visual Discrimination: 27	Visual Discrimination: 24	Visual Discrimination: 23	Visual Discrimination: 23	Visual Discrimination: 21
						Individual Checkout: 25 (30 wpm/3 errors)
Comprehension		Literal Questions: 23 Predict/Confirm Predictions: 24 Make Connections: 24	Literal Questions: 21 Predict/Confirm Predictions: 21 Make Inferences: 22 Make Connections: 22	Literal Questions: 20 Predict/Confirm Predictions: 21 Note Details: 21 Make Connections: 21	Literal Questions: 21 Note Details: 22 Make Connections: 22	Literal Questions: 19 Make Inferences; 19 Predict/Confirm Predictions: 20 Note Details: 20 Make Connections: 20
		Modified Cloze: 25 Match Sentences to Pictures: 27	Modified Cloze: 23 Match Sentences to Pictures: 24	Modified Cloze: 22 Match Sentences to Pictures: 23	Note Details: 26 Match Sentences to Pictures: 24 Modified Cloze: 26	Note Details: 22 Modified Cloze: 24

Key: (for Teachers) √= informal assessment   Numbers = exercise numbers   Bold face type = first appearance

		Lesson 126	Lesson 127	Lesson 128	Lesson 129	Lesson 130
Phonemic Awareness			Onset Rime: 10	Onset Rime: 13		
Print Awareness		Copying Text: 20	Copying Text: 25	Copying Text: 24	Copying Text: 22	Copying Text: 22
Letter Sound Correspondence		Review: 1 (sh, th, c, ŏ, r, l, w, ā), 3 Review: 4 (b, ing, ĕ, ch) √: 2	Introduction: 1 (ĭ) Review: 3 (ĭ, ĭ, l, ing) Review: 5 (ĭ, ŏ, b, ch, ĕ, ā, ō, h) √: 2, 4, 6	Review: 1 (ĭ) Review: 2 (ĭ, ĕ, ĭ, ing) Review: 4 (ĭ, ŏ, ch, v, w, k, p, b) √: 3, 5	Review: 1 (ing, ĭ, b, d, ĕ, p, ĭ, k) Review: 3 (l, ch, c, ĕ, ŏ, ŭ, ŏ, l) √: 2, 4	Review: 1 (b, ing, ĕ, ĕ) Review: 2 (ŏ, ā, g, ŭ, t, ĭ, s, p) √: 3
		Phonograms: 20	Phonograms: 25	Phonograms: 24	Phonograms: 22	Phonograms: 22
						Mastery Test 25 after L130
Phonics and Word Recognition	**Irregular**		nose: 8 to: 16 √: 17	**walk:** 12 **talk:** 13 √: 16	walk: 10 talk: 14 √: 11	walk: 7 **talking:** 9 √: 8, 10
					C-V-C: 2 (was)	
	Regular	Blending Sounds into Words: 5 (**be**), 6 (**big**), 7 (**getting**), 8 (**bed**), 9 (**bit**) Reading Words: 12 (**bugs**)	Reading Words: 7 (**sleeping, fishing, leaf**) Blending Sounds into Words: 10 (**slam**), 11 (**let's**), 12 (**but**), 15 (**slip**) Consonant Blend: 10, 15 (sl_)	Blending Sounds into Words: 6 (**pond**), 7 (**back**), 8, 9 (**bus**), 12, 14 Reading Words: 17	Reading Words: 5 Blending Sounds into Words: 8 (**bite**), 9 (**tub**), 15 (**stop**) Consonant Blend: 15 (st_)	Reading Words: 4 Blending Sounds into Words: 13 (**dive**), 14 (**like**), 15 (**sliding**) Consonant Blend: 15 (sl_)
		Reading Connected Text: 15 √: 16	Reading Connected Text: 20 √: 21	Reading Connected Text: 20 √: 21	Reading Connected Text: 18 √: 19	Reading Connected Text: 18 √: 19
		C-V-C: 1, 2, 3, 4 C-V: 4 C-V-C-C: 2	V-C: 1 C-V-C: 1 C-V-C-C: 1 V-C-C: 1	C-V-C: 2 C-V: 1 V-C-C: 3, 4	V-C: 5 C-V-C: 1, 4, 5 C-V: 1, 3 V-C-C: 5	C-V-C: 2, 3 C-V: 1 C-V-C-C: 3
						Reading Words
Fluency		Reading Words: 10, 13 √: 11, 14	Reading Words: 8, 13, 18 √: 9, 14, 19	Reading Words: 10, 15, 18 Rhyming: 13 √: 11, 16, 19	Reading Words: 6, 12, 16 √: 7, 13, 17	Reading Words: 5, 11, 16 √: 6, 12, 17
		Reading Connected Text: 17	Reading Connected Text: 22	Reading Connected Text: 22	Reading Connected Text: 20	Reading Connected Text: 20
		Visual Discrimination: 20	Visual Discrimination: 25	Visual Discrimination: 24	Visual Discrimination: 22	Visual Discrimination: 22
						Individual Checkoutg: 26 (36 wpm/3 errors)
Comprehension		Literal Questions: 17 Note Details: 18 Make Inferences: 18	Literal Questions: 22 Predict/Confirm Predictions: 23 Note Details: 23 Make Inferences: 23	Literal Questions: 22 Predict/Confirm Predictions: 22 Note Details: 23 Make Inferences: 23	Literal Questions: 20 Predict/Confirm Predictions: 20, 21 Note Details: 21 \Make Connections: 21	Literal Questions: 20 Predict/Confirm Predictions: 20, 21 Note Details: 21 Make Connections: 21
		Match Words to Pictures: 19, 20 Note Details: 20 Modified Cloze: 23	Match Words to Pictures: 24, 25 Note Details: 25	Note Details: 27 Match Words to Pictures: 24	Note Details: 25 Match Words to Pictures: 22	Note Details: 24 Match Words to Pictures: 22

		Lesson 131	Lesson 132	Lesson 133	Lesson 134	Lesson 135
Phonemic Awareness						
Print Awareness		Copying Text: 19	Copying Text: 23	Copying Text: 30	Copying Text: 22	Copying Text: 20
Letter Sound Correspondence		Introduction: 1 (y) Review: 3 (y, v, w, ĭ) Review: 5 (y, n, ŏ, ō, ĕ, ī, ing, b) √: 2, 4, 6	Review: 1 (y) Review: 2 (y, k, ĕ, ī) Review: 4 (y, ing, ŭ, sh, l, ch, ī, b) √: 3, 5	Review: 1 (y) Review: 2 (y, ī, ē, ĭ) Review: 4, (ch, d, ing, ā, y, ĕ, p, b), 6 √: 3, 5	Review: 1 (r, w, ĕ, b) Review: 2 (ā, g, y, ch, sh, ĭ, l, ing) √: 3	Introduction: 1 (er) Review: 3 (er, r, y, ĕ) Review: 5 (er, ing, ĭ, ī, v, p, b, w) √: 2, 4, 6
		Phonograms: 19	Phonograms: 23	Phonograms: 30	Phonograms: 22	Phonograms: 20
				Phonograms: 1 (c)	Phonograms: 1 (c)	
						Mastery Test 26 after L135
Phonics and Word Recognition	**Irregular**		do: 15 **doing**: 15	**into**: 7 park: 12 **dark**: 13 **you**: 19 √: 8, 14, 20	you: 7 **yard**: 11 √: 8, 12	
		C-V-C: 1 (has), 2 (was), 3	V-C: 1 (is) C-V-C: 1 (has, his), 2 (was)	C-V-C: 2	C-V-C: 3 (has), 4 (was)	C-V-C-C: 3 V-C-C: 2
	Regular	Blending Sounds into Words: 7 (**rabbit**) Reading Words: 8 (**sitting**), 11	Reading Words: 6 (having) Blending Sounds into Words: 9 (**slide**), 10 (**slid**), 12, 13 (**time**), 14 (**tell**) Consonant Blends: 9, 10 √: 11	Reading Words: 9 (**stops, rich, stopping**), 16 (led) Blending Sounds into Words: 15 (**digging**), 21 (**boy**) √: 22	Blending Sounds into Words: 4 (**told**), 5 (**hole**), 6 (**yes**) Reading Words: 13 (**line, lived**), 16 (**dig**) √: 17	Blending Sounds into Words: 7 (**dad**), 8 (**they**), 11 Reading Words: 9, 13 (**find**) √: 12
		Reading Connected Text: 14 √: 15	Reading Connected Text: 18 √: 19	Reading Connected Text: 25 √: 26	Reading Connected Text: 18 √: 19	Reading Connected Text: 16 √: 17
			Sentence Writing: 3	C-V-C: 3 C-V: 3 Sentence Writing: 4	C-V-C: 2, 5 C-V-C-C: 5 Sentence Writing: 6	C-V-C: 1, 3, 4 Sentence Writing: 4
						Reading Connected Text
Fluency		Reading Words: 9, 12 √: 10, 13	Reading Words: 7, 16 √: 8, 17	Reading Words: 10, 17, 23 Rhyming: 16 √: 11, 18, 24	Reading Words: 9, 14 √: 10, 15	Reading Words: 10, 14 √: 10, 15
		Reading Connected Text: 16	Reading Connected Text: 20	Reading Connected Text: 27	Reading Connected Text: 20	Reading Connected Text: 18
						Individual Checkout: 25 (37 wpm/3 errors)
Comprehension		Literal Questions: 16 Predict/Confirm Predictions; 16, 17 Note Details: 17 Make Connections: 17	Literal Questions: 20 Note Details: 21 Make Inferences: 21	Literal Questions: 27 Predict/Confirm Predictions: 28 Note Details: 28 Make Connections: 28	Literal Questions: 20 Predict/Confirm Predictions: 20 Note Details: 21 Make Connections: 21	Literal Questions: 18 Note Details: 19 Make Connections: 19
		Modified Cloze: 18 Note Details: 19 Match Sentences to Pictures: 19	Modified Cloze: 22 Note Details: 23 Match Sentences to Pictures: 23	Modified Cloze: 29 Note Details: 30 Match Sentences to Pictures: 30	Modified Cloze: 22 Note Details: 22 Match Sentences to Pictures: 22	Modified Cloze: 20 Note Details: 20 Matching Sentences to Pictures: 20

Key: (for Teachers) √ = informal assessment Numbers = exercise numbers Bold face type = first appearance

		Lesson 136	Lesson 137	Lesson 138	Lesson 139	Lesson 140
Phonemic Awareness						
Print Awareness		Copying Text: 26	Copying Text: 24	Copying Text: 22	Copying Text: 27	Copying Text: 24
Letter Sound Correspondence		Review: 1 (er) Review: 2 (er, ĕ, ĕ, r) Review: 4 (ŭ, ing, er, ā, ĭ, b, ch, y), 6 √: 3, 5	Review: 1 (y, b, er, c) Review: 2 (g, ā, l, v, ō, ing, ĕ, ī) √: 3	Review: 1 (y, ĭ, b, t) Review: 2 (er, ĕ, k, ing, th, h, v, l) √: 3	Introduction: 1 **(x)** Review: 3 (x, k, s, ch) Review: 5 (x, ĭ, y, ē, ō, ŭ, ing, er) √: 2, 4, 6	Review: 1 (x) Review: 2 (x, s, k, er) Review: 4 (x, l, sh, y, b, l, v, ĕ) √: 3, 5
		Phonograms: 26	Phonograms: 24	Phonograms: 22	Phonograms: 27	Phonograms: 24
						Mastery Test 27 after L140
Phonics and Word Recognition	**Irregular**	walk: 12 you: 18 √: 13, 19	**brother: 4 you:** 9 **other:** 11 **mother:** 12 **love:** 15 √: 5, 10, 14, 16	brother: 4 **card:** 10 love: 11 mother: 14 other: 16 √: 5	mother: 13 other: 19 √: 14, 20	**come:** 6 **some:** 7, 8
		C-V-C-C: 2 (farm) V-C-C: 2 (arm)	C-V-C-C: 2 (farm) V-C-C: 2 (arm)	C-V-C-C: 3 (farm) V-C-C: 1 (arm)	C-V-C: 3 (car) C-V-C-C: 1 (farm)	C-V-C: 3 (car) V-C-C: 2 (arm)
						Reading Words (you, card)
	Regular	Blending Sounds into Words: 7 **(hunt, hunting),** 11, 16 Reading Words: 8 **(ride, gun)** √: 17	Reading Words: 6 Blending Sounds into Words: 17 **(deer)**	Reading Words: 6, 15 Blending Sounds into Words: 9 **(her)**	Blending Sounds into Words: 7 **(beans),** 17 **(toys)** Reading Words: 8 **(ever, shopping, never),** 11 √: 12, 18	Blending Sounds into Words: 9 **(hop)** Reading Words: 12, 14, 17 **(shop),** 18 √: 13
		Reading Connected Text: 22 √: 23	Reading Connected Text: 20 √: 21	Reading Connected Text: 18 √: 19	Reading Connected Text: 23 √: 24	Reading Connected Text: 20, 21 √: 21
		V-C: 1 C-V-C: 3, 4 Sentence Writing: 5	C-V-C: 1, 3 V-C-C: 1 Sentence Writing: 4	C-V-C: 2, 4 V-C-C: 2 Sentence Writing: 5	C-V-C: 2, 4 C-V: 4 C-V-C-C: 4 Sentence Writing: 5	C-V-C: 1, 4 V-C-C: 1 Sentence Writing: 5
						Reading Words
Fluency		Reading Words: 9, 14, 20 √: 10, 15, 21	Reading Words: 7, 18 Rhyming: 12 √: 8, 14, 19	Reading Words: 7, 12, 17 √: 8, 13	Reading Words: 9, 15, 21 √: 10, 16, 22	Rhyming: 7 Reading Words: 10, 15, 19 √: 11, 16
		Reading Connected Text: 24	Reading Connected Text: 22	Reading Connected Text: 20	Reading Connected Text: 25	Reading Connected Text: 22
						Curriculum-Based Assessment 140 after L140
						Individual Checkout: 29 (37 wpm/3 errors)
Comprehension		Literal Questions: 24 Predict/Confirm Predictions: 24, 25 Note Details: 25 Make Inferences: 25 Make Connections: 25	Literal Questions: 22 Note Details: 23 Make Inferences: 23 Make Connections: 23	Literal Questions: 20 Predict/Confirm Predictions: 20 Note Details: 21 Make Inferences: 21 Make Connections: 21	Literal Questions: 25 Predict/Confirm Predictions: 25 Note Details: 26 Make Inferences: 26 Make Connections: 26	Literal Questions: 22 Note Details: 23 Make Connections: 23
		Modified Cloze: 26 Note Details: 26 Match Sentences to Pictures: 26	Modified Cloze: 24 Note Details: 24 Match Sentences to Pictures: 24	Modified Cloze: 22 Note Details: 22 Match Sentences to Pictures: 22	Modified Cloze: 27 Note Details: 27 Match Sentences to Words: 27	Modified Cloze: 24 Note Details: 24 Match Sentences to Pictures: 24

Key: (for Teachers) √= informal assessment   Numbers = exercise numbers   Bold face type = first appearance

		Lesson 141	Lesson 142	Lesson 143	Lesson 144	Lesson 145
Phonemic Awareness					Onset Rime: 9	
Print Awareness		Copying Text: 26	Copying Text: 22	Copying Text: 22	Copying Text: 23	Copying Text: 28
Letter Sound Correspondence		Review: 1 (x) Review: 2 (x, k, s, ch) Review: 4 (ā, ŏ, ē, ŏ, w, x, y, er), 6 √: 3, 5	Introduction: 1 **(oo)** Review: 3 (oo, r, ŏ, w) Review: 5 (oo, ŏ, ē, ĭ, er, x, y, ing) √: 2, 4, 6	Review: 1 (oo) Review: 2 (oo, w, ŏ, ō) Review: 4 (oo, er, ĭ, x, b, ē, ā, y) √: 3, 5	Review: 1 (oo, r, x, w) Review: 3 (v, n, er, y, ē, ĭ, ing, g), 5 √: 2, 4	Introduction: 1 **(j)** Review: 3 (j, g, sh, ch) Review: 5 (j, oo, y, er, ĭ, c, x, ŏ) √: 2, 4, 6
		Phonograms: 26	Phonograms: 22	Phonograms: 22	Word Completion: 21 Phonograms: 23	Word Completion: 26 Phonograms: 28
						Phonograms: 1 (b)
						Mastery Test 28 after L145
Phonics and Word Recognition	**Irregular**	come: 17 √: 18		car: 10 other: 12 you: 14 are: 16 √: 11, 13, 15, 17	you: 12 √: 13	**walk**: 7 **walked**: 7 **talked**: 8 **loved**: 9
		C-V-C: 1 (car, far, tar) C-V-C-C: 2 (farm) V-C-C: 2 (arm)	C-V-C: 2 (far, car) V-C-V: 1 (are)	C-V-C: 1 (car), 4 (was), 5 (far) V-C-V: 3 (are)	C-V-C: 3 (car) C-V-C-C: 2 (hard), 4 (card) V-C-V: 1 (are)	C-V-C: 4 (was, has) V-C-V: 3 (are)
	Regular	Blending Sounds into Words: 7 **(box)**, 8, 9 **(bike)**, 10, 13 **(topper)**, 14 **(stopper)** Double Medial Consonants: 14 (_pp_) Reading Words: 19 (fox)	Blending Sounds into Words: 7 **(over)**, 8 **(eagle)**, 13, 14 Reading Words: 9 **(hitting)**, 12, 15	Blending Sounds into Words: 6 **(shore)**, 9 **(slider)** Reading Words: 7 Consonant Blend: 9 (sl_)	Reading Words: 6 **(room)** Blending Sounds into Words: 9 **(broom)**, 10 **(dime)**, 11 **(chore)** Consonant Blends: 9 (br_)	Reading Words: 12 **(moon)**, 18 **(than)** Blending Sounds into Words: 13 **(chip)**, 14 **(better)**, 15 **(pile)**
		Reading Connected Text: 22, 23 √: 23	Reading Connected Text: 18, 19 √: 19	Reading Connected Text: 18, 19 √: 19	Reading Connected Text: 16, 17 √: 17	Reading Connected Text: 21, 22 √: 22
		Sentence Writing: 3	C-V-C: 3 C-V-C-C: 3 Sentence Writing: 4	C-V-C: 2, 4 Sentence Writing: 6	C-V-C: 5 (nod) Sentence Writing: 6	C-V-C: 2, 4 C-V: 2 Sentence Writing: 5
						Reading Connected Text
Fluency		Reading Words: 11, 15, 20 √: 12, 16, 21	Reading Words: 10, 16 √: 11, 17	Reading Words: 8 √: 8	Reading Words: 7, 14 √: 8, 15	Reading Words: 10, 16, 19 √: 11, 17, 20
		Reading Connected Text: 24	Reading Connected Text: 20	Reading Connected Text: 20	Reading Connected Text: 18	Reading Connected Text: 23
						Individual Checkout: 31 (36 wpm/3 errors)
Comprehension		Literal Questions: 24 Make Connections: 25	Literal Questions: 20 Note Details: 21	Literal Questions: 20 Note Details: 21 Make Connections: 21	Literal Questions: 18 Predict/Confirm Predictions: 18, 19 Note Details: 19 Make Connections: 19	Literal Questions: 23 Note Details: 24
		Modified Cloze: 26 Note Details: 26 Match Sentences to Pictures: 26	Modified Cloze: 22 Note Details: 22 Match Sentences to Pictures: 22	Modified Cloze: 22 Note Details: 22 Match Sentences to Pictures: 22	Modified Cloze: 20, 22 Picture Comprehension: 21	Modified Cloze: 25, 27 Picture Comprehension: 26

Key: (for Teachers) √ = informal assessment   Numbers = exercise numbers   Bold face type = first appearance

		Lesson 146	Lesson 147	Lesson 148	Lesson 149	Lesson 150
Phonemic Awareness			Onset Rime: 16	Onset Rime: 4		Onset Rime: 15
Print Awareness		Copying Text: 26	Copying Text: 26	Copying Text: 21	Copying Text: 22	Copying Text: 29
Letter Sound Correspondence		Review: 1 (j) Review: 2 (j, g, x, ch) Review: 4 (y, ĕ, p, j, oo, er, b, ing), 6 √: 3, 5	Review: 1 (j) Review: 2 (j, y, g, ch) Review: 4 (j, x, oo, er, ĭ, ĭ, ĕ, ü) √: 3, 5	Review: 1 (ĭ, ing, b, j) Review: 2 (y, t, l, x, ŏ, ā, ĕ, er) √: 3	Introduction: 1 (ȳ) Review: 2 (ȳ, y) Review: 3 (ȳ, y, ĭ, l) √: 4	Review: 1 (ȳ) Review: 2 (ȳ, j, ĕ, y) Review: 4: ȳ, f, ing, ch, v, x, oo, er) √: 3, 5
		Word Completion: 24 Phonograms: 26	Word Completion: 26 Phonograms: 26	Word Completion: 21 Phonograms: 21	Word Completion: 22 Phonograms: 22	Word Completion: 29 Phonograms: 29
		Phonograms: 1 (b)				Mastery Test 29 after L150
Phonics and Word Recognition	**Irregular**	talked: 10 was: 12 walked: 16 √: 11, 13	loved: 9 walked: 17 √: 10, 18	some: 12 √: 13	says: 5 **tart**: 12 **start**: 14 √: 6, 13, 15	talked: 9 says: 11 barn: 16 your: 19 other: 21 √: 10, 12, 17, 20, 22
		C-V-C-C: 5 (card) V-C-V: 2 (are)	V-C: 1 (is) C-V-C-C: 1 (card, farm)	C-V-C: 2 (his) C-V-C-C: 2 (card), 3 (cart) V-C-V: 2 (are)	C-V-C: 1 (was) C-V-C-C: 4 (farm)	C-V-C: 3 (his)
	Regular	Reading Words: 7 (**soon, must**) Blending Sounds into Words: 14 (**day**), 17 (**brush, brushed**) Consonant Blend: 17 (br_) Inflectional Ending: 17 (_ed)	Reading Words: 6 (**either**) Blending Sounds into Words: 11 (**jump**), 12 (**tore**), 13 (**pool**), 16 (**store**) Consonant Blend: 16 (st_)	Blending Sounds into Words: 4 (**swimming**), 9 (**broke**), 14 (**jumped**) Consonant Blends: 4 (sw_), 9 (br_) Reading Words: 5, 8 (**jumps**)	Reading Words: 7 (**fill**), 11 (**teacher**) Blending Sounds into Words: 10 (**bring, bringing**) Consonant Blend: 10 (br_)	Reading Words: 6 (**riding**) Blending Sounds into Words: 13 (**horse**), 15 (**stand**) Consonant Blend: 15 (st_)
		Reading Connected Text: 19, 20 √: 20	Reading Connected Text: 21, 22 √: 22	Reading Connected Text: 17, 18 √: 18	Reading Connected Text: 18, 19 √: 19	Reading Connected Text: 25, 26 √: 26
		C-V-C: 2, 3, 6 C-V-C-C: 4 Sentence Writing: 7	C-V-C: 2, 3 Sentence Writing: 4	C-V-C: 1, 4 Sentence Writing: 5	C-V-C: 1, 2, 5 C-V-V: 3 Sentence Writing: 6	C-V-C: 2, 4 C-V-V: 1 Sentence Writing: 5 Reading Words
Fluency		Reading Words: 8, 15, 18 √: 9	Reading Words: 7, 14, 19 √: 8, 15, 20	Reading Words: 6, 10, 15 Rhyming: 8 √: 7, 11, 16	Reading Words: 8, 16 √: 9, 17	Reading Words: 7, 14, 18, 23 √: 8, 24
		Reading Connected Text: 21	Reading Connected Text: 23	Reading Connected Text: 19	Reading Connected Text: 20	Reading Connected Text: 27
						Individual Checkout: 33 (38 wpm/4 errors)
Comprehension		Literal Questions: 21 Note Details: 22 Make Inferences: 22 Make Connections: 22	Literal Questions: 23 Make Inferences: 23 Predict/Confirm Predictions: 23, 24	Literal Questions: 19 Predict/Confirm Predictions: 19 Note Details: 20 Make Connections: 20	Literal Questions: 20 Predict/Confirm Predictions: 21 Note Details: 21 Make Connections: 21	Literal Questions: 27 Note Details: 28 Make Inferences: 28 Make Connections: 28
		Modified Cloze: 23, 25 Picture Comprehension: 24	Modified Cloze: 25, 26 Picture Comprehension: 26	Modified Cloze: 21 Picture Comprehension: 21	Modified Cloze: 22 Picture Comprehension: 22	Modified Cloze: 29 Picture Comprehension: 29

Key: (for Teachers) √= informal assessment   Numbers = exercise numbers   Bold face type = first appearance

		Lesson 151	Lesson 152	Lesson 153	Lesson 154	Lesson 155
Phonemic Awareness				Onset Rime: 11	Onset Rime: 12	Onset Rime: 12,16
Print Awareness		Copying Text: 27	Copying Text: 30	Copying Text: 30	Copying Text: 28	Copying Text: 31
Letter Sound Correspondence		Review: 1 (ȳ) Review: 2 (ȳ, u, y, ï) Review: 4 (ȳ, l, b, ē, j, x, er, oo), 6 √: 3, 5	Introduction: 1 **(wh)** Review: 3 (wh, w, oo, r) Review: 5 (wh, ch, ȳ, j, er, x, y, h) √: 2, 4, 6	Review: 1 (wh) Review: 2 (wh, ȳ, w, r) Review: 4: wh, h, j, oo, ï, x, ē, ing) √: 3, 5	Introduction: 1 **(qu)** Review: 3 (qu, k, wh, ch) Review: 5 (qu, ȳ, c, j, oo, x, y, er) √: 2, 4, 6	Review: 1 (qu) Review:2 (qu, wh, p, k) Review: 4 (ȳ, i, j, qu, ï, ĭ, oo, x), 6 √: 3, 5
		Word Completion: 27 Phonograms: 27	Word Completion: 30 Phonograms: 30	Word Completion: 30 Phonograms: 30	Word Completion: 28 Phonograms: 28	Word Completion: 31 Phonograms: 31
			Phonograms: 1 (th)	Phonograms: 1 (th)		Mastery Test 30 after L155
Phonics and Word Recognition	**Irregular**	your: 11 says: 12	your: 10 **book:** 12 says: 14 √: 11, 13, 15	**ouch:** 6 barn: 12 into: 14 **look:** 18 book: 19, 20 √: 7, 13, 15	**took:** 16 look: 17, 18 book: 17, 18	touch: 7 √: 8
			C-V-C-C: 4 (card)	V-C-V: 2 (are)	V-C-V: 4 (are)	C-V-C-C: 3 (barn) V-C-C: 2 (arm)
	Regular	Reading Words: 7 **(liked)**, 10 **(nine, fine)**, 15 Blending Sounds into Words: 15, 16, 17 **(bill)**	Reading Words: 7 **(gold)**, 19 **(my)** Blending Sounds into Words: 18 **(filled)**, 20 **(fly)** Consonant Blend: 20 (fl_)	Reading Words: 8 **(six)** Blending Sounds into Words: 11 Inflectional Ending: 11 (_ed)	Reading Words: 7 **(times)**, 13 **(when, tooth)** Blending Sounds into Words: 8 **(where)**, 9 **(white)**, 12 **(slipped)** Inflectional Ending: 12 (_ed)	Reading Words: 9 **(shine)**, 13 **(why)** Blending Sounds into Words: 12, 16, 17, 18, 21 **(smile, smiled)** Consonant Blend: 12 (st_), 16 (fl_) Inflectional Ending: 21 (_ed)
		Reading Connected Text: 20, 23, 24 √: 24	Reading Connected Text: 23, 26, 27 √: 27	Reading Connected Text: 23, 26, 27 √: 27	Reading Connected Text: 21, 24, 25 √: 25	Reading Connected Text: 24, 27, 28 √: 28
		C-V-C: 1, 3, 5 V-C-C: 4 C-V-V: 2 Sentence Writing: 6	C-V-C: 2, 4 C-V-V: 3 Sentence Writing: 5	C-V-C: 2 C-C-V: 3 C-C-V-C: 4 Sentence Writing: 5	C-V-V: 2 C-C-V: 3 C-C-V-C: 1, 5 Sentence Writing: 6	C-V-C: 5 C-V-C-C: 1 C-C-V-C: 4 Sentence Writing: 6
						Reading Connected Text
Fluency		Reading Words: 8, 13, 18 Rhyming: 10 √: 9, 14, 19	Reading Words: 8, 16, 21 √: 9, 17, 22	Reading Words: 9, 16, 21 Rhyming: 19 √: 10, 17, 22	Reading Words: 10, 14, 19 √: 11, 15, 20	Reading Words: 10, 14, 19, 22 Rhyming: 13 √: 11, 15, 20, 23
		Reading Connected Text: 21, 25	Reading Connected Text: 24, 28	Reading Connected Text: 24, 28	Reading Connected Text: 22, 26	Reading Connected Text: 25, 29
						Individual Checkout: 35 (40 wpm/3 errors)
Comprehension		Follow Written Directions: 22 Literal Questions: 25 Predict/Confirm Predictions: 26 Note Details: 26	Follow Written Directions: 25 Literal Questions: 28 Make Inferences; 28 Story Grammar: 28 Note Details: 29 Make Connections: 29	Follow Written Directions: 25 Literal Questions: 28 Predict/Confirm Predictions: 28, 29 Note Details: 29	Follow Written Directions: 23 Literal Questions: 26 Predict//Confirm Predictions: 26 Note Details: 27 Make Inferences: 27	Follow Written Directions: 26 Literal Questions: 29 Predict/Confirm Predictions: 30 Note Details: 30 Make Connections: 30
		Modified Cloze: 27 Picture Comprehension: 27	Modified Cloze: 30 Picture Comprehension: 30	Modified Cloze: 30 Picture Comprehension: 30	Modified Cloze: 28 Picture Comprehension: 28	Modified Cloze: 31 Picture Comprehension: 31

| Key: (for Teachers) | √ = informal assessment | Numbers = exercise numbers | Bold face type = first appearance |

		Lesson 156	Lesson 157	Lesson 158	Lesson 159	Lesson 160
Phonemic Awareness						
Print Awareness		Copying Text: 30	Copying Text: 29	Copying Text: 31	Copying Text: 23	Copying Text: 19
Letter Sound Correspondence		Introduction: 1 (**z**) Review: 3 (z, s, x, th) Review: 5 (z, qu, ȳ, j, wh, er, b, y) √: 2, 4, 6	Review: 1 (z) Review: 2 (z, s, v, qu) Review: 4 z, ā, ŭ, j, g, qu, wh, ȳ) √: 3, 5	Review: 1 (u) Introduction: 2 (ü) Review: 3 (ü, ō, ȳ, qu, j) √: 4	Review: 1 (**ü**) Review: 2 (ü, ŭ, oo, z) Review: 4 (ü, qu, wh, j, ȳ, y, er, ĭ) √: 3, 5	
		Word Completion: 30 Phonograms: 30	Word Completion: 29 Phonograms: 29	Word Completion: 31 Phonograms: 31	Word Completion: 23 Phonograms: 23	Word Completion: 19 Phonograms: 19
			Phonograms: 1 (p)	Phonograms: 1 (p)		
Phonics and Word Recognition	Irregular	looked: 19		look: 9 took: 18 √: 10, 19		took: 7 moon: 9 √: 8
		C-V-C-C: 4 (barn)		V-C-V: 4 (are)	C-V-C-C: 2 (barn)	C-V-C: 1 (bar)
	Regular	Reading Words: 7, 17 (**under**), 20 (**fatter**), 21 Blending Sounds into Words: 10 (**tree**), 11 (**from**), 12 (**tiger**), 15 (**yelled**), 16 (**after**) Consonant Blend: 10 (tr_)	Blending Sounds into Words: 6 (**steps**), 10 (**stands**), 17, 18 (**things**), 19 (**even**), 21 (**slow**) Consonant Blend: 6 (st_), 10, 17 (tr_), 21 (sl_) Reading Words: 7, 11, 14 (fast)	Blending Sounds into Words: 5, 12 (**picks**), 20 (**head**) Reading Words: 6, 11 (**wife, life**), 15 (**show**), 21 (**thing**)	Reading Words: 6, 9, 12 Blending Sounds into Words: 13	Reading Words: 1, 4
		Reading Connected Text: 23, 26, 27 √: 27	Reading Connected Text: 22, 25, 26 √: 26	Reading Connected Text: 24, 27, 28 √: 28	Reading Connected Text: 16, 19, 20 √: 20	Reading Connected Text: 12, 15, 16 √: 16
		C-V-C: 5 C-V-C-C: 3 C-C-V: 5 C-C-V-C: 2 C-V-V: 1 Sentence Writing: 6	C-V-C: 2 C-V-C-C: 3 C-C-V-C: 2 C-V-V: 4 Sentence Writing: 5	C-V-C: 4 C-V-C-C: 2, 3 C-C-V: 4 Sentence Writing: 5	V-C: 3 C-V-C: 4 C-V-C-C: 2 C-V-V: 1 Sentence Writing: 5	C-V-C: 2 C-V-C-C: 1, 2 Sentence Writing: 3
Fluency		Reading Words: 8, 13, 18, 22 √: 9, 14, 18, 23	Reading Words: 8, 12, 15, 20 √: 9, 13, 16, 20	Reading Words: 7, 13, 16, 22 Rhyming: 11 √: 8, 14, 17, 23	Reading Words: 7, 10, 14 Rhyming: 12 √: 8, 11, 15	Reading Words: 2, 5, 10 √: 3, 6, 11
		Reading Connected Text: 24, 28	Reading Connected Text: 23, 27	Reading Connected Text: 25, 29	Reading Connected Text: 17, 21	Reading Connected Text: 13, 17
						Curriculum-Based Assessment 160 after L160
						Individual Checkout: 25 (38 wpm/3 errors)
Comprehension		Follow Written Directions: 25 Literal Questions: 28, 29 Make Connections: 29	Follow Written Directions: 24 Literal Questions: 27 Predict/Confirm Predictions: 28	Follow Written Directions: 26 Literal Questions: 29 Make Inferences: 29 Note Details: 30	Follow Written Directions: 18 Literal Questions: 21 Note Details: 21, 22	Follow Written Directions: 14 Literal Questions: 17 Note Details: 17 Predict/Confirm Predictions: 18 Make Inferences: 18 Make Connections: 18
		Modified Cloze: 30 Picture Comprehension: 30	Modified Cloze: 29 Picture Comprehension: 29	Modified Cloze: 31 Picture Comprehension: 31	Modified Cloze: 23 Picture Comprehension: 23	Modified Cloze: 19 Picture Comprehension: 19